MEDIEVAL TRANSLATORS

AND THEIR CRAFT

MEDIEVAL TRANSLATORS
AND THEIR CRAFT

Edited by

Jeanette Beer

Studies in Medieval Culture, XXV
MEDIEVAL INSTITUTE PUBLICATIONS

WESTERN MICHIGAN UNIVERSITY

Kalamazoo, Michigan--1989

Library of Congress Cataloging-in-Publication Data

Medieval translators and their craft / edited by Jeanette Beer.
    p. cm. -- (Studies in medieval culture ; 25)
    Bibliography: p.
    Includes index.
    ISBN 0-918720-95-8. -- ISBN 0-918720-96-6 (pbk.)
    1. Translating and interpreting--History. 2. Translating and interpreting--Europe. I. Beer, Jeanette M. A. II. Series.
CB351.S83 vol. 25
[P306]
940.1'7 s--dc19
[418'.02'0902]

89-2535
CIP

Printed in the United States of America

Cover Design by Elizabeth King

Artist's Note: "I created the symbol used on the front cover as a representation of the concept behind the work of the translator. By using two opposite, yet equal aspects of the Moon, already a symbol of transmutation and change, and linking them with a symbol for the active intellect, I attempted to convey the striving of all translators to achieve equal meaning between two languages, with the ultimate goal of fairness to one Idea."

For my mother

ACKNOWLEDGEMENTS

I should like to thank Otto Gründler and the Medieval Institute at Western Michigan University, Kalamazoo, Michigan, for sponsoring both the session THE MEDIEVAL TRANSLATOR'S CRAFT and also the volume which resulted from it. I am grateful to Howard Mancing and to the Department of Foreign Languages and Literatures of Purdue University for providing their help as I assembled the manuscript. The informed and careful services of Margaret Hunt were particularly valuable in this regard, and to her I owe special thanks.

Jeanette Beer
Purdue University

CONTENTS

INTRODUCTION

At no time in the history of the West has translation played a more vital role than in the Middle Ages. Centuries before the appearance of the first extant vernacular documents, bilingualism, and preferably trilingualism, was a necessity in the scriptorium and chancery; and since the emergence of Romance had rendered the entire corpus of classical literature incomprehensible to all but the "litterati," both old and new worlds awaited (re)discovery or, to use Jerome's metaphor, "conquest." Paradoxically, the universality and vitality of the activity as well as the disparateness of its products have led some modern theorists to deny the existence of "real" translation until the "Renaissance."

But translation in the Middle Ages was not a literary sub-species, obeying (or *not* obeying!) certain presupposed requirements. It was not, in fact, and is not now a literary genre at all, and medieval translators never classified it as such, despite their strong generic awareness. No catch-all term denoted all its heterogeneous products. No manual legislated its requirements. Even its processes were described non-technically and unpretentiously, "metre en romanz / françois" being as satisfactory in France, for example, as the Latinism "translater." Similarly, the functions of translation were almost infinitely variable, although there was, broadly speaking, a dichotomy between the literal (scientific / legal) and the literary (where considerations other than the mere transmission of content might intervene).

Inevitably the function of servicing an unlettered public implied at first a degree of didacticism, and the conception of translation as a teaching activity was never more apt. In the fullest sense the medieval translator was master of the author. When responsibility to a pagan source conflicted with responsibility to a Christian public, the latter invariably had precedence.

1

A translator's responsibility toward himself *qua* translator was traditionally of lesser importance, since he had from the beginning fulfilled a service role. As late as 1213 the French compiler-translator of all known source materials about Julius Caesar meticulously named all sources and all switches between sources without thinking once to include his own name. Today, of course, the translator's responsibility toward his literary source, his public, and himself are in uneasy competition. As for the modern ideal of "audience response equivalence," it would, even if formulated, have been anathema. Appropriateness of form was determined from the predicted response of a particular target audience, never from an attempted match between presumed past response and presumed present one.

For similar reasons, structural equivalence between source and translation was not of prime importance. By the criterion of appropriateness to target audience a treatise properly could become poetry, epic become romance, and sermons drama--or vice versa! Such dramatic changes in form serve as irritants to those modern theorists who, for the sake of anachronistic criteria, categorize a millennium of translative vitality as one thousand years of non-translation. But the value judgments implied by such substitute terms as "adaptation," "paraphrase," or "imitation" must not be allowed to obscure the complexity of the translative process in the Middle Ages. The translators' assumptions usually remain implicit, but their lack of theoretical exposition must not be equated with a lack of theoretical principles. Their dialogue was not, after all, with one another, as had been the case between Augustine and Jerome, but with their public. Glosses, prologues, explanations, and inter-polated comments, if they existed at all, were addressed to that public, and must be interpreted in that light. Most frequently there were no explanations. The medieval translator required no argu-ments to justify either his authority or his activities. Moreover, his translation would not ultimately be judged against a self-justifi-catory prologue but rather in its own right. It remains therefore for us to analyze the dynamics of medieval translation from the practices themselves.

Clearly Ciceronian discussions, as well as the theories and

practices of Jerome and Augustine, had long been part of the translator's intellectual baggage. Acknowledgement of the literality versus freedom dilemma appears, for example, in the not infrequent claim of word-for-word translation. The claim should be interpreted with some caution. No age was closer to, or more aware of, the linguistic problems involved in transforming Latin's synthetic structure into the analytic patterns of Romance. Absolute correspondence, if sought at the level of the smallest sentence-units, was rarely possible by the later Middle Ages. And since this extrinsic difference between source and target languages annihilated the possibility of literal translation, all other changes were merely a matter of degree.

Closest to the literality ideal were early diplomatic documents (for example, the *Strasbourg Oaths*), renderings of Scripture (for example, the "Valenciennes fragment" of a bilingual sermon about Jonah), and (despite Roger Bacon's fulminations against Aristotelian translators!) scientific treatises. The reasons were several. In the case of diplomatic documents, the bilingualism or, often, trilingualism of the early chanceries encouraged an almost automatic transference between languages. The result, as visible in the formularies' stock phrases, was an efficient legal-diplomatic jargon which was readily transferable in various directions. Similarly, the pragmatic function of such early sermons as the *Jonas* fragment, which involved merely a transference from Vulgate to vernacular in the cause of comprehensibility, ensured that affective changes were minimal. Here again, since the translator's languages were vocationally interreactive, the possibility for close lexical, stylistic, and even structural equivalence was high.

Scientific translation began some centuries later and posed somewhat greater problems. The desirability of as close a trans-ference as possible was in conflict with the unfamiliarity of the subject matter. Although the target audience must be presumed to have had some acquaintance with the material to make vernacular translation viable, the highly technical nature of scientific vocab-ulary necessitated particular lexical strategies. Of these, outright borrowings and calques were the most efficient, and in this respect the medieval and the modern translator coincide in method.

Demonstrable need in a target language for technical terminologies, whether social, scientific, or philosophical, precipitates direct imports or closely calqued approximations. One hazard is, of course, incomprehensibility, as one unrecognizable item is substituted for or "cloned" upon another. The process is nevertheless an essential part of the translative process whenever the translator is faced with lexical superiority in a source text.

While the inherited legal formularies, Scripture, and philosophic / scientific treatises compelled translators toward close lexical equivalence, literary translation necessitated no such devices. Whether he recognized the debt or not, the literary translator was the true inheritor of Horace: not for him the literal minded-pedantism of the "fidus interpres" decried in the *Ars Poetica*! His reasons are often misrepresented, however. When he chose to use his sources selectively or freely, the creative liberties should not be viewed as errors in comprehension (although these did occur!). They derived rather from the shifting medieval attitudes toward authorship and authority in the Middle Ages.

The "auctoritas" of Scripture was absolute, its source obviously being beyond all reproach, but the status of other literary works in the inherited corpus was variable and varying. For some translators Isidore of Seville was part of "L'Escriture" and was quoted with the same deference as was Scripture (in its narrowest sense). But "L'Escriture," like the modern literary canon, has ever shifting boundaries even while recognized as an entity. Biblical material apart, the translator abrogated to himself the right to act magisterially with his "auctor." Explicit intervention through commentary was one possible technique in the process, but the translator's magisterial role often extended far beyond such superficialities. If his responsibility was to his public, not to his source, the authority of that text *qua* text was correspondingly minimized. No period (*pace* Ezra Pound!) has been less servile to the literalities of a text, because the authority of that text was not recognized as absolute.

Some mention should be made about the influence of rhetorical precept upon the medieval translator. Inevitably, rhetorical treatises had general relevance to all medieval writers, and a more particular relevance to medieval translators, who presumably never began their task without *some* knowledge of the rhetorical authorities. But the activity of translation was necessarily more than "inventio," a given text being more tyrannical in its demands than a topos. Thus the precepts of any given treatise cannot be accepted holus-bolus as a translator's manual. Particularities of context could easily supersede precepts.

The diversity of translation in the Middle Ages is illustrated, although not encompassed, by the diversity of chapters in the present volume. It comprises a selection of contributions which had previously been presented in the session THE MEDIEVAL TRANS-LATOR'S CRAFT which I convene annually at the International Congress for Medieval Studies, Kalamazoo, Michigan. An extensive bibliography has been placed at the end of the volume for those readers who are interested in the general theory and practice of translation. Items specific to individual chapters are appended to those chapters, where necessary, as Additional References.

Wace's *Brut* reflects an important stage in the formulation of the concept of vernacular translation; Nancy Vine Durling's "Translation and Innovation in the *Roman de Brut*" examines the implications of Wace's "translater" as against his source Geoffrey of Monmouth's "transferre."

By a comparison of five translations of the *Passio Sancte Katerine Virginis*, William MacBain shows the manner in which hagiographic translators might interpret their source for a particular public, a process which one of them calls "le tens selunc la gent user."

Robert Taylor examines a corpus of vernacular translations by the Cistercian order. The manuscripts, some of them luxuriously made, appear to have been intended for the edification of a cultivated lay audience.

Patricia A. McAllister exemplifies the popularizing techniques of the fifteenth-century vernacular bibles in Germany through the apocryphal elements in the Middle Low German manuscript Helmstedt 611.1.

Hans R. Runte examines the results of a double translation process: a version of the *Roman des sept sages de Rome* was translated into the *Historia septem sapientum*, which in turn was retranslated to French version H.

Raymond C. St-Jacques shows the influence of a French translation upon the *Middle English Glossed Prose Psalter*, contributing, by its freedom from the Latin versions, to a preservation of the native rhythms and textures of the English language.

In Brian A. Shaw's "The Old English Pheonix," the Old English rendering of Lactantius is seen to combine expansion and explanation, translation and exegesis.

Peter F. Dembowski compares two French derivatives of Andreas Capellanus's *De Amore*, Drouart la Vache's *Li Livres d'Amours* and *Le Livre d'Enanchet*, for their differing use of the Latin source.

Karen Pratt concentrates specifically upon the translation of direct speech passages from Old French into German romance, seeing them as a key to other translative practices. Although the German poets were able to parallel most of the stylistic and rhythmic effects of their models, they frequently chose to innovate or to incorporate features of German literary tradition in their translations.

English derivatives of French courtly romance contain their own modifications. Brenda Hosington analyzes the particular rejections and retentions which characterize Hue de Rotelande's Englishing of his comic source in *Ipomedon*.

Earl Jeffrey Richards treats an Italian derivative of *Le Roman de la rose*, the *Fiore*, both as a translation of a French original and as a literary work in its own right.

My chapter on *Le Bestiaire d'amour en vers* discusses a relatively unusual manifestation of translation, the self-translation of Richard de Fournival's *Bestiaire d'amour* to a *Bestiaire d'amour en vers*. His expressed intention "por miex plaire" and his eight-line prologue are ironically ambiguous, perhaps satirizing the contemporary vogue of romance.

Lys Ann Shore treats the subject of non-literary translation as it is illustrated in scientific treatises about the stars from the late thirteenth to the end of the fifteenth century.

Charity Cannon Willard's chapter on Raoul de Presles's

translation of St. Augustine's *De Civitate Dei* is of particular interest for its information about translation as commissioned and executed within Charles V's court. Raoul's prologues reflect one medieval translator's concern for problems of structure and for manuscript divergences.

Kenneth Lloyd-Jones concludes the volume with a discussion of Humanist concerns about translation. Although Dolet's *La Maniere de bien traduire d'une langue en aultre* may be considered the first translation manual in French, there is not as much discontinuity as might be supposed between Dolet's conceptualization of translation and that of our medieval translators. To quote Lloyd-Jones,

> There is something touching, even reassuring, in this sense of translation as being not so much a service to a monumentalized original, a homage to the past and a concession to our dependency on it, but rather a service to the present, an affirmation and consolidation of our own capacity for self-reliance and our ability to speak and to mean in ways that are at once like and unlike those of our forebears.

TRANSLATION AND INNOVATION IN THE *ROMAN DE BRUT*

Nancy Vine Durling

The generic status of Wace's *Roman de Brut* has long been a subject of scholarly debate. Current trends have favored classification of the work among the *romans antiques*. As Michel Zink
recently put it, "le *Roman de Brut* de Wace . . . par son titre, par son
sujet initial, par la teneur de son prologue, est bien un roman
antique."[1] This assessment, however, sidesteps a major issue in the
debate--the relation of the *Brut* to its model. While *Thèbes*, *Enéas*,
and *Troie* each claim a close connection with classical antecedents,
the *Brut* is based on a contemporary and highly problematic text,
Geoffrey of Monmouth's *Historia Regum Britanniae*. Although this
work enjoyed tremendous success in the twelfth century, contemporary historians generally took a dim view of Geoffrey's
innovations. He was charged with a number of sins, among them
distortion of the truth, self-aggrandizement, and fraudulent use of
translation.[2] It is not surprising then, that Wace begins his
reformation of the *Historia* by insisting on his own reliability as a
purveyor of truth:

> Maistre Wace l'ad translaté
> Qui en conte la verité.
>
> [Master Wace who tells the truth about it,
> has translated it.]   (lines 7-8)[3]

The connection which Wace here establishes between the concept
verité, the activity *translater*, and his own name raises a number of
questions. How are we to understand Wace's use of the term

translater? What does the term tell us about his reading of Geof-frey? More generally, what does this term teach us about the practice of translation in the mid-twelfth century?

The term *translater* is, in fact, relatively rare in twelfth-century OF texts. One of the first known uses of the OF term occurs in the *Psautier de Cambridge* (c. 1130), where it is used in the literal sense of transfer:

> Pur ceo ne crendrums cum serat translatée la terre,
> e dequassé li munt el quer de la mer.

> [Therefore, we will not fear when the earth will be moved
> and the mountains will be shaken into the heart of the sea.]
>
> (Psalmus XLV, 2)[4]

The *Brut* contains one of the first uses of the term to refer to linguistic translation.[5]

Wace refers to his activity as a translator in other works also. In the *Roman de Rou*, he claims to be translating a long and difficult *geste*:

> La geste est grande, longue et grieve a translater,
> mez l'en me porroit bien mon enging aviver,
> mout m'est doux le travail quant je cuit conquester.
> Lez Normanz et lor geste m'esteut avant mener.
> A jugleours oï en m'effance chanter
> que Guillaume fist jadiz Osmont essorber.
> . . . .
> ne sai noient de ceu, n'en puiz noient trover,
> quant je n'en ai garant n'en voil noient conter.

> [The "geste" is great, long, and hard to translate,
> but people could truly quicken my wit;
> the work is very sweet to me when I believe that I have
>   mastered it.
> It is necessary for me to make known the "geste" of the
>   Normans.
> I heard the jongleurs singing in my childhood

that long ago William overcame Osmond.

. . . .

I know nothing of this, and I can tell nothing about it.

When I have no witness to its truth, I don't want to
   recount anything about it.]

(Deuxième Partie, lines 1357-62, 1366-67)[6]

In this passage, Wace makes clear his distrust of oral tradition; in order to be reliable, material must come from a written source. Whether or not the *geste* he is "translating" is in Latin or in the vernacular is not, however, made clear; it is possible that *translater* here may refer either to translation from one language to another or to transcription from a written source. Another use of the verb *translater* occurs in a well-known passage of the *Roman de Rou*, where Wace complains that his services are not properly appreciated:

> Mult soleient estre onuré
> e mult preisé e mult amé
> cil ki les gestes escriveient
> e ki les estoires treiteient;
> suvent aveient des baruns
> e des nobles dames beaus duns
> pur mettre lur nuns en estoire,
> que tuz tens mais fust de eus memoire.
> *Mais or(e) puis jeo lunges penser,*
> *livres escrire e translater,*
> *faire rumanz e serventeis,*
> tart truverai tant seit curteis
> ki tant me duinst e mette en mein
> dunt jeo aie un meis un escrivein,
> ne ki nul autre bien me face
> fors tant: "Mult dit bien Maistre Wace;
> vus devrïez tuz tens escrire,
> ki tant savez bel e bien dire."
>
> [They used to be greatly honored
> and greatly prized and greatly loved
> those who wrote the "gestes"

11

and who told the tales.
They often had beautiful gifts from lords
and from noble ladies
in order that their names be included in the stories,
so that they would be remembered forever.
But now I can think for a long time,
write and translate books
make up romances and "serventeis,"
and it will be a long wait before I find anyone
   courteous enough
to give me and put into my hand
enough to pay a scribe for one month,
nor who would do anything else for me
except to say: "Very well said, Master Wace;
You really should write all the time,
<since> you know how to compose so beautifully
   and so well."]
          (Troisième Partie, lines 143-160, emphasis added)

Of particular interest is the juxtaposition of *translater* and *faire rumanz*. Is Wace equating the two activities, or is he distinguishing between them? The passage itself does not provide enough evidence to decide; however, examination of the term *romanz* within a broader context may help us.

The use of the term *romanz* in early vernacular texts has been a subject of intense interest among scholars. Wace is among the first to use the term; it appears in the *Brut*, for example, as part of an authorial intervention:

Ço testemonie e ço recorde
Ki cest romanz fist, maistre Wace

[Master Wace, who writes this "romanz"
witnesses and records it;]   (lines 3822-23)

and at the conclusion of the work, where he affirms his authorship:

Puis que Deus incarnatiun

12

Prist pur nostre redemptiun
Mil e cent cinquante e cinc anz,
Fist mestre Wace cest romanz.

[1155 years
after God became incarnate
for our salvation
Master Wace wrote this "romanz."]

(lines 14863-66)

Although Robert Marichal has claimed that Wace's use of *romanz* in lines 3823 and 14866 refers solely to his translation into French of the *Historia*, it may also refer to *genre*. The juxtaposition of the term *romanz* with *serventeis* in line 153 of the *Rou* suggests that it did indeed have a generic connotation in the mid-twelfth century.[7]

The expression *mettre en romanz* and its variants were widely used in twelfth-century vernacular texts to refer to the practice of translation.[8] In Benoît's *Chronique* (lines 13699 and 38590), *romanz* is used in opposition to Latin; lines 25832-35 imply that translation from Latin into Romance is not always possible:

Mais li latins dit e conprent
Od somme, od glose, ce m'est vis,
Ou ronmanz ne puet estre mis
Choses moutes; por ce m'est gref.

[But the Latin text says and includes,
with a summary, with a gloss; it seems to me
many things cannot be put into "romanz";
I am sorry for this.]

In the *Roman d'Alexandre* the term carries a didactic connotation:

L'estoire d'Alixandre vous voeil par vers tretier
En romans qu'a gent laie doie auques profitier.

[I want to write the story of Alexander for you in romance verse
so that lay people can also profit <from it>.]

(Branch I, lines 30-31)[9]

13

The term is also used in the twelfth century to refer to books written in the vernacular, whether translations or not. Gaimar, for example, uses the term *en romanz* (without a verbal antecedent) in this sense:

> [Gaimar] purchaca maint esamplaire,
> Liueres Engleis, e par gramaire,
> E en Romanz, e en Latin.

> [<Gaimar> obtained many copies,
> English books, and grammar books,
> In "romanz" and in Latin.]
> (*Lestorie des Engles*, lines 6442-44)

All of these instances of *en romanz* refer (1) to writings in the vernacular; (2) to translations into the vernacular; or (3) to a vernacular genre. The term *translater*, on the other hand, refers, in the instances before us (1) to translation into the vernacular or (2) to the transfer of material from one written form into another. This second use, of course, is closer to the original sense of the Latin etymon, *transferre*.[10] Given the close connection between the Latin term and its vernacular derivative, it may be useful to compare the way in which Geoffrey uses *transferre* and Wace uses *translater*.

Transferre is used in the *Historia* in the following passages:[11] (1) Geoffrey claims to be translating an old British book into Latin (Book 1:1); (2) Geoffrey refers to Gildas's translation (from British into Latin) of the Molmutine laws (later translated by King Alfred into English) (Book 3:4, 80-84); (3) Geoffrey refers to King Alfred's translation (into English) of the law written by Marcia (Book 3:12, 226-30); (4) Geoffrey refers to the transfer of Constans from a monastery to the kingship (Book 5:19, 542-44); (5) Geoffrey provides an introduction to his translation of Merlin's prophecies (Book 7:1-7:2, 1-15); (6) Geoffrey concludes his work with another reference to his translation into Latin of the *liber Britannici sermonis* (Book 11:18).

Of these six references, Wace retains the first, third, and fifth: (1) in the Prologue to the *Brut* (lines 1-8), Wace claims to be translating the truth about the genealogical succession of the English kings; (2) in lines 3345-48, Wace comments briefly on King Alfred's translation of Marcia's law; (3) in lines 7539-40, Wace refuses to translate the *Prophetia Merlini*.

In what follows, my procedure will be to examine the relevant passage in the *Historia* and then compare it with Wace's use of it in the *Brut*; to comment briefly on Wace's treatment of the other three instances of the term *transferre* in Geoffrey; and, finally, to attempt to draw some conclusions.

I

The verb *transferre* first appears in the *Historia* in Geoffrey's dedication of the book to his patrons. The passage which introduces the term is complex and merits quotation at some length:

> Cum mecum multa et de multis saepius animo revolvens, in historiam regum Britanniae inciderem, in mirum contuli, quod infra mentionem quam de eis Gildas et Beda luculento tractatu fecerant, nihil de regibus qui ante Incarnationem Christi inhabitaverant, nihil etiam de Arturo ceterisque compluribus qui post Incarnationem successerunt repperissem, cum et gesta eorum digna aeternae laudis constarent et a multis populis quasi inscripta iocunde et memoriter praedic(ar)entur. Talia mihi et multotiens cogitanti de talibus, obtulit Walterus, Oxinefordensis archidiaconus, vir in oratoria arte atque in exoticis historiis eruditus, quendam Britannici sermonis librum vetustissimum, qui a Bruto, primorum rege Britonum, usque ad Cadwaladrum, filium Cadwallonis, actus omnium continue (et) ex ordine pulchris orationibus proponebat. *Rogatu itaque illius ductus, tametsi infra alienos hortulos phalerata verba non collegerim, agresti tamen stilo propriisque calamis contentus, codicem illum in Latinum sermonem transferre curavi.* Nam, si in ampullosis dictionibus paginam illevissem, taedium legentibus ingererem, dum magis in exponendis verbis quam in historia intelligenda

ipsos commorari oporteret. Opusculo igitur meo,
Roberte, Claudiocestriae dux, faveas, ut sic, te doctore,
te monitore, corrigatur quod non ex Gaufridi Mone-
mutensis fonticulo censeatur exortum, sed sale Minervae
tuae conditum, illius dicatur editio, quem Henricus,
illustris rex Anglorum, genuit, quem philosophia
liberalibus artibus erudivit, quem innata probitas
militibus in militia praefecit: unde nunc Britannia, tibi
temporibus nostris, ac si alterum Henricum adepta,
interno gratulatur affectu.

[While turning over many things in my mind, I happened
upon the history of the British kings. It seemed
astonishing that, beyond such mention of them as Gildas
and Bede had made in illustrious treatises, I found
nothing concerning the kings who had lived before the
Incarnation of Christ, nothing either of Arthur and of the
many others who succeeded <him> after the Incarnation,
although their deeds are worthy of eternal praise and
they were entertainingly told from memory by many
peoples as if they had been written down. While I was
repeatedly thinking these thoughts about these matters,
Walter, Archdeacon of Oxford, a man learned in the art
of eloquence and in foreign histories, brought me a
certain very old book written in the British language
which, from Brutus, first king of the Britons, down to
Cadwalader son of Cadwallon, set forth the deeds of all
of them in elegant style and in continuous order.
*Induced by his request, though I do not gather verbal
ornamentation from other people's gardens, contenting
myself with my <own> rural style and my own reed pens,
I took pains to translate his book into the Latin tongue.*
For if I puffed up my page with swollen words, I would
cause tedium in my readers, since they would have to
delay more to disentangle words than to understand the
history. Therefore Robert, duke of Gloucester, favor my
little work so that, with you as teacher, you as guide, it
may be corrected and not be thought to have come forth
from Geoffrey of Monmouth's little fountain but,

seasoned with the salt of your wisdom, may be said to be
his publication whom Henry, the illustrious king of the
English begat, whom philosophy has formed with her
liberal arts, whom innate valor has placed in command of
the soldiers of the army: on account of which now
Britain rejoices with inward affection for you in our time
as if she had gained another Henry.]

(Book 1:1, emphasis added)[12]

This passage has given rise to an extraordinary amount of
speculation about Geoffrey's "source," the *liber vetustissimus*.[13]
Whether Geoffrey's "book" was real or a fiction does not concern us
here. We shall focus, instead, on the *claims* Geoffrey makes for his
source and the claims he makes for himself as its "translator."
Several important points emerge.

Nowhere in this passage does Geoffrey refer to truth. He
focuses, instead, on the claims of *oral* tradition, which, he implies, is
as reliable as written tradition. The old book is based on "deeds . . .
worthy of eternal praise . . . entertainingly told from memory by
many peoples *as if they had been written down (quasi inscripta)*." In
other words, the oral traditions of the "many peoples" are authentic
and worthy of transcription. Authoritative histories, such as the *De
excidio et conquestu Britanniae* of Gildas and Bede's *Historia
ecclesiastica gentis Anglorum*, have made only brief (and, one
gathers, unsatisfactory) mention of these *gesta*. Geoffrey's work,
then, is designed to remedy the lacunae in earlier written histories of
the kings of Britain by incorporating information derived from oral
tradition. It is of the utmost importance that the *liber* is said to be
written in the *vernacular*, and that it is given to Geoffrey by "a man
learned in the art of eloquence" (*vir in oratoria arte eruditus*) and in
"foreign histories." These details about the book and its donor help
to support Geoffrey's central claims in the first portion of the
dedication: i.e., oral tradition can be authentic and, once it has been
transcribed into a book, can contribute to authoritative history.[14]
Translation (*translatio*) from the vernacular into Latin can therefore
be a legitimate part of historical writing. These claims are extra-
ordinarily innovative and help to explain the extreme resistance to
the *Historia* among many twelfth-century historians.

17

A second aspect of Geoffrey's dedication is his discussion of style. First, he makes specific claims about the style of the book he is translating. He attributes to it a continuous, orderly narration and "elegant style" (*pulchrae orationes*). He then turns to his own role in the translation / transmission of this material. He will not choose ornaments of speech from external (*alienos*) sources;[15] instead he will rely on his own simple style. Flint has suggested that Geoffrey's omission of any reference to his own erudition and his protestations of rhetorical inadequacy constitute a parodic reformulation of dedications written by William of Malmesbury and Henry of Huntingdon, historians who underscore their learnedness.[16] Whether or not Geoffrey intended his dedication as a parody cannot be known. It is clear, however, that his claim to rusticity or "rural style" is a well-known topos, one which is designed to highlight the extraordinary erudition of the author.[17] It is noteworthy that the topos is compatible with the practice described as *transferre*. The author, then, claims the freedom to change or transform the rhetorical style of the work being "translated."

A third aspect of the dedication is Geoffrey's attempt to derive authority for his book from the status of the recipient. Robert of Gloucester, is asked to "correct" Geoffrey's work so that, with Robert's help, the work "may be said to be his publication whom Henry, the illustrious king of the English, begat. . . ." In other words, Geoffrey seeks to link his own position as author / translator with that of his patron. The association adds luster to the work by suggesting that it is authorized by one whose lineage Geoffrey is relating. By translating the lost *liber*, Geoffrey has rehabilitated Henry's family history. In doing so, he establishes himself as a crucial link in the chain of remembrance; in effect, Geoffrey attempts to situate himself and his book within the historical process of transfer which is his subject. Historical and literary genealogy are correlated. (As we shall see, this is an idea which is adopted, and greatly elaborated, by Wace.) The claims he makes are far-reaching and revolve around the process indicated by the term *transferre*.

We turn now to Wace's use of the passage. Unlike the *Historia*, the *Brut* contains no dedication. Instead, an eight-line prologue announces the subject and the author's intentions.

> Ki vult oïr e vult saveir
> De rei en rei e d'eir en eir
> Ki cil furent e dunt il vindrent
> Ki Engleterre primes tindrent,
> Quels reis i ad en ordre eü,
> Ki anceis e ki puis i fu,
> Maistre Wace l'ad translaté
> Qui en conte la verité.

> [He who wants to hear and who wants to know
> Those who first held England
> From king to king and from heir to heir
> Who these were and where they came from
> What kings there were and in what order
> Who came first and who came later
> Master Wace, who tells the truth about it,
> has translated it.]   (lines 1-8)

In the first part of the Prologue (lines 1-6), Wace appeals directly to a public as his audience and not to a patron; this fact establishes the position of the author in relation to his listeners and readers. Specification of *matière* follows: the text will relate the genealogy of the kings of Britain. The rhetorical repetition and hypotaxis of these lines (*vult...vult*; *rei...rei*; *d'eir...eir*; *Ki...Ki...Ki*) suggests the genealogical format of the subsequent narrative; a conflation of form and content is indicated. The second part of the Prologue (lines 6-8) names the controlling presence "Maistre Wace," who has "translated" the *matière*. By claiming that he is recounting the truth about the *matière*, Wace implies that others do not. By inserting his name, Wace asserts his own authority in the process of textual generation and continuation. The connection between his name, the process of "translation," and the *verité* of the text, legitimizes future authorial interventions, and allows Wace the freedom to transform his model.[18] Wace's claims, therefore, go beyond Geoffrey's; Wace reserves the right to modify the *matière* itself.[19]

II

Geoffrey uses the term *transferre* again in the central section of the *Historia*, where he inserts another dedication and another "translation": the *Prophetia Merlini*. The new dedication is an interruption of the narrative at a special moment. King Vortigern has just heard an explanation of Merlin's mysterious birth and has just witnessed Merlin's first act of divination:

> Credidit ergo rex, quia verum prius dixerat de stagno et fecit hauriri stagnum. Sed super omnia Merlinum admirabatur; admirabantur etiam cuncti qui aderant tantam in eo sapientiam, existimantes numen esse in illo.

> [The king therefore believed it, because he <Merlin> had told the truth about the pool earlier and he had the pool drained. But above all, he wondered at Merlin; everyone there wondered at the greatness of his wisdom, thinking that there was divinity in him.]   (Book 6:12, 334-37)

These lines are the conclusion of Book Six; it is at this point that Geoffrey interrupts the narration and turns to the Prophecies. The focus on the king and his admiration of Merlin is particularly suggestive. What better moment to disrupt the flow of the narrative and remind the reader of his debt to Geoffrey, who is "translating" this information about Merlin for the first time? Geoffrey highlights the importance of Book Seven by including another dedication passage, in which he discusses his reasons for translating the Prophecies.

> Nondum autem ad hunc locum historiae perveneram, cum, de Merlino divulgato rumore, compellebant me undique contemporanei mei prophetias ipsius edere, maxime autem Alexander Linconensis episcopus, vir summae religionis et prudentiae. Non erat alter in clero sive in populo cui tot nobiles famularentur, quos mansueta pietas ipsius et benigna largitas in obsequium suum alliciebat. Cui cum satisfacere praeelegissem, prophetias *transtuli* et eidem cum huiusmodi litteris direxi:
>> "Coegit me, Alexander, Lincoliensis episcopus,

nobilitatis tuae dilectio *prophetias Merlini de Britannico in Latinum transferre, antequam historiam perarassem, quam de gestis regum Britannorum inceperam.* Proposueram enim illam prius perficere et illud opus subsequenter explanare, ne, dum uterque labor incumberet, sensus meus ad singula minor fieret. Attamen quoniam securus eram veniae quam discretio subtilis ingenii tui donaret, agrestem calamum meum libello apposui et plebeio modulamine ignotum tibi *interpretatus* sum sermonem."

[But I had not yet reached this place in the story when, noise about Merlin having gotten about, my contemporaries urged me from all sides to publish his prophecies, but especially Alexander, Bishop of Lincoln, a man of the greatest religion and prudence. There was not another, whether among the clergy or among the people, who had so many nobles in his household, whom his gentle piety and benign largesse attracted to his service. When I had decided to satisfy him, I *translated* the Prophecies and sent them to him with this sort of letter:

"Love of your nobility, Alexander, Bishop of Lincoln, *has made me translate the Prophecies of Merlin from the British into Latin before finishing the history that I had begun of the deeds of the British kings.* For I had intended to finish that first and to set forth this work later lest while it was burdened with a double labor my wit should become less for each of them. Nevertheless, since I was sure of the pardon which the judgment of your subtle wit would give, I applied my rustic pen to the little book and with a plebian melody I have *interpreted* the language unknown to you."]

(Book 7:1-7:2, 1-15, emphasis added)

It is now believed that Geoffrey's translation of the Prophecies had been circulated independently, prior to the completion of the *Historia*.[20] The Prophecies, then, would have helped to establish Geoffrey's reputation as a writer, and the insertion of them at the physical center of the work served to highlight Geoffrey's reputation and his skill as an author.[21] They are carefully woven into the preceding narrative and become a natural part of the scene which concludes Book Six. The dedication, which introduces the Prophecies, underscores the importance of translation from the vernacular into Latin; the verb *transferre* is referred to twice, and the term *interpretatus* also refers to translation.

The corresponding passage from the *Brut* contrasts dramatically:

> Dunc dist Merlin les prophecies
> Que vus avez, ço crei, oïes,
> *Des reis ki a venir esteient,*
> *Ki la terre tenir deveient.*
> Ne vuil sun livre *translater*
> Quant jo nel sai *interpreter*;
> Nule rien dire ne vuldreie
> Que si ne fust cum jo dirreie.

> [Then Merlin spoke the prophecies
> Which you have, I believe, heard,
> *of the kings who were to come*
> *and who should govern the land.*
> I don't want to *translate* his book
> since I don't know how to *interpret* it.
> I wouldn't want to say anything
> unless it were just as I should say.]
> (lines 7535-42, emphasis added)

Wace's text is especially striking because, although he retains the reference to "translation", his use of the term *translater* is *negative*. Wace refuses to translate Merlin's "book" of prophecies, he says, because he does not know how to "interpret" it; in other words, without interpretation there is no translation and, therefore, no (new) text. Wace's refusal to translate the *livre* raises a number of questions. This passage, like Geoffrey's, is located near the physical center of the text; why does Wace refuse this act of translation here? Given the extraordinary popularity of the Prophecies, it at first seems somewhat surprising that Wace deleted them.[22] The importance of the midpoint helps to explain the deletion. Since the Prophecies are so closely identified with Geoffrey, it is logical that Wace would remotivate this central section in order to celebrate his own identity as an author. He accomplishes this, first, by using the midpoint, as Geoffrey does, to recall the beginning of his work, and, second, by establishing a crucial link between his own narrative presence and Merlin, an important authorial figure. A particularly striking parallel is created by lines 7537-38, which relate the narrative subject of Merlin:

> Des reis ki a venir esteient,
> Ki la terre tenir deveient

and lines 2-4 of the Prologue, which specify the *matière* that Wace will relate:

> De rei en rei e d'eir en eir
> Ki cil furent e dunt il vindrent
> Ki Engleterre primes tindrent.

The connection between Wace and Merlin is underscored by an act of clerkly interpretation which Wace highlights at the *exact* midpoint of his poem.

Instead of Merlin's Prophecies, Wace situates the story of Merlin's birth at the center of the *Brut*. As noted above, Geoffrey also relates the tale, but his account differs from Wace's in several important ways. In the *Historia*, Merlin's mother (a nun) confesses to King Vortigern that she does not know who Merlin's father is:

> "Unum autem scio, quia cum essem in thalamo parentum puella, apparuit mihi quidam in specie formosi iuvenis, ut videbatur, et amplectens me strictis bracchiis saepissime osculabatur et statim evanescebat, ita ut indicium hominis non appareret loquebaturque aliquando non comparens. Cumque in hunc modum me diu frequentasset, tandem in specie humana miscuit se mihi et gravidam dereliquit. Sciat ergo prudentia tua, me aliter non cognovisse virum."

23

["When, as a girl, I was sleeping in the bedroom of my parents, there appeared to me, as it seemed, someone in the shape of a handsome youth, and holding me tightly in his arms, he would often kiss me and suddenly disappear, so that a trace of a man would not appear; and he used to speak sometimes, without appearing. And when he had frequented me in this manner for a long time, finally, in human appearance he lay with me and left me pregnant. Let your prudence therefore know that I have not known a man except in this way."] (Book 6:11, 297-304)

The king calls "Maugantius magus" before him to determine whether what the woman claims is possible. Maugantius confirms the possibility, citing Apuleius's *De deo Socratis* on sublunar demons as his authority.

Wace makes a number of small but crucial changes in Geoffrey's account of Merlin's paternity. For example, in the *Brut*, Merlin's mother specifically *refuses* to speculate about the identity of Merlin's father:

> "Une chose veneit suvent
> Ki me baisout estreitement.
> Cumë hume parler l'oeie,
> Et cumë hume le senteie,
> E plusurs feiz od mei parlout
> Que neient ne se demustrout.
> Tant m'ala issi aprismant
> E tant m'ala suvent baisant,
> Od mei se culcha si conçui,
> Unches hume plus ne conui.
> *Cest vallet oi, cest vallet ai*
> *Plus n'en fu, ne plus n'en dirai.*"

> ["A thing often used to come
> which (embraced) me tightly and kissed me.
> I heard it speak as a man
> and I felt it as a man
> and it spoke with me several times
> without ever showing itself.

It so often came, approaching me in this way
and it so often came and kissed me,
that it lay with me and <I> conceived.
No other man have I ever known.
I had and I have this boy;
There was no more to it, <and> I will say no more
        about it."]   (lines 7423-34, emphasis added)

Her remarks, which constitute the exact midpoint of the *Brut* (line 7432), must be interpreted by Magant, *un clerc de lettres mult savant*, who is summoned by the king:

"Trové avum, dist il, escrit,
Qu'une manere d'esperit
Est entre la lune e la terre.
Ki vult de lur nature enquerre,
En partie unt nature humaine
E en partie suveraine.
Incubi demones unt nun;
Par tut l'eir unt lur regiun,
E en la terre unt lur repaire.
Ne püent mie grant mal faire;
Ne püent mie mult noisir
Fors de gaber e d'escharnir.
Bien prenent humaine figure
E ço cunsent bien lur nature.
Mainte meschine unt deceüe
E en tel guise purgeüe;
Issi puet Merlin estre nez
E issi puet estre engendrez."

["We have found it written, he says
That a type of spirit exists
between the moon and the earth
which, if you want to inquire about their nature,
they have, in part, a human nature,
in part a supernatural one.
These demons are called incubi;
their region is throughout the air,

25

their dwelling is in the earth.
They cannot cause any great trouble,
nor can they do much harm
apart from joking and mocking.
They often take on human form;
their nature permits that.
They have deceived many a young girl,
and in such a way made her pregnant.
In this manner Merlin
could have been engendered and born."]

(lines 7439-56)

Where Geoffrey cites a specific philosophical authority, Wace instead appeals more generally to the existence of texts. The placement of this passage at the physical center of Wace's work underscores the importance of interpretation as a clerkly activity. Interpretation must be based on the clerk's knowledge of texts. There are, of course, no external texts to support Merlin's Prophecies, and this makes the interpretation of them problematic for Wace. At the same time, the act of interpretation on the part of the "learned clerk" links him to Wace, whose function in the poem is to explain the truth about genealogical succession and, consequently, the truth about antecedents.

Wace introduces in this passage an important theme, that of genealogical subversion. In a world where paternity (both physical and textual) is in doubt, genealogical history (and narrative) become problematic. Merlin, however, is a crucial link in the chain of textual transmission, and his importance in the narrative must ultimately be confirmed. His role is made clear in the following passage:

> *Maistre Wace, ki fist cest livre,*
> *Ne volt plus dire de sa fin*
> *Qu'en dist li prophetes Merlin;*
> Merlin dist d'Arthur, si ot dreit,
> Que sa mort dutuse serreit.
> *Li prophetes dist verité;*
> Tut tens en ad l'um puis duté,

26

E dutera, ço crei, tut dis,
Se il est morz u il est vis.
Porter se fist en Avalun,
Pur veir, puis l'Incarnatiun
Cinc cenz e quarante dous anz.
Damage fud qu'il n'ot enfanz.

[*Master Wace, who made this book*
does not want to say any more about his end
than the prophet Merlin says about it.
Merlin says of Arthur, and he is right,
that his death must remain in doubt.
The prophet speaks the truth;
people have always doubted
and always will doubt, I think
<whether> he is dead or alive.
He had himself carried to Avalon
it is true; 542 years after the Incarnation.
It was a pity that he had no children.]

(lines 13282-94, emphasis added)

Through his prophecies about Arthur, Merlin links the king to the present rulers of Britain. In other words, Merlin's prophecies act as a poetic substitute for natural paternity, which is unavailable to Arthur (*Damage fud qu'il n'ot enfanz*). It is Merlin (through the intermediary of Geoffrey and Wace) who makes available the link between the glorious Arthurian past and the reality of the present reign. It is no accident that Merlin became one of the most powerful figures associated with writing in the Middle Ages, and it is a measure of Wace's genius that he focused on and exploited this association so quickly and so expertly.[23] Wace's manipulation of the concept *translater* as translation, interpretation, and transfer allows this association to be articulated.

III

The *Brut* offers one other example of the verb *translater*, in lines 3335-48. As in the other two passages, the power of the

translator's craft is underscored. This passage relates the story of
Marcia, the wife of Guincelins, the grandson of Belin; again, it is
striking when compared to the corresponding passage in the
Historia.

> Post hunc Gwntelinus diadema regni suscepit, quod satis
> modeste omni tempore vitae suae rexit. Erat ei nobilis
> uxor, Marcia nomine, omnibus artibus erudita, quae inter
> plurima, proprio ingenio reperta, legem quam Britones
> Marcianam appellant, invenit. *Hanc rex Aluredus inter
> cetera transtulit et Saxonica lingua Marchenelaga vocavit.*

> [After him Guithelin received the crown of the kingdom,
> which he ruled virtuously all the time of his life. He had
> a noble wife named Marcia, who was learned in all the
> arts. This woman, among the many things she used her
> talent to create, wrote a law which the Britons call the
> Marciana. *This law, among other things, King Alfred
> translated and <he> called it the mercian law in the
> Saxon tongue.*]   (Book 3:12, 226-30, emphasis added)

Wace's version is as follows:

> Guincelins fu de bone vie,
> E sa moiller out num Marcie,
> Lettree fu e sage dame,
> De buen pris e de bone fame.
> Sun enging mist tut e sa cure
> A saveir lettre e escriture.
> Mult sout e mult estudia,
> Une lei escrit e trova,
> Marcïene l'apela l'on
> Sulunc le language breton.
> *Li reis Alvret, si cum l'en dist,*
> *Translata la lei e escrist.*
> Quant il l'out en engleis tornee,
> Marcenelaga l'ad nomee.

> [Guincelins led a good life

and his wife was named Marcia.
She was a lettered and wise lady,
most worthy and of good repute.
She brought all her wit and all her care
to bear on learning texts and writings.
She learned much and studied a great deal.
She wrote a law,
which was called the Mercian
in the British language.
King Alfred, so they say,
translated the law and wrote it out.
When he had turned it into English
he named it the Marcian law.]
                    (lines 3335-48, emphasis added)

As Tatlock has explained, the passage from the *Historia* must be situated within its political context. Marcia is an invention, her name "coined with a glance at Roman history, from an existing scheme of English law, the Mercian" (p. 283). Geoffrey may have gotten his idea from Gildas, who is cited in connection with the translation of another law, the Molmutine:[24]

> Si quis autem desiderat scire omnia quae de eis prae-
> ceperit legat Molmontinas leges, quas Gildas historio-
> graphus de Britannico in Latinum, rex vero Aluredus de
> Latino in Anglicum transtulit et reperiet luculenter
> scripta quae optat.

> [Whoever wants to know everything which he set forth
> about them, let him read the Molmutine laws, which the
> historian Gildas translated from British into Latin, and
> which King Alfred translated from Latin into English,
> and he will find most clearly written what he wishes.]
>   (Book 3:4, 80-84)

Marcia is one of several strong female rulers depicted in the *His-toria*; it has been argued that these women were created in homage to Mathilda, daughter of Henry I, who, like Marcia, acted as regent

29

for her young son.[25] The attributes of the figure Marcia are those of a wise ruler; they are, in addition, qualities prized in literary patrons. Like Geoffrey's patrons and benefactors, Marcia is learned (*erudita*); Walter, who gave the original *liber* to Geoffrey, is described as *eruditus*, and Robert of Gloucester is *philosophia liberalibus artibus erudivit*.[26] Marcia has *ingenium*, as does Alexander of Lincoln. She has also written a law which has been translated (and therefore adopted) by a British king. It seems possible that Geoffrey, through this flattering portrait of a ruling regent similar to Mathilda, sought to stress that the reputation of rulers and patrons is dependent, in part, upon the process of translation.

Wace modifies the meaning of this passage in several ways. Since the context of patronage is not referred to in the *Brut*, qualities associated with patrons and donors are, instead, attributed directly, and exclusively, to Marcia (i.e., to the writer herself). Wace deletes the earlier reference to the Molmutine laws and amplifies Geoffrey's brief reference to Marcia's erudition (*omnibus artibus erudita*), devoting a full three lines of the passage to the description of her learnedness. It is implied that her good reputation and her worth are linked to her knowledge of *lettre* and *escriture*; this knowledge results from conscientious study (*mult sout e mult estudia*). It is also stressed that we know about Marcia *because* of writing--not only her own scholarly activity, but also that of the translator (who renames the law Marcia wrote) which perpetuated her memory. The claims are therefore very similar to Geoffrey's; however, Wace underscores the importance of learning and of texts.

It is evident that Geoffrey's use of the term *transferre* and Wace's use of the term *translater* are complex and reveal much about their theories of writing. For Geoffrey, translation is a powerful process through which oral tradition may become legitimized. It allows free reign of rhetorical expression, is a crucial part of the process of genealogical transfer and genealogico-historical memory, and is closely linked to the concept of patronage. For Wace, translation is a vision of truth which allows the author to add or to delete material. It implies interpretation based on the author's own erudition, is suggestively linked to paternity, and is not discussed as a product of patronage. Geoffrey's reference to his translation of the *liber* at the conclusion of the *Historia* is omitted from the *Brut*, as is his single reference to *transferre* as a process of physical transfer (Book 5:19). Wace includes only those examples of *transferre* which in the *Historia* refer to rulership or patronage, and, as we have seen, these passages are all significantly reformulated. Wace's choice of passages is a natural one, since the *Brut* is, in large measure, a celebration of the translator's independence and authority. The *Brut* is clearly an important stage in the development of a concept of translation in the mid-twelfth century. It is, indeed, difficult to imagine such texts as *Thèbes*, *Enéas*, and *Troie* without the claims for translation which are outlined in the *Brut*. As the first great Old French translation of the twelfth century, it is not only an innovative, but also a most authoritative text.

NOTES

1. Michel Zink, "Une mutation de la conscience littéraire: Le langage romanesque à travers des exemples français du XIIe siècle," *Cahiers de civilisation médiévale* 24 (1981):3-27; here, p. 8.

2. The mixed reception of the *Historia* in the twelfth century is well known. (See, e.g., J. S. P. Tatlock, *The Legendary History of Britain* [New York: Gordian Press, 1950; 1974], pp. 422-32; Nancy F. Partner, *Serious Entertainments: The Writing of History in Twelfth-Century England* [Chicago and London: Univ. of Chicago Press, 1977], pp. 62-68; and Valerie I. J. Flint, "The *Historia Regum Britanniae* of Geoffrey of Monmouth: Parody and its Purpose. A Suggestion," *Speculum* 54 [1979]: 447-68; here, pp. 447-48.) The attack on Geoffrey's use of translation is particularly interesting. The claim is made by William of Newburgh in the *Prooemium* to his *Historia Rerum Anglicarum*: "Gaufridus hic dictus est, agnomen habens Arturi, pro eo quod fabulas de Arturo, ex priscis Britonum figmentis sumptas et ex proprio auctas, per superductum Latini sermonis colorem honesto historiae nomine palliavit. . . ." [He was called Gaufridus with the nickname Arturus because, taking up the myths about Arthur from the early figments of the British and increasing them with some of his own, he cloaked them with the virtuous name of history, casting over them the color of the Latin language. . . .] The text of the *Prooemium*, along with

several other twelfth- to fourteenth-century discussions of Arthurian material, is found in E. K. Chambers's *Arthur of Britain* (1927; rpt. Cambridge: Speculum Historiale, and NY: Barnes and Noble, Inc., 1964), pp. 246-82. William of Newburgh is cited on pp. 274-75.

3. *Le Roman de Brut de Wace*, ed. Ivor Arnold, 2 vols. (Paris: SATF, 1938, 1940). All references are to this edition.

4. *Le Livre des Psaumes: Ancienne traduction française*, ed. Francisque-Michel (Paris: Imprimerie Nationale, 1876).

5. Other examples of this second meaning of the term occur in Gaimar's *Lestorie des Engles* (c. 1150). Robert of Gloucester--Geoffrey's patron for the *Historia*--had commissioned the translation of one of the manuscripts used by Gaimar. The author notes that Robert:

> Fist translater icele geste,
> Solum les liueres as Waleis
> Kil aueient des Bretons reis
>
> [had this "geste" translated
> according to the books about the British kings
> they had in Welsh;]   (lines 6451-53)

and he then says, with reference to his source:

> Geffrai Gaimar cel liuere escrit,
> Les translad anfes i mist,
> Ke li Waleis ourent leisse.
>
> [Geoffrey Gaimar wrote this book.
> He translated them, put in deeds
> which the Welsh had left out.]   (lines 6460-62)

(Trans. and ed. T. D. Hardy and C. T. Martin, *Lestorie des Engles solum la translacion Maistre Geffrei Gaimar*, 2 vols. [London: Eyre and Spottiswoode, 1888-89]. This passage is reprinted in Chambers [n. 2 above], pp. 260-61.) Although the term does not occur in *Enéas* or *Thèbes*, it is used by Benoît in *Troie* to explain the reception of Dares's manuscript into the

Latin tradition:

> Lonc tens fu sis livres perduz,
> Qu'il ne fu trovez ne veüz;
> Mais a Athenes le trova
> Cornelius, quil translata:
> De greu le torna en latin
> Par son sen e par son engin.

> [His book was lost for a long time;
> it was neither found nor seen.
> But Cornelius, who translated it,
> found it in Athens.
> He turned it into Latin from the Greek
> with his cleverness and wit.]   (lines 117-22)

Benoît insists that his own work is a faithful copy, although he does not refer to it as a translation:

> Ceste estoire n'est pas usee,
> N'en guaires lieus nen est trovee:
> Ja retraite ne fust ancore,
> Mais Beneeiz de Sainte More
> L'a contrové e fait e dit
> E o sa main les moz escrit.
> . . . .
> Ci vueil l'estoire comencier:
> Le latin sivrai e la letre,
> Nule autre rien n'i voudrai metre,
> S'ensi non com jol truis escrit.

> [This story is not well known
> nor is it found in many places.
> It was never written out before,
> but Benoît of Sainte More
> has found it, made and created it,
> and written the words with his hand.
> . . . .
> I want to begin the story here:

33

I'll follow the Latin and the letter,
I don't want to include anything else at all unless it is
just exactly as I have found it written down.]
(lines 129-34, 138-41)

(*Le Roman de Troie, par Benoît de Sainte-Maure*, ed. Léopold Constans, 4 vols. [Paris: Firmin-Didot et Cie, 1904-08].) Benoît uses the term *translater* more frequently in the *Chronique des Ducs de Normandie*, where it is connected with hard work and study:

Granz est l'estuide e li labors,
Granz esmais sereit as plusors
De si faite ovre translater,
Mais ne m'i puis desconforter:
Se mi senz est humle et petiz,
Je crei que li Sainz Esperiz
I overra ensemble od mei.

[Great is the study and the labor,
most people would have great distress
to translate such a work.
But I can't be sad <about it>;
though my wit is humble and small
I believe that the Holy Spirit
will work together with me.]   (lines 2123-29)

(*Chronique des Ducs de Normandie par Benoît*, ed. Carin Fahlin, 3 vols. [Uppsala: Bibliotheca Ekmaniana, 1951-1967].) (See also Aimé Petit, who notes that Benoît "souligne qu'il procède à une traduction en recourant au verbe *translater* et en mettant l'accent sur les difficultés de la traduction d'un texte latin" [*Naissances du roman. Les Techniques littéraires dans les romans antiques du XII*[e] *siècle*, 2 vols. (Paris and Geneva: Champion-Slatkine, 1985), 2:790].)

It is also associated with truth and accuracy:

Tant puis bien dire, sanz mentir,
Translatee ai l'estoire e dite
D'eissi cum l'ai trovee escrite;
N'ai mis fauseté ne mençonge.

[This I can certainly say without lying:
I have translated the story and I have written it
just as I have found it written.
I have put no falsehood or lie.]

(lines 42034-37)

Other uses of the term *translater* occur in lines 2159, 14781, 42049, and 44502.

6. *Le Roman de Rou de Wace*, ed. A. J. Holden, 3 vols. (Paris: SATF, 1970-73).

7. Robert Marichal, "Naissance du roman," in *Entretiens sur la Renaissance du XIIe siècle*, ed. Maurice de Gandillac and Edouard Jeauneau (Paris and The Hague: Mouton, 1968), pp. 449-82; here, p. 450. I want to thank Jeanette Beer for bringing this point to my attention.

8. Several examples of the expression in the *romans antiques* are given by Petit [n. 5 above], 2:789-92. See also Marichal [n. 7 above], pp. 450-51.

9. *The Medieval French* Roman d'Alexandre (Vol. 2, Version of Alexandre de Paris, Text), ed. E. C. Armstrong, D. L. Buffum, Bateman Edwards, and L. F. H. Lowe (Princeton: Princeton Univ. Press, 1937).

10. On the concept of *translatio* and its relation to translation, see Douglas Kelly, "Translatio Studii: Translation, Adaptation, and Allegory in Medieval French Literature," *Philological Quarterly* 57 (1978):287-310. According to Kelly, "There are three prominent modes of *translatio* in medieval French: translation as such, including scribal transmission; adaptation; and allegorical or extended metaphorical discourse. In each case, a source, an extant *materia* surviving from the past, is re-done by a new writer who is, in effect, the translator. . . . *Translatio* is in fact rarely only close translation. The translator has a specific intention in making the translation. And that intention may differ from the original author's" (pp. 291-92). Laurie Scott Tomchak has made note of the connection between the term *translater* and *translatio* in Wace's *Roman de Rou* ("Wace's Work: Patronage, Repetition and Translation in the *Roman de Rou*" [Ph.D. diss., University of California, Irvine, 1983], pp. 33-37, 55).

35

11. *Geoffrey of Monmouth* Historia regum Britanniae: *A Variant Version Edited from Manuscripts*, ed. Jacob Hammer. (Cambridge, MA: The Medieval Academy of America, 1951). The chronology of the various versions of the *Historia* has been a vexing problem in Galfridian studies. Hans-Erich Keller has discussed the merits of the several editions. He strongly supports the *Variant Version* published by Hammer as the chief source for Wace's *Brut*. ("Wace et Geoffrey de Monmouth: Problème de la Chronologie des Sources," *Romania* 98 [1977]:1-14. See in particular pp. 7-8).

12. A second dedication to Waleran of Mellent follows. There is still some question whether the double dedication preceded a single dedication to Robert. Acton Griscom (*The Historia Regum Britanniae of Geoffrey of Monmouth* [London, New York, and Toronto: Longmans, Green and Co., 1929]), favors the double dedication as the earliest version of the *Historia* (pp. 42-44). See, however, Neil Wright, who, in the preface to his recent edition of the *Historia* (*The Historia Regum Britanniae of Geoffrey of Monmouth, I. Bern, Burgerbibliothek, MS. 568* [Cambridge: D. S. Brewer, 1985]), states: "in fact, the relationship of the Robert and Robert-Waleran dedications cannot be resolved with certainty, although it is possible that that to Robert alone is the earlier" (p. xiv). I would like to thank Robert M. Durling for contributing the translation of Book 7:1-7:2, lines 1-15 of the *Historia*. All other translations of the *Historia* are my own.

13. For a résumé of the scholarship concerning the *liber* see Tatlock [n. 2 above], pp. 422-32; Geoffrey Ashe, "'A Certain Very Ancient Book': Traces of an Arthurian Source in Geoffrey of Monmouth's *History*," *Speculum* 56 (1981):301-23; and Wright [n. 12 above], pp. xvii-xviii. Flint [n. 2 above] views the reference as an elaborate joke: "As Latin literature was accumulating round him when Geoffrey was writing, so too was anxiety about translation. . . . There is an element of pure delight in the thought that the single source which Geoffrey claimed his learned contemporaries lacked . . ." (p. 460). Griscom [n. 12 above] criticizes a similar, earlier approach by R. H. Fletcher and W. Lewis Jones and vehemently defends the seriousness of Geoffrey's purpose: "to suggest that . . . 'his appeal to his *liber* is chiefly a joke' . . . is to read modern theories and standards of historical writing back into the XII century." (p. 52).

14. As Robert Hanning has suggested, "the appeal to the *vetustissimus liber*, of which he is but the translator, is very possibly an indication that Geoffrey was aware of the radical nature of his departure from the fall of Britain tradition and sought to soften the impact of his approach by giving it a pedigree of its own" (*The Vision of History in Early Britain from Gildas to Geoffrey of Monmouth* [New York: Columbia Univ. Press, 1966], p. 223 n. 11).

15. It is unclear exactly what Geoffrey means by *alienos*. The term could imply treatises, other writers, or even the *liber* itself. The ambiguity is no doubt intentional.

16. "In their prefaces both William and Henry lay stress upon the quantity and breadth of their reading. . . . Geoffrey, in words not too far removed from those of William, sounds in his own preface a first clear note of discord: 'infra alienos ortulos falerata verba non collegerim, agresti tamen stilo propriis calamis contentus.'" (Flint [n. 2 above], pp. 452-53).

17. On the topos of affected modesty see E. R. Curtius, *European Literature and the Latin Middle Ages*, trans. Willard R. Trask (Princeton: Princeton Univ. Press, [1953] 1973), pp. 83-85. On Geoffrey's learnedness, see Hammer [n. 11 above], pp. 265-69, and Flint [n. 2 above], pp. 459-60.

18. Cf. Ebba Kristine Brightenback who has noted that "the juxtaposition of *translaté* and *vérité* . . . permits us to understand that the narrator's reliability and authority are inseparably linked to his clerkliness rather than specifically to the truth he professes to 'translate'" ("Aspects of Organicity in Old French Romance Narrative: The Prologue and Narrative Modalities in the Lais of Marie de France" [Ph.D. diss., Princeton University, 1974], p. 24). For Brightenback, translation serves two main functions in the *Brut*: (1) it "provides an occasion for a display of erudition" and (2) "it serves as a pretext for the poetic exploitation of latent authorizations" (pp. 27-28).

19. On this point see Zink [n. 1 above] (p. 4), who notes that "l'irruption de l'auteur en tant que tel et de la conscience qu'il a de lui-même au sein de la littérature définit à la fois le moment où la littérature mérite ce nom et celui où la vérité de l'œuvre est celle-là seule que lui

concède l'auteur, qui a seul *autorité* pour définir sa nature et qui en porte la responsabilité"; and Norris J. Lacy: "Wace adopts from Geoffroy's text certain elements, and adds others, which undermine the historian's authority. By reporting what a chronicler cannot know, he is signaling that he is now working primarily in the realm of literature, from the point of view of the omniscient author. This is true not only of the *kind* of material but also of its arrangement: a conscious ordering of events, being necessarily artificial, works against any impression of historical accuracy" ("The Form of the *Brut's* Arthurian Sequence," in *The Jean Misrahi Memorial Volume: Studies in Medieval Literature*, ed. Hans R. Runte, Henri Niedzielski, and William L. Hendrickson [Columbia, SC: French Literature Publications Co., 1977], pp. 150-58; here, p. 152). The problem of historicity in the *Brut* is complex and beyond the scope of this essay. For an overview of the theoretical issues involved see Suzanne Fleischman, "On the Representation of History and Fiction in the Middle Ages," *History and Theory: Studies in the Philosophy of History* 22 (1983):278-310. On the relation of truth and fiction in twelfth-century narrative, see Jeanette M. A. Beer, *Narrative Conventions of Truth in the Middle Ages*, Etudes de Philologie et d'Histoire (Geneva: Droz, 1981).

20. This is the view of Wright [n. 12 above] (p. xi), who states: "Evidence that this was indeed the case is provided by the *Historia Ecclesiastica* of Orderic Vitalis. In Book 12, chapter 47, Orderic quotes parts of the *Prophetie* . . . [He] states that his source was a *libellus Merlini*. This book of Orderic's *Historia* was written in 1135-36; so the *Prophetie* were available separately, in the form of a *libellus*, in Normandy at this date--a date fully concomitant with their probable completion by 1135." That the prophecies were circulated independently of the *Historia* after its publication is well-known. See, e.g., Caroline D. Eckhardt, *The Prophetia Merlini of Geoffrey of Monmouth: A Fifteenth-Century Commentary* (Cambridge, MA: The Medieval Academy of America, 1982), pp. 4-6.

21. As Tatlock [n. 2 above] has noted: "seldom does Geoffrey show his architectonic ability more than by his seventh book. When the *Historia* has completed half of its steady advance, comes this pause, to look back a little and forward even to the time of writing. Thus he carries the blood of his own present into the withered past. . . . From Virgil, who does the same half-way through the *Aeneid*, also by means of a marvelous prophecy . . . he may have got the idea" (p. 403). The *Aeneid* connection is also noted by

Wright [n. 12 above], p. xvii.

22.　See Eckhardt [n. 20 above], pp. 1-15.　Ivor Arnold, editor of the *Brut*, cites three thirteenth-century Anglo-Norman manuscripts in which scribes have emended Wace's text by adding the prophecies.　These interpolations attest to the enduring popularity of the prophecies and suggest that the deletion of them in the *Brut* was somewhat surprising--at least to later readers of Wace.　See Arnold's "Introduction" [n. 3 above], pp. vii-xii.　The manuscripts in question are: Durham Cathedral C. IV. 27.I; Lincoln Cathedral, no. 104; a ms. from the private library of Mr. Boies Penrose.　There are no surviving twelfth-century mss.

23.　See, for example, the recent discussion of Merlin as author in R. Howard Bloch, *Etymologies and Genealogies: A Literary Anthropology of the French Middle Ages* (Chicago: Univ. of Chicago Press, 1983), pp. 1-6 and 212-17.　For an in-depth study of the figure of Merlin, see Paul Zumthor's *Merlin le prophète*, (Lausanne: Payot, 1943; Rpt. Geneva: Slatkine, 1973).

24.　Tatlock [n. 2 above], p. 283.

25.　See, e.g., Tatlock [n. 2 above], p. 288.

26.　It is worth noting that Robert was Mathilda's chief supporter in her struggle for power. See Tatlock [n. 2 above], p. 288.

FIVE OLD FRENCH RENDERINGS OF
THE *PASSIO SANCTE KATERINE VIRGINIS*

William MacBain

Of the many Latin versions of the legend of St. Catherine of Alexandria which have survived into modern times, one--the *Passio Sancte Katerine Virginis*, also known as the *Vulgata* text (ed. Knust, *Geschichte*, pp. 231-314)--is the source of at least five different renderings into Old French, all dating from the twelfth and thirteenth centuries. A comparison of these Old French texts with their Latin source and with one another casts light on the manner in which different medieval translators approached their task and to what extent they perceived the need to reinterpret the message--or perhaps the medium--of the eleventh-century Latin version geared to learned clerics, for the society of a different period and for a different kind of audience.

The Old French texts in question are as follows: (1) the twelfth-century Anglo-Norman rhymed version by Clemence, a Benedictine nun from the Abbey of Barking, which is preserved in three manuscripts (ed. MacBain, *Life of St Catherine*); (2) the thirteenth-century rhymed version by Gui which is preserved in a single manuscript in the Bibliothèque Nationale, Paris (ed. Todd); (3) the thirteenth-century rhymed version by Aumeric in the dialect of Poitou preserved in a single manuscript in the Bibliothèque Municipale, Tours (ed. Naudeau); (4) an anonymous thirteenth-century rhymed version in Picard preserved in seven manuscripts and a fragment (ed. MacBain, *De Sainte Katerine*); and (5) a thirteenth-century prose version preserved in four manuscripts (ed. Knust, *Geschichte*, pp. 232-314).

Two of the Old French texts (the version by Gui and the prose version) appear to be based on an abbreviated version of the *Vulgata* dating from the twelfth century. Two of the translators (Gui and Clemence) claim to be reworking existing translations of an earlier period (Clemence) or in another dialect (Gui). All of the Old French texts cut out much of the apologetic material thought to date back possibly to the second century A.D. Several of the versions add their own special touches to appeal to contemporary listeners. The longest version is that of Aumeric, although the sole manuscript of this text lacks the beginning section. This is especially unfortunate in that, in the absence of a prologue of some kind, we have no way of knowing how the author approached his task or what sources he claimed to be using. Was he, like Clemence and Gui, aware of earlier translations? Naudeau claims (p. 8) that Aumeric has used an unknown "source secondaire" in addition to the *Vulgata*, but the one piece of evidence he adduces in support of this hypothesis is not especially convincing. Aumeric's original poem must have run to over 2,900 lines. It is followed by that of Clemence with 2,700 lines. Gui's version, based as it is on the abbreviated form of the *Vulgata*, is understandably shorter with 1,971 lines, but the anonymous Picard working from the full-length *Vulgata* delivers the shortest text of all with only 1,616 lines, saying repeatedly: "Ne vos en voil fere lonc plet" and "Ne sai que face lonc sermon" and cutting the disputations down to their bare bones.

The plot of the St. Catherine legend may be rapidly summarized as follows: Catherine, only daughter of King Costus, lives in Alexandria where she had devoted her early years to the study of pagan philosophy until her conversion to Christianity. At the outset of the narrative she is eighteen years old. The Emperor Maxentius, following his defeat by Constantine, has fled to Alexandria and has ordered a general sacrifice to his gods. Catherine disrupts the ceremonies and disputes with him in the temple concerning the validity of their respective faiths. Unable to hold his own in debate with her, he summons fifty of his best orators, but they are vanquished by Catherine in public debate and converted to Christianity, for which they suffer martyrdom. After an unsuccessful attempt to win Catherine over by blandishments, Maxentius has her imprisoned for twelve days without food or drink. She is visited secretly by the queen and Porphirius, the emperor's chief of staff. Both are converted but keep silent out of fear of Maxentius. Starvation having failed, the emperor unveils a terrifying machine composed of rotating wheels and sharp blades with which he hopes to assure Catherine's apostasy or her destruction. Instead, it is the machine that is destroyed by a thunderbolt from heaven resulting in the death of four thousand pagans. Encouraged by this miracle, the queen and later Porphirius proclaim their new faith and suffer martyrdom. Catherine, who resolutely refuses to give up her faith even when Maxentius offers to make her his new queen, is beheaded, and her body is transported by angels to the summit of Mt. Sinai where it becomes the source of healing miracles.

In the prose version (hereafter referred to as *Prose*) and in those of Aumeric and the anonymous Picard (=*Picard*), the approach of the translator to his task is not explicit and must be inferred from a comparison of the text with its Latin source. *Prose* is indeed prosaic, occasionally glossing an already transparent image. Thus when Porphirius accuses the emperor of sparing him, the "principem et caput," and punishing his men, the "membra inferiora," the translator renders his model word for word but adds a phrase to explain what is meant by "membra inferiora":

> "Que veus tu fere, empereres, qi me lesses em pes qi princes sui et chies de ces? . . . et ces bas membres *et ces petites genz* fez mal . . ." (Knust, p. 305, emphasis added)

> ["What is your purpose, Emperor, in leaving me their prince and head in peace? . . . and you harm those lower limbs *and those little people* . . ."]

Aumeric, for his part, likes to add to the suspense of the narrative by interjecting his own emotional reaction to the situation. Thus when Catherine is about to begin her disputation with the philosophers, Aumeric exclaims: "Deus, per cui il i est, la gart!" [line 480; May God, for whose sake she stands there, protect her!], and after the death of Porphirius and his men, he remarks: "Damideus d'euz las armes ait!" [line 2436; May the Lord God keep their souls!]. Aumeric appears to feel that his model is at times insufficiently explicit. In the *Vulgata*, Catherine, in her initial confrontation with the emperor, is content to say that the sun, moon, and stars have no intrinsic power and simply do the bidding of their Creator. But Aumeric adds a whole series of explanations of natural phenomena going beyond the sun, moon, and stars to the firmament itself, the sea and tides, the effects of heat and rain on the earth, earthquakes, etc. The emperor is understandably overwhelmed by such scientific expertise in a mere woman and responds weakly and with anachronistic and somewhat misplaced chauvinism that if Catherine had only studied in France, there would be none more knowledgeable than she with regard to the pagan faith (lines 141-46).

Aumeric stresses much more than does the *Vulgata* the theme of male-female confrontation. At the beginning of the debate with the philosophers, the question arises as to who shall speak first. Catherine calls upon the philosophers to open the debate, but they refuse saying that they have been summoned to hear her. Their attitude is clearly one of contempt. They have already announced that any one of their apprentices would be perfectly capable of defeating fifty Catherines. Aumeric chooses, however, to stress Catherine's surprise that a woman may speak before a man.[1] Again, at the conclusion of the debate (lines 939-50), the emperor reminds them of their boast. He too had thought that a hundred such women, "saives, clerzesses, cristianes" [wise, educated, Christian women], would not have dared to speak with even one of the philosophers. Instead, one such woman has single-handedly made all fifty of them look foolish.

When the queen is about to be put to death, she asks for Catherine's prayers lest she succumb under torture, and by way of explanation she adds a remark to the effect that woman is a fickle thing ("chosa muabla"). This is picked up by Catherine in her reply as she urges the queen to have the heart of a man, not of a woman: "Aies cor d'ome, nun de fenne" (line 2243).

Perhaps the most curious aspect of Aumeric's version is that once he has recounted Catherine's martyrdom he ends the work with a brief postscript in Latin verse describing Catherine's miraculous burial by angels on Mt. Sinai and the migration of her soul to heaven to be united with Christ. He continues with a brief personal prayer, likewise in Latin, and finally reveals his name, Aumericus, "a friend of the people of Poitou and a monk at the monastery of St. Michel."

The change to Latin at this point would seem to indicate that Aumeric is now addressing his brother monks rather than the general public for whose edification the translation is destined. The information which it contains on the burial of Catherine comes directly from the *Vulgata*, and Aumeric makes clear with his remark "ut presens pagina dicit" that he is still working from the same text. Why he chooses to deny this information to his general audience is a matter for speculation. The fact that he ends the translated section with a double "Amen" seems to indicate that, in his view, he had fulfilled his task as translator, and that what followed would be of interest only to other clerics.

We are indeed fortunate that the three extant manuscripts of Clemence's version and the sole manuscript of Gui's poem have preserved their authors' prologues in which the matter of translation is explicitly dealt with. Clemence asks the help of God as she sets about her task, and she speaks not simply of translating a Latin text--"De latin respundre en rumanz / Pur ço que plus plaise as oianz" (lines 33-34)--but also of amending into "rumanz" a previous translation that had lost favor with her contemporaries, who, she remarks, are excessively difficult to please:

> Ele fud jadis translaté
> Sulunc le tens bien ordené;
> Mais ne furent dunc si veisdus
> Les humes, ne si envius
> Cum il sunt la tens ki est ore
> E aprés nus serrunt uncore.
> Pur ço que li tens est mué
> E des humes la qualité
> Est la rime vil tenue
> Car ele est asquans corrumpue.
> Pur ço si l'estuet amender
> E le tens selunc la gent user.   (lines 35-46)

[It was translated before, and quite well according to the

45

standards of the day, but the people of those times were
not as clever nor as critical as they are nowadays, and
doubtless will be even more after we are gone. Since
times have changed, and with them the quality of people,
the verse of the old translation is held in contempt, for it
is imperfect in parts. For this reason it is necessary to
amend it, and to deal with the world as befits the people
who inhabit it.]

In her view the earlier translation was "bien ordené" for the
period in which it was done, and she admits that the rhyme is
"asquans corrumpue," which may suggest that a more primitive
verse form had been used, possibly the assonanced *laisses* of the
chansons de geste now out of favor in courtly circles.[2] At all events,
Clemence seems less than enthusiastic about the need for a new
translation. She associates the poor reception of the earlier text with
the lowered moral quality of her contemporaries--something which
is only going to get worse as time goes on. Esthetic judgments, she
seems to think, are conditioned by moral values. She reluctantly
acknowledges that one must move with the times ("le tens selunc la
gent user"), and she disclaims any false pride in her desire to
"amend" this earlier translation:

> Ne l'aiment pas pur mun orgoil,
> Kar preisie estre n'en voil;   (lines 47-48)

> [I do not amend it because of my own pride,
> for I seek no praise on account of it.]

Only God should be praised from Whom she has received her "povre
saveir."

At the end of the poem when Clemence reveals her identity and
asks her audience to pray for her, she speaks of herself only as
translator ("Jo ki sa vie ai translatee," line 2689), and she makes no
further reference to her source in "rumanz." This is hardly
surprising since she has added so much of her own moral
commentary to the text and has so transformed the character of the

46

emperor that, at times, even the *Vulgata* is lost from view.

Gui also claims to be reworking an existing translation. After an opening remark that saints' lives should be rendered into the vulgar tongue,[3] he goes on to say that he has undertaken to translate from Latin into "romanz" ("de latin en romanz traire," line 16) the life and saintly character ("saint estre") of one of Christ's special friends. He will do so in order that it may be pleasing to the audience ("que plus delite a escouter / a cels qui l'oent raconter," lines 17-18). He explains that this is not the first translation into "romanz"; an earlier rendering by a Norman cleric was not pleasing to the "François," and so a friend passed this version on to him in order that it might be put into "françois." He does not say that the French could not understand the Norman dialect when they heard it; indeed, he does not say that the "rime" was in the Norman dialect. The suggestion is, rather, that the earlier version bore traces of the translator's Norman origins. In any case it did not find favor with the French, and since the saints are "la delitable pleigne / par ou l'on vet en la monteigne" (lines 7-8), there should be pleasure involved in listening to accounts of their lives. Clearly such accounts are more pleasing to the listeners in "romanz" than in Latin, and more pleasing to a French audience if they are in French rather than in Norman. It is interesting to note that Gui stresses pleasure rather than comprehension, the esthetic rather than the purely practical.

At the end of the poem (lines 1940-71), Gui reveals his name and congratulates himself on a job well done. He gives thanks to Christ both for the trouble ("peine") he has had, and for this composition ("escrit") which he has brought to such a successful completion ("si bien achevé"), and in which he has "damaged" nothing ("ne li a riens grevé"). It was not for vainglory that he carried out this task, but in memory of St. Catherine. On her behalf and on account of her merit, he has "renewed" the passion which she suffered so that it would not be withheld from the public.

In order to illustrate in some detail how these various translators carried out their task, I shall focus principally on the treatment of one specific episode in the legend: the reaction of the emperor to what he sees as his betrayal, first by his wife, then by his friend and confidant, Porphirius. In their treatments of this episode, the Old

French translators run the gamut from mere transmission of the *données* of the Latin text, as in the case of the prose version, Gui, and the anonymous Picard, through limited modification, as with Aumeric, to a total transformation of the sense of the episode, as in the version of the aristocratic nun of Barking.

The *Vulgata* tells how the queen had observed the miraculous destruction of the machine of wheels from a tower window. No longer afraid of her husband, she descends rapidly and charges him publicly with waging a hopeless struggle against God and those who serve Him. At this, many of the pagans who had observed the miracle were converted to Christ and proclaimed with one voice:

> "Vere magnus est Deus christianorum cujus nos servos ab hodierno die constanter profitemur, nam dii tui idola vana sunt que nec cultoribus suis aliquid prestare possunt." (Knust, p. 298)

> ["Truly, great is the God of the Christians whose servants we shall be from this day forward, but your gods are vain idols, incapable of coming to the aid of those who worship them."]

The emperor reacts to these events with great anger and accuses the queen of having been seduced by the magic arts. If he now permits "amor conjugalis" to weaken him so that he lets the queen's insult to the gods go unpunished, other Roman wives will imitate her example, divert their husbands from the cult of the gods, and turn the whole empire over to the Christians. He warns her that if she does not immediately abandon this foolishness and make sacrifice to the gods, he will have her beheaded after lengthy tortures and her body abandoned to birds and wild beasts:

> His auditis tirannus collegit se in omnem furorem adversus eos, sed vehementius adversus reginam, in vocem hujusmodi erupit: "Quid tu," inquiens, "regina, ita loqueris? Nam te quoque magicis artibus seductam christianorum aliquis subvertit *ut et tu quoque omnipotentes deos nostros relinqueres, per quos imperii*

nostri summa consistit. Quae mala infelicitas mea ut qui ad culturam deorum nostrorum alienos coartabam, jam pestiferum subversionis venenum familiarius domui mee inserpere videam et unicam lectuli mei consortem hujus morbi contagione[4] vexari contuear! Porro si me ita amor conjugalis emolliverit ut pro regine erronea mutabilitate deorum contumeliam ita negligam, quid restat nisi ut cetere imperii romane matrones hujus ejusdem erroris exemplum imitantes viros proprios a cultura deorum evertant et ad fabulosam christianorum sectam totum regni corpus incurvare presumant? Juro *ergo* tibi per magnum deorum imperium, o regina, quod nisi maturius ab hac stulticia resipiscens diis immolaveris, caput tuum a cervice recisum et carnes feris et volatilibus dilacerandas hodie rejiciam. *Nec tamen tu celeri morte vitam finisse letaberis, quam ego, extortis primo mamillis, longo faciam cruciatu interire!*

(Knust, pp. 298-99, emphasis added)[5]

[On hearing this, the tyrant summoned up all his rage against them, but he burst out even more violently at the queen in this manner: "What are you saying, Queen?" he asked. "For one of these Christians has by sorcery led you astray, *causing you to abandon our omnipotent gods by whom our entire empire is sustained? What evil misfortune has befallen me that I who used to force others to worship our gods should ever see the pestilential poison of subversion creep into the very bosom of my household, and attack with its contagion the sole companion of my bed? Yet if conjugal love weakens me such that I overlook on account of the queen's heretical fickleness this affront to the gods, the sole result will be that other Roman wives, following the same wrong example, will turn their husbands too away from the worship of the gods, and will proceed to make the entire nation bow to this absurd Christian cult.* I swear to you, *therefore*, O Queen, by the power of the great gods, that if you do not swiftly repent of this folly and make sacrifice to the gods, I shall this very day have

your head severed from your body, and your remains cast
out to be torn up by birds and wild beasts. *And do not
rejoice that your life will end in a swift death; I shall see
to it that you die a slow and painful death, having first
had your breasts torn from your body.*"]

When, later, Porphirius proclaims his conversion, the emperor's
reaction is one of deep personal distress rather than anger:

Hinc tirannus, velut alto vulnere saucius, pro planctu
rugitum, velut amens, altum emisit quo tota regio
pertonuit. "O! o! me miserum! o omnibus miserandum!
ut quid me in hanc erumpnosam vitam natura mater
edidit [cui] tollitur omne quod nostri imperii precipue
summa requirit! *Ecce Porphirius qui erat unicus anime
mee custos et totius laboris solatium, in quam ab omni
cura et sollicitudine reclinabar, velut singulare mihi
presidium, ecce hic, nescio qua demonum infestatione
supplantatus, deorum nostrorum culturam aspernatur et
illum Jhesum quem vesana turba christianorum pro Deo
colit, utpote mente captus, publica voce confitetur! Hic
nimirum reginam a lege patria et cultura deorum,
subvertit, nec alius querendus nobis est conjugalis
dementie architectus. Et quamvis irreparabile mihi
dampnum de conjuge ab eo constet illatum, hoc potius
eligo ut, resipiscens ab hac stultitia, deos sibi placabiles
reddat et in nostra, ut ceperat, amicitia perduret quam
nostre animadversionis sententiam experiatur.*"

(Knust, pp. 303-04, emphasis added)

[Then the tyrant, as if afflicted with a deep wound,
uttered, like one gone mad, a great roar of lamentation
which resounded throughout the whole region. "Oh! Oh!
pitiful man that I am! Oh! worthy to be pitied by all!
Why did Mother Nature ever thrust me forth into this
wretched life when everything really essential to our
power is taken from me? *Behold Porphirius who was the
sole keeper of my soul and my solace from all toil, to
whom I retreated from every care and worry as to my*

50

*only protection. I do not know what onslaught of demons
has caused him to stumble. He spurns the worship of our
gods and, his mind in bondage, confesses publicly this
Jesus whom the mad throng of Christians revere as God!
He it is, undoubtedly, who turned the queen away from
the law of the land and from the worship of the gods, and
we need seek no farther the author of our wife's
madness. Yet however irreparable is the harm he has
done me through my wife, it is my preference that,
turning away from this foolishness, he placate the gods
and continue as hitherto in our friendship, than that he
taste the sentence that we shall otherwise pronounce."*]

In the *Vulgata*, there is a marked contrast between the emperor's
reaction to the conversion of his wife and to that of his friend.
Porphirius is much more important to him. His use of the term
"amor conjugalis" in reference to his relationship with his wife
suggests duty rather than inclination, more especially in the absence
of any words of love or indications of personal distress. The
emotion he expresses is one of anger, nothing more. Nor does he
hesitate to proceed immediately with her torture and execution. But
when he hears of the defection of Porphirius, he roars as if deeply
wounded. Porphirius is his closest friend and counsellor, and now
he has confessed *publica voce* that he has abandoned the gods.
Maxentius is convinced that Porphirius is responsible also for the
conversion of the queen, no doubt on the grounds that a mere woman
would be incapable of such action by herself. Porphirius, therefore,
is doubly at fault, and yet he is offered a complete pardon and return
to the good graces of the emperor, if he will but placate the gods.
Moreover, even after Porphirius fails to respond to his offer,
Maxentius goes on to punish not Porphirius but his men, and when
Porphirius, fearful that they may yield under torture, demands that
he, their commander, be punished instead, Maxentius gives him a
second chance to choose between living in imperial glory with him
or dying by the sword.

Dicit ei tirannus: "Tu caput et princeps horum es, ut
asseris, opportunum est ut tu de te istis prebeas exem-

plum, videlicet ut primus ab hac stulticia resipiscas et
nobiscum gloriose vivas aut certe primus gladio
intereas."   (Knust, p. 305)

[The tyrant said to him: "You are their prince and head
as you say; it is right that you should set them an
example, namely that you be the first to turn back from
such foolishness and live gloriously with us, or you will
surely be the first to die by the sword."]

There is no mention of torture in his case, although, as in the case of
the queen, the bodies of Porphirius and his men are to be left
unburied.

As we turn to the Old French translations of this episode, it must
first be pointed out that the abbreviated form of the *Vulgata* used by
Gui and by the author of the prose version omits the reference to
"amor conjugalis" and also the words of affection addressed to
Porphirius. The prose version, in this episode as elsewhere, adds
nothing and subtracts nothing. It gives a straightforward account of
the basic facts as presented in the shorter *Vulgata* text:

Quant li tiranz oi ce si fu toz forsenez envers eus, mes
plus durement envers la roine, et parla a li en ceste
maniere: "Roine," fet il, "coment paroles tu einsint? Ja
ne t'a aucuns des crestiens souzduite et subvertie par art
d'enchantement avec les autres? Roine, ie te iur par
l'empire des granz dex qe, se tu tost ne te repenz de ceste
folie et sacrefies as dex, ie geterai hui en cest ior ta teste,
qe ie te ferai trenchier parmi la gorge et ton cors devant
les bestes sauvages et devant les oiseaus por despechier
et por deschirer."   (Knust, pp. 298-99)

[When the tyrant heard this, he reacted with fury toward
them, but with even greater harshness toward the queen,
and spoke to her in these terms: "Queen," he said, "how
is it that you speak in this way? Surely you have not
been misled and subverted through sorcery by any of the
Christians along with those others? Queen, I swear to

52

you by the empire of the great gods that if you do not forthwith repent of this folly, and sacrifice to the gods, I shall this very day throw your head, which I shall have severed at the neck, and your body to the wild beasts and the birds that they may tear them into small pieces."]

The Porphirius episode is treated with similar brevity:

> De ce fu li tyranz aussi come navrez de la plaie parfonde et en liu de pleinte mist fors come dervez un cri dont toz li pais tonna: "Oi mi chetif dont totes genz doivent avoir pitié! Porqoi me mist nature mere en ceste crimineuse vie? Donc ne m'est tolue tote chose qe nostre empire avoit a li governer? Et perdue ai la some de l'empire."
>
> (Knust, p. 303.)

> [At this the tyrant reacted as if stricken by a deep wound, and in place of lamentation he uttered like one gone mad a cry which resounded throughout the whole country: "Ah! wretched me on whom all must have pity! Why did Mother Nature bring me into this wicked life? Now is not everything needed to govern our empire taken from me? And I have lost what was best in the empire."]

In like manner, Gui, writing in verse, moves rapidly from the astonished inquiry to the threat and on to its execution:

> "Qu'est ce, reïgne, que tu diz?
> Por coi t'es tu de ce ventee?
> Li Crestien t'ont enchantee,
> Mes je te jur par mes granz Diex
> Que se tu es longuement tiex,
> Et tu ne lesses ta foleur,
> Je te ferai a grant doleur
> La teste du cors desevrer;
> Et si ferai ton cors livrer
> Et au[s] bestes et aus oisiax
> Qui en feront toz leur aviaus."
> Lors commende que l'en la praigne.   (lines 1571-82)

53

["What is this you are saying, Queen? Why have you boasted of this? The Christians have cast a spell on you, but I swear to you by my great gods that if you remain so for long and do not abandon your folly, I shall have your head severed painfully from your body, and I will have your body thrown to the beasts and birds who will do with it what they will." Then he commands that they take her.]

Later, in the Porphirius episode, Gui feels the need, for purposes of meter and rhyme, to add a line in which Maxentius, having cursed the day he was born, asks Death to strike him down:

> ". . . Chetis, l'eure fu male
> Que je onques cheï sus terre.
> *Male mort, car vien, si m'aterre,*
> Quant je pert tout a la reonde
> Ce que j'amoie en tot le monde."
>
> (lines 1673-77, emhasis added)

["Wretch that I am, it was in an evil hour that I dropped on this earth. *Evil death, come strike me down*, when all around I lose what I loved most in all the world."]

The anonymous Picard, with the entire text of the *Vulgata* at his disposal, makes no mention of love, even conjugal love, in connection with the queen. The emperor's reaction is purely one of anger. He does not even address the queen directly except in his initial outburst. Whereas the *Vulgata* moves from direct address to indirect when Maxentius speaks about his dilemma and back to direct speech when he makes his threats to the queen, the Picard poet continues in the indirect form to the end:

> "Une riens sace me moulliers:
> De li me vengerai premiers.
> Car s'ele as dix ne sacrefie,
> Et envers aus ne s'umelie,
> Je li ferai le kief trenkier,
> Et les mameles esracier."
>
> (lines 1275-80)

54

["Let my wife be aware of one thing: I shall avenge
myself first on her, for if she does not make sacrifice to
the gods and humble herself before them, I shall have her
head cut off and her breasts torn out."]

With regard to Porphirius, it is distress rather than anger that he
feels, just as his source had indicated: "De duel cuide vis esragier"
[line 1370; He thinks he will go out of his mind with grief]. He
refers to Porphirius as his "ciers amis," and despite the latter's
"responsibility" for the loss of the queen, he begs him (in the third
person, as in the Latin text) to abandon his folly and return to his
(Maxentius's) love, assuring him that he will enjoy a high position
in the imperial household:

> "Mais or li wel dire et proier
> Qu'il deguerpisse ceste errour,
> Et si se traie a nostre amour.
> S'il veut laier ceste folie,
> Ja nen iert pis de ma maisnie."   (lines 1380-84)

["But now I will tell him and implore him to abandon
this false doctrine and return to our love. If he will give
up this madness, he will in no way be the least important
person in my household."]

Aumeric goes beyond the *données* of the *Vulgata*, adding
touches which betray more real sadness than is suggested by the
Latin reference to "amor conjugalis." He announces to her
immediately that, if what she says is true, then her death is
imminent, and he goes on to lament what has happened to him.

> "Las, fait il, que soi devenuz?
> O est ma forza e ma vertuz?
> Las, qui m'a malmené ma fenne?
> Mais volguisse perdre mon regne.
> Ja iso non cuidei veer.
> Que fairei? toz me desesper,
> E per l'amor que ai o lei
> A martire la livrarei."   (lines 2183-90)

55

["Alas, he said, what has become of me? Where is my strength and my power? Alas, who has taken my wife away from me? I would rather have lost my kingdom. I never thought that I would see such a thing. What shall I do? I am in utter despair, and for the love I share with her I shall hand her over to be martyred."]

Finally, after describing the slow and painful manner in which she will meet her death, he adds a revealing comment which has no basis in the *Vulgata*:

> "Aisi me vengerei de tei,
> Des quant tu n'as cura de mei." (lines 2211-12)

["Thus I shall avenge myself on you since you have ceased to care for me."]

Her death will serve as an example to other women who might be tempted to subvert their husbands, but the torture she will undergo before her death will be his vengeance on her for her abandonment of him. "Amor conjugalis" has become "l'amor que ai o lei," and from angry despot Maxentius has become a spurned lover, an interesting and potentially fruitful development. But when Aumeric comes to treat the Porphirius situation, he faces a problem. Having already belabored the emperor's love for his wife and his jealousy at losing her to the Christians, he tries to follow the *Vulgata* in suggesting an even greater degree of distress in the case of Porphirius's betrayal. He translates faithfully every image of the Latin which serves to stress the confidence which the emperor has in Porphirius and then adds one or two remarks of his own which represent a kind of gloss on the Latin text:

> "M'lt l'ai amé, il o sat bien;
> En sa man ait trestot lo men.
> Ma fenna est morta, il est vis;
> Non quer mais qu'il me seit amis,
> Rei e seinor siam amdui;
> Non me voil pas iraistre o lui." (lines 2365-70)

["Much did I love him, and he knows it well. Let all that
I possess be in his hands. My wife is dead, he is alive.
All I want henceforth is that he should be my friend. Let
us be king and lord together; I do not wish to be angry
with him."]

Nothing can bring back the queen. He knows now the answer to the
question he had asked at the outset: "Las, qui m'a malmené ma
fenne?" (line 2185), but now Porphirius is all that he has left, and he
does not want to pursue his anger against him.

But it is Clemence, the nun of Barking, who makes the most
radical modifications to this episode. In the Porphirius sequence she
follows the Latin text faithfully, neither cutting nor adding, but in
the earlier sequence the account of the emperor's reaction to the
queen's conversion is greatly expanded. It occupies 102 lines of the
text as opposed to 16 in Gui, 26 in the Picard text, and 40 in
Aumeric who is not otherwise noted for his brevity. With Clemence
it is no longer the "amor conjugalis" of the original Latin, nor even
the suggested vengeance and jealousy of Aumeric which is
highlighted, but rather the despair of the abandoned lover. He
knows from the outset that he has no choice but to put his wife to
death with the others who had all too publicly proclaimed their
conversion. But already, like Racine's Berenice, he tries to imagine
what life will be like without the one he loves. Despite the length of
the passage, it is worthwhile quoting it in its entirety in order to
appreciate the rhetoric of lamentation which it displays and the
astonishing similarities with the style of some of the fragments of
Thomas's *Tristan*:

	"Reine, u averai ge confort
2172	Aprés ta doleruse mort.][6]
	Laissier ne pois que ne t'ocie;
	Assez m'ert pur mort puis ma vie.
	[Coment viveras tu sanz mei,
2176	Et ge coment viverai sanz tei?]
	Tu esteies sule ma cure
	De desirer bone aventure,
	[Et pur tei suleie duter

2180   Mal aventure et eschiver,
       Mes malement l'ai eschivee,
       Kant de tei l'ai encuntree.]
       Las, que me valt ore m'amur,
2184   Quant n'i receif el que dulur.
       En grant tristur demenrai ma vie,
       Quant jo vus perdrai, bele amie.
       [Kar sule esteies mun delit,
2188   Et jeo le ten, [si] cum jeo quit.]
       Mais ore sai bien e entent,
       Que surquidance noist suvent;
       Pur co que tant vus poi amer,
2192   Suleie altel de vus quider;
       Mais bien crei par ceste pruvance,
       Que el ne fud fors surquidance.
       [Chaitifs ore sui, tut deceu,
2196   Mort et trai et confundeu.
       Or n'arai mais nul reconfort;
       Or ne desir el que la mort.
       Mei ne purra [ja] rien guarir,
2200   Kant le plus pert de mun desir;
       Et quant li plus averai perdeu,
       De[l] meins serrai puis susteneu?]
       Poi me valdra [puis] mun poeir,
2204   Quant perdu avrai mun voleir;
       [Kar desque mun voleir me faut,
       De ceo ke ne voil, mei ke chaut?]
       Quel joie purrai jo aveir
2208   De poissance cuntre voleir?
       [Las, tut puis ceo ke ne ruis,
       Et ceo ke plus voil, pas ne puis.]
       Cuntre voleir poeir acoil,
2212   Mais cest voleir senz poeir doil.
       Car si jo en usse poissance,
       Dunc fust fenie ma grevance.
       Ore ne sai jo a quel fin traire,
2216   Quant [jo] mun voleir ne pois faire,
       [N'a quele cure mun quer juenge,
       Kant tute honur de mei s'esluinge.]"

["Queen, where shall I find comfort from the anguish of your death? I have no choice but to kill you, but afterwards my life will be a form of death. How will you live without me? And as for me, how shall I live without you? You were my sole reason for desiring good fortune, and it was on your account that I feared ill fortune and tried to avoid it; but how poorly I have avoided it when it was through you that I encountered it. Alas, what good is my love to me now when all I get from it is pain. In great sadness I shall lead my life when I lose you, fair friend. For you alone were my delight, and I yours, I believe. But now I know well and understand that presumption is often harmful. Since I had so much love for you, I thought that you felt the same for me, but I firmly believe, as a result of this experience, that that was nought but presumption on my part. Now I am wretched, totally discomfited, slain, betrayed, and undone. Now I shall never again find solace. Now I desire nothing but death. Nothing can ever make me well again when I lose the greater part of what I desire; and when I lose the greater part, can I then be sustained by the lesser? My power will be of little value to me once I have lost what I desire. For when I no longer have what I desire, what do I care about what I do not desire? What joy can I have from power which is contrary to desire? Alas, I can do everything that I have no real urge to do, and what I most desire, that I cannot have. I accumulate power which is contrary to desire, but this powerless desire makes me grieve. For if I had the power to obtain these desires, then my grieving would be over. Now I know not what to aim for when I cannot carry out my will, nor do I know to what to attach my heart when all honor deserts me."]

There are a number of curious features in this extended meditation. Maxentius states that his whole life has been centered around his love for his wife. Life without her will henceforth be bereft of meaning. But what is even more noteworthy is his conviction that she shared the intensity of his devotion, that their

59

love was mutual. He goes as far as to ask how she will ever be able to live without him, forgetting momentarily that she is not going to have a chance to find out.

We noted above that Aumeric had added a few touches to this scene to flesh out a little the rather passionless reference to "amor conjugalis" in the *Vulgata*. He may have felt it inappropriate that Maxentius should be more distressed by the betrayal of his friend than by that of his wife. If this is so, he is changing the spirit and the intent of the eleventh-century author of the Latin text who is clearly much closer both in time and in psychology to the poet who has Roland grieve for his friend Oliver, his king, his companions, and *douce France*, and who not once spares a dying thought for *la belle Aude*, his betrothed. Clemence, for her part, is writing some sixty or seventy years earlier than Aumeric, closer certainly in time to the *Roland*, but at a time when *courtoisie* and *fin'amors* had just swept into England in the wake of Henry II and Eleanor of Aquitaine. Her poem appears to be written quite deliberately in the style of this "new wave."

It is perhaps in her comments in the prologue on the need to be pragmatic ("le tens selunc la gent user") that we may find the clue to her reinterpretation. Realizing that the assonanced text with its variable meter was, despite its dramatic possibilities, unsuited to aristocratic ears already well tuned to the smooth flow of octosyllabic rhyming couplets, she undertook to rewrite the legend, interpolating from time to time her own views on society and its injustices, but sugar-coating her bitter truths with the language, rhetoric, and at times even the emotions of the highly popular *Tristan* romances. It is unlikely that changing *mores* demanded that Maxentius show more distress over the loss of his wife than over that of his friend. It is historically much too early for this to have been a determining factor, and in any case the anonymous Picard, considerably later in date than Clemence, feels no such constraint. Nor can it be because Clemence is a woman and feels moved to redress the balance between what is owed to the wife and what is owed to the friend. Rather, by presenting Maxentius as an abandoned and heartbroken lover, Clemence engages the sympathy of her aristocratic audience. Maxentius is torn between what he perceives to be his duty to the state and to his gods on the one hand and his personal happiness on the other. But Clemence's purpose goes, I believe, even further. By having the emperor witness to the mutuality of the love he shared with his wife, we become aware of *her* sacrifice also. In the dungeon scene, Catherine advises the queen not to fear her husband:

> "Ne ergo verearis regis temporalis aut mortalis sponsi . .
> . ne verearis, inquam, ejus consortium aspernari pro rege
> eterno et inmortali sponso domino Jhesu Christo."
>
> (Knust, pp. 282)

> ["Have no fear on account of your temporal king or mortal
> husband . . . do not be afraid, I say, to spurn him in favor of
> your eternal king and immortal husband, Jesus Christ."]

But in Clemence's translation, she tells the queen not to fear her husband *nor any longer to desire his love*, a comment not found in the *Vulgata* nor in any of the other translations:

> "Ne dutez pas l'empereur
> *N'aiez mais desir de s'amur.*
> S'amur est fraille e decevable,
> E sa poeste trespassable."
>
> (lines 1641-44, emphasis added)

> ["Do not fear the emperor. *Do not desire his love.* His
> love is fragile and unreliable, and his power ephemeral."]

And both admonitions are repeated a few lines later without any further support from the Latin source:

> "Dame reine, pur co pri,
> Ne dutez cest mortel mari.
> Sa poissance ne deis duter,
> *Ne s'amur guaires desirer.*
> Mais met en lui tut tun desir,
> Ki dampner te puet e guarir."
>
> (lines 1653-58, emphasis added)

61

["Lady Queen, for that reason I implore you: fear not this mortal husband. You must not fear his power *nor even desire his love*. But put all your desire in him who can damn and save you."]

The emperor's love is "fraille e decevable," and later Catherine tells the queen and Porphirius that even the happiness of the world brings great suffering to those who have it:

"Meeimes la boneurté del munt
Est grant dulur a cels ki l'unt."   (lines 1679-80)

["Even the happiness of the world is great affliction to those who have it."]

What we see in the emperor's bitter anguish is proof of the validity of this remark. Worldly love, however deeply felt, is subject to the whims of fortune. The more intense, the more genuine the emotion, the more painful will be its loss. The love of God, on the other hand, is immutable, and the joys of Paradise are assured. As Catherine tells the queen when the latter is about to go to her grisly death:

"Tu recevras un tel ami
Pur le tuen qu'as guerpi,
De qui belté le mund resplent,
E si est rei sur tute gent."   (lines 2283-86)

["In return for the lover you have abandoned, you will receive one whose beauty illumines the world, and who is king of all nations."]

Her use of "ami" to render the Latin "sponsus" is again indicative of her concern to translate into the idiom of her aristocratic and courtly audience. The sacrifice of a mere husband might not have seemed too great a price to pay for a reward in the next life, but if the husband were also a lover, and one whose passionate devotion rivaled that of Tristan, the story might be quite different. Cle-

62

mence's concentration on "amur" (lines 1642, 1643, 1656) and "ami" (line 2283) and her reference to the presence in Paradise

> Des virges e des chastes pulceles
> Ki les *mortels amanz* despistrent,
> E la *chaste amur* Deu eslistrent
> > (lines 1780-82, emphasis added)

> [of those virgins and chaste maidens who rejected *mortal lovers* and chose instead the *chaste love* of God]

for which there is no evidence in the *Vulgata*, underline this concern. Perhaps she realizes that *fin'amors* is the new enemy to be faced. Perhaps it was not only the form of the earlier translation which needed to be amended, but the message as well?

Clemence's *Vie de sainte Catherine* is, I believe, one of the most remarkable works of the latter half of the twelfth century, in its originality worthy to stand alongside those of Chrétien de Troyes and Marie de France. Clemence has taken a popular tale of Christian martyrdom in which good and evil are presented in stark opposition, as convention demanded, and by some deft touches has added the *agréments* needed to gain the attention of her courtly audience, and by means of these same *agréments* has thrust home her message that even the highest joys of this world are ephemeral and insubstantial.

The measure of Clemence's genius is evident when her accomplishment, of which we have seen here only a part, is compared in its entirety with that of other translators, even Aumeric, in whose hands the dross of the *Vulgata*, despite some sifting and sorting, remains essentially dross. Clemence, for her part, has achieved that delicate balance between the permanence of the Christian message and the need to adapt its form and expression to the mutability of human society. For her, translation is far from being an automatic process. It is essentially a reinterpretation into the idiom of the time with a specific audience in mind. Is this not precisely what her contemporary Marie de France was attempting in her retelling of Celtic legend?

NOTES

1. I have some difficulty in accepting Olivier Naudeau's remark (*La Passion de sainte Catherine d'Alexandrie éditée d'après le ms. 945 de la Bilbliothèque municipale de Tours avec Introduction, Etude de la langue et Glossaire*, Beihefte zur Zeitschrift für Romanische Philologie 186 [Tübingen: Max Niemeyer, 1982], p. 117 n.) that "Aumeric s'exprime ici avec une politesse toute poitevine."

2. It is interesting in this connection to note that Fawtier-Jones saw in the curious, multi-metered, assonanced Manchester fragment of the late eleventh or early twelfth century the very source to which Clemence refers, and drew attention to one or two *formules* in it which Clemence may have incorporated into her translation; see E. C. Fawtier-Jones, "Les Vies de sainte Catherine d'Alexandrie en ancien francais," *Romania* 56 (1930): 80-104, esp. pp. 100-03.

3. That is how I interpret the lines:

> Pour l'amitié de Jhesu Crist
> Doivent estre en nostre escrist
> Li servise de ses amis   (lines 1-3)

Quotations are from Henry Alfred Todd, "La Vie de sainte Catherine d'Alexandrie," *PMLA* 15 (1900):17-73, but I have corrected occasional typographical errors or misreadings of the manuscript.

4. The reading in Hermann Knust, *Geschichte der Legenden der h. Katharina von Alexandrien und der h. Maria Aegyptiaca nebst unedirten Texten* (Halle: Niemeyer Verlag, 1890) is "contagine," which I have emended to "contagione."

5. Extracts from the *Vulgata* are printed as they appear in Knust's edition [n. 4 above]. The italicized sections are those which are absent from the abbreviated version of the *Vulgata*. The entire *Vulgata* text has been recently reprinted in my *De Sainte Katerine: An Anonymous Picard Version of the Life of St. Catherine of Alexandria* (Fairfax, VA: The George Mason Univ. Press, 1987).

6. Brackets indicate lines supplied from another manuscript to fill lacunae in the base manuscript.

7. See William MacBain, "The Literary Apprenticeship of Clemence of Barking, *AUMLA* (*Journal of the Australasian Universities Language and Literature Association*) 9 (1959):1-23.

ADDITIONAL REFERENCES

Boykin, Robert W. J. "The Life of Saint Katherine of Alexandria: A Study in Thematic Morphology Based on Medieval French and English Texts." Ph.D. diss., University of Rochester, 1972.

Bronzini, Giovanni. *La Leggenda di S. Caterina d'Alessandria: Passioni greche* e *latine.* Rome: Accademia Nazionale dei Lincei, 1960.

Jarník, Jan Urban. *Dvě verse starofrancouzské legendy o sv. Katěrině Alexandrinské.* Prague: Nákl. české akademie císaře Františka Josefa pro vědy, slovenost a umění, 1894.

Legge, M. Dominica. *Anglo-Norman Literature and Its Background.* Oxford: Clarendon Press, 1963.

MacBain, William. *The Life of St. Catherine of Alexandria by Clemence of Barking.* Anglo-Norman Text Society 18. Oxford: Blackwell, 1964.

Manger, Karl. *Die französischen Bearbeitungen der Legende der h. Katharina von Alexandrien.* Zweibrücken: A. Kranzbühler, 1901.

Trenkle, Mary Patricia. "A Critical Edition of *Le Vie me damne sainte Kateline Vierge*, MS. 10295-304, Bibliothèque Royale, Bruxelles, a Versed Old French Passion of Saint Catherine of Alexandria, Known as an Anonymous Version." Ph.D. diss., University of Alabama, 1976.

THE OLD FRENCH
"CISTERCIAN" TRANSLATIONS

Robert Taylor

With exceptions, scholars of French culture have not always given medieval translations their due. Albert Henry has shown that a judicious examination of translations can yield rich rewards for semantic and dialectal study,[1] and, in a few cases, the study of multiple or successive translations of the same Latin text has yielded valuable insight into the evolution of social attitudes and concerns.[2] A specialized group of translators was examined by Léopold Delisle in an attempt to clarify the intellectual climate at the court of Charles V.[3] Still, the corpus is somewhat neglected, and much remains to be learned from a systematic study of medieval translations. In what follows, I attempt to identify a close-knit group of a dozen translations of pious texts from the late twelfth and early thirteenth centuries and to consider how they may be utilized to gain some insight into the history of religious movements and religious training in the period when lay pious organizations rapidly spread through northeastern France and Belgium.

It is known that the Cistercian movement expanded rapidly in this area from the mid-twelfth century, the same period which saw the rapid growth of the Benedictines and the mendicant preaching orders. But little is known of the precise nature of the impact that these movements had on their milieu or of the ways in which the religious enthusiasm of the organized orders was transmitted to the cultivated levels of lay society.

Some insight into these matters may be gleaned by examining a series of interrelated translations produced in the area during the period in question. Most of the texts are little known and have not previously been linked together as a meaningful corpus. It is necessary, therefore, to begin by identifying them, pointing out similarities and distinguishing features.

MS. 5, Musée Dobrée, Nantes[4] dates from the end of the twelfth or the beginning of the thirteenth century. Numerous dialectal traits clearly indicate Walloon origin, the area of Liège according to earlier scholars, though there may be reason to place its origin further south, perhaps in the area of the Cistercian Abbey of Orval. It contains vernacular renderings of the first forty-four of Bernard of Clairvaux's sermons on the Song of Songs as well as two other texts by Bernard--*De diligendo Dei* and the sermons on the *Missus est*. Four shorter anonymous texts are also contained in the manuscript: a sermon-treatise on Psalm 150,[5] a version of the Legend of Mary Magdalene,[6] a treatise of meditation on the nature of Christ, and a sermon on Saint Agnes.[7] Although these latter texts are not translations, they are closely linked in subject matter, style, and language to the other texts in the manuscript.

B.N. fr. 24768, Paris contains forty-five of Bernard's sermons arranged for the liturgical year--from late November (Advent) through March (Annunciation).[8]

Meermann 1925, Berlin contains forty-three sermons, again arranged for the liturgical year, but this time running from March (Annunciation) through August (Assumption).[9] Although this collection and B.N. fr. 24768 follow upon one another and have obvious similarities, they are not two parts of a former set now separated. They share three overlapping sermons in common, but these, while very similar, are not identical. Perhaps both were copied from the same original. Dialectal traits in both indicate that they were prepared in the Lorraine area, possibly in the region of Metz.

B.N. fr. 24764, Paris is closely related in language to the Walloon features of the Nantes manuscript, though a number of consistent minor differences indicate that they were not prepared by the same translator. Included in the manuscript are translations of the *Moralia in Job* and *Dialogues* of Gregory the Great,[10] a fragment of the anonymous *Elucidarium*[11] in a vernacular adaptation, and a tiny fragment of a sermon.

MS. 79, Bürgerbibliothek, Bern,[12] a late twelfth-century translation made in the Lorraine area, contains the twelve homilies of Book One of Gregory's homilies on *Ezekiel*, the last of the twelve interrupted in mid-sentence approximately half-way through. In vocabulary and dialectal traits this is closely related to B.N. fr. 24768 and Meermann 1925, although it was not produced by the same translator.

MS. 244, Municipal Library, Laon,[13] a Latin Pontifical, has as end-papers two fragments of a translation of the same homilies on *Ezekiel* as are contained in the Bern MS.--two folios from homily 8 and one from homily 9. The dialectal features of the text are clearly Walloon, are similar to those of the Nantes MS. and the Gregorian texts in B.N. fr. 24764; however, it does not appear that any translator was responsible for more than one text.

Arsenal 2083, Paris, a manuscript from the Lorraine area, contains seventeen homilies: thirteen are vernacular translations of homilies from the standard Latin collection the *Homiliae de tempore* of Haimo of Auxerre, a Benedictine monk of the ninth century whose works remained influential throughout the Middle Ages;[14] two are extracts from Haimo's commentary on the Epistles; and two more are by an unknown author. Evidently, the translator took pains to choose appropriate homilies from the Latin collection and to adapt suitable extracts from the commentary.

MS. 72, Municipal Library, Verdun, the final manuscript in the corpus being considered here, contains a translation into Old French of the so-called *Golden Epistle*, the *Epistola de vita solitaria ad fratres Montis Dei*, of William of Saint-Thierry.[15] According to its editor, the translation was probably produced c. 1200 in St. Paul's Monastery, Verdun. Since the Latin original circulated mostly among the Cistercians, the French version may have been made for the lay brothers of St. Paul's.

Some of the texts from this corpus have been studied individually in regard to dating or localization; some have been compared with other texts in the group in order to determine their relative independence or to discover if any of them have been prepared by the same translator or in the same place; but the corpus as a whole has not until now been examined in depth. Michel Zink has approached a coherent study of the group,[16] but the aim of his research--as opposed to mine--was, on the one hand, more wide-ranging both in time and place and, at the same time, more restricted since it was limited, in principle, to sermons; as a result, he was unable to give particular attention to this corpus and thus fully explore its nature and importance. I believe that a detailed study of these texts reveals that they are clearly linked to the Cistercian movement and that examining them can tell us much about the nature and goals of the Cistercian mission, particularly in relation to that of rival mendicant orders.

The texts do in fact have a great deal in common. All of them belong to what may be called predicatory literature; that is, sermons and sermon-like texts meant for the moral instruction of Christian believers. Many of them are sermons, such as those of Bernard, Gregory, and Haimo, but others are moral treatises, like those of Isidore, Gregory, and William of Saint-Thierry. In any case, there is no clear separation between the two types, since a number of the "sermons" are made up of extracts from treatises, like the *Lucidarium* or Haimo's commentaries on the Epistles, and some of the texts found alongside the translated sermons may indeed be labelled sermons and have all the structural characteristics of sermons, while being far too long and involved to have ever been presented orally.[17] When account is taken of these additional texts which sometimes accompany our chosen group in their manuscripts and of other similar composite manuscripts from other areas and other time periods, it seems evident that they belong to a very large family of collections which were put together to be read rather than to be delivered orally. Whether they were meant as inspiratory texts from which preachers could take their sermon material or as exemplary readings for the instruction of pious individuals by way of personal reading is not clear, and it is possible that both intentions, and others, may have been involved in the creation of the collections. The texts themselves, in any case, function as written texts, not as the mere transcription of spoken texts. Our whole corpus shares this characteristic and may profitably be expanded slightly to include the compatible texts which accompany some of the translations within their manuscripts.

The unity of function which holds the corpus together is

reinforced by the unity of time and place which has already been mentioned but which merits further attention. All of the texts have been dated approximately to the late twelfth or early thirteenth century; none can be dated with precision, in spite of the various hypotheses that have been advanced. On paleographical and linguistic grounds alone, it is not possible to peg them any more closely than the fifty years or so centered on 1200.

Some interior groupings can be identified, which narrow the relative time-span, at least within the sub-groups. The Berlin and Paris manuscripts of Bernard's sermons are linked in complex ways. P and B form a kind of continuum, as has been mentioned, P covering the liturgical year from November to March, B from March to August, with three sermons at the end of P overlapping with the first three of B. However, the overlapping sermons are not identical in the two copies, though they are close enough in language and expression that they may well have been copied from the same original translation. This would still link the two very closely, but a further examination of P reveals that the three final sermons were copied in a different hand from the rest of the collection and that they interrupt the succession of sermons that might have been expected to follow number 42, which is a kind of prologue for a lengthy series of sermons based on the ninetieth Psalm. A further complication is added by the fact that sermon 40 of P is found again in B (number 29) but is obviously an independent translation, the work of a second translator.[18] A third complication adds a final twist to the problem: manuscript B is not unified in language as P is. Sermons 1 to 28 and 39 to 43 are by one translator; sermons 29 to 38 are by another. It is evident that the larger group is the work of the same translator who prepared P's copy-text, since the language in the two series is extremely uniform. We are led to postulate a lost original translation from which P and B were separately copied. But does the presence of two separate versions of one sermon (no. 40 in P, no. 29 in B) indicate that there were two separate translations of the whole collection? Perhaps, but not necessarily, because the repeated sermon 29 in B lies within the section (sermons 29 to 38) that has been shown to be the work of a second translator. This intercalated series of ten sermons is intrusive not only in language usage, but for other reasons as well. Sermons 30, 31, and 32 are not by Saint Bernard at all: 31 is by Nicolas of Clairvaux; the other two are of unknown authorship. All ten break with the normal ordering of the manuscript, which arranges the sermons in chronological order according to the liturgical year. The regular order is interrupted by number 29 and does not resume until number 39. Furthermore, the rubrication of the sermons in B is done by two different hands, nine titles being written by the copyist who is responsible for the entire text, the other thirty-two by a second rubricator. Curiously, most of the titles written in by the copyist himself (*before* the other thirty-two titles),[19] are within the intercalated section, and three of these titles are erroneous. Sermons 29 and 32 are claimed wrongly to be about the Virgin (*de nostre damme*) and 38 about Peter and Paul (*des apostles*). At the beginning and end of the intercalated section, the copyist seems to have tried purposely to hide the fact that the chronological ordering of the collection had been interrupted. Since number 28 was about Peter and Paul, it was made to appear that four sermons on the Virgin followed, as would be proper, although in fact it was not so. At the end of the interruptive section, it was made to appear that a sermon on Peter and Paul (no. 38 falsely titled *des apostles*) preceded four sermons on the Virgin, numbers 39-43 being in fact, and properly, about the Virgin. Among the seven sermons in the intercalation that are by Saint Bernard, five are taken from the *De diversis* collection, whereas all the others in B and all but one in P are from the *De sanctis*. The intercalation is, therefore, an obviously foreign insert within the collection, in language, in subject matter, and in authenticity. The awkward attempt to disguise the fact by manipulation of the titles indicates that the copyist was aware of its inappropriateness, but the reason for its inclusion does not leap immediately to mind. It is possible to postulate that sermon 29, the second version of a sermon already translated (and copied) in its proper place in P and found at the start of this intercalated section, indicates the existence of two separate translations of the whole series; but the eclectic nature of the group of ten interlopers may point, rather, to a collection made up of a wide range of sermons, including some by authors other than Saint Bernard, which happened to contain one that was already in P. Whatever its nature, the collection of translations from which the ten inserted pieces were selected has not been preserved; its postulated existence, however, does add to the proof of a wide-ranging interest in the translation of predicatory materials at the time and place which are under investigation. As for our detective mystery, it seems plausible to me that the copyist may have mixed up his copy-texts, mistakenly copying ten sermons from the eclectic collection before realizing his error and returning to the chronologically arranged *De sanctis* exemplar. We can only speculate whether his amateurish attempts to hide his mistakes (from the rubricator?) were successful.

Whatever may lie behind the intricacy of their interrelationship, it is clear that the P and B manuscripts of Bernard's sermons are closely connected and that they reveal a well-developed local interest in the preparation of vernacular translations; moreover, their complex interconnections point to a copying activity which may have been part of an organized propagation of texts and collections of an educational nature, possibly connected with the rapid spread of religious orders and communities in northeastern France and southern Belgium at this precise period.

Other texts in our corpus have been linked to the P and B Bernardian texts because of similarities in vocabulary and dialectal forms. The translation of Haimo of Auxerre's homilies and that of Gregory's sermons on *Ezekiel* are close enough to them in language that it is plausible to think of them as products of the same workshop, or at least as part of what may have been a co-operative effort among several interrelated communities to produce a library of useful volumes for the nourishment of a religious education.

The area most frequently named as the home of this translation activity is the city or the region of Metz, though this localization has not been accepted by all scholars. The other Lorraine text in our corpus can be localized more precisely. The translation of William of Saint-Thierry's *Golden Epistle* was apparently prepared in St. Paul's monastery in Verdun,[20] some sixty kilometers to the west of Metz but still very solidly within the north-west quadrant of the Lorraine dialectal area. A note at the front of the volume indicates that there was a second copy of the text at Mont-Dieu, but this is now lost. The nature of the *Golden Epistle* itself makes it fit very closely into the family of predicatory texts; it was addressed to the novices and younger members of the Carthusian monastery at Mont-Dieu and discusses the problems and rewards of dedication to the contemplative life in a gentle, fatherly manner. The original Latin work was long attributed to Saint Bernard, as in our text, a fact which helps account for its popularity within a corpus dominated by Bernard's writings. Interestingly, the lost copy of Mont-Dieu apparently had an attribution to William of Saint-Thierry which was scratched out and replaced by the name of Saint Bernard. The very fact that there was a second copy of the translation reinforces the impression already gleaned of a sustained effort to make available in multiple copies a varied collection of moral and didactic texts.

The rest of the texts in the corpus form a separate but very coherent group, closely related in language and all strongly colored by Walloon traits of spelling, morphology, and vocabulary. These are the sermons of Saint Bernard on the Song of Songs and related texts in the Nantes manuscript, the translations of Gregory the Great's *Dialogues* and *Moralia in Job* and related texts in the Paris manuscript 24764, and the fragment from Gregory's homilies on *Ezekiel*. The dialectal characteristics of all these texts are very similar, leading me to believe that they were all prepared in the same general area. Close comparison of grammatical usage and lexical habits indicates that the three units--Bernard group, Gregory group, and *Ezekiel* fragment--are the work of three different translators from the same area. All three have been localized by several scholars to Liège, largely because of a forcefully propounded hypothesis of Maurice Wilmotte.[21] Other scholars, however, have seen no compelling reason to prefer Liège over other areas, and recently Albert Henry has published a number of very close dialectal investigations which tend to point to an area south of Liège. While Henry does not draw any firm conclusions, he wonders if the Cistercian abbey of Orval (or perhaps that of Signy-l'Abbaye) might have been the center of translation activity not only for the Walloon group but possibly even for the so-called Metz group.

In fact, the early and persistent localization of a number of the Lorraine translations to the area of Metz is the result of an unfortunate hypothesis championed by many scholars, especially Hermann Suchier.[22]   In 1199, Pope Innocent III officially condemned the translation activity of a group of Waldensian heretics in the diocese of Metz and ordered the texts destroyed. In the pope's letter are mentioned specifically the Gospels, the Epistles, *Moralia in Job*, "et plures alios libros." Samuel Berger had earlier decided that the translation of Haimo's sermons, which he did not identify as such, belonged to this heretical list,[23] and he baptized the translation as the "Evangéliaire des laïques de Metz"; other scholars added the P and B series of Bernard's sermons and Gregory's homilies on *Ezekiel.* Many of the texts were dated to the late twelfth century on the basis of the Waldensian hypothesis rather than on more objective linguistic or paleographical grounds, and Suchier completed the tendency by drawing in the Walloon texts as well. Since the pope's letter had named specifically the *Moralia in Job*, he concluded that the surviving text in B.N. fr. 24764 must be the Waldensian one mentioned.   Suchier removed the problem posed by the text's Walloon dialectal features by reasoning that the Waldensian translations had been identified with the diocese of Metz rather than with the city itself; since he believed that in the twelfth century the diocese boundary had extended into the southern edge of the Walloon area, all doubts were dispelled and the hypothesis gained wide acceptance. Alfred Schulze (see n. 19) saw this identification as the key which drew the translations in the Nantes manuscript and that of Gregory's *Dialogues* into the Waldensian group.   The fragility of the original hypothesis may now be recognized as wishful thinking and a gross over-simplification of the facts.

It is clear that our corpus of translations had no connection with the heretical activities of the Waldensians. Instead, its collective purpose, as we have seen, was to make available to a literate audience a collection of texts in the vernacular to be read as a part of the process by which intelligent Christians could be led into a fuller understanding of the moral life. Two important questions remain to be answered: who prepared these translations, and for what audience?

A few modern scholars have begun to attach some of the impetus for translation to the Cistercian order, which has not been known hitherto to have had a didactic mission as clearly defined as that of the mendicant orders but which does seem to be connected in various ways to our corpus. The importance of Bernardian works to the Cistercians is immediately obvious; three lengthy series of his sermons and two of his treatises were made available in the vernacular, along with the *Golden Letter*, which was thought to be by him. Of course Bernard was known and revered on all levels of society, not only within his own order; thus, the prominence given to his works in the corpus would certainly neither speak against a Cistercian connection nor impose it. The presence of a manuscript at Clairvaux containing vernacular sermons of Saint Bernard was noted in 1746.[24] Since the P and B manuscripts were known to be held elsewhere in 1746, the Clairvaux manuscript could be the one now preserved in Nantes, or a fourth. In any case, there is proof of a direct connection between vernacular translation activity and Clairvaux. The *Laudate* text in the Nantes manuscript (see n. 3) is also found in other manuscripts, one of which is known to have come from the library of Clairvaux. The Latin *Lucidarium*, from which the two sermons *de sapientie* in B.N. fr. 24764 are drawn, was also the source of a *Lucidaire* in verse form composed by the Cistercian monk Gillebert de Cambres.[25] Gillebert's *Lucidaire* is a pious didactic work aimed at a lay audience anxious to seek instruction in the proper way to live a moral Christian life; as such, it is similar in purpose and tone to the texts of our corpus. The whole manuscript B.N. fr. 24764, containing Gregory's *Dialogues* and *Moralia in Job* as well as the *Lucidarium* sermons, has been identified as a Cistercian volume.[26] Finally, the Latin original of the *Golden Epistle* circulated mostly among Cistercians, and it is therefore natural to assume that its translation was prepared in a Cistercian milieu.

The intended audience of these translated works is more difficult to identify. It has already been shown that all the texts in the corpus are meant to be read, but by whom? The Cistercians were known for their emphasis on learning. In a significant passage, Alain de Lille reproached the Waldensians for preaching without sufficient preparation and gave, as an example, the Cistercians, who were better versed in Scriptural study but did not preach.[27] Zink is right to point out that this reference to popular preaching would in no way rule out the possibility that the energetically expanding Cistercians saw a particular mission to respond to the demand on the part of educated lay Christians for reading material in the vernacular which would help them enrich their understanding of the Christian life. The intellectual level of the Cistercians themselves and the fact that serious study would be unthinkable in anything but Latin rule out any possibility that the texts were prepared for internal use. It may be possible that the vernacular texts were used occasionally for the instruction of novices and lay brothers in the monasteries, but this could not have been their principal use, since they were so costly to produce. Some of the volumes are luxuriously made, with skilled illumination and gold embossing; one would envisage a more frugal presentation, probably calling for improvisation by the spiritual guide, in the case of lay brothers. The principal audience must have been a cultivated, independent, secular one, possibly of elevated social position. Such a group seems to be addressed in the prologue of the Sermon on Saint Agnes in the Nantes manuscript--". . . je pri toz cels ki le liront u ki l'escoteront ke il prient por moi"[28]--and the last piece in the same manuscript--a treatise on meditation which suggests an appropriate theme of contemplation for each of the liturgical hours through the day--is structured in imitation of the regulated liturgical observances of monks and nuns governed by a Rule, a fact which proves that the text is addressed not to these but to a secular audience. Zink takes this hypothesis further to propose that the texts of our corpus, and many others, were prepared for the use of the Beguines,[29] but this may be going too far. There appear to have been numerous communities of women in the southern Walloon and northern Lorraine areas in the late twelfth century under the patronage and tutelage of the Cistercians, who would have formed, together with the lay brothers and the Beguines, a natural audience, eager to read collections of moral readings and capable of profiting from their instruction. Much research remains to be done on the individual works in this rich corpus, on the questions raised by the corpus itself, and on the society in which the works were produced, before the validity of these hypotheses can be fully tested and refined. But I hope to have shown already that the corpus itself is a rich and suggestive one, and that the translation activity is one which may well lead us into a fuller understanding of the social movements that called it into being.

NOTES

1. For complete references, see "Saint Bernard traduit vers 1200 en pays wallon," *Les Dialectes de Wallonie* 8-9 (1981):99-100 (note).

2. For example, the study by Howard R. Patch, *The Tradition of Boethius, A Study of his Importance in Mediaeval Culture* (New York: Oxford U.P., 1935).

3. *Recherches sur la librairie de Charles* V, 2 vols. (Paris: H. Champion, 1905); cf. especially 1:82-120.

4. G. Durville, *Catalogue de la bibliothèque du Musée Thomas Dobrée*, tome I: *Manuscrits* (Nantes: Musée Thomas Dobrée, 1904), pp. 223-61. Robert Taylor, ed., "Li sermon saint Bernart sor les Cantikes," Ph.D. diss., University of Toronto, 1964. Publication in progress.

5. Robert Taylor, "Li sermons sor Laudate, texte anonyme de la fin du XIIe siècle," *Travaux de linguistique et de littérature* 20 (1982):61-100.

6. Cindy Corcoran, et al., "De la Madelaine, vie anonyme de Marie-Madeleine en prose française de la fin du XIIe siècle: édition critique," *Zeitschrift für romanische Philologie* 98 (1982):20-42.

7. Robert Taylor, "Sermon anonyme sur sainte Agnès, texte du XIIIe siècle," *Travaux de linguistique et de littérature* 7 (1969):241-53.

8. Wendelin Foerster, *Li sermon saint Bernard* (Erlangen, 1885); also in *Romanische Forschungen* 2 (1886):1-210.

9. Alfred Schulze, *Predigten des heiligen Bernhards in altfranzösischer Übertragung*, Bibliothek des litterarischen Vereins in Stuttgart 203 (Tübingen: Litterarischer Verein in Stuttgartt, 1894)

10. Wendelin Foerster, *Li Dialoge le pape Gregoire* (Halle: Niemeyer, 1876).

11. Yves Lefèvre, *L'Elucidarium et les Lucidaires* (Paris: E. de Boccard, 1954).

12. Konrad Hofmann, "Altburgundische Übersetzung der Predigten Gregors über Ezechiel," *Abhandlungen der Philosophisch-Philologischen Classe der königlichen bayerischen Akademie der Wissenschaften, München* 16, 1 (1881), 3-126.

13. Jacques Chaurand, "Deux fragments d'homélies sur Ezechiel," *Romania* 88 (1967):91-112.

14. Karl Storchenegger, *Les 17 Homélies de Haimon. Première édition de la version française* (Zurich: Juris, 1973).

15. Volker Honemann, *Die 'Epistola ad fratres de Monte Dei' des Wilhelm von Saint-Thierry: lateinische Überlieferung und mittelalterliche Übersetzung.* Münchener Texte und Untersuchungen zur deutschen Literatur des Mittelalters 61 (Munich, 1978). See pp. 221-81.

16. Michel Zink, *La Prédication en langue romane avant 1300* (Paris: Champion, 1976). See pp. 65-70 (Bernardian group), 72-74 (Gregory's homilies on *Ezekiel*), and 130-37 (the Cistercian connection).

17. *Laudate* covers eighteen folios, about five times the average length of Saint Bernard's sermons in the same manuscript.

18. Schulze [n. 9 above], lx-xiii.

19. Alfred Schulze, "Zu den altfranzösischen Bernhardhand-schriften," *Beiträge zur Bücherkunde und Philologie August Wilmanns zum 25. März 1903 gewidmet* (Leipzig: Harrassowitz, 1903), pp. 389-404. See pp. 400-02: Schulze demonstrates by an ingenious bit of detective work that the nine titles rubricated by the copyist must have been in place before the other rubricator did his job.

20. Honemann [n. 15 above], pp. 98-119.

21. Maurice Wilmotte, "Le dialecte du ms. f. fr. 24764," *Etudes de philologie wallonne* (Paris: Droz, 1932), p. 168.

22. "Zu den altfranzösischen Bibelübersetzungen," *Zeitschrift für romanische Philologie* 8 (1884):413-29.

23. *La Bible française au moyen âge* (Paris: Imprimerie nationale, 1884), p. 40.

24. *Histoire littéraire de la France*, 7 (Paris, 1746), p. xliv.

25. Lefèvre [n. 11 above], pp. 311-15.

26. Zink [n. 16 above], p. 130.

27. Passage quoted by Zink [n. 16 above], pp. 133-34.

28. Taylor [n. 7 above], p. 246.

29. Zink [n. 16 above], p. 137.

APOCRYPHAL NARRATIVE ELEMENTS IN THE *GENESIS* OF THE MIDDLE LOW GERMAN *HISTORIENBIBEL* HELMSTEDT 611.1

Patricia A. McAllister

Some one hundred manuscripts represent the body of late medieval German literature referred to as *Historienbibeln*. These texts are vernacular prose paraphrases of biblical material, predominantly from the Old Testament, marked by extensive omissions of Vulgate material as well as supplemental additions which can in large part be traced to patristic writings, popular histories, and rhymed chronicles such as Rudolf von Ems's *Weltchronik* of the mid-thirteenth century. The *Historienbibeln* are a fifteenth-century phenomenon in German literature, most of the manuscripts dated in the period from 1440-75. These vernacular bibles reflect a more popular side of biblical study in the late Middle Ages, documenting the relevance of passages from the Bible as well as the varying need for, and methods of clarification of, such passages. One witnesses in these texts different styles of compilation of biblical traditions which can lend insight into the interests of the respective audiences and their acquaintance with popular biblical traditions.

To date, research in this genre has been sorely handicapped by the lack of editions. With the exception of selected excerpts such as Psalm texts or the *Song of Solomon*, the *Historienbibeln* texts remain available only in manuscript form and are thus largely inaccessible to the modern scholar. We remain dependent on the work of the early twentieth-century scholar Hans Vollmer, who indexed and categorized over one hundred *Historienbibel* manuscripts according to content and dialect, providing physical descriptions of and sample lines from the manuscripts--in essence, describing the genre while offering no full example of it. According to this index, the styles range from the totally vernacular to re-Latinized renditions.[1] Based on his study of these manuscripts, Vollmer postulates as major sources Petrus Comestor's widely known *Historia scholastica*, Isidore of Seville's *Etymologiae*, Honorius Augustodunensis's *De imagine mundi*, and Gottfried von Viterbo's *Pantheon*. The medieval German rhymed bibles, such as Rudolf von Ems's *Weltchronik*, reflect the same sources and, in their own right, may have acted as more immediate sources of such material for the redactors of the fifteenth-century vernacular bible paraphrases.[2] One can, of course, also trace occasional details and explanations to the traditional glosses to the Vulgate, such as the *Glossa ordinaria*, which had essentially become part of the Bible in many medieval manuscripts, included as marginalia or interlinear notes.

Vollmer postulates as audiences for these texts the lay brothers or nuns who were involved in the study of the Bible but had no knowledge of Latin and were thus dependent on the vernacular. These vernacular bibles were then intended for daily reading in the refectory at mealtimes. As anthologies of biblical traditions, they may also have been used for the preparation of sermons.[3]

That the traditions of the *Historienbibeln* did not survive beyond the late fifteenth century is most likely attributable to the advent of the Humanist movement and the Reformation, both of which espoused a loyalty to the original text of the Bible.[4] The increasing popularity of the printed book may also have contributed to the waning of this popular genre, providing a more fertile soil for "legitimate" books written in a standardized German.

Of the over one hundred texts critiqued by Vollmer, only five are written in Middle Low German, i.e., in the dialect of northern Germany during the Middle Ages. One such text is the manuscript indexed as Helmstedt 611.1, currently in the holdings of the Herzog August Bibliothek in Wolfenbüttel, one of many manuscripts which were previously housed in Helmstedt. H 611.1 records selections from the first seven books of the Old Testament, starting with the tale of Abraham and Lot (Gen. 13). Supplementary material traceable to Petrus Comestor, Vincent of Beauvais, and the *Glossa ordinaria* is very much in evidence here. That a German version of excerpts from the *Historia scholastica* appeared in print shortly after 1460[5] offers additional evidence of the popularity of Petrus Comestor's work among a German-speaking audience and may even have been a source for the redactor of H 611.1, who wrote in the year 1472.

This dating of the manuscript as well as information about the redactor of H 611.1 have been supplied by the redactor himself, who concluded his text with the following lines in Latin:

> Ffinitus et conpletus est liber iste sub annis D(o)m(ini)
> millesimo quadringentesimo septuagesimo secundo per me
> Iohannem Hasen clericum Bremens(is) dioce(sis), tu(n)c
> temp(or)is incola civitat(is) Kilonen. Orate pro eo.

> [This book was finished and completed in the year of the
> Lord 1472 by me, Johannes Hasen, cleric of the diocese
> of Bremen, at that time a resident of the city of Cologne.
> Pray for him.]

Of this Johannes Hasen there is nothing more known than what he writes here himself, unless a carelessly written or read pen stroke --entirely possible in the case of the bastarda *r* and long *s*--might allow us to identify him with Johannes von Haren, a prebendary of the order of St. John (Hospitallers) at Bredehorn, who translated in abbreviated form the *Chronica archicomitum Oldenburgensium* of Johannes Schiphower into Low German. That manuscript, also signed, is dated 1506.[6] The year is feasible, the locality close, the type of manuscript--unattributed, free translation of "historical" material into Middle Low German--the same. As the manuscript of 1506 has not yet been edited, this identification must for the time being remain conjecture.

H 611.1 is not an elegant manuscript. Its 189 folios are written on paper, each page measuring 21 x 14.2 cm. The written surface, 15.4 x 9.2 cm, is covered by, in most cases, twenty-five lines of text. Latin inscriptions and the first few lines of each book are written in Gothic block lettering, while the majority of the text is recorded in a bastarda script, a more rounded, almost cursive style. The ink is now brown, with occasional initial letters, underlining, and simple flourishes--as well as some corrections--in red ink. The manuscript is devoid of illumination or illustration. In short, H 611.1 was a working text rather than a showpiece. It could well have been used as a textbook for the preparation of sermons or for individual or group study, as suggested by Vollmer.

Judging from the content and style of the text, the intended audience would not have been well versed in the Vulgate or the patristic writings. The episodes are more narrative than theological in nature, and didactic digressions serve to clarify contradictions in the text or draw associations with contemporary religious practices. One can assume that the audience was not well educated.

The inherent and ultimate source of H 611.1 is, of course, the Vulgate. Indeed, the redactor implies this source in his opening lines: "Hir begi(n)net sic de vyf boke Moyses, de ghesatet synt uthe deme latino" [Here begin the five books of Moses, which are translated from the Latin]. Beyond this introduction, there is no evidence that the redactor was working directly from the Vulgate--or, for that matter, from any Latin text. Those episodes clearly identifiable with the Vulgate tradition are richly supplemented with material found only in more popular biblical traditions. Nor does the redactor take the scholarly precaution of marking extra-Vulgate material as such. Tales from the Vulgate appear here in much modified form, with increased use of dialogue and better development and motivation of character. Editorial digressions are uneven and unpredictable, ranging from a short definition of "mugghe"--one of the insects sent as a plague upon the land of Pharaoh--to a lengthy prefiguration of the role of the Virgin Mary.

The form of Middle Low German used by Johannes Hasen does not betray Latin influence. No tell-tale Latinized constructions stand out as inconsistent with German syntax or semantics. The language reflects the style of other Middle Low German literature. Simplified syntax lends a tone of informality, as do the floating adverbial prefixes and occasionally omitted verbal endings which are, even today, typical of Low German. This linguistic style, as well as the content of the text, argues for the redactor's independence from a Latin source and from the Vulgate form of the biblical material. It is more likely that his source was also in Middle Low German--or, at least, in some dialect of German. As Vollmer has classified three other Middle Low German *Historienbibel* manuscripts together with H 611.1, of which the oldest is dated 1466,[7] there is some evidence that Johannes Hasen was working within an established tradition.

This, then, is the context within which a Middle Low German prose paraphrase of the Bible took shape. Within this genre, popular histories were as valid a source as the Vulgate. Tales and commentary were melded into a more or less flowing narrative. The tale of Joseph as narrated in H 611.1 illustrates the types of variations that were made to the Vulgate text by the genre *Historienbibel.*

The story of Joseph begins with a dream. The dreamer and interpreter of dreams is--if only by this God-given gift--favored by God. The seventeen-year-old Joseph tells his brothers of his dream in which his brothers' sheaves bowed down to his own, then tells his father and brothers of another vision, in which the sun and the moon and eleven stars bowed to him. The reaction is his father's rebuke and his brothers' hatred and jealousy (Gen. 37).

Both dreams are reproduced in the Helmstedt Genesis, but with differences in detail, interpretation, and reaction. The sixteen-year-old Joseph tells of a vision of the sun, the moon, and twelve stars. As he watched, the sun impregnated the moon, from which twelve additional stars were born. The eleven stars bowed to and served the twelfth. The inconsistency of numbers, as twenty-four stars are then reduced to twelve, could suggest an uneasy assimilation of two distinct traditions. Since, however, the literary tradition of the Joseph story contains no other instance of twenty-four stars in the dream, it seems likely that the redactor or scribe was in error. The birth of *twelve* stars has been substituted for the birth of a *twelfth* star.[8]

While the Vulgate Joseph makes no secret of who bows to whom, the Helmstedt Joseph is discreet. Asked for an interpretation of his dream, Joseph refuses with the words: "Leue vader, hadde gy noch ene(n) sone, so wolde ik juw dat ghesichte wol beduden . . ." [21r, lines 20ff.; Dear father, if you had one more son, I would interpret the vision for you . . .].[9] Until a twelfth son is born, the parallel cannot be seen. Joseph's reticence provokes even greater anger in his brothers, who interpret the dream antagonistically:

> Myt der su(n)nen, dar mede menet he vnsen vader,
> vn(de) vnse moder meynet he by der mane(n); we(n)te
> wy synt va(n) vnseme vader thelet an dem(e) licha(m)me
> vnser moder vnde va(n) eer gheberet to der werlde; vnde
> dat leuent hebbe wy va(n) dem(e) he(m)mele vntfanghen.
> Vn(de) wy broder(e) synt de sternen; vn(de) he menet de
> schoneste sterne tho wesende. Wanner wy noch enen
> broder kreghen, so meynet he, dat wi eme noch alle xj
> scholen deyne(n).   (21v, lines 4ff.)

> [By the sun he means our father, and by the moon our
> mother; for we were begotten by our father in the body
> of our mother, and she brought us into the world; and
> from heaven have we received life. We brothers are the
> stars, and he thinks of himself as the greatest star. If we
> get one more brother, he thinks that all eleven of us
> should serve him.]

The character portrayal of the Helmstedt text thus attributes dissension to the brothers without any suggestion of arrogance in Joseph.

The dream of the twelve sheaves is postponed in the Helmstedt text:

> Do yd der tyd nalede, dat Got de Here Josephe den
> bedroueden losen wolde vnde trosten, do dromede
> Josepe, wo elffen garwen vppe deme velde stu(n)den;
> vnde de leste was aller schonest, vnde de theyne
> negheden der elfften. Do vornam Joseph dat wol, dat syn
> dynk gud werde(n) scholde.   (27v, lines 15ff.)

> [When the time neared when the Lord God would release
> and comfort the troubled Joseph, Joseph dreamt of eleven
> sheaves which stood in a field; and the last one was the
> most beautiful, and the ten bowed to the eleventh. Then
> Joseph knew that his affairs would turn out well.]

Its postponement eliminates Joseph's second display of superiority over his brothers, while strengthening the significance of each dream.

The two dreams and their interpretation remain essentially the same in the Helmstedt text. The interaction among the three prisoners is, however, subtly different. The Vulgate Joseph offers his services as interpreter of the dreams of his fellow prisoners with the comment that interpretations belong to God (Gen. 40:8), and he again asserts the divine source of his gift before the pharaoh. The Helmstedt Joseph makes no comment about his God-given gift and speaks as a man to fellow men. Furthermore, his attitude is more deferential before the pharaoh, and he begins his response with a plea of innocence, the most natural of statements from one wrongly imprisoned. That such a comment is lacking in the Vulgate reflects the relatively impersonal nature of the Bible as compared to the Helmstedt manuscript.

The narration of the episode with Potiphar's wife also shows subtle modifications of plot and character portrayal. In the Vulgate, the accusation of Potiphar's wife (Gen. 39:13ff.) remains ambiguous, whereas the Helmstedt text provides clear motivation:

> Do wort eer hone, vnde se vruchtede, dat yt Joseph scholde ghesecht hebben vnde hebben se tho schanden ghemaket. Des begreep se de vorclaghe vnde reep joduthe ouer den vromeden mynschen Josephe, dat he wolde eer benomen hebben an der kameren ere eere; vnde tho warteke hadde se syn ouerste kleet beholden, do he eer entleep uthe deer kameren. (25v, lines 16ff.)

> [Then she grew ashamed and feared that Joseph might have told it and put her to shame. So she made the accusation first and cried for help against the righteous Joseph, claiming that he wanted to rob her honor in the room; and as evidence she had kept his topmost garment when he ran away from her and out of the room.]

The figure of Joseph, the bridegroom, varies radically from the Vulgate. Gen. 41:45 announces the marriage of Joseph to Asenath, daughter of Potiphar priest of On. Nothing more is said of Asenath. The Helmstedt text incorporates a lengthy episode of the heathen woman's conversion.

Its content is not original, going back to a second-century A.D. original Greek version which was later translated into Syriac and Latin.[10] A more accessible source for a medieval redactor would have been the abbreviated Latin version of the tale incorporated into Vincent of Beauvais's *Speculum Historiale* in the thirteenth century.[11] From a religious point of view, the episode justifies Joseph's marriage to a heathen, but the richly detailed story is its own narrative justification. Another narrative addition is the Egyptian "stone-herb" which Joseph surreptitiously supplies to his visiting brothers and which, they are told, will hasten Joseph's forgiveness (37v, lines 23ff.).[12] The brothers accept the herb, and Joseph is thus drawn conspicuously into the process of reconciliation.

Not only narrative but also didactic elements are added to the Helmstedt text. According to the Vulgate tradition, twenty pieces of silver were exchanged for Joseph when he was sold into slavery. The redactor rejects the Helmstedt redaction's variation of thirty pennies but assimilates the Vulgate's use of prefiguration by the following explanation:

> . . . dat was to ener figuren, dat Godes sone Jhesus Christus, dat vnschuldighe, durre bloet, scholde van syneme broder Judas Scharyot vorraden vn(de) vorkofft werden v(m)me xxx penni(n)ghe.   (23v, lines 24ff.)

> [. . . that was a figura of the fact that God's son Jesus Christ, that innocent and dear blood, should be betrayed and sold by his brother Judas Iscariot for thirty pennies.]

Explanatory commentary is added also to Jacob's lament for Joseph in order to correct Jewish error.

> Dar moste(n) alle patriarchen vnde p(ro)pheten in, de dar vorstorue(n) vor Ghodes boert, vn(de) ok Abraham. Hir an(e) synt de yoden sere tho straffende, wente se

spreken, wenner dat se steruen, so willen se to
he(m)mele varen in Abraha(m)mes schoet. Dar v(m)me
so mach se ene yewelich my(n)sche straffen vn[de]
spreken tho en aldus: Nu gy meyne(n), dat Christus
Messias nicht ghekomen sy, de juw an der ee ghelouet
was. We hefft denne de sone ghemaket, dat Abraha(m)
in den he(m)mel ghekome(n) is; wente do he starff, do
voer he io in de helle. Hir vmme so mothe gy ok
yu(m)mer varen to deer helle, edder gy mothen louen,
dat Messias was de sone Godes, Jh(es)us Chr(ist)us. . . .

(35v, lines 7ff.)

[All patriarchs and prophets who died before God's birth,
including Abraham, had to go there. In this the Jews are
very much at fault, for they say that they will go to
heaven, to the lap of Abraham, when they die. For this
reason, everyone may punish them and speak to them in
this way: Now you claim that Christ the Messiah, who
was promised to you in the testament, has not come.
How, then, did the son arrange for Abraham to enter into
heaven; for when he died, he surely went to hell, or else
you must believe that Messiah was the son of God, Jesus
Christ. . . .]

With such devices the Helmstedt version modifies its source. Its
retelling is at times unpolished, its style uneven, and its additions
intrusive. Didactic digressions concerning the prefigurative significance of certain characters or episodes are the most explicit form
of instruction. Subtler clarifications come from the interpolated
plots and from additional character details. Such modifications have
the overall effect of humanizing the text, even if they endanger the
unity of it. The figure of Joseph in Helmstedt 611.1 is a synthesis of
traditions which reveals much about the medieval translator's craft.

NOTES

1. See Hans Vollmer, *Materialien zur Bibelgeschichte und religiöse
Volkskunde des Mittelalters*, 2 vols. (Berlin: Weidmannsche Buchhandlung, 1912-27).

2. Hans Vollmer, ed., *Neue Beiträge zur Geschichte der deutschen Bibel im Mittelalter* (Potsdam: Akademische Verlagsgesellschaft m.b.H., 1938), p. 36.

3. Vollmer, *Neue Beiträge*, pp. 58, 73.

4. Christoph Gerhardt, "Historienbibeln," in *Die deutsche Literatur des Mittelalters. Verfasserlexikon*, ed. Kurt Ruh, 2nd ed. (New York: Walter de Gruyter, 1978-), vol. 4, col. 73.

5. Vollmer, *Neue Beiträge* [n. 2 above], p. 83.

6. Thomas Frenz, "Johannes von Haren," in *Die deutsche Literatur des Mittelalters. Verfasserlexikon* [n. 4 above], vol. 4, col. 637.

7. Vollmer, *Materialien* [n. 1 above], vol. 1, pt. 2, p. 1.

8. The Helmstedt text reads here: "Van dem(e) mane(n) treden xij sterne(n) men der ande(re)n sternen" (21r, lines 14ff.). This line could with justification be emended as: "Van dem(e) mane(n) tred(e) en xij. sterne men der ande(re)n sternen."

9. The text of Helmstedt 611.1 exists as yet only in the original manuscript form. The quotations which appear here, both in the original and in English translation, are drawn from my own work with the manuscript. Publication of a critical edition of the entire manuscript is forthcoming.

10. Manfred Derpmann, *Die Josephgeschichte. Auffassung und Darstellung im Mittelalter* (Düsseldorf: A. Henn, 1974), pp. 146-54.

11. Dieter Sänger, *Antikes Judentum und die Mysterien, Religionsgeschichtliche Untersuchungen zu Joseph und Asenath* (Tübingen: J. C. B. Mohr, 1980), p. 12.

12. Neither dictionaries nor context offer any help in identifying this mysterious "stone-herb," but the following note in *Biblia sacra cum glossa ordinaria a Strabo Fuldensi et Postilla Nic. Lirani Franc*, vol. 1 (Antwerp: Ioannes Meursius, 1634), col. 601, with reference to Ex. 12:22, sheds light

on a possible definition of the word:

> Hyssopus herba est humilis, nascens in petris, purgans pectus
> et pulmonem: et significat veram humilitatem, cujus exemplum
> Christus nobis in semetipso praebuit. Fasciculum ergo hyssopi
> sanguine tingimus, quando memores humilitatis Christi, eum
> imitari studemus.

> [Hyssop is a humble plant, found in rocks, which cleanses the
> chest and the lungs; and it signifies true humility, an example
> of which Christ offered us in himself. For this reason we soak
> a bundle of hyssop in blood when, remembering the humility of
> Christ, we seek to imitate him.]

See also Walafrid Strabo, *Glossa ordinaria. Patrologia Latina*, ed. J.-P. Migne, vol. 113 (Paris: J.-P. Migne, 1855) and Petrus Comestor, *Historia Scholastica. Patrologia Latina*, ed. J.-P. Migne, vol. 198 (Paris: J.-P. Migne, 1855). If it was indeed hyssop with which Joseph supplied his brothers--and the context certainly accommodates an herb signifying humility--the above note would clarify the etymology of the Middle Low German *steencrude*.

ADDITIONAL REFERENCES

Bluhm, Heinz. "Martin Luther and the pre-Lutheran Low German Bibles." *Modern Language Review* 62 (1967):642-53.

Brodführer, E. "Bibelübersetzung." In *Reallexikon der deutschen Literaturgeschichte*. Ed. Werner Kohlschmidt and Wolfgang Mohr. Vol. 4, cols. 145-52. Berlin: De Gruyter, 1958-84.

Ising, Gerhard, ed. *Die niederdeutschen Bibelfrühdrucke.* Berlin: Akademie-Verlag, 1961.

Josephus, Flavius. *Opera.* Ed. Guilelmus Dindorfius. Paris: Firmin-Didot, 1929.

Lasch, Agathe. *Mittelniederdeutsche Grammatik.* Halle a. S.: Verlag von Max Niemeyer, 1914.

Lübben, August. *Mittelniederdeutsche Grammatik nebst Chrestomathie und Glossar.* Leipzig: T. O. Weigel, 1882.

_____. *Mittelniederdeutsches Handwörterbuch.* Norden / Leipzig: Diedr. Soltau, 1888. Rpt. Darmstadt: Wissenschaftliche Buchgesellschaft, 1980.

Maurer, Friedrich. *Studien zur mitteldeutschen Bibelübersetzung vor Luther.* Heidelberg: Carl Winter's Universitätsbuchhandlung, 1929.

Merzdorf, Theodor. *Die deutschen Historienbibeln des Mittelalters.* Stuttgart: Anton Hiersemann, 1870. Rpt. Hildesheim: Georg Olms, 1963.

Reuss, Eduard. *Die deutsche Historienbibel vor der Erfindung des Bücherdrucks.* Stuttgart: Fischer, 1855. Rpt. Wiesbaden: Sändig, 1966.

Schiller, Kurt, and August Lübben. *Mittelniederdeutsches Wörterbuch.* 6 vols. Bremen: Verlag von J. Kühtmann's Buchhandlung, 1875. Rpt. Münster: Aschendorffsche Verlagsbuchhandlung, 1931.

Smalley, Beryl. *The Study of the Bible in the Middle Ages.* 3rd ed. (rev.) Oxford: Basil Blackwell, 1983.

Walther, Wilhelm. *Die deutsche Bibelübersetzung des Mittelalters.* Braunschweig: Verlag von Hellmuth Wollermann, 1889-92.

FROM THE VERNACULAR TO LATIN AND BACK: THE CASE OF *THE SEVEN SAGES OF ROME*

Hans R. Runte

he Seven Sages of Rome is a medieval collection of stories a-bout wise counselors and wicked women. It was, throughout the Middle Ages and beyond, an extremely popular work which spread into virtually all European languages. Campbell[1] summarizes it as follows:

> A young prince is tempted by his stepmother [the empress]. She, being rebuffed by him, accuses him of attempting to violate her, and he is condemned to death. His life is saved by seven wise men, who secure a stay of execution . . . by entertaining the [emperor] through seven days with tales showing the wickedness of woman, the [empress] meantime recounting stories to offset those of the sages. On the eighth day the prince, who has remained silent up to that time, speaks in his own defense, and the [empress] is put to death.   (pp. xi-xii)

The collection has its ultimate roots in the East, where it is usually known as *The Book of Sindbad*. The oldest extant Western text, French Version K, was probably written about 1155. Campbell counted at least forty different Western versions, upwards of two-hundred manuscripts, and nearly 250 editions of *The Seven Sages of Rome*.[2]

In this great wealth of versions, manuscripts, and printings lies hidden a literary curiosity which has not yet been fully studied. Towards the turn of the thirteenth to the fourteenth century, one of several French *Romans des sept sages de Rome*, Version A, was translated into the very influential *Historia septem sapientum* (Latin Version H), from which almost all European versions were to derive, including the retranslated French Version H. The reasons for and methods of this remarkable double translation[3] are the subject of the following investigation.

Structurally, *The Seven Sages of Rome* resembles, as the French generic term *roman à tiroirs* suggests, a chest of fifteen drawers. Drawers 1, 3, 5, 7, 9, 11, and 13 contain the empress's tales, while drawers 2, 4, 6, 8, 10, 12, and 14 hold the sages' rebuttals. In drawer 15 lies the prince's summation.

The longevity, popularity, and adaptability of *The Seven Sages of Rome* derive ultimately from this sturdy yet flexible narrative construct. Imitators, adaptors, and translators everywhere recognized easily that in terms of the story they were writing, a fifteen-slot frame represents the logically optimal dimensions of their work; attempts at adding drawers to the ideal chest have remained inconsequential. On the other hand, they also realized that there was within the outer shell of the text a certain amount of creative freedom: as long as they respected the inner logic of the frame story and the basic principle of alternating argumentation, they could adapt drawer content to their liking or resourcefulness, or rearrange odd-numbered and even-numbered drawers in a variety of sequences. In fact, so pervasive was this tendency to vary the order of tales that in Campbell's tabulation (p. xxxv) of eight different versions of *The Seven Sages of Rome*, only one of the fifteen tales, *canis*,[4] can be seen to occupy consistently the same slot, drawer 2.

Accidents inevitably occurred in the transmission of tales, the worst offender in this respect being the redactor of French Version M. He filled drawers 7, 9, 10, 11, 12, and 13 with tales which are totally alien to the *Seven Sages of Rome* tradition and run counter to the internal logic of the frame story.[5] While Version M is an aberration, its exceptionalness does not necessarily confirm the rule. *Inclusa*, for example, fits drawer 14 very badly, yet that is its place in most versions. Indeed, the seventh sage's tale about the jealous man's immured wife who elopes through a secret passageway devised by her husband's friend cannot be construed as an *exemplum* of feminine wickedness without unduly twisting the tale's motivational mechanics.

Long before Gaston Paris and Professor Gilleland drew attention to this flaw, the redactor-translator of Latin Version H had already noticed and set out to correct it. He moved *inclusa* into the empress's drawer 13, rearranged *vidua* into drawer 14, and filled drawer 12 with new material (*amatores*); *Roma* from drawer 13 he squeezed in with *senescalcus*.

		French Version A	Latin Version H
1	Empress	arbor	arbor
2	Sage	canis	canis
3	Empress	aper	aper
4	Sage	medicus	puteus
5	Empress	gaza	gaza
6	Sage	puteus	avis
7	Empress	senescalcus	sapientes
8	Sage	tentamina	tentamina
9	Empress	Virgilius	Virgilius
10	Sage	avis	medicus
11	Empress	sapientes	senescalcus + Roma
12	Sage	vidua	amatores
13	Empress	Roma	inclusa
14	Sage	inclusa	vidua
15	Prince	vaticinium	vaticinium + amici

A number of initial, general conclusions may be drawn as to the transformation of French Version A into Latin Version H. The rearrangement of drawers up to tale 11 (4 moved to 10, 6 to 4, 7 to 11, 10 to 6, 11 to 7) is so common an occurrence in the *Seven Sages of Rome* tradition as to be hardly worthy of further analysis, especially since none of the empress's tales is cross-attributed to the sages, or vice versa. Immeasurably more is revealed about the writer of Latin Version H in the chain-reaction reorganization triggered by the movement of *inclusa* from drawer 14 to 13. He was clearly not "just" translating blindly one tale after another, but had a full and detailed understanding of the structure and meaning of his source. He had likely read the French text *in toto* before setting his translator's quill to parchment, had realized and accepted that a sage has to have the last word, and had recognized in *vidua* the ultimate weapon against the empress. Closing the debate with the incomparable "Matron of Ephesus" instead of *amatores* is an unrivaled masterstroke and suggests, perhaps in conjunction with the realignment of the preceding tales, a conscious attempt at building up narrative and didactic momentum.

Roma is not one of the empress's more convincing tales, and Latin Version H could well have done without it. (According to the empress, her imperial husband resembles the Saracens who, fooled and frightened by one of the Roman sages' histrionics, abandon their siege of the city and are massacred.) Was it faithfulness to the French model that made the translator hold on to left-over *Roma*? It could be that sage Genus's (French Version A) construction of a giant mirror, his squirrel-tail cloak, and his shadow-swordmanship on Rome's ramparts were deemed worthy of retention. Or perhaps *Roma* was meant to echo *Virgilius*, a tale with too many similar motifs not to worry text editors weary of internal contamination. (Virgil sets up a high mirror as an early-warning-system against invaders such as the king of Puille--already featured in French Version A's *senescalcus*--whose spies compromise the emperor by sabotaging the Roman defense installation.) *Virgilius* could have absorbed *Roma* seamlessly, were it not for the fact that greed is the motive in the former tale (a great treasure is rumored to be buried under the mirror), and gullibility in the latter. To be retained, *Roma* needed to be attached to a tale about easy deception, such as *sapientes* (seven wise men hoodwink Herod until they are unmasked by a boyish Merlin; French Version A). Unfortunately, the translator of Latin Version H missed this ideal connection, first by taking *sapientes* out of drawer 11 and moving it up four slots, second by being unwilling or unable to have *Roma* travel the distance from drawer 13 to drawer 7.

In *Senescalcus*, with which the translator of Latin Version H paired *Roma,* the Empress tells about the greed of a seneschal who sells his wife to the king of Puille for twenty marks. French Version A reads:

"Ore, sire, n'avez vous oï que li seneschaus fist par
convoitise d'avoir?   Or esgardez conment il l'en est
avenu: il est desheritez a tout jourz et sa fame bien
mariee. Autresi vous devez vous prendre garde de vous,
car vous estes si convoiteus de oïr les paroles a ces
sages, et convoitise vous vaincra, si que vous en seroiz
essilliez et chetis et honteus seur terre."[6]

["Now then, Sire, have you not heard what the seneschal
did out of greed? Now look what happened to him: he
has forever lost his wealth and his properly married wife.
You must therefore watch yourself, for you are so eager
to hear these sages' tales, and eagerness will undo you,
so that you will end your life on this earth in exile,
miserable and shameful."]

The transition from the greedy seneschal to the easily fooled
Saracens of *Roma* cannot have been obvious, but the translator of
Latin Version H cleverly developed the transition. *Senescalcus* ends
thus in French Version A and Latin Version H:

Li seneschax s'en foï, et li rois maria sa fame bien et bel
en sa terre.   (19[d])

[The seneschal fled, and the king happily married his
wife in his land.]

Senescalcus vero hoc audiens fugit nec ultra comparuit;
rex vero, quamdiu vixit, uxorem eius in honore et gaudio
secum tenuit.[7]

[But the seneschal, upon hearing this, fled and did not
appear again; the king, on the other hand, kept his wife
by his side in honor and joy as long as he lived.]

Latin Version H continues immediately:

Post amocionem senescalci exercitum collegit et Romam
obsedit tam diu, quousque Romani corpora sanctorum
Petri et Pauli volebant ei dare, ut discederet;   (51)

[After the removal of the seneschal he assembled his army and besieged Rome until the Romans would be willing to give him the bodies of Saint Peter and Saint Paul in order to make him leave;],

which corresponds to the beginning of *Roma* in French Version A:

"Sire, Rome fu moult guerroiee jadis, car set rois païens l'avoient asise en tele maniere qu'il voloient avoir la chaiere Saint Pere et l'apostele metre a torment et a mort, et toute crestienté destruire."   (36[a])

["Sire, Rome was once fiercely attacked by seven pagan kings who had besieged her because they wanted to take Saint Peter's see and to torture and kill the apostolic community and to destroy Christendom altogether."]

French Version H renders the whole transition thus:

Cecy estre dit, le seneschal incontinant s'en ala hors du royaulme, ne jamais plus ne se trouva. Et le temps que le roy vesquist, tint avec soy la femme du seneschal, a laquelle fit des honnours et donna pluseurs biens. Mais sy tost que le seneschal s'en fut allé il se mist en armes trespuissament pour combattre les Romains, lesqueux il asiega soubz condicion que jamais ne les habandonneroit jusques il eust les corps de saint Pierre et saint Pol, don il furent tenus sy de près qu'il estoient contens de luy delivrer lesdis corps saints et qu'i s'en ala.[8]

[This having been said, the seneschal immediately left the realm and never again returned. And as long as the king lived he kept with him the seneschal's wife on whom he bestowed honors and to whom he gave many possessions. But as soon as the seneschal had left he raised a mighty army in order to fight the Romans whom he besieged; his conditions were that he would under no circumstances lift the siege until he had received the bodies of Saint Peter and Saint Paul. The Romans were

kept under such close watch that they were glad to give
him the said bodies and see him leave.]

The solution is ingenious in its simplicity: the seneschal leaves
senescalcus and enters *Roma* as the protagonist, replacing the seven
pagan kings and thus knitting the two tales indissolubly together.

There remains, however, the question of the explicatory moral(s)
to be drawn from the double tale. The empress's conclusion to
senescalcus [quoted above, p. 97] is given thus in Latin Version H:

> "Nonne primo audivisti quomodo senescalcus, in quem
> rex tantum confidebat, propriam uxorem propter
> cupiditatem prodidit et confudit et ideo de regno fuit
> expulsus? Simili modo filius tuus propter cupiditatem,
> quam habet ad imperium, ut regnet, te intendit con-
> fundere ac destruere. Sed dum es in tua potestate, fac tu,
> sicut fecit rex cum senescalco suo. Si eum occidere non
> vis, saltem sit exulatus, ut de cetero nunquam com-
> pareat; et tunc in pace poteris quiescere."   (52)

> ["Did you not hear, first of all, how the seneschal in
> whom the king had so much confidence, gave up and
> confounded his own wife out of greed, and how he was
> therefore expelled from the realm? Similarly your son,
> who is eager to reign over the empire, intends to
> confound and destroy you. But while you are in all your
> power, do as the king did with his seneschal. If you do
> not want to kill him, at least banish him, so that he may
> never reappear; and then you will be able to live quietly
> in peace."],

while in *Roma*, she tells the emperor:

> "Autresi fetes vous, sire. . . . Cil set sage vous deçoivent
> par leur art et par leur engin, dont vous morroiz a honte.
> Et ce sera a bon droit."   (37$^{a\text{-}b}$)

> ["You do exactly the same thing, Sire. . . . Those seven

sages deceive you with their artifice and with their
stratagems, and you will die a shameful death because of
it. And that would not be unjust."]

"Deinde audisti quomodo rex [senescalcus!] civitatem
romanam obsedit et quomodo per sapientes deceptus fuit
et civitatem perdidit et in fine per cautelam unius senis
[no longer named Genus] occisus et devictus totus
exercitus fuit. Eodem modo iam isti .VII. sapientes
intendunt tecum agere i.e. per cautelas te decipere et in
fine te occident, ut filius tuus regnare poterit." (52)

["Then you heard how the king (the seneschal!) besieged
the citizens of Rome and how he was deceived by the
sages and lost the city, and how in the end the whole
army was killed and conquered because of one single old
man's (no longer named Genus) cunning. In the same
manner these seven sages intend to deal with you, i.e., to
deceive you with their cunning, and in the end they will
kill you so that your son may reign."]

The silly confusion concerning "senescalcus" / "rex" and the
belabored enumeration of the two lessons (". . . primo . . . deinde . . .")
make it clear that drawer 11 contains two distinct if connected tales
after all. French Version H translates the Latin as follows:

"N'avés vous pas veu comment le roy premiérement se
confioit du tout en son seneschal, et ce nonobstant il fut
si desloyal qu'i luy mena sa propre femme pour la honter
et deshonnorer pour sa faulce convoitise, don il fut
bangny du royaulme? Semblablement je vous dis que
vostre filz pour la grant convoitise qu'il a d'avoir
l'empire il entent vous confondre et destruyre du tout.
Pour quoy, tant que vous estes en puissance, vengés vous
de luy et en faites comme le roy fit du seneschal; au
moings se vous ne le voulés faire morir deffendés lui
vostre royaulme et le banizés, a celle fin que vous
puissiez vivre en pais et sans doubte en vostre pais. Puis
aprés vous avés ouy comment le roy mist le siége devant

Romme, et comment par ces cept sages yl fut depceu et
abusé tellement qu'i fut confus avec ses gens et mors
honteusement.   Soyés seur que semblablement vous
fairont ces sept sages, lesqueux vous decepvront par
leurs cautelles, et vous fairont morir affin que vostre filz
plus tost puisse regner."   (131)

["Did you not see how the king first trusted his seneschal
in all things, and nevertheless the seneschal was so
disloyal that because of his sinful greed, he brought his
own wife to him, to her shame and dishonor, for which
he was banned from the realm? Similarly I tell you that
your son, who is very eager to have the empire, is
planning to confound and destroy you totally. Therefore,
as long as you are in power, seek revenge on him and
deal with him as the king dealt with the seneschal; at
least, if you do not want to kill him, forbid him your
realm and banish him so that you may live in peace and
without fear in your land. Then you heard how the king
besieged Rome, and how he was so deceived and abused
by those seven sages that he and his people were
confounded and shamefully killed. You can be sure that
the same will be done to you by these seven sages who
will deceive you with their cunning and will kill you so
that your son may reign sooner."]

The empress would seem to emerge from this arrangement with
a definite advantage, having been attributed an eighth tale against
the sages' seven.   The counterweight given *vidua* as the clinching
argument is therefore all the more justified and significant.

Keenly aware as he surely was of the narrative power play
opposing sages and empress, the author of Latin version H continued
to balance his translatory biases within the frame he had set up for
himself.   An analysis delving more deeply into the tales than did
Paris's preface will show that he is as much a translator as a restruc-
turer of his French source material; that he is more of both than the
author of French Version H; and that through judicious realignment,

amplification, and contraction of plot and plot elements, he created the "classic" *Seven Sages of Rome* version on which subsequent retellings, including French Version H, could improve but little.

"The translator," Paris observed, ". . . has everywhere noticeably lengthened" the text of French Version A (p. xxxii; my translation). The impression casual reading leaves of verbosity in Latin and concision in French needs nuancing, for it does not, or only in part, originate in the translation of the individual tales. Rather, it stems mainly from Version H (in any language) having an "extravagant fondness for pointing the moral" as soon as certain tales have been told.[9] *Arbor* in French Version A and Latin Version H offers a good example:

"Sire," dit l'empereriz, "or est il coupez, or est il del tout a honte menez par icelui qui issi de lui. Ausi est de vostre filz qui issi de vous, qui vous met ja a honte, car touz li empires est ja contre vous de vous desheriter, et vous estiez avant ier el point de vous delivrer. Et pour ce vous en puisse il ausi avenir conme il fist au pin de son pinel." (7^{a-b})

["Sire," said the empress, "so now it is cut down, now it is totally brought to shame by the offshoot which sprung from it. The same is true of your son who sprung from you and who dishonors you already, for the entire empire is already against you and wants to strip you of your power. And yesterday you had the opportunity to rid yourself of him. Therefore may happen to you what happened to the pine tree because of its offshoot."]

"Iam exponam que dixi. Arbor ista tam nobilis est persona tua. . . . Pinella sub arbore est filius tuus maledictus, qui iam incipit per doctrinam suam crescere. Ille vero studet, in quantum potest, ramos potentie tue evellere, ut aerem i.e. famam ac laudem humanam habeat. Deinde personam tuam propriam destruet, ut post decessum tuum regnet. . . . Consulo ergo, dum es in tua potestate ac sanitate, ut eum destruas." (15)

["Now let me explain what I said. That noble tree is
you. . . . The little pine tree under the tree is your cursed
son who through education is beginning to grow. He is
eager, as much as he can, to break the branches of your
power in order to receive air, i.e., fame and human
praise. Thereafter he is going to destroy yourself so that
he may reign after your death. . . . I advise you therefore
to destroy him while you are still in power and health."]

Such "allegorizing" (Paris, p. xxxviii), or "pointing the moral," as
Professor Gilleland has rightly noted (pp. 230-32), characterizes
exclusively the empress's tales; the sages content themselves with
much simpler lessons, as illustrated in *canis*:

"Sire, se vous par le conseil de vostre fame volez
destruire vostre filz sanz le conseil de vos barons, si vous
em puisse il ausi avenir conme il fist au chevalier de son
levrier." (10^{a-b})

["Sire, if upon your wife's advice you want to destroy
your son without your counselors' advice, may the same
happen to you that happened to the knight because of his
greyhound."]

"Amen dico vobis, si vos filium vestrum propter verbum
uxoris vestre occiditis, peius vobis eveniet quam illi de
leporario suo." (18)

["Verily I tell you, if you kill your son on your wife's
word, may you fare worse than the one with his
greyhound."],

or in *medicus*:

"Sire, autretel volez vous faire. Vous n'avez que un filz,
et celui volez vous destruire pour le dit de vostre fame.
Vous estes viel home et savez bien que jamés n'en aurez
plus enfant. Et se vos ainsint le volez destruire, si vous en

103

aviegne il ausint conme il fist Ypocras de son neveu." (13ᶜ)

["Sire, you want to do the same. You have only one son and you want to destroy him because of what your wife said. You are an old man and you know very well that you will never have another child. And if you want to destroy him in this way, may the same thing happen to you that happened to Hippocrates with his nephew."]

"Et ego dico vobis, peius vobis continget, si propter verbum uxoris vestre filium vestrum unicum occiditis, qui tempore necessitatis, si contingeret, vos saluaret." (49)

["And I tell you, may worse befall you if because of your wife's word you kill your only son who in times of need, should it come to that, would protect you."]

One effect of belaboring the empress's morals is to establish the tale collection firmly and irrevocably in the domain of didactic writing and to deny the tales, many of which were once *fabliaux*, even the slightest entertainment value. The second effect may be more significant still. The sages' tales about "maliciam mulierum" [women's wickedness]--in *vidua* for example--are quickly understood by emperor and reader; their antifeminism is easily recognizable. But what of the empress's tales? Do they not shift the didactic thrust from the social into the political domain, warning against filial usurpation and bad counselors and needing extensive explanations in order to drive the less familiar lessons home? It seems far from impossible that the author of Latin Version H wanted to enrich *The Seven Sages of Rome* by taking the empress's tales out of the shadow of the misogynistic sages and giving at least parts of his work the appearance of a *Fürstenspiegel*.

Before examining a further shift of focus in Latin Version H, it must be confirmed that the translator has indeed "followed his model quite faithfully" (Paris, p. xxxii; my translation). A quantitative scan of the text shows that on average an unexpected 25% of each tale (from 13% for *Roma* to 33% for *arbor*) has been translated *literally*. This includes not only narrative fillers such as:

et dirent a la dame [and said to the lady]   (*puteus*)

dixeruntque ei [and said to her];

or

a celui jour que cil viscuens fu morz [the day the
viscount died]   (*vidua*)

accidit quod illo die, quo miles sepultus erat   [it
happened that on the day the knight had been buried];

but also important and often lengthy plot elements:

et se tint a une des mains aus branches et a l'autre
conmença a grater le sengler.   (*aper*, 11ᵃ)

[and he held on to the branches with one hand and with
the other began to scratch the boar.]

et cum una manu aprum scalpebat, cum alia se per
arborem tenuit.   (19)

[and with one hand he scratched the boar, with the other
he held on to the tree.];

or

Et quant le borjois venoit de hors, la pie li disoit quanque
ele savoit et ooit et veoit.   (*avis*, 27ᶜ)

[And when the burgher returned home, the magpie told
him whatever it knew and had heard and seen.]

Pica ista, quidquid poterat audire, videre, totum domino
suo narravit.   (28)

[The magpie told its master everything it could hear and
see.];

or

> Lors fist Genus faire un vestement et le fist taindre en
> arrement, puis fist querre queues d'escureus plus d'un
> millier et les fist atachier a cel vestement . . . (*Roma*, 36ᶜ)

> [So Genus had a garment made and had it dyed black.
> Then he collected over a thousand squirrel tails and had
> them attached to the garment . . .]

> Magister quadam tunica mirabili se induit habensque in
> tunica pennas pavonis et parva tintinabula et alios
> colores aliarum avium, caudas surellorum . . .   (51)
> [The master put on a marvelous garment and had on this
> garment peacock feathers and little bells and varied
> colors of different birds, squirrel tales . . .].

Second-degree literalness may be observed in about one third of the
tales' textual mass. Here the translator renders the exact content of
French Version A either in more (1) or in fewer (2) words or by
drastically summarizing his source (3):

> (1) La dame manda son ami.   (*avis*, 27ᵈ)

> [The lady invited her friend.]

> Illa statim nuncium ad amasium destinavit, ut sine
> ulteriori dilacione ad eam veniret.   (28)

> [She sent at once a messenger to her lover telling him to
> come to her without further delay.]

> (2) Lors conmença a ferir des deux espees et a fere une
> escremie et une si fiere bataille que li feus et les
> estancelles voloient des espees.   (*Roma*, 36ᵈ)

> [Then he started to strike the two swords together and to
> joust and fight so fiercely that fire and sparks flew from
> the swords.]

Incepit se hinc inde movere, duos gladios in ore tenere et
miro modo splendere. (51)

[Then he started to move around there, holding the
swords in his mouth and making them sparkle in an
amazing way.]

(3) Et tant que un jour avint que li sires tenoit en sa main un
coustel qui novelement li avoit esté donez, dont il voloit
doler un boudon. (*vidua*, 32^c)

[Finally, it happened one day that the sire was holding in
his hand a knife which had recently been given to him,
with which he wanted to whittle down a stick.]

Miles a casu cultellum parvum in manu tenebat . . . (64)

[The knight happened to hold a small knife in his hand.]

It is in the remaining 40% of the tale material that the Latin
translator reveals himself most clearly. As can be expected, there is
not a single tale to which he has not added new narrative features, or
from which he has not eliminated certain narrative elements.
Surprisingly, however, his additions and omissions fall easily into a
pattern which reflects his particular interpretation of the collection
and his personal intent in translating it.

As judged by the non-traditional motifs with which he em-
broiders his tales, the translator must have been uncommonly
inventive, or else more widely read than those who have attempted
to unearth his sources. Even the unrelenting Campbell (followed
more recently by Professor Buuren[10]) was reduced to stating merely
that the tree in Latin *arbor* has "the peculiar virtue of curing
leprosy" (p. lxxviii); that *canis* has added "a pet falcon to the actors"
(p. lxxix); that in *aper* "the emperor of the land had offered his
daughter and his throne to any one who would slay the boar" (p.
lxxxiii); that *vidua* adds "to the mutilations normally recorded" (p.
ci); etc. Professor Buuren notes that the knight in Latin *canis* breaks
his spear and removes himself to the Holy Land (p. 142; also in *avis*,

p. 148); that in *puteus* the jealous husband keeps the keys to the house under his pillow (p. 148); that in *avis* both the wife and her maid climb on to the roof to fake a thunderstorm (p. 162); etc. Many more instances of narrative amplification could complement such lists: in Latin *gaza* the son's willingness to help his thriftless father defraud the emperor is motivated by fear of poverty; in *senescalcus* the ailing king is planning to rob Rome's sacred relics ("corpora apostolorum Petri et Pauli"); in *vidua* husband and wife are playing dice at the beginning of the tale; etc. The origins of such motifs are lost in the timeless traditions of popular culture; when they are traceable, features such as the trio of nurses in *canis* (most versions) have taken written form in Etienne de Bourbon's stories, in *fabliaux*, in the *Gesta Romanorum*. Self-mutilation designed to escape detection (most versions of *gaza*) is featured in *Berinus* and in *Mélusine*, removal of ears (Latin *vidua*) in the tradition represented by Brantôme, and the execution of one instead of several robbers (Latin *vidua*) in fables (Aesop, Marie de France, Ysopets), *fabliaux*, *Matheolus*, Vitry's *exempla*, etc.

Ultimately, the search for sources and analogues reveals less of the translator than may close scrutiny not of plot amplification but of the translator's work habits. For example:

> leva uns petiz pinniaus . . . qui vint a volenté. En ce que li borjois le vit, si en ot grant joie et fist querre de la meilleur terre qu'en poïst trover, et la fist metre au pié du pin. (*arbor*, 6^c)

> [a little pine tree rose up . . . which grew satisfactorily. When the burgher saw it, he was very happy about it and had the best available soil brought in and had it put at the foot of the pine tree.]

> vidit quandam pinellam pulchram crescere, vocavit ortulanum et ait: "Karissime, curam de ista pinella specialem habeas, *quia spero meliorem arborem habere quam ista est.*" (14, emphasis added)

> [he saw a beautiful little pine tree grow forth, called his

gardener and said: "Dearest friend, take special care of
this little pine tree *because I hope to have a better tree
than that one is.*"];

or

"Que a, fet il, ce grant pin qui est sechiez?"--"Sire, fet il,
ce fait l'ombre de vostre petit pinel."   (*arbor*, 7[a])

["What is the matter, he said, with the big pine tree
which is dried up?" "Sire, he said, the shadow of your
little pine tree is doing that."]

"Karissime, quomodo est hoc? Pinella ad libitum meum
non crescit." Qui ait: "Domine, mirum non est. *Altitudo
arboris pluviam et solem impedit*, per que duo pinella
crescere deberet."   (14, emphasis added)

["Dearest friend, how is this happening? The little pine
tree is not growing as I wish." He said: "Sire, that is not
surprising. *The height of the tree keeps away rain and
sunshine,* and the little pine tree needs both to grow."]

The translator has thought a good deal about these passages and
many others like them. The "special care" instruction not only
avoids an awkward repetition (in French the preceding sentence
reads: "Li preudons si fist querre des meilleurs terres qu'en poïst
trouver et metre au pié du pin" [6[b-c]]), but it is also given an
explanatory justification in the moral-pointing subordinate clause
(*ista* is the emperor, *melior arbor* his son). The old tree does not
simply overshadow its offshoot, observes the translator, it more
accurately deprives it of water and sunshine. Attention to details of
time and space fixes events and situations firmly on the story line:

Puis vint en haut aus fenestres et s'escria et dist . . .
          (*puteus*, 17[b])

[Then he went to the upstairs windows and shouted and
said . . .]

109

Hoc facto solarium domus ascendit et in quadam fenestra, *que ultra plateam communem erat, appodiavit, ut uxorem videret, quando ab amasio recederet. Post hoc erga tercium gallicantum venit mulier, et cum hostium firmiter clausum invenit, pulsabat.* Ait miles . . .

(21, emphasis added)

[After that he went up to the veranda of the house *and leaned against* a window *which gave on to the common square, in order to see his wife when she came back from her lover's. After that, around the third cock-crow, the wife came and finding the house firmly locked, knocked.* Her husband said. . . .]

Characters and relations between them are frequently described more fully and with more nuance:

Quant li amis a la dame avoit esté avec lui . . . (*avis*, 27[c])

[After the lady's friend had been with her . . .]

Civis vero quendam iuvenculam in uxorem habebat pulchram, sicut vos habetis, que non dilexit maritum suum, quia non poterat ei placere per omnia, eo quod potens non erat debitum carnale reddere, quociens volebat. Mulier ista quendam alium sub marito suo dilexit et omni tempore, quo maritus ad negociandum extra civitatem pergeret, tam cito pro amasio suo mittebat, ut secum omni nocte dormiret.

(28, emphasis added)

[*But the burgher had as his wife a beautiful young girl, as you do, who did not like her husband because he could not please her in all things, being in particular unable to do his carnal duty as often as she wanted. While married to her husband, the wife loved another man, and whenever her husband left the city on business, she quickly sent for her lover* to sleep with her all night.]

About the knight in *canis*, om. French A, the translator of Latin
Version H says:

> Miles iste miro modo hastiludia ac torneamenta dilexit. . . .
>
> (17)
>
> [The knight enjoyed jousting and tournaments ex-
> ceedingly . . .],

and about the thriftless sage in *gaza*, om. French A, he says:

> Torneamenta ac hastiludia sicut prius frequentabat . . .
> Miles iste miro modo torneamenta ac hastiludia dilexit.
>
> (23, 24-25)
>
> [He attended tournaments and jousts just as before. . . .
> The said knight enjoyed tournaments and jousts very
> much.]

The preceding examples from *canis* and *gaza* show that the translator is not beyond belaboring a point, often by uninspired repetition. Additional examples include:

> Le sarpent leva la teste et le mordi el col.   (*canis*, 8^d)
>
> [The serpent raised its head and bit it in the neck.]
>
> Dum vero sic pungnassent, serpens leporarium momor-
> dit, *quod sanguis ab eo exiit in magna copia, ita quod
> tota superficies terre in circuitu cunabuli plena sanguine
> erat leporarii.*   (17, emphasis added)
>
> [But while they were thus fighting, the serpent bit the
> greyhound *so that a great amount of blood streamed
> forth from it, so much that the entire surface of the
> ground around the cradle was full of the greyhound's
> blood.*];

or

. . . et eles respondirent que li levriers estoit enragiez, si avoit son enfant estranglié et mort.   (*canis*, 9[b-c])

[. . . and they replied that the greyhound was crazy and had strangled and killed her child.]

At ille: "O domina, heu nobis et vobis! Leporarius, quem tantum diligit dominus noster, filium vestrum occidit *et ibi iuxta murum satiatus de sanguine pueri iacet. Et tota superficies terre in circuitu cunabuli de sanguine pueri est plena.*"   (17, emphasis added)

[They said: "O mistress, woe on us and you! The greyhound our master loved so much has killed your son *and is lying there next to the wall all covered with the boy's blood. And the entire surface of the ground around the cradle is full of the boy's blood.*"]

At the same time, the translator of Latin Version H excels in enlivening his tales by transforming arid descriptive passages into spirited dialogues, or by creatively inserting additional dialogue:

Lors vint a sa pie si li dist: "Par mon chief, vous ne me mentiroiz ja mes."   (*avis*, 28[c])

[So he went to his magpie and said to it: "I swear, you will never lie to me again."]

Civis perrexit ad picam et ait ei: *"Nonne propriis manibus singulis diebus pascebam te? Et tu mendacia inter me et uxorem posuisti, in tantum quod per mendacia tua uxor mea per totam civitatem est diffamata." Ait pica: "Novit deus quod nescio mentiri; sed sicut audivi et vidi, sic tibi retuli!" At ille: "Mentiris! Nonne michi dixisti quod nocte ista fuissent grando, nix et pluvia, in tantum quod fere vitam tuam amisisti? Cum tamen a vicinis meis, qui te diligunt, veritatem quesivi et totum oppositum michi dixerunt; immo, quod plus est, per totum annum non erat nox tam*

112

amena sicut nocte ista. Ammodo talia mendacia nec discordiam inter me et uxorem non facies."

(30, emphasis added)

[The burgher went to his magpie and said to it: *"Did I not feed you with my own hands every single day? And you have put lies between me and my wife to such an extent that because of your lies my wife is defamed throughout the whole city."* The magpie said: *"God has learned that I do not know how to lie; but what I have heard and seen I report to you as is!"* He said: *"Liar! Did you not tell me that last night there was so much hail, snow, and rain that you almost lost your life? Yet when I asked the truth of my neighbors who like you, they told me the exact opposite: on the contrary, moreover, all year long there has not been such a nice night as was the last one.* From now on you shall no longer put such lies and discord between me and my wife."]

Finally, it cannot be overlooked that the translator works into his text, wherever he deems it appropriate, the common phrases of the day's ecclesiastico-didactic discourse:

"Dahaz ait, dame, qui en chaut."   (*puteus*, 17[b])

["Lady, cursed be he who cares about that."]

Ait miles: *"Recole quociens lectum meum violasti et adulterium commisisti! Melius est tibi hic pro peccatis tuis penam sustinere quam in purgatorio vel in inferno permanere."* Que ait: *"Domine, amore illius, qui pependit in cruce, miserere mei et permittas me intrare!"*

(21-22, emphasis added)

[The burgher said: *"Remember how often you have violated my bed and committed adultery! It is better for you to bear the punishment for your sins here than to stay forever in purgatory or in hell."* She said: *"Master,*

113

for the love of Him who hung on the cross, have mercy
on me and let me in!"];

or

"Ha, bele suer, pour Dieu merci, ja sonera cuevre feus, et
se je sui pris, je serai demain fustez."   (*puteus*, 17^d)

["Ha, beautiful sister, for the grace of God, the curfew
will soon be sounded and if I am taken, I shall be
punished tomorrow."]

"Si in pillorio crastina die positus ero, erit tibi et michi
opprobrium pro sempiterno. *Ideo dei amore permittas*
me intrare ut non confundar in eternum!" Que ait: "In
vanum loqueris! Melius est tibi hic penam sustinere
quam in purgatorio permanere. . . . Mendax es et tamen
dives; quid fuit necesse michi mendacium inponere?
Infatuatus es, quia florem iuventutis mee pro libitu tuo
habuisti et adhuc ad meretrices tuas perrexisti. Ideo
magna dei gracia est quod hic deus permittit te penam
sustinere, ut in eternum parcat, et ideo peccatis tuis
penam hic sustineas pacienter!" At ille: "O domina,
deus est misericors, et nichil a peccatore querit nisi
satisfaccionem. Permittas me intrare, et me volo
emendare, ex quo talia michi inponis." Que ait: "Quis
dyabolus te talem predicatorem constituit? Magna dei
misericordia est, ex quo permittit quod hic puniaris . . ."
                                        (23, emphasis added)

["If I am put on the pillory tomorrow, you and I will be
disgraced forever. *For the love of God let me in so that I*
may not be confounded for all eternity!" She said: "You
speak in vain! It is better for you to bear your
punishment here than to endure it in purgatory. . . . You
are a liar and yet wealthy; what made it necessary to
accuse me of lying? You are a fool because you had the
flower of my youth at your pleasure and still you went to
your prostitutes. Great is therefore God's mercy that he
lets you bear your punishment here in order to spare you

in eternity and therefore lets you bear the punishment for
your sins patiently here!" He said: "Dear wife, God is
merciful and all He asks of a sinner is amends. Let me
in, and I wish to make amends as to the things of which
you accuse me." She said: "Which devil has made you
into such a preacher? God's mercy is great, wherefore
he permits you to be punished here. . . ."]

The Latin translator may well have been a churchman. Ready-made liturgical and biblical expressions and phrases come naturally to him--"He who hung on the cross"; "confounded for all eternity"; "it is better to do penance here and now than to remain forever in purgatory or in hell"; "great is the Lord's mercy"; "for the love of God"; etc.--even though such a vocabulary is quite inappropriate in the context of his secular tales. (The translator of French Version H later supplements this technique by the standard medieval amplification of verbal matter through multiplication of synonyms.)

Remarkably, the Latin translator's interpolations do not permit any speculation as to which of some thirty extant manuscripts of French Version A, or which group of manuscripts, he may have used. He seems to have covered his tracks well, taking his additional material from anywhere but his immediate model. Speculation becomes quite irresistible, however, and possible, when one studies his omissions. There are naturally in each tale a good number of exclusions dictated by personal choice; the author is intelligent and skilled enough to be permitted such translatory license. But the instances of parallel omissions in the French and the Latin tales are too numerous to be entirely coincidental.

The evidence suggests that the translator worked with two strands of the French manuscript tradition. He consistently reproduced the greatest number of omissions from text 1, using text 2 in the significantly less numerous cases where he did not want to keep a lacuna. Text 2 has many fewer omissions in common with the Latin translation, and instances of filling blanks found in text 2 with material from text 1 are proportionately less frequent still. Finally, examples of Latin passages corresponding to lacunae in both text 1 and text 2 are virtually non-existent.

115

canis	om. in Latin text	not om. in Latin text
om. French text 1	52.6%	26.3%
om. French text 2	15.7%	21.0%
om. French texts 1 & 2	10.5%	5.2%

vidua	om. in Latin text	not om. in Latin text
om. French text 1	36.6%	23.3%
om. French text 2	33.3%	20.0%
om. French texts 1 & 2	6.6%	3.3%

In the manuscript tradition of French Version A, text 1 is represented by MSS. Paris, Bibl. Nat. f. fr. 20040 (thirteenth century); Paris, Arsenal 3516 (formerly B.L.F. 283) (thirteenth century); and Saint-Etienne, Bibl. mun. 109 (fifteenth century, incomplete). Text 2 can be found in MSS. Cambridge, Fitzwilliam Museum, McClean 179 (end of the thirteenth century); and Paris, Arsenal 3152 (formerly B.L.F. 246) (thirteenth century).[11] It could be argued that of the two pertinent manuscripts of text 1, the translator worked with Bibl. Nat. 20040, since Arsenal 3516 is an amalgam of French Versions A and L replacing *Roma* with *filia* and adding *noverca* after *vaticinium*; he may nevertheless have used the totally regular manuscripts of text 2 as a control while translating Arsenal 3516. Too little is known about Bibl. Nat. 20040 to turn speculation into assertion; yet Le Roux de Lincy[12] observed that this "text . . . has been copied from an older manuscript. *The tales* [are] *somewhat abridged*" (p. xxxi; my emphasis and translation), which corroborates the results of the preceding omission analysis.

In adding to and subtracting from his French model, the Latin translator has been guided by personal preference and material necessity. It must be noted, however, that his originality is not gratuitous, nor his compliance absolute. Rather, in reshaping *The Seven Sages of Rome* through translation, he seems to be following a definite overall plan according to which additions and omissions fall into a clear pattern: he amplifies the empress's tales less than he condenses them, and conversely he adds more to the sages' tales than he subtracts from them. The net result may well reflect his attempt at rebalancing the contestants' respective moral and didactic weight by reducing the aggressive and subversive empress and bolstering the ineffective old sages.

The characters' relative impact on the intended, now irre-trievable medieval reader or listener can of course be estimated by the usual stylistic analysis. In the case of *The Seven Sages of Rome*, it can also be measured quantitatively since the tales the debaters tell and the story in which they live exist only as long as, and in the way in which, the protagonists keep debating. Restricting the empress's narrating time limits her presence in the audience's mind more directly and more concretely than is the case in most texts. The sages derive prominence from being attributed the seven longest tales in the translation, including *vidua* and its elaborate and detailed account of the mutilation and hanging of the robber's body.

In the Latin translation, the empress's *aper* has been stripped of enough narrative elements to reduce the tale to the skeleton of its French model version (untranslated passages in italics, alternate Latin motifs in brackets):

> [En cest païs] ot jadis une forest *grant et merveilleuse et plenteïve de fruiz et de boschages.* Si i fu uns sengliers *norriz en repost, granz et parcreüz* [et orgueilleus], si que [nus n'osoit entrer en la forest cele part. En mi cele forest en une place avoit un alïer qui fu bien chargiez d'alies meures. Li sengliers s'en saouloit chascun jour une foiz. Un jour ot adiré] uns pastres [une soe beste, et s'en fu foïe en la forest. Li pastres] vint cele part *et vit l'alïer, si convoita moult des alies qui jurent a terre. Il s'abessa si en comença a cueillir tant qu'il en ot plain son giron. En tant conme il emploit l'autre giron,* es vous venir le sengler. *Quant li pastres le vit venir, si ot poour et il ot droit, si s'en vost foïr. Mes il vit le sengler si aprouchier de lui qu'il n'osa, si fu si esbahiz qu'il ne sot que fere. Lors regarda contremont l'alïer et* monta sus. *Li sengliers vint desouz l'alïer. Il se merveilla moult conme il n'avoit trouvé autant des alies conme il*

soloit, puis regarda contremont l'alïer si vit le pastour.
Lors *s'aïra, si conmença a maschier et a estreindre les
denz et ses deus piez a aguisier contre la terre, et* feri des
denz contre l'alïer *si que touz trambla.* Ce fu avis [a celui
qui desus estoit] qu'il deüst brisier par mi. . . .   (10^c-11^a)

[(In this country) there once was a *great and marvelous*
forest, *full of fruits and bushes.* In it there lived a *great
and powerful* (and fierce) boar *feeding there secretly,*
and (nobody dared enter the forest in these parts. In the
middle of this forest there was in a certain place a
service-tree heavy with ripe sorb-apples. The boar filled
itself with them once every day. One day) a shepherd
(had lost one of his animals which had fled into the
forest. The shepherd) came into the forest, *saw the
service-tree and coveted the sorb-apples lying on the
ground. He lowered himself and started to pick them up
until he had filled his apron. While he was filling
another apron,* all of a sudden the boar came. *When the
shepherd saw it coming, he was afraid, and rightly so,
and wanted to flee. But he saw the boar coming so close
that he did not dare and was so perplexed that he did not
know what to do. He looked at the service-tree and*
climbed up it. *The boar came under the service-tree. It
wondered why it had not found as many sorb-apples as it
usually did, then looked up into the service-tree and saw
the shepherd.* Whereupon *it became angry, started
moving and gnashing its teeth and sharpening its two
feet against the ground and* hit the service-tree with its
teeth *and made it shake from top to bottom.* (He who was
in the tree) thought it would break down the middle. . . .]

In *puteus*, the unfaithful wife, pretending to drown herself in a
well, has locked her worried husband out of the house. The second
sage continues in this manner (amplifications in italics, alternate
wordings in square brackets):

(Domina) *solarium ascendit et in fenestra se appodiavit.*
Interim miles *ultra fontem stetit et* flevit amare atque

dixit: "[Heu michi! iam uxore mea sum privatus].
*Pereat hora, in qua hostium contra eam clausi!" Domina
hoc audiens subrisit et ait:* "[O maledicte senex, cur ista
hora iam ibi stas?] Nonne corpus meum tibi sufficiebat?
*Cur ad meretrices tuas sic omni nocte vadis et lectum
meum dimittis?" Ille, cum audisset vocem uxoris sue in
fenestra superius, gavisus est valde et ait:* "Benedictus
deus quod salvata es! Sed bona domina, dimidium anime
mee, quare michi talia inponis? Ego volebam te
castigare et ideo hostium clausi. Sed quando sonitum
audivi,* credebam quod tu esses in fonte *et ideo ad fontem
currebam, ut te iuvarem." At illa: "Mentiris! Novit
deus quod nunquam talia commisi, que michi inponis!
Modo apparet quod dicitur in antiquo proverbio: 'Si
quis fedatus fuerit, vellet quod omnes fedati essent.' Iam
inponis michi crimen, quod tu ipse usitatus es. Amen
dico tibi, ibidem exspectabis, donec pulsetur campana et
tunc venient pervigiles et beneficium legis in te inple-
bunt." At ille: "Cur michi talia inponis? Senex sum
miles et in ista civitate per multos annos mansi;
nunquam de talibus scandelizatus fui.* Si in pillorio
crastina die positus ero, [erit tibi et michi opprobrium
pro sempiterno]. . . ." (22-23)

[(The lady) *went up to the veranda and leaned against
the window.* Meanwhile the burgher *was standing
beyond the well and* cried and said: "(Woe on me! I am
deprived of my wife.) *May the hour be undone at which
I shut the house on her!" The lady heard this, laughed,
and said:* "(Cursed old man, why are you standing there
at this hour?) Was my body not enough for you? *Why
do you go every night long to your prostitutes,
abandoning my bed?" When he heard his wife's voice at
the upper window he was very happy and said: "Praised
be the Lord, you are safe! But good wife, half of my
soul, why are you doing these things to me? I wanted to
punish you and therefore I locked the house. But when I
heard the noise I thought you had fallen into the well,
and therefore I ran to the well in order to help you."*

119

She said: "Liar! God knows that I never committed the things you allege! Now is clear what is said in the old proverb: 'He who is corrupt wants everybody else to be corrupt too.' You are accusing me of a crime you are yourself committing. Verily I tell you, you will wait there until the bell rings and then the watchmen will come and will give you the benefit of the law." He said: "Why do you do this to me? I am an old man and have lived in this city for many years; never have I been humiliated by such things. If I am put on the pillory tomorrow, (you and I will be disgraced forever). . . ."]

In the end, the Latin translator achieves thus a reasonable balance between the empress, whose tersenesss is amply compensated by the haranguing explications of her tales, and the sages who make up for their pitiful role in the frame story by tales well enough told to render their foregone conclusions acceptable and convincing.

The universal popularity of *The Seven Sages of Rome* is largely based on the translation known as Latin Version H, and while a text in the *lingua franca* of the age may have lent itself more readily to vernacular adaptations than an Old French model, those who could have known both versions--the French one was surely circulated widely enough--may well have deemed the recast Latin story more appropriate for their particular narrative and didactic purposes.

French literature itself provides a telling example of a possible preference of this kind. At the time of French Version H (first printed in 1492), there existed already in French the voluminous body of Versions K (rhymed), L, M, D, and A (plus six continuations), disseminated in at least forty manuscripts. To satisfy popular demand, any one of these texts, especially a manuscript or group of manuscripts of Version A, could have been copied or later printed with the greatest of ease. Instead, someone chose to translate Latin Version H.

The redactor of French Version H, Professor Gilleland suggests (p. 229), may have been a churchman: not only does he enjoy reproducing and expanding the lessons to be learned from the tales (especially *vaticinium-amici*), but he also revels in "sermonizing" (Gilleland, p. 231) after the moralizing (*canis*, *puteus*). On the whole, his translation "was done with great faithfulness" (Paris, p. xli), although Paris went too far by saying that it "can replace the original in comparing the texts" (p. xli; my translation). Professor Gilleland (p. 235) has demonstrated, for example, that tales 1 through 8 are closer to the Latin source than tales 9 through 15, and further analysis will show that the French translator's literalness by no means precludes individuality and originality. On the whole, however, his arsenal of translation techniques is much less impressive than the one used by the author of Latin Version H. The latter had transformed *The Seven Sages of Rome* into an explicitly didactic work by pointing the moral and suggesting the possibility of a political interpretation; the French translator fails to surpass this achievement by adding sermons to the moral. Where Latin Version H shows traces of ecclesiastical rhetoric, the French translation resorts to the tautological style of uninspired preaching. The art of dialogue and the attention to logical details of events, time, space, and characters in Latin Version H are unmatched in the French version, and the French translator is much less adept at manipulating the text through amplification, contraction, or omission, his Latin predecessor having perhaps beaten him to the goal of reinventing *The Seven Sages of Rome*.

Most of the omissions in French Version H are of little narrative consequence; they concern descriptive details (in italics below) which have been excised to make room for the translator's tautological mania:

> "Veritatem tibi dicam: *dum essem iuxta te in lecto*, venit quedam ancilla ex parte matris mee, *que michi nunciavit* ut eam sine ulteriori dilacione visitarem, *eo quod in extremis laborabat*." (*puteus*, 21)

> ["Let me tell you the truth: *while I was next to you in bed*, a maid servant came from my mother's, *who told me* to go to her without further delay *because she was close to death*."]

121

". . . sur mon ame je vous diray la verité: ceste nuyt quant vous fustes endormy j'ai esté demandée de la servante de ma mére pour aler a elle hactivement. . . ." (83)

[". . . upon my soul I will tell you the truth: last night when you were asleep I was asked by my mother's maid servant to go to her quickly. . . ."];

or

Statim testiculos eius abscidit; *hoc facto canibus ad commedendum proiecit.* . . . (*vidua*, 68)

[She cut off his testicles immediately; *after that she threw them to the dogs for food.* . . .]

Elle prist le cousteaul et les luy coupa. (154)

[She took the knife and cut them off.]

Rarely do important elements (in italics below) such as the husband's age in *puteus* get lost:

Dudum erat in quandam civitate quidam miles *senex* qui quandam iuvenculam . . . accepit. (21)

[Some time ago there was in a city a certain *old* burgher who married . . . a young girl.]

En une cité avoit ung chevalier qu'avoit espousé une jeune damoiselle. . . . (82)

[In a city there was a knight who had married a young lady. . . .]

Sometimes the translator pays more attention to the plot than to his source:

"Latro . . . *duos* dentes in superiori parte amisit. . . ."

Lapidem accepit et *eum in dentibus percussit, quousque omnes* dentes *superiores* amisit.

(vidua, 67, emphasis added)

["The thief lacked *two* upper teeth. . . ." She took a stone and *struck him in the teeth until* he had lost *all upper* teeth.]

"Le larron . . . avoit perdus *deux* de ses dents de la partie dessus. . . ." Et lors elle prist une pierre et luy fit tomber *deux* de ses dens. . . .   (153-54, emphasis added)

["The thief . . . had lost *two* of his upper teeth. . . . And so she took a stone and knocked out *two* of his teeth. . . .]

(French Version A reads: "si em brisa a son seigneur *les* denz en la gueule" [35ᵇ; "and broke her husband's teeth in his mouth"].)

While only close comparison can show the translator's good judgment, even a cursory reading of his text reveals one of his most obvious and least attractive characteristics: his inability, which may be a mark of his profession, to leave well enough alone, stylistically speaking. In *aper*, for instance, he renders "contristatus" as "triste *et mal content*," "occideret" as "occiroit *et deffaroit*," and "aprum scalpebat" as "se mist a gracter *et adoulcir* le porc." In *puteus* he translates "adulterium perpetrasti" as "tu as [commis] *pechié et* adultére," "Amen dico tibi" as "je te jure *et soie certaine*," "penam sustinere" as "soustenir reprouche *et effacer tes pechiez en cestuy monde*," "me ipsam submergere volo" as "je me veulx noyer *et me gecter en l'aigue du puis*," "lego omnibus sanctis animam meam" as "je donne *et remectz* a tous les saintz *de paradis* mon ame," "secundum disposicionem tuam" as "en vostre disposicion *et volenté*," "uxor mea est submersa" as "ma femme est noyée *et tombée*," "clausit" as "ferma *et serra la porte fort et seurement*," "benedictus deus" as "Dieu soit loué *et begnyt*," and "ut te iuvarem" as "pour toy aider *et saulver*." In *vidua*, "presencia sua carere non potuit" becomes "i[l] ne la pouvoit habandonner *ne laisser de veuhe*," "lex" becomes "coustume *et usance*," "auxilium" becomes "conseil *et reméde*," "socius meus" becomes "mon compagnyon *et*

123

bon amis," "in uxorem ducere" becomes "espouser [*et*] *prendre a femme*," "tu eum deturpasti" becomes "tu l'as defiguré *et si villeynement navré*," and so on.

Unattractive as this tendency may appear to the modern reader, it was accepted, even prescribed, practice in the Middle Ages. Medieval arts of preaching list this oratorical device under the rubric of amplification, as in the anonymous Dominican *Tractatulus solemnis de arte et vero modo predicandi* (*A Short Formal Treatise on the Art and True Method of Preaching*):

> the sermon is expanded through multiplication of synonyms, particularly when the matter in hand is reproving, laudatory, or exhortative. . . . Amplify by synonyms as follows: Man is filled with woes in that he is oppressed by cares, beset by worries, irritated by adversity, choked by perils, and the like. Expand in this way also in eulogy. . . . Likewise in exhorting to emulation of the examples of our ancestors. . . . This use is clear in the passage of the Psalms: 'O come, let us sing unto the Lord, let us make a joyful noise,' and so forth.[13]

The translator is more creatively inventive in adding nuancing touches (in italics below) to many a dry Latin passage:

> "Nolui te a sompno excitare et ideo satis occulte exivi, ac eam visitavi."   (*puteus*, 21)

> ["I did not want to rouse you from sleep and therefore I left quite secretly and went to her."]

> ". . . *quant je vous senty ainsy dulcement dormir*, je ne ousaye vous reveillier ne prendre congié de vous, *et ainsy je pris les clefz* et alay a ma mére, *laquelle est sy tresfort malade que je doubte que demain ne la faille oindre et donner ses sacrements*."   (83)

> [". . . *when I felt you sleeping so sweetly*, I did not dare

wake you nor ask your leave, *and so I took the keys* and
went to my mother *who is so very sick that I doubt she
won't receive tomorrow the last rites and sacraments.*"];

or

. . . illa sic inclusa recesserunt.   (*vidua*, 65)

[. . . after she had been thus settled in, they left her.]

. . . puis s'en alérent affin que *quant* elle se trouveroit
ainsy seule *elle fut contrainte de venir a la compagnye
des gens.*   (151)

[. . . then they left so that she, *when she* was thus alone,
would be obliged to seek the company of people.]

The freezing guard on night duty in *vidua* is well observed:

Dum vero ibidem esset, tantum geluerat, quod videbatur
militi spiritum emittere. . . .   (65)

[While he was there it was so cold that the knight's
breath could be seen. . . .]

Et estoit le temps qu'i faisoit grant froit; *luy aloit et
venoit pour se eschauffer.*   (151, emphasis added)

[And it was the time when it was very cold; *he walked
back and forth to keep warm.*]

Vidua also manages to let the hypersensitive husband die properly:

Famuli hoc videntes unus post alium ad ecclesiam
cucurrit pro sacerdote, ut secum corpus Christi portaret;
sed ecce tantum dolorem accepit, quod, antequam
sacerdos venit, emisit spiritum.   (64-65)

[Seeing this, the attendants ran one after the other to the

church to get the priest, that he might bring the body of
Christ; but he was in such great pain that he gave up his
spirit before the priest arrived.]

*Le chapellain vint hactivement, sy tost qu'i l'eut
administré*, il va morir. . . .　　　　　(151, emphasis added)

[*The chaplain came hastily, and as soon as he had
administered to him*, he died. . . .],

which proves that the translator is not above meddling with the Latin
facts to suit his thinking on death and the Church.

As Paris has pointed out (p. xlii), the translator seems to admit
in his preface that his knowledge of Latin is not perfect (Gilleland p.
229):

> j'ay entencion de translater au plus près de l'entende-
> ment de celluy qu'a le latin composé, en contemplant
> aucune foys par vraysemblable interpretation la chose
> facilement faite selon la signification du terme posé en
> latin, qui plus signifie d'une chose en françoys reduyte
> pour estre bien entendable.
>
> [I intend to translate as closely as possible to the under-
> standing of him who composed the Latin, by contem-
> plating every time by true interpretation the thing easily
> done according to the meaning of the term in Latin, which
> means more than a thing reduced in French to be well
> comprehensible."]　　　　　(Paris, p. 56; my translation)

While worse could be said of his prefatory French, the fact remains
that his "translation is good" (Gilleland, p. 229) and perfectly
readable. His linguistic doubts and approximations may be flaws for
some, elegant solutions for others (paulatim: bellement; private: tout
bellement; inconveniencia: fole parole; audacter: seurement; uno
ictu: trespuissamment; toto conanime: incontinant; dei amore: en
l'onnour de Dieu; etc.) He is an accomplished summarizer and
adaptor: (coram toto populo: devant mes amis; salvata es: tu n'ez

point morte; permittas me intrare: ouvre moy; hic: en cestuy monde; in platea: devant sa maison; mobilia et immobilia: biens; absit ut: a Dieu ne plaise que; tibi constat quod: vous sçavés que; etc.)

Most important, however, he is an intelligent reader. He has read and knows a given Latin tale before he begins translating it, for he sometimes assembles his story line from disparate pieces picked in total disregard for their place in the Latin text (the same occurs frequently in the Latin translation of French Version A). *Vidua* (Latin H, 65; French H, 151) offers a good example:

(1)	Domina vero, ultra quam credi potest, gemitus et suspiria emittebat nec consolari volebat.	(1)	La dame sus tous mena grant deul et tellement ploura
	*	(1a)	sus sa tombe†
	**	(2)	qu'i n'estoit personne qui l'en peut oster. Et quant on la reprenoit et qu'on luy disoit que c'estoit mal fait.
(6)	illa vero votum deo vovit quod nunquam de illo recederet.	(3)	elle respondoit qu'elle avoit voé a Dieu de non jamais s'en aler de celluy lieu.
(2)	sed cottidie clamabat: "Heu michi, heu! quid faciam ego? Ego sicut turtur de cetero ero!"	(4)	mais pour l'amour de son mary elle fairoit comme la torterelle en cas de viduité
(3)	Cum magna solempnitate eum sepelierunt.		[not translated]
(4)	Ipso sepulto domina super sepulcrum eius cecidit.		[not translated] ‡
(5)	Amici volebant eam ammovere.		[not translated]
(7)	sed propter amorem viri sui ibi spiritum emitteret.	(5)	et que la elle prendroit fin.
(8)	Dixeruntque amici. . . .	(6)	Ses amis luy dirent. . . .

---

* French A: sus la fosse
** Not in Latin, but see (5)

† See Latin (4)
‡ See (1a)

In this discussion of the translation of Latin Version H into French Version H, the mention of the source of Latin H, ever-present though side-lined French Version A, raises the tantalizing question of whether the French translator knew of, and indeed used, Version A occasionally. A respectable number of his additions (in italics below) seem to stem from that source:

Ille vero arborem ascendit. *(aper*, 19)

[He climbed up into the tree.]

Cestuy pastoriaul *de paour* incontinant monta sus ung arbre . . .   (H, 81)

[The shepherd *out of fear* quickly climbed up a tree . . .]

. . . li pastres . . . *ot poour.* . . . Lors regarda contremont l'alïer et monta sus.   (A, 10^d)

[. . . the shepherd . . . *was afraid.* . . . So he looked at the service-tree and climbed up it.];

or

"Illum de sepulcro extrahe et in loco latronis suspende!"
                                   (vidua, 67)

["Pull him out of the grave and hang him up in the place of the thief!"]

"Ostés le du sepulchre *et le portés au gibet,* et le mestés au lieu *de celluy qu'estoit pendu.*"   (H, 153)

["Take him out of the grave *and carry him to the gallows,* and put him in the place *of the one who had been hanged.*"]

"Desterrons le meintenant *et le portons aus fourches,* et soit penduz en leu *de celui qui a esté emblez.*"   (A, 34a)

["Let's unbury him now *and let's carry him* to *the gallows,* and let's hang him in the place *of the one who has been carried off.*"]

The French translator's rephrasings echo Version A just as frequently:

Pastor continue proiecit, ita quod aper est repletus et ad
terram iacuit.   (*aper*, 19)

[The shepherd continuously threw them down so that the boar was full and collapsed on the ground.]

. . . aprés qu'il eust assés mangié *se mist a dormir.*
                                    (H, 81, emphasis added)

[. . . after it had eaten enough *it began to sleep.*]

En ce que li senglers menjoit, *si s'endormi.*   (A, 11[a])

[While the boar was eating *it fell asleep.*]

Many of these atavisms may be purely coincidental, the effect of loose translation or of phrasal conventions governing the narration of certain contexts and therefore inconclusive as to a possible direct link between French Versions A and H. However, it must be noted that virtually all passages the author of French Version H left out of his translation of Latin Version H are also absent from French Version A, i.e., the translator seems to have disliked a great many of the additions meant to improve Latin H over French A. Unfortunately, whenever Latin H omits more than a few words of French A, French H follows the former rather than the latter.

Whether he worked with or (more likely) without an occasional glance at Version A, the French translator has left his mark on *The Seven Sages of Rome.* Paris has noted his typographical re-arrangement of the collection into books, chapters with rubrics, and an "epylogacion" (p. xlii). Professor Gilleland has shown how he has set slightly varying accents in some portions of the frame story and in some tales, and this present study shows the translator to be a competent if less innovative craftsman than was the Latin translator of French Version A. A more wide-ranging and complete test of his contribution to the *Seven Sages of Rome* tradition will some day be a comparison of his translation with that of his counterparts in Denmark, Holland, England, Germany, Hungary, Poland, Russia, Spain, Sweden, and elsewhere.

Because of the nature and purpose of the collection, *The Seven Sages of Rome* does not qualify as an example of the highest mode of medieval *translatio* in France, "allegorical or extended metaphorical discourse."[14] It does contain, especially in the transition from French Version A to Latin Version H, noteworthy instances of the second mode of *translatio*, adaptation, "revision . . . in the meaning of . . . [a] work . . . new arrangements and combinations" of source material, "adaptation of old material to new ideas and . . . ends" (Kelly, pp. 294, 297). For the most part, though, *The Seven Sages of Rome* offers ideal opportunities to observe the basic mode of "translation as such," a kind of *translatio* having "received relatively little study, in comparison to the two other modes, by . . . literary and textual scholars" (Kelly, p. 291). Perhaps the foregoing can be a small step toward redressing this imbalance.

NOTES

1. 'Killis Campbell, *The Seven Sages of Rome: Edited from the Manuscripts* (Boston: Ginn, 1907; rpt. Geneva: Slatkine, 1975).

2. Paragraph summarized from Hans R. Runte (with J. Keith Wikeley and Anthony J. Farrell), *The Seven Sages of Rome and the Book of Sindbad: An Analytical Bibliography*, Garland Reference Library of the Humanities, 387 (New York: Garland, 1984), pp. xi, xiii, xiv.

3. Franciscus Modius's *Ludus septem sapientum* (c. 1560), a Latin translation of German Version H, would seem to present a similar case (see ibid., p. 121).

4. The tales are traditionally referred to by Latin titles; they may be summarized as follows (in the order of French Version A):

Arbor (*The Tree*): In the shadow of one of its offshoots an old pine tree dries up and is cut down.

Canis (*The Dog*): A faithful greyhound, having saved an infant by killing a serpent, is falsely accused of having killed the child and is beheaded.

Aper (*The Boar*): A boar is lured into submission and killed.

Medicus (*The Physician*): Hippocrates, being surpassed in knowledge by his pupil, his nephew, kills him and later dies himself despite his great medical skills.

Gaza (*The Treasure*): A Roman sage is risking discovery while breaking into the imperial treasury and orders his son to decapitate him. The body is dragged through the streets, but the thief's family pretends not to recognize him.

Puteus (*The Well*): An unfaithful wife, having been shut out of the house by her husband, lures him into the market square by pretending to drown herself in the village well, then locks him out in turn and has him arrested for curfew violation.

Senescalcus (*The Seneschal*): Out of greed a seneschal offers his wife to the king and is expelled from the realm.

Tentamina (*The Trials*): Before seeking satisfaction elsewhere, a wife tests her husband's patience and affection three times, then is cured of her passion by a generous bloodletting.

Virgilius (*Virgil*): In order to warn Rome of approaching enemies, Virgil has erected a giant mirror which is destroyed in the course of a treasure hunt authorized by the greedy emperor. The defenseless city executes the emperor.

Avis (*The Bird*): A speaking magpie is deceived in order to protect her unfaithful mistress from its denunciations. The jealous husband kills the bird.

Sapientes (*The Sages*): Emperor Herod is cured of blindness by Merlin who rids Rome of seven corrupt sages and the curse they had put on the city.

Vidua (*The Widow, The Matron of Ephesus*): An easily consoled widow remarries quickly and against all earlier promises desecrates her husband's memory.

Roma (*Rome*): Rome under siege relies on one of the sages' histrionic powers to disperse, pursue, and kill the enemy.

Inclusa (*The Immured Lady*): An overprotective husband marries his disguised wife to her friend who has been seeing her by means of a secret

131

passageway.

Vaticinium (*The Prophecy*): A boy's prediction that one day his parents will be like servants to him, causes his father to abandon him. The boy grows up to become a king's trusted counselor and his son-in-law whom his visiting parents would be honored to serve.

5. Hans R. Runte, *Li Ystoire de la male marastre: Version M of the Roman des sept sages de Rome*, Beihefte zur Zeitschrift für romanische Philologie, 141 (Tübingen: Max Niemeyer, 1974).

6. French Version A (here fol. 19^d) is quoted throughout from MS. Paris, Bibl. Nat. f. fr. 2137. O. Derniame (with M. Henin and H. Nais), *Les Sept Sages de Rome: Roman en prose du XIIIe siècle d'après le manuscrit no. 2137 de la B.N.* (Nancy: Université de Nancy II, 1981) is a computer-generated transcription rather than an edition.

7. Latin Version H (here p. 51) is quoted throughout from Georg Buchner, *Die "Historia septem sapientum" nach der Innsbrucker Hand-schrift v. J. 1342*, Erlanger Beiträge zur englischen Philologie, 5 (Erlangen: A. Deichert, 1889; rpt. Amsterdam: Rodopi, 1970). The punctuation conforms to German usage; "u" has been replaced by "v" where appropriate.

8. French Version H (here p. 129) is quoted throughout from Gaston Paris, *Deux Rédactions du "Roman des sept sages de Rome,"* SATF (Paris: Firmin Didot, 1876).

9. Brady B. Gilleland, "The French and Latin Versions of *Historia septem sapientum*," *Classica et Mediaevalia* 33 (1981-81):229-37, quoting Campbell; see also Paris, ibid., p. xxxviii.

10. Catherine van Buuren, *The Buke of the Sevyne Sagis: A Middle Scots Version of "The Seven Sages of Rome,"* Germanic and Anglistic Studies of the University of Leiden, 20 (Leiden: Leiden Univ. Press, 1982).

11. For descriptions see the following:
20040: Antoine-Jean-Victor Le Roux de Lincy, *Roman des sept sages de Rome en prose* (Paris: Techener, 1838), pp. xxx-xxxi; Paris [n. 8 above], p. xvi; *Cat. gén. des mss fr.: Ancien St-Germain fr.* (Paris: Ernest Leroux,

1900), vol. 3, pp. 468-70.

3516: L.-J.-N. Monmerqué and F. Michel, *Lai d'Ignaurès* (Paris: Silvestre, 1832), pp. 35-41; F. Michel, *Lai d'Havelok le Danois* (Paris: Silvestre, 1833), p. 15; H. A. Keller, *Li Romans des sept sages* [Version K] (Tübingen: Fues, 1836), p. lxix; Le Roux [this note, above], pp. xxxix-xliii; Paris [n. 8 above], pp. xxi-xxiii; Henry Martin, *Cat. des mss de la Bibl. de l'Arsenal* (Paris: Plon, 1887), vol. 3, pp. 395, 402-05.

109: J.-B. Galley, *Cat. de la bibl. de la ville de St-Etienne* (St-Etienne: Urbain Balay, 1885), p. 209; *Cat. gén. des mss des bibl. publ. de France* (Paris: Plon, 1893), vol. 21, pp. 241, 266-67.

179: M. R. James, *A Descriptive Cat. of the McClean Coll. of Mss. in the Fitzwilliam Museum* (Cambridge: Cambridge Univ. Press, 1912), pp. 340-46.

3152: Le Roux [this note, above], p. xxxviii; Paris [n. 8 above], p. xx; Martin [this note, above], vol. 3, pp. 270-71, and vol. 7, pp. 284-85.

12.   Le Roux de Lincy [n. 11 above].

13.   Harry Caplan, *Of Eloquence* (Ithaca, NY: Cornell Univ. Press, 1970), p. 71.

14.   Douglas Kelly, "*Translatio Studii:* Translation, Adaptation, and Allegory in Medieval French Literature," *Philological Quarterly* 57 (1978):291.

THE *MIDDLE ENGLISH GLOSSED PROSE PSALTER* AND ITS FRENCH SOURCE

Raymond C. St-Jacques

Although men like Chaucer and Wyclif gave the English language new credence as a vehicle for artistic and scholarly thought during the fourteenth century, many still felt that the language as it stood was not yet ready to deal adequately with Scripture. As Geoffrey Shepherd writes: "The English language had slowly acquired cultural standing and was seeking to become coterminous with contemporary life. But its range was still limited."[1] In fact, when we look for translations into English of the complete Bible or even of one complete book of the Bible before Wyclif, we find little before the English Psalter now generally referred to as the *Middle English Glossed Prose Psalter*. This is not so of translations from Scripture into French, which are numerous during the thirteenth and fourteenth centuries. Not surprisingly, then, the pioneering translator of the *MEGPP* made extensive use of a French translation of the Latin glossed Psalter that he was rendering into English. Surprisingly, however, the resulting prose version of the Psalms was unusually successful in preserving the native rhythms and texture of the English language, and for this success the intermediate source was largely responsible.

A cautious attitude to things Scriptural and a lack of confidence in the English language were assuredly the causes for the small number of Biblical translations into Middle English before the great Wycliffite versions of the 1380s and 1390s. Apart from paraphrases of the Bible, such as the ME *Genesis and Exodus*, or works where possible translations of brief excerpts from the Vulgate are submerged beneath a great weight of apocryphal, legendary, liturgi-

135

cal, or catechetical materials (for example, the *Northern Homily Cycle* or the *Southern Temporale*), there were only seven translations of Scriptural books. The most important was the Psalter, with three distinct complete versions; the so-called *Surtees Psalter* (1250-1300), the translation and commentary made some time between 1337 and 1349 by Richard Rolle, and the *Middle English Glossed Prose Psalter* (1325-50). Also popular, judging from its seventeen surviving manuscripts, was the ME *Apocalypse and Commentary*, the earliest versions dating from 1340-70. Finally, there were four other major translations from the New Testament, only one of which pre-dates the work of the Wycliffites; the *Commentary on Matthew, Mark, and Luke* (1325-75), Clement of Llanthony's *Harmony of the Gospels* (1375-1400), the *Commentary on the Four Gospels* or *Glossed Gospels* (1375-1400), and the *Prose Versions of Epistles, Acts, and Matthew* (1380-1400). No ME translation of the complete Bible exists before the Wycliffite versions of the later fourteenth century.[2]

A strikingly different situation obtained in thirteenth- and fourteenth-century France. By the early twelfth century, several Old Testament books had been translated. A French text of the Gallican Psalter, which was to exert great influence on subsequent translations, existed before 1200. A superb translation of Kings, made some time in the second half of the twelfth century, was later included in the first complete French Bible. At least one of the many versions of the Apocalypse also dates from this period. The first extant major compilation, the Acre Bible, containing the Old Testament historical books and some sapiential books, was probably made for St. Louis during his mid thirteenth-century stay in the Holy Land. Another similar work was prepared in Flanders c. 1275. The first French translation of the complete Bible, the *Bible du treizième siècle*, appeared no later than 1280. By 1297, Guyart des Moulins had produced his *Bible historiale*, a translation of Comestor's *Historia Scolastica* and the relevant portions of the Old Testament, together with a Gospel Harmony and Acts; Guyart's work was to be completed, possibly as early as 1312, by the addition from the *Bible du treizième siècle* of those books that he had not translated. Before 1355, Jean de Sy had begun his translation of the Bible, only to leave it unfinished at Jeremiah 18, and shortly after the middle of the fourteenth century, a Bible in the Anglo-Norman dialect began circulating.[3]

That at least some fourteenth-century Englishmen were aware of the wealth and variety of translations of Scripture into French is abundantly clear from a survey of extant fourteenth-century manuscripts of such works in English libraries. Berger and Robson (see n. 3) list copies of four different Bibles: four manuscripts of the *Bible du treizième siècle*, two of which are in an English hand (there exist also three manuscripts of the Gospels from this Bible, one of which is in an English hand); ten manuscripts of the *Bible historiale*, including one in an English hand (a second manuscript in an English hand exists in the Bibliothèque nationale); and one manuscript each of the Anglo-Norman Bible and the incomplete revision by Raoul de Presles of the *Bible du treizième siècle*. In addition there are twelve extant manuscripts of various French Psalters, including two written in whole or in part in an English hand, and six French translations of the Apocalypse, one of which is in an English hand (two other such manuscripts in English hands are now in the Bibliothèque nationale and in the Bibliothèque de l'Arsenal). This large number of French manuscripts corroborates the view based on bequests in fourteenth-century wills that before 1400 "French books [of piety] were still commoner than English ones."[4] Also, among religious scholars, whether they were monks, friars, or secular clergy, one finds many who, like Peter of Langtoft, Nicholas Bozon, Robert Mannyng, Nicholas Trivet, John of Canterbury, or Dan Michael of Northgate, either wrote in Anglo-Norman or translated French works into English.[5] It was inevitable, then, that a translator of Scripture from Latin to English would eventually make use of a French version of his text if he had one at hand. His own linguistic proclivity and the experience of other scholars would support this approach. As Paues writes:

> It would in fact be no great matter of surprise to learn that the English translator found it an easier and more congenial task to turn a familiar French text of the psalms into English than the more difficult Latin psalter.[6]

This is clearly the route chosen by the English translator of the *MEGPP*, with remarkable results.

Four manuscripts of this Psalter exist, each with a Latin and Middle English text. While the Latin presents essentially a Gallican text, about one third of the verses contain short glosses, generally signalled by an abbreviated form of *id est* after the lemma, or by the underlining of the gloss, or most frequently by both. The accompanying ME does away with the lemma and the signals to the glosses, silently incorporating the glosses into the position occupied originally by the lemma.[7] In 1902, a fifteenth-century copy of a lost earlier French translation of the glossed Latin came to light. Since this text treated lemma and glosses exactly as did the ME translation, scholarly opinion came to favor the lost French as one of the principal sources of the ME.[8]

The most striking feature of the *MEGPP* (GP) at a first reading is the modernity of its English. This is due in large part to its independence from the Latin (L), insofar as word-order is concerned. The French translation (F), which treats L in exactly the same way, is obviously the source of this independence. While L tends to favor what has become the normal word order in English statement clauses, with subject-verb in initial position (for convenience referred to here as "type 1" clauses), even using this order for interrogative clauses on occasion, it almost as frequently employs constructions where elements other than subject-verb are positioned initially or where subject-verb are inverted ("type 2" clauses). An analysis of the 116 main and subordinate clauses contained in the opening verses of the first fifty Psalms in L reveals that 63 are of type 1, while 53 are of type 2, a rough 55 / 45 division that generally holds true for the entire Psalter. F and GP, however, almost always prefer type 1 statements, employing type 2 generally only for questions. Of the 116 clauses described above, for example, they retain 59 of L's type 1 clauses and transform 43 of L's type 2 clauses, 3 of which are interrogative, into type 1 clauses. In only 7 cases out of 116 do F and GP disagree, one siding with L against the other, with F most often favoring type 1 where GP follows L's type 2 construction. In the complete Psalter, approximately 90% of type 2 statement clauses in L are made over into type 1 by GP and F.

Clearly, then, GP sides with F in its word-order preferences with respect to major clausal elements.

This appears all the more striking when GP is compared to other translations of the Psalter that favor L, such as Rolle's (R) or the earlier Wycliffite (eW) version.[9] Psalm 20.1 provides a good example of the results of these transformations, the 2 / 2 construction of L becoming 1 / 1 in F and GP but remaining unchanged in R and eW:

> L. Domine in virtute tua letabitur rex; et super salutare tuum exultabit vehementer.

> F. Sire, le roy esjouyra en ta vertu et gravement esjouyra en ta sainctete.

> GP. Lord, þe kyng shal gladen in þy vertu, and he shal greteleche ioyen vp þyn helpe.

> R. Lord in thi vertu the kynge sall ioy; and on thi hele he sall glad gretly.

> eW. Lord, in thi vertue shal the king gladen; and vpon thin helthe ȝuere ful out ioȝen hugely.

The later Wycliffite version (lW) also favors type 1 constructions and is, therefore, at least in word-order, much closer to GP and F than to R and eW: "Lord, the kyng schal be glad in thi vertu; and he schal ful out haue ioye greetli on thin helthe." The word-order of GP and of lW contributes largely to the modernity of their English, although it must be remembered that GP is earlier by as much as half a century.

The manner in which F and GP handle a large number of nouns in the vocative case represents another interesting departure from L. Where L places a vocative at the beginning of a clause, F and GP follow suit, as in 4.3, 8.1, 8.9, etc.; however, where L's vocative appears elsewhere in a clause or at the end of a clause, F and GP, like lW, frequently replace it at the beginning, generally introducing it by the interjection "Ha" (P writes "A"; T frequently omits "Ha" or often prefers "O"), as for example in 44.8:

L.   Sedes tua deus in seculum seculi;

F.   Ha Dieu, ton sieige est ou siecle du siecle;

GP.   Ha God, þy sege is in þe worlde of worldes.

This practice can be seen in 55.12, 64.1, 64.6, etc.; in 108.25 ("Ha, Sire" / "Ha Lord"); in 58.1 ("Ha mon Dieu" / "Ha my God"); in 75.6 ("Ha tu Dieu de Jacob" / "Ha þou God of Jakob"); in 65.1 ("Ha toute terre" / "Ha alle þe londe"); in 112.1 ("Ha vous enfans" / "Ha ȝe childer"), etc. R and eW, on the contrary, almost always follow L, although on occasion--in 112.1 for example--disregards L's order and places the vocative at the beginning ("Laudate pueri dominum" / "Barnys louys oure lord").

Less obvious but nevertheless exhibiting further independence from L and closer ties between F and GP is their handling of the adverbs "autem," "vero," and "verumptamen." These words occur fifty-one times in the first one hundred Psalms, with L giving them either the initial or second position in their clause, for example in 21.3 and 38.8: "Tu autem in sancto habitas, laus israel" / "Verumptamen vniuersa vanitas." F and GP, translating "adecertes" (more rarely, "vraiement") and "for-soþe," agree with L twenty-two times. However, in another fourteen cases, F and GP use the initial position where L uses the second; in five cases they choose the second position while L prefers the first; and in three cases--39.9 and 23, 81.7--they prefer a position after the verb to L's choice: "aures autem perfecisti michi" / "tu feiz adecertes a moy entendement," "þou madest for-soþe vnderstondyng to me"; "Ego autem mendicus sum et pauper" / "Je suis adecertes mandiant et pouvre," "Ich am for-sorþe beggand and pouer"; "Vos autem sicut homines moriemini": "Vous mourrez adecertes comme hommes," "ȝe shul dye for-soþe as men." Finally, in the fifty-one occurrences of these adverbs, F and GP disagree only seven times as to positioning: each agrees with L three times against the other, while all three disagree once. The situation differs considerably with the three other translations considered so far. When he translates "sothly," R follows L's order; frequently, however, he uses "bot" at the beginning of the clause, independently of L's order. "But" and less frequently "forsothe" are used by lW always in initial position; eW almost always uses "forsothe" and follows L's order scrupulously.

Interesting as well, although falling into no distinct patterns such as those described above, are the many verses where GP chooses F's ordering of elements over L's. Space permits the presentation of only two examples, but others equally varied and original can be found in almost every Psalm. The full effect of the F / GP renderings is better felt if other translations of L are examined first. Psalm 64.6 provides the first example:

L.   Exaudi nos deus salutaris noster: spes omnium finium terre et in mari longe.

R.   Here vs god oure hele; hope of all the endes of erth and in the see fere.

eW.   Ful out here vs, God, oure helthe ȝiuere; hope of alle the coostis of erthe, and in the se afer.

lW.   God, oure heelthe, here thou vs; thou art hope of alle coostis of erthe, and in the see afer.

With the exception of the words "Ful out" and "ȝiuere" both R and eW show great fidelity to L, even in word order; lW prefers to reposition the vocative to the beginning and to add "thou art" to the second clause. The versions of F and GP are remarkably close to this later and more modern form:

F.   Ha Dieu, nostre sainctete, oyes; tu nous es espoir de toutes les contrees de la terre, et loing en la mer.

GP.   Ha God, our helþe, here us; þou art hope of alle þe cuntres of þerþe and fer in þe see.

141

Like IW, both have replaced the vocative at the beginning and added "tu es"; but both also have placed the adverb "longe" before "in mari," contrary to all other versions. It should be noted that GP does not follow F exactly, however, leaving the direct object "nos" after its verb "exaudi," whereas F seems to have moved it to the next clause, inserting it between "tu" and "es" without any authority from L. The second example is taken from Psalm 86.7; again, L and other translations are given first:

L. Sicut letancium omnium: habitacio est in te.

R. Als of all Joyand: wonnyng is in the.

eW. As of alle gladende; dwelling is in thee.

IW. As the dwellyng of alle that ben glad; is in thee.

Of the three translations, only IW attempts to put words into a more usual order for an English reader. Here again the "modern" flavor of F and GP is apparent:

F. Habitacion, Dieu, est en toy ainsi que de tous esjoissans.

GP. Wonynge, Lord ys in þe as of alle gladeand.

GP has followed F's order faithfully; it even inserts a reference to God on the authority not of L but of F, although it uses "Lord" (generally reserved for F's "Sire") for "Dieu." Also worth noting is the opening verse of the same Psalm, where GP follows F in reversing the order of the two clauses of the verse while the other translations remain faithful to L.

If GP is heavily indebted to F in matters of clausal word-order and positioning of vocatives and certain adverbs, it does not blindly follow F in all matters related to word-order. It does not, for instance, accept the typically French placing of a pronominal direct object between verb and subject, but prefers the English manner, as in 4.1:

F.   Quant je appellay le Seigneur de ma droiture, il me ouy, tu,
        Sires, me eslargis en tribulacion.

GP.   As ich cleped, God of my ryȝt herd me; þou, Lord, forbare me
        in my tribulacioun.

Interestingly in this case GP also correctly makes "deus iusticie
mee" subject of "exaudiuit" rather than object of "inuocarem" as
does F: "Cum inuocarem exaudiuit me deus iusticie mee: in tribu-
lacione dilatasti michi." R here, although it normally follows L
closely, places the pronominal object before the verb in the first
clause, but after the verb in the second: "When .i. incald me herd god
of my rightwisnes; in tribulacioun thou made brad til me." Both eW
and lW follow the more traditional English practice exhibited by GP.

A second category of borrowings from F consists of terms used
idiosyncratically by F or based on traditional French practice, which
GP takes over literally into English although they do not conform to
common English forms or usage. The most evident because of its
frequency is the phrase "our(e) Lord," a literal translation of F's
"Nostre Seigneur," for all cases of "dominus," except for the
vocative, whether or not "noster" accompanies it in L. Unless L also
has "dominus noster," R translates "Lord" alone, without even the
article "the" used by eW and lW in such cases. Closely linked to
this practice is GP's generally consistent imitation of F's "Ha Sire"
or "Ha Dieu" for the vocatives "domine" or "deus" (GP "Ha Lord"
and "Ha God" and even "Ha Sir" at 12.1). Needless to say, such
forms are not found in the other translations discussed so far.

Similar treatment is afforded to "ecce," "quid," and "numquid"
by F and GP. R, eW, and lW all have "lo" for "ecce." According to
the *MED*, eW's "lo" is the ME form of the OE interjection "la" (the
illustrative quotation is eW's Jer. 13.7). A second term for "ecce,"
the homograph "lo," a shortened form of the imperative "loken"
(v.2, 4c) is recorded as early as c. 1200 for "ecce." The metrical
Surtees Psalter (SP),[10] follows this tradition, favoring "loke" but
occasionally (50.7 and 8, etc.) employing "lo." F's "voy," a
currently acceptable French translation together with "voi cy,"
occurs as "vez," "vez ci," etc., for example, in three MSS. of the

"Psautier lorrain."[11]   Although this was not a common English
rendering, GP regularly prefers translating F's "voy" literally as "se"
("lo" in 7.15 only). The *MED* ("sen" 8b) cites the *Midlands Prose
Psalter*, that is GP, as the first recorded user of "se" for "ecce" but
does not point out its French source. The handling of "quid" by GP
is also at variance with that of all the other English Psalters
considered here. Where they uniformly write "what," GP writes
"what þyng(e)," paralleling F's "quelle chose." The same is true of
the negative interrogative particle "numquid," which appears as
"wher" in SP and as "whether" in R, eW, and lW. The "Psautier
lorrain" and the Oxford[12] and Cambridge[13] Psalters simply use an
interrogative clause, although Oxford and Cambridge occasionally
begin the clause with "dum." However, F always employs either
"savoir" or "asavoir" at the beginning of L's clauses containing
"numquid." GP imitates F exactly through the English form "þyng
to witen" ("ys to witen" once at 29.12). As with "ecce" and "quid,"
GP prefers to follow F's practice, although it does not correspond to
a standard English form.

Finally, the word "super" deserves special attention. "Upon"
(with its variants "vp" and "vpe") or "on" is generally used, but
alternatives appear in certain contexts. For example, "over" (SP,
eW, lW) or "abouen" (R) translate this preposition in 96.10 "nimis
exaltatus es super omnes deos," or again in 94.3 "et rex manus super
omnes deos" (SP and eW "over"; R "abouen"; lW, "aboue" and
"ouere"). In 83.10 "Quoniam melior est dies una in atriis tuis *.i.
gaudijs* super milia *gaudia pravorum*," SP and eW write "over," R
uses "abouen," and lW prefers to leave it out: "For whi o dai in thin
hallis is bettere; than a thousynde." Similarly in 8.6 "constituisti
eum super opera manuum tuarum," SP and eW employ "over," with
R and lW preferring "aboue." However, F uses "sur" for every
instance of "super," as does the "Psautier lorrain," in the tradition of
the Oxford and Cambridge Psalters. The A text of GP is faithful to
F in its use of "vp" exclusively; T and P also write "vp" for "super"
in the preceding examples but occasionally replace A's "vp" with
"aboue" as in 8.2 "super celos," agreeing with R and lW (SP "upe,"
eW "ouer"). Although all other ME translators select prepositions
more idiomatic than "upon" for "super" in certain phrases, GP

follows the practice of F, its model in so many other ways. A thorough study of GP's use of French loan-words, a third important form of influence, can be found in Reuter (see n. 8), which must, however, be used with caution when attempting to determine the relationship between F and GP. Reuter lists some 652 French words in GP. Of these he sets aside 343 as being in such wide circulation by the mid-fourteenth century that they can tell us little about GP's sources. On the authority of the *OED* he divides the remaining 309 into words that are rarely recorded in ME before their appearance in GP, those that GP employs in a new way, and those whose first recorded appearance is in GP. However, 123, more than a third of the words in all three groups, are so similar in form in Latin, French, and English, that one can not determine whether they were borrowed from F or from L, with F possibly providing only some reinforcement and support. These include words such as "asper" (90.3: L "asper," F "aspre"), "corupcioun" (15.10: F "corruptio," F "courrupcion"); "distribucioun" (77.60: L "distributionis," F "distribucion"), etc. Another 87 do not appear in F at all, although in fact they are borrowed from French. They include "aliened" (57.3: L "alienare," but F "esloignez"), "chalangeours" (71.4: L "calumniator," but F "contredisans"), "environ" (87.17: L "circumdare," but F "compasser"), etc. Reuter's argument that they may well have been contained in the version of F used by GP is not to be discounted, but it certainly offers no firm proof of an F-GP link. Finally, 99 are found in F and GP, but translating a Latin term formally very different. "Gorge" (13.5: L "guttur," F "gorge"), "remembraunt" (102.18: L "memores," F "remembranz"), "reproce" (30.14: L "opprobrium," F "reprouche"), etc. are examples of these. Since GP and F could not in all probability happen by chance upon these same words in their respective versions of precisely the same psalm verses, these last 99 provide much more solid evidence of F's influence on GP than do Reuter's categories and should be culled from each of his divisions by anyone wishing to study more closely GP's borrowings from F.

Reuter's study, focusing as it does on French loan-words, can also mislead the reader into believing that, to the detriment of its English elements, GP makes use of many more French words than it actually does. If we set aside the strong French influence on word order or on the handling of certain recurring expressions or forms discussed above, we find a basically conservative text, which makes judicious use of French loan-words here and there but remains faithful to native vocabulary to much the same extent as does R or eW. Psalm 58, 1-10, provides a good illustration of this:

Eripe me de inimicis meis deus meus: et ab insurgentibus in me libera me.

Ha my God, defende me fram myn enemis, and deliuere me from þe ariseand oӡains me.

Eripe me de operantibus iniquitatem et de viris sanguinum *.i. pollutis mortalibus peccatis* salva me.

Defende me fram wirchaund wickednes, and saue me fram men defouled wiþ dedelich sinnes.

Quia ecce ceperunt animam meam; irruerunt in *.i. contra* me fortes.

Se, for hij token my soule; þe stronge fel oӡains me.

Neque iniquitas mea neque peccatum meum domine; sine iniquitate cucurri et direxi *hoc verbum.*

Ne my wickednes, Lord, ne my sinne; ich ran wiþ -outen wickednes, and dresced þis worde.

Exurge in occursum meum, et vide: et tu domine deus virtutum deus israel.

Aryse, Lord, in myn oӡain-erning, and se; and þou, Lord, art God of uertuӡ, God of Israel.

Intende ad visitandas *animas* omnes gentes; non miseriaris omnibus qui operantur iniquitatem.

ȝif entent to uisiten al folkes; ne haue þou nouȝt mercy on alle þat wirchen wickednes.

Conuertentur ad vesperam et famem pacientur ut canes: et circuibunt ciuitatem.

Hii shul ben turned at euen, and shul suffren hunger as hundes; and hij shul cumpassen þe cite.

Ecce locuntur in ore suo et gladius *.i. asperitas verborum* in labijs eorum, quoniam *dicent*, Quis audivit.

Se, hij shul speken in her mouþe, and sharpnes of wordes his in her lippes; and hij shul saien, Who herd it?

Et tu domine deridebis eos: ad nichilum deduces omnes gentes.

And þou, Lord, shalt scornen hem, and þou shalt bringe to nouȝt alle folkes.

Fortitudinem meam ad te custodiam, quia deus susceptor meus es: deus meus misericordia eius preueniet me.

Y shal kepe to þe myn strenþes, for God is my taker, my God; his mercy shal come tofore me.

Here GP follows F only in the use of "defende" to render "eripe" (R "out tac me," eW "tac me out"). The choice of "shul cumpassen" for "circuibunt," although sanctioned by F elsewhere (17.5, for example), seems a personal one since F prefers "environneront," as does eW ("enuyroune"). For the rest, GP employs the same native words that R and eW do ("wickednes," "hundes," "mouþe," "lippes," "scornen," etc.); if the occasional French loan-words occur ("deliuere," "uertuʒ," "uisiten," "cite," etc.), they are words well established in the language by this time and are used either by R or eW or both in their renderings of the same verse.

The use of "cumpassen" in 58.7 does illustrate an interesting aspect of the indebtedness of GP's vocabulary to F, however: the use of English and French synonyms or synonymous expressions to translate L in different places. In 17.5, 21.11, or 114.3, for example, where F has "compasser" for "circumdare," GP selects "ʒede aboute" but employs some form of "cumpassen" in 31.9, 39.16, 87.18, and 90.5, where F does the same; however, in 29.14, 31.13, 47.11, and 54.10, where F uses a form of "environner," GP continues to employ "cumpassen." Similarly, GP has "alas, alas" (F "helas, helas") for "euge, euge" in 34.24, but in 34.28 and 69.4 the translator chooses the native "sorrow, sorrow," probably imitating F's "douleur, douleur," but with an English equivalent. Pairs such as "bed-couche" (4.5, 35.4 / 6.6, 62.7), "dite-songe" (39.4 / 65.1 and 3), "gorge-þrote" (13.5 / 5.11), "malice-wickednes" (49.20, 51.1 / 35.4, 106.33) abound, with GP at times imitating F's translation and at other times providing an English synonym where F continues to use the same French word that GP had borrowed elsewhere to translate the identical Latin. In borrowing from F, then, the English translator seems to have been at pains to select judiciously as a help in rendering difficult terms and as a means of increasing the number and variety of his word choices.

One final group of similarities between F and GP, which constitutes perhaps the best proof of F's influence because such similarities cannot simply be attributed to coincidence, is made up of F's omissions from or additions to L and those of F's erroneous or inaccurate translations that GP has taken over apparently on F's sole authority. Again only a few examples must suffice. Omissions and additions in F with GP in agreement range from one to several words; in all cases the text of L accompanying GP either contains the word or words omitted by F and GP or does not contain the word or words they add. In 107.2, for example, L's opening short clause is omitted:

Exurge gloria mea, exurge psalterium et cythara:
exurgam diluculo.

Levez psalterion et harpe; je leveray au matin.

Aryse sautrie and harpe, and y shal arysen in þe
morwenyng.

In 4.7 and 9.35 "domine deus" appears as "Sire" / "Lord" only,
whereas the full translation appears elsewhere when L uses the same
expression. If GP on F's authority seems freely to omit other words
such as "semper" in 15.8, it seems on the same authority freely to
add words, such as "Lord" (F "Sire") in 4.1 and 35.11, for instance.
Both F and GP repeat their translation of "vocem dederunt" in 76.16
without L's sanction and for no apparent reason:

Multitudo sonitus aquarum *.i. gencium* vocem
dederunt nubes *.i. obscurati in lege.*

La grandeur des sons des gens donnerent a toy
voix, les obscureiz en ta loy te donnerent voix.

þe gretness of þe soune of men ȝaf voice to þe,
and þe derked in by lawe ȝaf voice to þe.

In 76.7 they add "mon esperit" / "my gost":

Numquid in eternum projiciet deus: aut non
apponet vt complacicior sit adhuc.

Savoir se Dieu deboutera mon esperit pardur-
ablement, ou qu'il ne mecte point qu'il soit
encores plus plaisant?

þynge to witen, ȝif God shal put owai my gost
wiþ-outen ende, oþer he ne sett nouȝt þat he ȝit be
more pleisant?

Though this addition clarifies the sense of the verse, R, eW, and lW are quite willing to allow L to stand without such clarification.

More telling are F's errors or inaccuracies picked up by GP. On occasion F seems to have misconstrued a grammatical construction in L and produced a very different text, which GP has copied. In 26.1, for example, the interrogative clause "quem timebo" is made into a subordinate clause modifying "dominus," the subject of the previous clause:

> Dominus illuminatio mea: et salus mea, quem timebo? Nostre Seigneur, lequel je doubte, est ma lumiere et mon salut.
>
> Our Lord, which ich shal douten, is my liȝtyng and my helpe.

Less serious is the confusion of "domine" and "deus," with "Dieu" / "God" used for "dominus" in 77.25 and "Nostre Seigneur" / "our Lord" or "Sire" / "Lord" used for "deus" / "deo" in 11.1 and 146.7. The rather simple-minded confusion between first and third person possessive adjectives and pronouns is frequent in F but rare in GP; noteworthy, however, is the erroneous "ses" for "meas" in 15.2, corrected to "my" in A but left as "his" in P.

Finally, GP occasionally accepts a rendering by F that does not, in fact, give quite the correct sense of L and that can not easily be excused by F's avoidance of a too great literalism. In 15.4, for example, "conuenticula eorum de sanguinibus" becomes in F "les convenans de leurs pechez" and in GP "her wicked felawe-shippes of synȝes." The "super peccatorum" of 108.5 appears in F as "sur le mauvais" and in GP as "vp þe wicked," and GP's "synners" in 1.7 follows F's "pecheurs" for L's "impiorum." For the term "fines," often in the expression "fines terre," which other translators have as "endes" (R) or "coostis" (eW, lW), GP prefers "cuntres" in 64.6, 66.6, 94.4, etc., accepting F's "contrees."

F is undoubtedly the source of these and many other inaccuracies and similar departures from L, as well as of certain infelicitious or unidiomatic translations such as those of "super" discussed above. However, these are far outweighed by F's positive influence on GP's prose style, a style that has led the scholar who first brought GP's French source to light to describe GP as "in every way a readable production" (Paues [n. 6], p. lx). It well deserves the praise of another of its devoted students, who commenting on the "modern impression" it gives because of its French borrowings writes: "Indeed, it is no mean product, and its sentences often strike one as idiomatic and beautiful" (Reuter [n. 8], p. 11). In the balance, then, the influence of a French text that took an approach to its Latin source more liberal than literal has enabled the English translator to produce a remarkable prose translation.

NOTES

1. Geoffrey Shepherd, "English Versions of the Scriptures before Wyclif," in G. W. H. Lampe, ed., *The West from the Fathers to the Reformation*, vol. 2 of *The Cambridge History of the Bible* (Cambridge: Cambridge Univ. Press, 1969), p. 387. There were, of course, other factors that mitigated against the use of English for biblical translation. Papal or conciliar pronouncements against the biblical translations of specific sects such as the Albigensians (Lampe, pp. 391-92, 432, 441, 473) seem to have been interpreted much more narrowly by English than by French church officials. Wyclif points out this difference in attitude in his *De Officio Pastorali* (c. 1378): "Also þe worþy reume of fraunse, not-wiþ-stondinge alle lettingis, haþ translatid þe bible & þe gospels wiþ oþere trewe sentensis of doctours out of lateyn in-to freynsch, why shulden not engliȝsche men do so? as lordis of englond han þe bible in freynsch, so it were not aȝenus resoun þat þey hadden þe same sentense in engliȝsch" (F. D. Matthew, ed., *The English Works of Wyclif Hitherto Unprinted*, rev. ed., Early English Text Society, o.s. 74 [London: Kegan Paul, Trench, Trubner, 1902], p. 429). This cautious official attitude to translation continued into the fifteenth century, with Archbishop Arundel prohibiting, in 1407, anyone "on his own authority" from translating "any text of Holy Scripture into English or any other language" (Lampe, p. 393) and "prohibiting, in 1408, the reading of English Bibles without *episcopal licence*" (Margaret Deanesly, "Vernacular Books in England in the Fourteenth and Fifteenth Centuries," *Modern Language Review* 15 [1920]:350-58, esp. p. 354).

151

2.   This information is derived from Laurence Muir, "Translations and Paraphrases of the Bible, and Commentaries," in *A Manual of the Writings in Middle English 1050-1500*, vol. 2, ed. J. Burke Severs (Hamden, CT: The Connecticut Academy of Arts and Sciences, 1970), pp. 381-409, 534-52.   Muir also lists a number of partial translations of the Psalter, either late fourteenth- or fifteenth-century, and some few fifteenth-century translations, but these do not significantly alter the picture I have presented.

3.   The best survey of French prose translations of the entire Bible or parts of it remains Samuel Berger, *La Bible française au moyen âge* (1884; rpt. Geneva: Slatkine Reprints, 1967).   This should be corrected and supplemented by C. A. Robson, "Vernacular Scriptures in France," in Lampe [n. 1 above], which adds 10 manuscripts to the 190 described by Berger and provides additional information on the Acre Bible, the Flanders compilation, and the *Bible du treizième siècle*.   Also extremely useful is Guy De Poerck and Rika Van Deyck, "La Bible et l'activité traductrice dans les pays romans avant 1300," in *La littérature didactique, allégorique et satirique*, ed. Jurgen Beyer, vol. 6, pt. 1 of *Grundriss der Romanischen Literaturen des Mittelalters* (Heidelberg: Carl Winter Universitatsverlag, 1968), pp. 21-48.   Part 2 of this same work, ed. Jurgen Beyer and Franz Koppe (1970), pp. 54-69, lists manuscripts and provides bibliographical information on editions and critical studies in the field.   For Guyart des Moulins see Raymond St-Jacques, "French Translations of the Bible in the Fourteenth and Fifteenth Centuries: Guyart des Moulins and his Contemporaries," *University of Ottawa Quarterly* 55 (1985):75-86.

4.   See Deanesly [n. 1 above], p. 351.

5.   The earlier view that French was used practically everywhere in England and was even in the ascendant in the fourteenth century has been convincingly refuted by numerous scholars.   See, for example, the excellent discussion in Albert C. Baugh and Thomas Cable, *A History of the English Language*, 3rd ed. (Englewood Cliffs. NJ: Prentice-Hall, 1978), pp. 134-50; the text is unchanged from Baugh's original statement in the first edition of 1957.   For an extremely useful review of the evidence on the question and a reinterpretation of the texts on which earlier views were based, see Rolf Berndt, "The Period of the Final Decline of French in Medieval England (Fourteenth and Fifteenth Centuries)," *Zeitschrift für Anglistik und Amerikanistik* 20 (1972):341-69, who admits almost grudgingly that

"French was still known to and used by a certain number of English monks and nuns of different Orders throughout the fourteenth century, and to a much more limited extent even later than that" (p. 365). However, the impressive number of French works circulating in English translations or adaptations indicates clearly a good knowledge of French by at least a fair proportion of the well-educated, lay and religious alike.

6. A. C. Paues, *A Fourteenth-Century English Biblical Version* (Cambridge: Cambridge Univ. Press, 1902), p. lx.

7. Karl Bulbring has edited the Middle English from BL MS. Additional 17376 (hereafter A) and printed significant variants from Trinity College Dublin MS. 69 (hereafter T); see Karl Bulbring, ed., *The Earliest Complete English Prose Psalter*, Early English Text Society, o.s. 97 (London: Kegan Paul, Trench, Trubner, 1891). In his introduction (pp. vii-ix) he summarizes the evidence against the earlier attribution of the Psalter to William of Shoreham, whose poems also appear in A. The glossed Latin verses from A with variants from T have been edited by Freeman Burket Anderson, "The Latin and Middle English Glosses in the Psalter of MS. Additional 17376," Ph.D. diss., Stanford University, 1952. For Magdalene College, Cambridge Pepys MS. 2498 (hereafter P), and Princeton University Scheide MS. 143 (hereafter S), which remain unpublished, see n. 8 below. Sarah Dodson, "The Glosses in *The Earliest Complete Prose Psalter*," *University of Texas Studies in English* 12 (1932):5-26, provides a general discussion of the nature and value of the glosses. Further bibliography can be found in Muir [n. 2 above], 537-38.

8. See Paues [n. 6 above], pp. lvi-lx, and Ole Reuter, "A Study of the French Words in the *Earliest Complete English Prose Psalter*," Societas scientiarum Fennica, *Commentationes humanarum litteraturum* 9, no. 4 (1938):1-60. The French MS., B.N. fr. 6260, is described in Berger [n. 3 above], pp. 350-51; it is, of course, a late copy of the French translation to which the English translator had access, and when we speak of F's influence on GP, we are referring to the influence of F's ancestor and not to that of the extant F. At present, Robert Black and I are preparing an edition of the ME text from P with significant variants from S, together with the glossed Latin verses from P and the French text from B.N. MS. fr. 6260. By printing the texts on facing pages, Middle English on the left, Latin and French on the right, we hope to enable the reader to follow the process of translation from Latin to French to Middle English.

9. Quotations from Rolle are taken from H. R. Bramley, ed., *The Psalter or Psalms of David and Certain Canticles With a Translation and Exposition in English by Richard Rolle of Hampole* (Oxford: Clarendon Press, 1884). Rolle himself admits, "In the translacioun .i. folow the lettere als mykyll as .i. may" (p. 4). Quotations from the early and later Wycliffite versions are taken from Josiah Forshall and Sir Frederic Madden, eds., *The Holy Bible, Containing the Old and New Testaments, with the Apocryphal Books, in the Earliest English Versions Made from the Latin Vulgate by John Wycliffe and His Followers*, 4 vols. (Oxford: Oxford Univ. Press, 1850). Although many of the conclusions reached in that edition have since been challenged, it seems reasonable to accept the existence of at least one early version completed by about 1384 and of a thorough revision by 1390 or a year or two later. Quotations from *MEGPP* (GP) are taken from A as printed in Bulbring [n. 7 above]; readings from T, always identified as such, are taken from Bulbring's collation in the same edition; readings from P, always identified, are taken from the MS., as are those from S (with regularized capitals, i / j, u / v, and punctuation). For convenience I quote unglossed L verses from Bramley and glossed verses from Anderson [n. 7 above]; verse numbers used correspond to those in Bulbring, which are generally faithful to the traditional medieval verse divisions, but the numbering of Forshall and Madden corresponds to that of the modern text of the Vulgate.

10. J. Stevenson, *Anglo-Saxon and Early English Psalter*, 2 vols., Surtees Society, 16 and 19 (London: J. B. Nichols and Son, 1843, 1847).

11. François Bonnardot, *Le Psautier de Metz* (Paris: F. Vieweg, 1884).

12. Francisque Michel, ed., *Libri Psalmorum versio antique gallica, e cod. ms in Bibli. Bodleiana asservato, una cum versione metrica aliisque monum. pervetustis, nunc primum descripsit et edidit.* (Oconii: e typographeo academico, 1860).

13. Francisque Michel, ed., *Le livre des Psaumes ancienne traduction française, publiée d'après les manuscrits de Cambridge et de Paris* Collection des Documents inédits sur l'histoire de la France (Paris: Imprimerie nationale, 1876).

THE OLD ENGLISH *PHOENIX*

Brian A. Shaw

When, in 1072, Bishop Leofric gave Exeter Cathedral a "large book in English about various topics," he could hardly have foreseen its significance, for this book, even though it is now damaged, remains one of the most important and enjoyable works of Old English poetry to be preserved. The volume contains perhaps as many problems for modern scholars as it does solutions. While no one questions that *The Exeter Book* of today is the original gift, the history of how that volume came into being, its organizing principles (if any), and the date of composition for the various poems in the miscellany remain obscure. It is usually thought that the scribe who made the actual presentation copy was working from an already compiled anthology, but beyond this little can be said with any confidence. The book contains poems "signed" by Cynewulf with his name worked into them in runic letters, and the case has sometimes been made that *The Phoenix* is an unsigned work by this author, or at least has been influenced by the Cynewulfian school. Conservative scholarship, however, presently regards only poems actually signed by the runic alphabet inclusions as genuine.

The codex is defective, but in all probability it began with the trilogy of poems about Christ. More might be missing than just the beginning of the first poem about Christ, but if this is not the case, then the first few poems in *The Exeter Book* all deal with religious topics; the poems about Christ are followed by two poems about the hermit saint, Guthlac, two poems dealing with the children in the fiery furnace, and then *The Phoenix*. None of the poems in the volume has a title (this being a modern editorial convention), but the separation between poems and the sections within each poem (if long enough to merit such division) is unambiguous because large

155

capitals, sometimes more than one line high, are used to denote the break between poems or the division of the poem into sections. Moreover, smaller capitals are often used for all or part of the rest of a line with a large initial capital, and the ends of poems in the manuscript are frequently signalled by a blank line and, in some cases, by punctuation and / or ampersand marks. Even though, perhaps owing to space limitations, the use of signalling devices between poems decreases later in the codex, *The Phoenix* occurs near the beginning of the manuscript, and there can be no doubt that the poem is intentionally divided into eight manuscript divisions.

The manuscript appears to be the work of a single scribe and shows a consistent attempt to regularize the language. It is far less clear whether the scribe who copied the single extant manuscript of *The Exeter Book* as now preserved regularized the texts himself or whether he was merely making a copy of a manuscript in which the changes had already been made. It is thus impossible to know whether the poems as initially recorded were characterized by internal divisions. Given the fact that the poems are from different dates, it would appear unlikely that the divisions recorded in the manuscript are necessarily those of the original poets, although any conjectures based on the manuscript divisions must, of necessity, remain highly speculative.

Many of the works in the *Exeter Book* are translations, yet the poets never overtly announce this fact, and much of the early Old English criticism dealt with tracing the various sources used by the poets. Among others, biblical, antiphonal, and hagiographic sources can be found for much of the poetry of *The Exeter Book*, but the term "translation" is quite misleading when one deals with Old English poetry. Poets usually paraphrased more than translated, as we currently understand the word. The opening verse of *The Phoenix* might suggest that the poet is admitting to a source, for the narrative begins "Hæbbe ic gefrugnen" [I have heard tell; line 1.1].[1] But such formulaic openings occur elsewhere in Old English and do not, I think, consciously call attention to a source but rather serve to evoke a heroic sense, for this opening, or at least a variant of it, occurs often enough to suggest that it is more the sort of rhetorical flourish associated with epic poetry than a statement of fact. The

Phoenix-poet is not looking to a source; he is letting his reader (or listener) know that the material will be heroic, that the actions of the bird, as emblematic of Christ's deeds and of the Christian soul, are of a certain importance.

The Phoenix falls into two basic portions: first, a description of the bird, its habitat, and its actions; second, an application of this information to various aspects of the Christian's life. There is no discernible change in diction or syntax between the two; these two halves deal simply with the phoenix as a bird and then with the phoenix as symbol. The second half of the poem functions as a sort of exegesis or explanation of the first half of the work. For the first part of the poem there is a source, the "Carmen de ave phoenice" of Lactantius. The poem by Lactantius--and it is unclear whether he wrote it before or after his conversion to Christianity--deals only with the bird and makes no interpretation of it in Christian terms. The Old English poet's "translation" of Lactantius is obviously close enough that there can be no doubt that he used it as the source, but the Old English version tends to elaborate and repeat ideas so that the 170 lines of Latin become the first 380 lines of the 677-line Old English poem. Yet the Old English version does not include about one-third of the material contained in Lactantius; missing are such things as the references to the classical gods and goddesses that Lactantius had included as part of what he must have considered proper poetic style, even if he had already converted by the time he composed the "Carmen."

The treatment of the first line of the "Carmen" may serve to illustrate the general expansion of the Latin. Lactantius is terse and merely gives the fact: "Est locus in primo felix oriente remotus."[2] The *Phoenix*-poet expands this to six lines:

> Hæbbe ic gefrugnen   þætte is feor heonan
> eastdælum on   æþelast londa,
> firum gefræge.   Nis se foldan sceat
> ofer middangeard   mongum gefere
> folcagendra,   ac he afyrred is
> þurh meotudes meaht   manfremmendum.

[I have heard tell that far hence in the east-regions is the
noblest of lands, renowned among men. That portion of
land is not open to many rulers of people over middle-
earth, but it is removed by God's might from those who
perpetrate evil.]   (lines 1-6)

In part, readers of Old English expect this sort of prolixity, the
variation and repetition that would appear to be an integral part of
Anglo-Saxon aesthetics. In addition, the poet is preparing for the
interpretation of the poem that will follow. The fame of the land and
the exclusion of evil-doers from it will be necessary comments for
the allegorical significance of the phoenix story. Even if the poet
were not preparing for an interpretation of the Latin work, the style
of *The Phoenix* is characteristic of Old English poetry, circuitous
and yet progressive as detail and nuance are constantly piled up in a
way that would be totally alien to Lactantius, a classically trained
teacher of rhetoric in the latter stages of the Roman empire.

The second half (lines 381-677) of *The Phoenix* is an interpretation of the material translated from Lactantius. For this portion
of the poem, the question of a source becomes more vexed. Long
before the Old English poet allegorized the phoenix story at length,
church fathers had seen the potential for reading the legend as
illustrating various doctrinal truths: a unique bird that returns to life
after its death and is thus eternal could hardly fail to strike any
Christian reader as significant. As far as can be determined,
however, there is no sustained allegorical treatment of the phoenix
myth, although a substantial number of references to the tale can be
found throughout patristic literature. It may be that early Christian
thinkers were too occupied with harmonizing the Old and New
Testaments to attempt a comprehensive explanation of classical
stories, or it may be that earlier Christians still felt sufficiently
threatened by pagan religion and ideas not to venture into this area.
The most elaborated treatment of the phoenix story occurs in the
Hexameron of Ambrose, and it is almost certain that the Old English
poet had access to this document, or at least knowledge of it. There
are enough similarities of thought to allow a reader to conclude that
the *Phoenix*-poet was familiar with Ambrose, yet there are no

similarities in style between the two, a fact which is not unexpected given the characteristics of Old English verse. Nor are the correspondences exact. While it is impossible to do more than conjecture about such matters, it would appear that the poet was almost certainly familiar with Ambrose, but it is unlikely that he had the document before him as he composed.[3]

At first glance, the poem might seem to contradict this assertion, for in the explanation of the significance of the phoenix, the poet claims: "Is þon gelicast, þæs þe us leorneras / wordum secgað , ond writu cyþað" [it is most like that which learned men say to us with words, and in writing make known; lines 424-25]. Rather than acknowledging that the material is translation from a source, the poet is, I think, acknowledging the general observations about the meaning of the phoenix that he could have found in a number of patristic sources and, most significantly, in Ambrose. Old English poets are reluctant to trust what we would consider originality: even *Beowulf*, hardly likely to be literally true, is presented as part of a historical framework, even if modern readers have not discovered anything closer than analogues. Again, a reader must, I think, accept such claims of the existence of "sources" as rhetorical rather than factual. *Guthlac B* and *Juliana*, poems standing close to *The Phoenix* in *The Exeter Book*, make the same type of reference to authority without specifying a precise source; such is the convention in which the *Phoenix*-poet is writing.

If, as I believe, the poet has taken up a general interpretation of the significance of the phoenix without merely producing a translation of some identifiable source, then the relation between that portion of the poem dealing with the bird and that concerned with interpreting its existence must be crucial to our understanding of what the poet was doing when he translated Lactantius. In other words, looking at the relation between the two halves may very well illuminate the process of "translation" as the poet conceived of his art. He has taken a source and rephrased and edited it into the vernacular, but with an eye to creating a first half that will bear the burden of the second. He must have had more liberty in the second portion, the response to the first, because the second half of the poem is not as reliant on already existing material. He has, in a sense, used the framework provided by Lactantius as the foundation upon which can be constructed the ultimate meaning of the phoenix, not totally out of his imagination but rather out of the general allegorical treatment of the story available from Ambrose or other brief references to the phoenix that occur elsewhere. Whatever the poet's accomplishment, it is not a simple compilation of Lactantius and Ambrose; it is the accomplishment of a sensitive poet aware of the total structure he creates, but not by a simple "cut-and-paste" method.

Looking at the large ornamental capitals in the manuscript, we see that the poem is divided into eight obvious sections (lines 1-84; 85-181; 182-264; 265-349; 350-423; 424-517; 518-58; 589-677). The existing manuscript divisions give a pleasing symmetry to the poem. Of the manuscript divisions, the shortest (seventy lines) and the longest (ninety-six lines) are close enough in length to look roughly equivalent on the manuscript page. The average section length is eighty-four lines so that no section deviates from the norm by more than fourteen lines, a difference that would not immediately strike a reader used to the convention of lineation used in *The Exeter Book*.[4]

The thematic division of the poem, however, does not correspond quite so neatly to the manuscript divisions as one could wish. For example, in the fourth manuscript division, we are told that the phoenix "gewiteð wongas secan, / his ealdne eard" [departs to seek the fields, his old dwelling; lines 320-21]. In the beginning of the fifth manuscript division, the phoenix is safely home: "eft geneosað / fægre foldan" [again visits the beautiful land; line 351]. There is a curious sense of telescoped action here, for the adoring humanity that watches the phoenix and the other birds that accompany it for part of the journey are strangely dropped from the poem's focus, while a new division of the manuscript merely to state that the phoenix has arrived seems out of proportion and lacking in continuity, even if the poet later returns to the idea in the exegetical section of the work. Similarly, at the end of the second manuscript division, the author notes the glory of the eternal tree linked to the phoenix and then, at the beginning of the third manuscript division, tells of the phoenix and its nest building. These ideas seem so

160

closely linked that it is difficult to justify the embellishment necessary for a complete new division.

The final three manuscript divisions, in contrast, seem to make perfect sense, as they reflect major transitions in thought. The sixth manuscript division begins the exegesis of the phoenix story with a simile: "Is þon gelicast" [that is most like; line 424], a rhetorical device that is not generally characteristic of much Old English poetry (there is, however, another instance of a simile at line 302 of *The Phoenix*). The penultimate manuscript division again makes sense, since it reveals the culmination of the judgment motif in the separation of the good from the bad. Finally, the last manuscript division shows Christ in glory surrounded, as had been the phoenix, with those who wish to make the journey. A separate division here seems warranted because it reiterates and interprets the meaning of the earlier portion of the story where the phoenix must abandon the followers, who now appear, in their typological fulfillment, as the rightful inhabitants of the New Jerusalem.

If we look at the content rather than just the manuscript divisions, it is obvious that the thematic break between the phoenix as bird and as symbol occurs in the fifth division of the manuscript, yet this particular manuscript division is the least thematically cogent in the whole poem. It begins with the phoenix's return home and continues with the strange detail (found in other versions of the story) of the ambiguity of the bird's gender, while noting that God is responsible for the power of this remarkable bird. Then, slightly less than half way through the section--at line 381--the tone shifts and the bird is likened to the ideal Christian who stands in opposition to Adam and Eve, whose sin caused their expulsion from Eden. Unlike the phoenix, which can return to its literal home, Adam and Eve's descendants must await the coming of Christ before the doors to the new paradise will be opened. It would thus appear that line 381 is the pivotal one in the theme and bridges the two halves of the poem, the rough translation of the work by Lactantius and the exegesis proper, which begins at line 424 (clearly intended to herald a shift in focus, since it begins with one of the poem's capital letters).

Each of the final three manuscript divisions breaks down into three basic lines of thought each, while the third has a meditation at the end. While the manuscript divisions do not fall quite so neatly into place in the first half of the poem, I hope to demonstrate that there are, in fact, three major thematic sections in the first part (up to the transitional pivot). In fact, two of these three thematic divisions that I should like to hypothesize do begin with the capitals that mark the other manuscript divisions. Furthermore, I hope to demonstrate that each of these thematic sections contains three principal threads of thought and that the third likewise contains a meditation. In other words, I should like to "schematize" the poem as follows: A (lines 1-84); B (lines 85-215); C (lines 216-380); transition (lines 381-423); D (lines 424-517); E (lines 518-88); and F (lines 589-677): sections A, B, D, and E each contain three principal ideas, while C and F each contain three ideas and a meditation added to the end of each.

Once this convenient scheme has been drawn, it seems to me obvious that the poet has constructed a work that is chiastic in form--a shape that is most appealing for a poem dealing symbolically with the resurrection and its consequences--for part A corresponds with part F, part B with part E, and part C with part D. Finally, I should like to suggest that each section of three main ideas deals with the material in the same order in its corresponding section; that is, section A has three principal themes which are handled in the same sequence in the corresponding section, F. The poet could not make the individual divisions into chiastic structures to mirror the larger shape of the poem because the meditations must come at the end of the two basic halves; hence a chiastic structure is not possible on this level. In other words, I would contend that there are six major divisions (five of which are marked by manuscript capitals), each developing ideas in the same basic progression as its corresponding division. Furthermore, there are two minor portions, a meditation and transition between the two halves of the poem and a separate meditation to complete the "translation" and explanation of the significance of the "Carmen." The six major and two minor divisions have been presented in a chart (see Appendix).

In the remainder of this essay, I should like to outline the main patterns of images, verbal repetitions, and themes that link the corresponding sections of the poem.

The first section of Part A (lines 1-27) deals with the habitation of the phoenix in a description which sets it within the tradition of images connected with the Edenic paradise, "eastdælum on æþelast londa" [in the eastern regions in the best of lands; line 2]. Parallel to this setting of part A is section F, which functions to establish the idea of the heavenly kingdom, the fulfillment in eternity of the temporal. The rejoicing of the souls serves to complement the beauty of the first paradise which, although a typical *hortus conclusus*, seems to have no other inhabitants than the phoenix. There is, however, one puzzling reference to mankind: Ðær bi∂ oft open eadgum togeanes / onhliden hleoþra wyn, heofonrices duru" [there is often open for the blessed, clear the joy of harmony, the door of heaven; lines 11-12]. In spite of the possibility of the joy manifest to the blessed, there is a sense that this earthly realm is just a "duru" and that only on the other side is true bliss to be found, and it is in the first part (lines 589-610) of section F that the poem celebrates the eternal realization of the type that the garden of the phoenix had celebrated in the corresponding section of part A:

> þær gæsta gedryht
> hælend herga∂   ond heofoncyninges
> meahte mærsia∂,   singa∂ metude lof.

> [there the band of spirits praise God and celebrate the
> power of the heavenly king, proclaim in song their love
> to the Lord.]   (lines 615-17)

The author of *The Phoenix*, not content to rely solely on these general similarities between the two sections, has specific echoes which more fully interweave the broader ideas of the two passages. The first and most important of these to be developed (lines 1-27) is the exclusion of evil from the abode of the phoenix: "ac he afyrred is / þurh meotudes meaht manfremmendum" [but he is removed from evil-doers by the might of the Lord; lines 5-6]. This idea helps to prepare for the theological interpretation of the poem, the movement from innocence, to the fall, to subsequent regeneration. Thus the notion that such a land is denied to those who have accomplished evil is echoed and amplified in the corresponding passage where not only is this land closed to the evil ones but also their evil itself has been overcome as they are granted the final peace of the blessed souls; those who could not join the phoenix in the beginning of the poem are now granted an eternal home where evil no longer exists:

>   þær him yfle ne mæg
> fah feond gemah   facne sceþþan,
> ac þær lifgað a   leohte werede,
> swa se fugel fenix

> [there in evil the hostile malicious foe may not harm them by guile, but there they ever live, surrounded by light, just as the bird, the phoenix.]   (lines 594-97)

The uniqueness of the phoenix, as seen in the initial portion of part A, has been replaced by a different sort of uniqueness. No longer does the poem celebrate the androgynous phoenix alone, but rather all the blessed souls, perhaps now also purified of such mundane concerns as sexual identity, who have demonstrated their uniqueness in their faith to Christ. In fact, the chosen, prefigured in the birds of part A who were unlike the phoenix in its ability to return home, now are likened to a flock of birds all participating in the uniqueness of the Christ / phoenix image, for they are all unified by salvation. Also, neither the home of the phoenix nor the New Jerusalem is going to be granted to all. Parallel to the assertion that it is not "mongum gefere / folcagendra" [accessible to many men; lines 4-5] is the description of the heaven which is inhabited by "gæstas gecorene" [chosen spirits; line 593] and which shines only for "soðfæstum sawlum" [truthfast souls; line 589].

The second, though less concrete, link between the first parts of sections A and F, is a tonal similarity. Part A, describing the earthly paradise of the phoenix, notes that it is "feor heonan" [far hence; line 1], while there is a world of hail and downpours, of heat and winter "her mid us" [here among us; line 23]. This same feeling of wistful longing is present in the description of heaven in part F where it is moderated by the notion that the separation is not absolute: rather it is simply temporal. There is an increased use of images of light and bliss in part F because joy is distanced from man on earth only in his separation from the blessed of the celestial realm, for which he now has reason to hope: "ac hy in wlite wuniað " [but they will dwell in splendor; line 609]. The tone thus moves from acute longing in part A, with the phoenix as symbol, to joyful expectation in part F, through the mediation of Christ. The poetic vision has enlarged from earth-bound and unattainable to eternal and accessible bliss.

After the poet has successfully evoked the garden-home of the phoenix, the ideas of the ephemeral are emphasized; the spot, while it is the greatest that can exist on earth, must eventually pass away. Thus the next thematic note of part A (lines 28-49) serves to deflate some of the magnificence of the garden. The transient, as the prophets have foretold, will be replaced by the final order, the heavenly kingdom which will be the permanent form of the garden. The celebration of this unending realm serves as the organizing principle of the middle portions of part A (lines 28-49) and part F (lines 611-31).

The second section of part A begins with an appeal to authority, for the prophets ("witgan" line 30) have proclaimed that the land of the phoenix is higher, by the measure of twelve cubits, than any of the hills among men. Even though the number twelve is the one used by Lactantius ("per bis sex ulnas imminet ille locus; line 8), the poet of *The Phoenix* has given it a definite Christian connotation by mentioning the prophets (who proclaim in the wisdom of their writing), a detail absent from Lactantius. The "gæsta gedryht" [the band of souls; line 615] of part F, who sing (or perhaps proclaim) the love of the Lord, may very well refer to the twelve disciples, the obvious typological fulfillment of the prophets earlier mentioned as the recorders of the significance of the life of the phoenix. The prophets of part A are able to foresee heaven, even if it is the unique abode of the phoenix; in the corresponding section of part F there is the praise for that heaven, now established and opened by the ministry of Christ as proclaimed by the disciples to all (as the prophets of part A had made known the wonders of the phoenix); in the exegetical portion, the inaccessible home of the phoenix is now made accessible to those who follow Christ.

One further important detail is the term employed in part A ("sigewong" [plain of victory; line 33]), for it hints at the victory on the cross, an idea strengthened by the use of the word "beamas" [trees; line 35], for we are told that they stand at God's behest. Surely the close proximity of these two words should remind any reader of Old English of the similar nexus of images to be found in *The Dream of the Rood*.

The victory of Christ leads the poet again to stress the temporal nature of this garden in part A and its counterpart, eternal heaven, in part F. The author recalls the flood, partly because its inability to destroy the home of the phoenix is remarkable (yet another instance of the providential order that pairs the type and the reality) and partly because the flood will be realized in the apocalypse where the shadows of the temporal world will be replaced by the actual:

> Swa iu wætres þrym
> ealne middangeard   mereflod þeahte,
> eorþan ymbhwyrft,   þa se æþela wong . . .
> gehealden stod.

[as long ago the rush of water, the seaflood engulfed all
the world, the region of the earth, while the noble field
. . . stood protected.]   (lines 41-45)

Thus, while the phoenix's home was able to resist the flood through God's grace, when the second destruction comes, the result will be different, for even this earthly paradise will not stand unscathed:

> bideð swa geblowen   oð bæles cyme,
> þryhtnes domes,   þonne deaðræced,
> hæleþ a heolstorcofan,   onhliden weorþað.

[it will thus wait, blooming, until the coming of fire, the
judgment of the Lord, when death-chambers, the graves
of men, will become open.]   (lines 47-49)

The home of the phoenix as a type of Eden serving to link Eden with paradise is blessed but doomed, replaceable only by the eternal where "ne biঠ him on þam wicum wiht to sorge" [there will be for them in those abodes nothing to their sorrow; line 611].

The third and final section of part A (lines 50-84) and the third portion of F (lines 632-54) serve mainly to amplify the ideas that precede and to introduce an important new way of thinking about the transition from the temporal to the eternal and its importance for mankind.

It was seen that, in the earlier two sections of A and F, the earthly home of the phoenix is destined to perish at the time of the final judgment to be replaced by the everlasting. This concept is clearly stated and repeated in both the final section of part A and the corresponding section of part F. In section A, the poet reiterates the transience of the phoenix's home, even though it is destined to stand for all of finite time; he also stresses that, by the end of time, even the type of the New Jerusalem will have become no longer valid:

> þæt onwended ne biঠ
> æfre to ealdre,   ærþon endige
> frod fyrngeweorc   se hit on frymþe gescop.

> [that will never be changed, ever in eternity, until He end the old ancient work that which He in the beginning created.]   (lines 82-84)

What must be evident is the double emphasis on the term "old" with its implication that the old law will end and be replaced. Thus the passage can be seen as a reference both to the end of the world and also to the crucifixion and resurrection of Christ, the establishment of the new order. The passage anticipates the praise for this deed in part F: "Swa se hælend us helpe gefremede / þurh his lices gedal, lif butan ende" [as the Lord accomplished help for us, life without end, by the death of His body; lines 650-51].

Linked in theme to the creation and destruction pattern is the destiny of the garden. It had a beginning dependent on the godhead ("se hit on frymþe gescop") who will destroy it to fulfill the plan.

The phoenix in its unique island is always in need of regeneration and so a direct contrast to Christ, of whom the poet writes:

> næs his frymð æfre,
> eades ongyn.   þeah he on eorþan her
> þurh cildes had   cenned wære
> in middangeard,   hwæþre his meahta sped
> heah ofer heofonum   halig wunade,
> dom unbryce.

[there was never an origin for Him, a beginning of His bliss. Though He on earth here through a child's form were born into the world, nevertheless, the power of His might high over the heavens remained holy, a glory undefiled.]   (lines 637-42)

The Old English poet picks up the motif of the well of life from Lactantius ("Sed fons in medio est, quem 'vivum' nomine dicunt, / Perspicuus, lenis, dulcibus uber aquis"; lines 25-26) but uses the epithet "brimcald" [sea-cold; line 67] for the waters which "brecað, bearo ealne geondfarað" [burst, flow through all the grove; line 67]. The notion of the sea-cold water evokes the archetypal journey, for one need look no further than *The Wanderer* or *The Seafarer* in the same anthology to note that the sea and the journey over it are inextricably linked in the Old English poetic imagination. This, then, helps to prepare both for the phoenix and its flight and for the souls which must, through the bitterness and coldness of death, prepare for their journey to heaven. The corresponding section of part F focuses these concepts into the new heaven. The archetypal "sea-coldness" that in much of Old English poetry is almost a synonym for the journey of death has been evoked; the physical regeneration of the phoenix has offered hope to mankind as it evokes the crucifixion (with the flowing of water and blood). The death, descent to hell, and resurrection of Christ are the logical extensions to terminate the almost endless cycle of the phoenix:

> þeah he deaþes! cwealm
> on rode treow   ræfnan sceolde,

þearlic wite,   he þy þriddan dæge
æfter lices hryre   lif eft onfeng
þurh fæder fultum.   Swa fenix beacnað,
geong in geardum,   godbearnes meaht.

[though He the agony of death on the rood-tree had to
suffer, dire tribulation, on the third day after the
destruction of the body He life again received from the
hands of the Father. So the phoenix demonstrates, young
in the dwelling place, the might of the Son of God.]

(lines 642-47)

After establishing the correspondences between the island of the
phoenix and the heavenly realization of the type, the poem moves on
to consider the role of the individual in both the prefiguration and
the actual. Thus two figures are introduced in parts B and E in order
to show that the way is open for humanity. The phoenix functions as
a type of Christ by demonstrating the physical regeneration of the
body from the ashes of death. Job, also, in the complementary
section, suggests renewal, yet shows it in a nobler manifestation, the
rebirth of the spirit through faith. The images of fire and journey,
already established in parts A and F of the poem, are augmented by a
new Christian motif, the total destruction of the body and the
subsequent restoration of life.

The first section of part B (lines 85-103) serves to introduce the
phoenix. As already noted for the habitation of the bird, the
temporal is brought into tension with the eternal, and in the corresponding section of E (lines 518-45) the earthly exile of the individual is counterbalanced by the prospect of reward: "þaer þa eadgan
beoð / æfter wræchwile weorcum bifongen, / agnum dædum" [there
the noble, after a period of exile, will be clothed in works, in their
own deeds' lines 526-28]. In fact, the poet makes it clear that the
salient features of the phoenix's home have their typological
fulfillment in the home of the blessed. Even if lesser birds are not
allowed to nest with the phoenix, nonetheless his abode contains the
promise for the election of the worthy. The good deeds of redeemed
men are like the joy that the phoenix takes in the plants associated

169

with its regeneration: "mid þam se wilda fugel / his sylfes nest biseteð utan" [with which the wild bird his own nest surrounds from without; lines 529-30].

The principal metaphors used in these two passages to describe the process are light and fire. No sooner is the phoenix introduced into the setting than the idea of the light, joined to the journey, is presented:

> se sceal þære sunnan   siÐ behealdan
> ond ongean cuman   godes condelle,
> glædum gimme.
>
> [it shall behold the journey of the sun and come towards
> God's candle, the joyous gem.]   (lines 90-92)

Parallel to the light which precedes the journey of the phoenix is the purgation by fire that must come before the souls are received into heaven:

> þær þa lichoman,   leahtra clæne,
> gongaÐ glædmode,   gæstas hweorfaÐ
> in banfatu,   þonne bryne stigeÐ
> heah to heofonum.
>
> [there the bodies, clean from iniquity, will go glad in
> heart, the spirits will pass from the bodies, when the fire
> rises high to the heavens.]   (lines 518-21)

Because the phoenix is a symbol of the divinity of Christ, it shows no fear of the ordeal that is to come while joyfully anticipating the arrival of the sun, herald of its rebirth; yet there is a characteristic sardonic understatement in the passage dealing with the exegesis of the phoenix. The bird had been glad in its expectation of renewal, but others may not be quite so joyous: "hat biÐ monegum / egeslic æled" [the dreadful pyre will be hot for many; lines 521-22].

The next pair of comparable passages of B and E (lines 104-81; 546-69) serves to introduce another major consideration. Balanced against the need for the bird to go on its quest is the controlling

170

reference to Job which suggests the stability of scripture. This idea of the authority of the written word (the fable of the phoenix and the prophetic utterances which had already occurred earlier) again is stressed as the poet reiterates the story of the bird in the familiar journey motif, the archetypal image of the larger quest which the phoenix foretells in its actions:

> þær se tireadga   twelf siþum hine
> bibaþað in þam burnan   ær þæs beacnes cyme,
> sweglcondelle,   ond symle swa oft
> of þam wilsuman   wyllgespryngum
> brimcald beorgeð   æt baða gehwylcum.

> [there the glorious one twelve times bathes itself in the river ere the coming of the sign, heaven's candle, and ever so often of the delicious well-spring tastes the sea-coldness at each bathing.]   (lines 106-10)

The sea-linked images of the departure of the bird recur in the second section of part E where now the Bible is evoked as the culmination of the miraculous phoenix; the fabled bird prefigures the divinely authored truth of its typological signficance:

> Ne wene þæs ænig   ælda cynnes
> þæt ic lygewordum   leoð somnige,
> write woðcræfte.   Gehyrað witedom
> Iobes gieddinga.

> [let not any of the race of men think that I in lying words compose my song, write my verse; hear the wisdom of Job's songs.]   (lines 546-49)

Just as the bird becomes "gearum frod [old in years; line 154], so has Job become "hrawerig" [weary in body; line 554] and must depart "hean þonan / on longne sið [go abject thence on a long journey; lines 554-55]. To heighten further the link between the phoenix story and the divinely inspired, the poet stresses another aspect of the bird's legend, one that helps to join it to the narration of Job, the tree motif. In order to effect the cycle of rebirth, the phoenix must seek a high tree (lines 171-73). So Job seeks his "neobed" [deathbed; line 553] in a "neste" [nest; line 553]: as the tree of the phoenix foretells Christ's sacrifice through a secular story, so Job's faith serves as the prophecy of Christian revelation in the biblical narrative. Just as the tree of the phoenix suggests the cross, so Job's tree echoes the rood and adumbrates the reward of those faithful to the cross. The bird's tree is alone "ealra beama . . . beorhtast" [of all trees brightest; lines 177-79]. This clearly is balanced by Job's confidence:

> þeah min lic scyle
> on moldærne   molsnad weorþan
> wyrmum to willan,   swa þeah weoruda god
> æfter swylthwile   sawle alyseð
> ond in wuldor aweceð.

[though my body shall in the grave become decayed, the sport of worms, yet the God of Hosts will redeem and deliver into glory my soul after a time of death.]

(lines 563-67)

With the establishment of the necessity for a journey and the comment made upon it in the mid portions of parts B and E, the final sections of these two divisions (lines 182-215; 570-88) build to a climax. Following the description of the gathering of the plants with which the phoenix surrounds itself, the bird is then ready for its consummation. But only five lines are given to the description of the most spectacular feature of the allegory, the actual fire (lines 211-15). In some ways the pyre scene seems to be a release, for the bird's preparation is presented as an almost frenzied activity. While the garden and tree will last to the end of time, the moment of preparation for immolation is quite intense:

> Bið him neod micel
> þæt he þa yldu   ofestum mote
> þurh gewittes wylm   wendan to life,
> feorg geong onfon.

172

[for him is the great need that he from age with great
haste through the impulse of knowledge journey to life,
seize youth.]   (lines 189-91)

The movement of part B is from an elaborate preparation for
death to its rapid accomplishment.   The corresponding passage,
following the reference to Job, can deal with the other half of the
idea, since Job's song itself (lines 552-69) provides the means by
which the reader is to understand the phoenix. Part B leaves the bird
in cinders, while by the end of part E the moral has been made
explicit with a quiet affirmation of the realization of Job's prophetic
utterance. The tree and garden may last only to the end of time;
however, the poem moves to beyond time in its exegesis of the
passage, and so the frenzy of the bird can be judged in the new light
of the period after the temporal:

> Ðus frod guma [Job]   on fyrndagum
> gieddade gleawmod,   godes spelboda,
> ymb his æriste   in ece lif,
> þæt we þy geornor   ongietan meahten
> tirfæst tacen   þæt se torhta fugel
> þurh bryne beacnað.

[Thus the wise man in days of old, God's seer, wise in
heart, sang about his resurrection into eternal life so that
we the more eagerly might understand the glorious
meaning that the radiant bird, by burning, betokens.]

(lines 570-75)

But the lesson is also expanded beyond Job alone to demonstrate
that all may participate in the pattern initiated by the phoenix and
exemplified by Job:

> swa nu æfter deaðe   þurh dryhtnes miht
> somod siþiaþ   sawla mid lice,
> fægre gefrætwed,   fugle gelicast,
> in eadwelum.

173

[so now after death, through the might of the Lord,
together the soul with the body, beautifully adorned,
journeys most like the bird, into blessedness.]

(lines 583-86)

Because this is the most important lesson of the poem, the artist is careful to bring the elements into a heightened balance. The preparation for and journey into death in part B are played against the preparation for and journey into life eternal in part E: "þær seo soþfæste sunne lihteð / wlitig ofer weoredum" [there the truthfast sun shines, beautiful over the hosts; lines 587-88].

Parts C and D (lines 216-380; 424-517) serve to lead from the climax, the actual burning, to the resolution of the problem of the ephemeral joys within the context to the phoenix's temporal regeneration and the establishment of the reality of the heavenly kingdom for the blessed souls.

The first section of part C (lines 216-64) introduces new ideas connected with the immolation of the phoenix and links them to the theme of purging away the flesh. The movement is needed because of the sins associated with Eden and the necessity to consider the former splendour of that place as a mere typological shadow. Thus the poem exploits a cyclical pattern. The return of the phoenix to its homeland might sound appropriate for a description of the ascension, yet it is a physical world to which the phoenix returns; its journey is a cycle that only foreshadows a larger truth. It travels in time: "oþþæt fyrngesetu, / agenne eard, eft geseceð " [until it again seeks its own abode, the old home; lines 263-64]. The phoenix, in other words, is eternal yet finite, caught in a cycle. This fact may very well be the reason for the envelope pattern[5] that exists between lines 264 ("agenne eard, eft geseceð " [again seeks its own abode]) and 275 ("agenne eard eft to secan" [again to seek its own abode]). Mankind, on the contrary, is not like the phoenix, for human regeneration will lead, not back to the old paradise, but on to the new. Rebirth of the phoenix is mirrored in the physical image of the restoration of the body so that the phoenix becomes "swylc he æt frymðe wæs" [just as he was at the beginning; line 239].

Perhaps most noteworthy about the first section of part C is the

174

long agricultural simile used to express the alternation of life and death. Each time humanity collects the autumn harvest to sustain itself during the winter and then finds rebirth in the spring, it re-enacts, in the microcosm (as does the phoenix), the divine plan of salvation. Just as "of þam wæstmum sceal / eorla eadwela eft alædan" [from the fruits shall man's riches again be brought forth; lines 250-51], so from the fruit of the womb will the ultimate "eorla eadwela" be brought forth. The old sins of Adam and Eve will be expiated, even if there is a tragic note about their departure from Eden:

> swa ða foregengan,
> yldran usse,   anforleton
> þone wlitigan wong   ond wuldres setl,
> leoflic on laste.

> [so the original parents, our ancestors, abandoned behind
> them the beautiful and marvellous realm and the seat of
> glory.]   (lines 437-40)

Surely the expulsion of Adam and Eve makes possible the final resolution, not simply a return--as is the case of the phoenix--but a genuine new life. The agricultural simile (as well as the cycle of the phoenix) is really only a shadow of the cosmic cycle of regeneration.

Showing far more poetic genius is the particular way in which the phoenix is reborn from the ashes. Lactantius tells of the rebirth from the cinders as "animal . . . sine membris" (line 101). The *Phoenix*-poet expands this to anticipate later developments of the idea:

> þonne of þam ade   æples gelicnes
> on þære ascan bið   eft gemeted,
> of þam weaxeð wyrm,   wundrum fæger.

> [then from the fire the likeness of an apple in the ashes is
> again found, from which grows a worm wondrously
> beautiful.]   (lines 230-32)

The loss of Eden has become connected with the apple; the "wyrm," which replaces the legless animal, calls to mind the serpent. The loss of Eden is the story of a serpent and an apple. The regeneration of the phoenix acts as a mirror of this; for the apple is now the agent of renewal, and the serpent, in its miraculous quality, reverses the harm of the old foe. It must be no accident that the *Phoenix*-poet adds this detail--that the ashes of the phoenix come together to resemble an apple--to the material found in Lactantius. It is also interesting to note the "æppel," this time offered by Satan, appears again in the transitional passage.

Near the beginning of part C, fire consumes the bird, and the author notes that "lif bið on siðe, / fæges feorhhord" [life is on a journey, the spirit of the fated one; lines 220-21]. By the end of this passage, regeneration is complete, and the phoenix "agenne eard eft geseceð" [his own land seeks again; line 264]. The long "sið " and the final arrival, however, are only half complete at the end of the corresponding portion of D (lines 424-42) when Adam and Eve:

> tugon longne sið
> in hearmra hond,   þær him hettende,
> earme aglæcan,   oft gescodan.

> [took a long journey into the hands of the evil one; then
> the hateful one, the wretched adversary, often harmed
> them.]   (lines 440-42)

While humanity may have to journey through the realm of foes, the travail is worth the effort, for the regeneration will see not just the repetition of the cycles, but rather the termination of the pattern and the destruction of the "aglæcan." The reversal hinted at in the image of apple and serpent in the Old English version of the phoenix will be completely reversed for Adam and Eve and their descendants.

In C and D the comparison continues between the regained bliss of the phoenix and the hope of those who have pleased God. The defeat of the old flesh by the bird symbolizes the need for man likewise to reject the old. The middle portion of C (lines 265-319) ends with the bird, full of glory, rejoicing in its paradise (lines

314-18) while man, in the middle portion of D (lines 443-90), is
exhorted to good in order to win heaven and, at the same time, is
cautioned not to hope long to possess the goods of this earth. He
must remember that the journey is yet to come before he may truly
rejoice:

> þonne deað nimeð,
> wiga wælgifre,   wæpnum geþryþed,
> ealdor anra gehwæs,   ond in eorþan fæðm
> snude sendeð   sawlum binumene
> læne lichoman.

> [then death will quickly take, that bloodthirsty warrior
> armed with weapons, the life of each one, and into the
> bosom of the earth quickly send, deprived of soul, the
> transitory body.]   (lines 485-89)

In the final two sections of parts C and D (lines 320-49; 491-517),
the parable and exegesis deal with joy manifest. The third section of
part C pictures the bird's actual flight back to its paradise with men
gathering to behold the phoenix:

> swa se fugel fleogeð,   folcum oðeaweð
> mongum monna   geond middangeard,
> þonne somniað   suþan ond norþan,
> eastan ond westan,   eoredciestum,
> farað feorran ond nean   folca þryþum
> þær hi sceawiaþ   scyppendes giefe
> fægre on þam fugle.

> [so the bird flies, manifest to people, to many men
> throughout earth, when they assemble from south and
> north, east and west, in crowds journey far and near,
> people in troops, where they perceive God's gift,
> wondrous in that bird.]   (lines 322-28)

Picking up the phrase "sigora soð cyning" [true king of victories;
line 329] which had established the primacy of the phoenix among

birds because it is a type of Christ, the author shows mankind gathered together for a different purpose in part D.:

> Đonne monge beoð   on gemot læded
> fyra cynnes;   wile fæder engla,
> sigora soðcyning,   seonoþ gehegan,
> duguða dryhten,   deman mid ryhte.

> [then many of the race of men will be led into an assembly; the true king of victories will hold counsel, Lord of Hosts, to judge rightly.]   (lines 491-94)

The meditative passages which end each of the two halves serve as a reminder of and meditation on the whole. The first of these, which occurs in part C (lines 350-80), notes several aspects of the phoenix not really comparable to the Christian story. The author makes the point that the phoenix returns home, yet the rest of the birds merely go back to their own homes, sad in mind. The phoenix is young; nonetheless, soon his thousand years have passed, and he must again depart. He is the eternal symbol, but he lacks efficacy.

The last passage of the poem, the meditation at the end of part F (lines 655-77), relies for a degree of heightened feeling on the use of Latin in the poem and the liturgical echoes, while dealing solely with Christ and his fulfillment of what the phoenix had promised. Christ, now on the right hand of God, is the "lucis auctor" [author of light; line 667] who enables man to obtain a place among the "sedibus altis" [the high abodes; line 671] and to have life eternal in the joy of peace. The profusion of light images clearly pales any glory of the mere symbol of this blessed state.

Finally, the transition makes use of many of the images from the first half of the poem to prepare for the treatment of these ideas in the second. There are introduced in the transition a number of concepts not found in Lactantius but which are crucial for the allegory. The transition exploits an almost ready-made set of images such as Christ and his thanes and the relation of this to the phoenix and its entourage. Also, parallels between the bird's paradise and the garden of Eden are a natural transitional device, as are Adam and

178

Eve, reference to the serpent, and the forbidden fruit:

> Habbaþ we geascad   þæt se ælmihtiga
> worhte wer ond wif   þurh his wundra sped,
> ond hi þa gesette   on þone selestan
> foldan sceata
>
> . . . .
> þær him niþ gescod,
> ealdfeondes æfest,   se him æt gebead,
> beames blede,   þæt hi bu þegun
> æppel unrædum   ofer est godes.

> [We have learned that the Almighty made man and
> woman by the might of his power and then placed them
> in the best of the regions of earth. . . .   There hatred
> harmed them, envy of the old fiend who offered them
> food, fruit of the tree, so that they tasted, unwisely
> against God's command, the apple.]   (lines 393-403)

While perhaps mechanical, the transition does allow us to see the
linkage between the Latin original and its "translation." Clearly, the
Old English *Phoenix* is far more than a translation--it is the art of
seeing in the old the basis of the new.

In the introduction of the poem, N. F. Blake observes:

> The poet has failed to select and arrange his material
> satisfactorily, for the overlapping interpretations some-
> times confuse the reader . . . but nevertheless one cannot
> help feeling that a greater poet would have been able to
> order the various allegorical strands into an organic
> unity.[6]

In reply to the criticism that *The Phoenix* is not well organized, it
would seem that many of the details of the first part were dictated by
the use of a source; yet the poet has been able artfully to counter-
balance these with his exegesis. The result is that the movement
from the fable to the explanation seems to be accomplished
smoothly. The poet's real art, then, has been to expand suggestions

179

and themes from the first part into logical explanations in the second. His use of the sources for the first section, however, has not merely produced a paraphrase; what alterations he makes can be seen as definite preparation for the Christian moral that follows.

The tension between these two, the translation and the exegesis, helps to impart the rich texture that characterizes the poem. In view of this complexity, the criticism that the poet shows little artistic selection and arrangement of material is unfounded. There is indeed a superb control of imagery apparent in the work, a control that arises chiefly from the two well-structured halves which produce a truly remarkable unity.

NOTES

1. *The Phoenix* as printed in *The Exeter Book*, ed. G. P. Krapp and E. V. K. Dobbie, The Anglo-Saxon Poetic Records, vol. 3 (New York: Columbia Univ. Press, 1936). All references follow this edition, with slight modifications to the capitalization. I have appended rough working translations of the material for the convenience of non-specialists in this area.

2. "Carmen de ave phoenice" as printed in *The Phoenix*, ed. N. F. Blake, Old and Middle English Texts Series (Manchester: Manchester Univ. Press, 1964). Subsequent references to Lactantius are from this edition of the poem.

3. Some further possible minor sources for ideas found in the second half of the poem can be found in the preface to Professor Blake's edition [n. 2 above].

4. While I have suggested that the manuscript divisions are more or less random and principally decorative, such a view does not, of course, represent the only possible interpretation of the manuscript divisions in this, or any, Old English poem. Because we cannot be certain whether the divisions are scribal flourishes or represent the original authors' intentions, the use to be made of the manuscript divisions must, for now, remain conjectural. Professor Robert D. Stevick has argued that the number of lines in the first manuscript division (eighty-four) is significant as the average of other groupings of divisions and that a complex geometrical

pattern can be established for the poem. I am grateful to Professor Stevick for making available to me a draft version of an article in which he refines his analysis of the significance of the number eighty-four in *The Phoenix*. See also Professor Stevick's "Mathematical Proportions and Symbolism in *The Phoenix*," *Viator* 11 (1980):95-121.

5. An envelope pattern, a term fully explained in Adeline C. Bartlett's work on Old English rhetoric (*The Larger Rhetorical Patterns in Anglo-Saxon Poetry* [New York: Columbia Univ. Press, 1935; rpt. New York: AMS Press, Inc., 1966]), refers to two verbal repetitions, either of a whole verse or a significant part of a line, positioned closely enough together to call attention to themselves to a reader (or, more likely, to a listener). They are usually thought to signify that the material so enveloped is of particular importance. I would like to express my thanks to Professor Constance B. Hieatt for calling this particular envelope pattern to my attention.

6. N. F. Blake, ed., *The Phoenix* [n. 2 above], pp. 33f. Professor Robert D. Stevick argues cogently for a more important rationale for the manuscript divisions [see n. 4 above].

APPENDIX

*Part A

lines 1-27
   habitation of phoenix
   evil folk excluded
   inaccessible
   sense of longing
lines 28-49
   prophets speak of phoenix

lines 50-84
   the symbol as transient

*Part B

lines 85-103
   eternal phoenix
   light / journey motif
lines 104-81
   departure and tree image

lines 182-215
   immolation of phoenix

Part C

lines 216-64
   phoenix returns to old home
   agricultural simile

lines 265-319
   joy in bird's return to paradise
lines 320-49
   men assembled to see phoenix
   (as type of Christ)

*Meditation

lines 350-80
   phoenix remains only as symbol

Transition

lines 381-423
   Christ and his followers parallel to phoenix and its followers

*Part D

lines 424-42
   reference to Adam and Eve
   expelled

lines 443-90
   man's possession of joy temporary
   need to strive for higher order
   journey yet to come

lines 491-517
   assembly for judgment

*Part E

lines 518-45
   reward for faithful
   purgation of souls
lines 546-69
   Job's song about departure and
   tree image
lines 570-88
   Job foresees beyond death

*Part F

lines 589-610
   heavenly kingdom
   evil overcome
   agriculture simile "fulfilled"
lines 611-31
   disciples' proclaiming
lines 632-54
   mankind eternally fulfilled
   (by Christ's sacrifice)

Meditation

lines 655-77
   Latin used to heighten effect and
   make symbol seem less valid

*Denotes thematic divisions that have manuscript capitals.

182

ADDITIONAL REFERENCES

Calder, Daniel G. "The Study of Style in Old English Poetry: A Historical Introduction." In *Old English Poetry: Essays on Style*. Ed. D. G. Calder. Berkeley: Univ. of California Press, 1979. Pp. 1-65.
[In addition to the enlightening study, the essay includes an extensive bibliography of material dealing with Old English stylistics.]

Chambers, R. W.; Forster, Max; and Flower, Robin, eds. *The Exeter Book of Old English Poetry*. (Collotype Facsimile). London: P. Lund, Humphries and Co., 1933.

Greenfield, Stanley B. "Esthetics and Meaning and the Translation of Old English Poetry." In *Old English Poetry: Essays on Style*. Pp. 91-110.

Stanley, E. G. "Two Old English Poetic Phrases Insufficiently Understood for Literary Criticism: *Ðing Gehegan* and *Seonoþ Gehagan*." In *Old English Poetry: Essays on Style*. Pp. 67-90.

TWO OLD FRENCH RECASTINGS / TRANSLATIONS OF ANDREAS CAPELLANUS'S *DE AMORE*

Peter F. Dembowski

The editor of this volume was kind enough to invite me to participate in a session on translations from Latin to Old French organized by her at the 1982 Congress on Medieval Studies at Western Michigan University. I am grateful to her, for as a result of our deliberations, I published an article on "Learned Latin Treatises in French: Inspiration, Plagiarism and Translation,"[1] in which I tried, perhaps somewhat rashly, to suggest that certain patterns of development in thirteenth- and fourteenth-century France permit us to offer at least a sketch of a history of translation. Without repudiating the main body of the arguments presented, I realize now perhaps more fully that it is very difficult to talk about "translation" in general in regard to certain thirteenth-century works. Every work considered as translation (in the broadest sense of the term) must be closely examined on its own merit. This examination should be carried out as free as possible from the interference of our modern concepts of translation, for, as we shall see, certain thirteenth-century works traditionally classified as translations would hardly be considered as such in later epochs. Such Old French borderline cases of the art and craft of translation are important in their own right, for they often can throw some light on the complex problems of the coexistence of Latin and vernacular cultures. They are essential, I believe, to our understanding of the long and complex process of development of the idea of translation as we know it today.

I wish to examine here two such borderline cases. Both have been classed as translations of the famous treatise *De Amore*[2] composed, probably in the 1180s, by Andreas Capellanus, usually identified with a certain André, chaplain at the court of Marie de Champagne, daughter of Louis VII of France and Aliénor d'Aquitaine. This famous treatise in the form of a long dissertation addressed to the friend of the author, Gualterius, is divided into three books. Book 1 is the longest. It offers a definition of love, describes the type of persons capable of "serving Venus," and, most importantly, presents eight dialogues about love. These dialogues, a veritable *ars dicendi*, follow a well-defined sociological pattern. People capable of love belong to three classes: bourgeois (*plebeii*), nobility (*nobiles*), and higher nobility (*nobiliores*). The first three dialogues present a bourgeois conversing with a bourgeois, with a noble woman, and with a lady of the higher nobility. In the next two, a nobleman speaks with a bourgeois and with a noble lady. The last three show a man of higher nobility debating with a bourgeois woman, with a noble lady, and with a lady of his own class. The fifth dialogue, "Loquitur nobilis nobili" [A nobleman speaks with a noblewoman], contains a short story in which a lone courtly hero is allowed to visit the palace of the King of Love and his court representing a vision of an afterlife. Ladies who used to be good servants of love are rewarded here, and those who refused love in this life are punished. The hero receives from the king twelve rules or commandments of love. The seventh dialogue, "Loquitur nobilior nobilii" [A man of higher nobility speaks with a woman of simple nobility], concludes with a letter to the Countess of Champagne containing a query about a love case and her answer (dated May 1174) resolving the case. Book 1 ends with brief discussions of problematic or forbidden forms of love: the one practiced by clerks, by nuns, acquired by money, attained too easily, and, finally, involving prostitutes.

Book 2 discusses the problems of retaining love. Here too, we have direct references to the contemporary life, for the Countess of Champagne, her mother Aliénor, the Countess of Flanders, and the Viscountess of Narbonne pronounce decisions, as supreme judges, in twenty-one love cases (*judicia amoris*). The book ends with an Arthurian tale in which a valiant Briton, following some adventures in what seems to be the Other World, receives from the King of

Love thirty-one rules of love (*regulae amoris*), in order to make them known to all lovers.

Book 3 of Andreas is, like the *De remediis amoris* of Ovid, a repudiation of his *De Amore*. Andreas's *De reprobatione* [*The Rejection of Love*] is a repudiation of adultery and fornication in the name of traditional Christian morality. This book is a veritable collection of not only anti-love, but also misogynic clichés.

The two earliest known French versions of Andreas's treatise are the subject of this chapter. They are: (1) Book 3, "La dotrine d'amor" [The Doctrine of Love], of the moral-doctrinal treatise composed sometime after 1250 in Franco-Italian prose by a certain Enanchet[3] (or Annanchet); and (2) a version in 7,640 octosyllabic couplets composed in 1290 by Drouart la Vache.[4] While some problems of translation encountered in the second work have been analyzed by the editor of Drouart in an introductory volume to the edition,[5] much less has been said about the nature of translation, strictly speaking, in regard to the work of Enanchet.

Let us abandon chronological order and examine first the work of Drouart. His long *roman* would not pass for a real translation in our times. The very fact that he has written in verse and in the form of a romance precludes his being faithful to the letter of the source-text. We know that, from the early thirteenth century on, there was a strong current of clerical opinion according to which verse was associated with imaginative literature, that is to say, with lies. Thus, any serious work, including, of course, a serious translation, should be composed in prose (or written "without rhyme," as one of the translators of what was deemed to be the "true" history put it), for prose alone allows one to express the truth.[6] Now Drouart la Vache has chosen verse, because he did not want to (re)compose a *treatise* but a *romance* of his own. He states this in his opening lines. Suppressing Andreas's *Prefatio* which establishes the *personae* of Andreas, the teacher, and of Gualterius, the pupil, Drouart writes his own introduction, which is important for us, because while explaining the genesis of his book to his readers, he explains his concept of translation. He learned to rhyme so well that, says he:

Encor weil je, aveigne qu'aveigne,
Translater en françois .i. livre,
Qui enseigne comment doit vivre
Cil qui veut amours maintenir.   (lines 4-7)

[And I wish, come what may, to translate in French a
book, which teaches the one who wants to support and
serve love how he must live.]

The reasons for this undertaking, he says, are of a purely romance
character: in the Autumn of 1290, one of his two companions
showed him a book ("Mout bien fait . . . / En latin" [lines 46-47;
very well composed . . . in Latin]). The book impressed him:

Quant je l'oi veü
Et il en ot .i. poi leü,
La matere trop durement
Me plot, sachiez, certainement,
Tant, que j'en commençai a rire.   (lines 47-51)

[When I had seen and he had read from it a little, the
subject matter pleased me, indeed, so much, that I began
to smile.]

The two friends beg him to translate the book *en rommans* (line 54)
[in French], and Drouart decides to accomplish this work "Que
n'entreprist omques mais hons" [line 65; that no one has ever
undertaken].[7] And he adds:

Assez i a d'autres raisons,
Que je pas or ne vous descuevre,
Qui me font commencier ceste oevre:
A ce me muet meësmement
Cele qui j'aimme entierement
Et amerai toute ma vie,
Sans penser nule vilonie;
Et se je pooie tant faire
Que mes rimes peüssent plaire

188

A ma tres douce chiere amie,
Bien seroie ma rime emploïe.   (lines 66-76)

[There are many other reasons, which I do not disclose,
for making me begin this work: the lady, whom I love
sincerely and whom I shall serve all my life without
thinking any vile thoughts, moves me particularly to do
it; and if I could only accomplish so much that my
rhymes could please my very dearly beloved, they would
be well used.]

Besides the entreaties of his companions, and the inspiration of his
ladylove, there are other reasons for his work, which the poet does
not wish to disclose. He asks us, however, not to blame him for
anything objectionable in his book, for he had no "entencion / De
dire nule vilonie" [lines 96-97; no intention to say any vile thing],
but if the reader finds a "vile thing," it is because "elle a mon livre
affiere, / Prenez vous en a la matiere, / Non pas a moi" [lines
99-101; it belongs to my source book, criticize my subject matter,
but not me].

Drouart's introduction is important to the understanding of his
concept of translation. He found *De Amore* "joyful" and containing
many "beautiful words" (lines 56-57). He dedicates his own book
(rather than its matter) to his beloved. But he also knows that there
will be other readers to whom the matter of the work might be
offensive. As so many of us, Drouart wishes to have the best of both
worlds. As an expert "rhymer" he is proud to offer his own work to
his lady, but as a recaster of somebody else's subject matter he
wishes to be free of any blame. If Drouart thought about himself in
terms of a modern translator, his non-responsibility for the offensive
aspects of his subject would have been self-evident. Rather, he is
using the well-known procedure of the romance writers. Like
Chrétien de Troyes, who insists that Marie de Champagne or
Philippe de Flandre supplied him either with the subject matter or
even with a specific book which he was to elaborate, Drouart treats
Andreas's work as such a romance source. The important difference
lies, of course, in the fact that Chrétien's sources probably did not

amount to more than some general indication of the plot, or were totally fictitious, but Drouart had a real model. He translates this model, and he says so explicitly (the verb *translater* is used twice in the preface), but he does not name it and presents his translation as his own romance.

The change in the genre between *Li Livres d'Amours* and the *De Amore* constitutes the greatest difference between Drouart's work and his model, and, consequently, between his idea of translation and ours. Since Bossuat has devoted a chapter to the analysis of "Le *Livre d'Amours* et son modèle,"[8] let us only touch upon Drouart's ability to translate, as well as upon certain fundamental "liberties" that he took with the text of *De Amore*. First of all, it must be said that he knows not only how to "rhyme" but also how to translate. This point is important, because the studies of his text, as well as of other translations into Old French, have been profoundly influenced by the contempt with which the nineteenth-century scholars considered them. According to their view, works such as *Li Livres d'Amours* possessed two fatal flaws: they were "unoriginal," i.e., they were "mere" elaborations of (a) known model(s), and they were inexact, i.e., "unfaithful" rendering of their models.[9] Such fundamentally unsympathetic attitudes to this mixed genre of recasting / adaptation / translation, to which many early Old French translations belong, prevented a serious scholarly interest in this genre until well into our century.

What has to be stated first of all is this: Drouart certainly was capable of translating faithfully. He knew Latin and was capable of rendering Andreas's thought in the clear language of the Old French *roman*. Let us take but one example, from the famous opening line of Book 1 of Andreas:

> Amor est passio quaedam innata procedens ex visione et immoderata cogitatione formae altrius sexus, ob quam aliquis super omnia cupit alterius potiri amplexibus et omnia de utriusque voluntate in ipsius amplexu amoris præcepta compleri.   (p. 3)

> [Love is a certain inborn suffering derived from the sight

of and excessive meditation upon the beauty of the
opposite sex, which causes each one to wish above all
things the embraces of the other and by common desire
to carry out all of love's precepts in the other's
embrace.]

Tele est la dyffinicions
D'Amours: Amours est passions
Ou maladie dedenz nee
Par vision desordenee
Venans de forme d'autre sexe
Et de commun assent connexe,
Ainsi com Venus le commande,
Par qui chascuns amans demande
Plus l'acoler et le baisier
Qui lui d'autre chose aaisier.   (lines 137-46)

[Such is the definition of Love: Love is a passion or
sickness born in by a disorderly vision of the form of the
opposite sex and closely related to a common consent,
commanded by Venus, because of which each lover
strives more for embraces and for kisses than any other
pleasure.]

I believe that this example will suffice to demonstrate that our early
translators were capable. We should, therefore, simply assume that
the numerous divergences between the models and the translations
resulted not so much from their incapacity as translators, but rather
from their unwillingness to follow the text exactly, or, better still,
from their desire to recast their models in order to adapt them to
their own needs.[10] Drouart's divergences from the text of *De Amore*
are numerous. The most important are the suppression of the
personae of Andreas and Gualtarius, not only, as we have seen, in
the preface, but throughout the book. Instead Drouart presents the
deciple who asks questions and receives answers from the *maistre*
(see lines 4017-4120). He abridges the long dialogues (which
represent about 55% of *De Amore*),[11] but he presents all eight of
them. He suppresses both of Andreas's *lais*: there is no mention of

the palace of the King of Love and the first set of rules of love. Similarly, he omits the Arthurian short story culminating in our reception of the full set of rules. But he presents twenty-nine of them, missing only the two most idealistic and abstract: "XXIV. Quilibet amantis actus in coamantis cogitatione finitur" and "XXVI. Amor nil posset amori denegare" [p. 311; Every act of a lover ends in the thought of his beloved and Love can deny nothing to love].[12] Thus, it could be easily argued that Drouart reproduced quite faithfully the first two books of Andreas. In a sense, he "improved" them by "unifying" the didactic, discursive, popular, and un-sophisticated character of his poem through the elimination of the two short stories. He apparently did not believe in the desirability of the obviously fictitious *exempla* in the body of a *tractatus*.

But Drouart took real liberties with the Latin model in his rendering of Book 3, *De reprobatione Amoris* [*The Rejection of Love*].[13] First of all, the rejection is not offered, as in Andreas, *ex abrupto*. Drouart prepares us by recalling the condition in which he undertook the work, and insists:

> por ce ne vous lo ge mie
> Que vous menez d'Amours la vie,
> Qui n'est pas bonne ne honeste. . . ."   (lines 6589-91)

[I do not advise you so to lead the life of Love, which is neither good nor honest. . . ."]

He then presents twenty *rationes* (under Latin rubrics) which reproduce, in a somewhat abridged form, the main argument of Andreas, but with a most important change: the anti-feminine stance is greatly reduced. Drouart seems to be aware of the incongruity of Andreas's antithetic position, for he states in his *Enseignemens* [*Teachings*] (part of *16a ratio*):

> Mais por ce ne weil ge pas dire
> Que les dames doie despire,
> Car je Nature acuseroie,
> S'en tele oppinion estoie

Qu'elles despites estre doient;
Et tuit cil errent qui le croient. . . .   (lines 7161-66)

[But I do not say it because I must despise ladies; if I
held the opinion that they must be despised, it would be
accusing Nature; and all who believe it are in error. . . .]

Similarly the short attack on the avarice, gluttony, lust, envy,
disobedience, scandelmongering, etc. of women (which follows the
20a ratio) is immediately followed by an important and final[14]
disclaimer. I cite it here, because it gives a good idea of the general
tone of Drouart's book and expresses the essential ideological
difference between him and his Latin model:

Après ce que j'ai dit des dames,
Vous devez des mauvaises fames
Entendre, qui sont diffamees;
Les autres, qui sont honorees,
Bonnes dames et glorieuses,
Entre toutes gens precieuses,
Celes doivent mestre lor cure
A maintenir bonne amour pure,
Par loial delectacion;
Car omques n'oi entencion
Que je des bonnes mesdeïsse,
Qu'il n'est chose que ne feïsse
Por les bonnes, se je savoie
Qu'elles dou faire eüssent joie.   (lines 7533-46)

[After what I said of the ladies you must understand that
I meant the bad women who are dishonored; the others,
who are honored, good, and glorious ladies, precious
among all others, must take all care to maintain good and
pure love, by a faithful enjoyment; because I have never
had any intention to speak ill of the good ones; since
there is nothing that I would not do for the good ladies, if
I knew that by doing it they could have joy.]

193

This forceful disclaimer rejoins thus the initial dedicatory statement, in which Drouart insists that the book was inspired by and undertaken to please his "very dearly beloved."

I am in agreement with Bossuat[15] as to the general nature of Drouart's work. It is essentially a "translation," since most of Andreas's ideas are reproduced in it more or less in the same pattern. But it is not what I described in my article (see n. 1) as a "service translation." Unlike the translator of *Li Fet des Romains* who explicitly acknowledged the various classical sources of his work,[16] or unlike Nicolas de Senlis who admitted the authority of the anonymous writer of the *Pseudo-Turpin*, or unlike Jean de Meun who granted, in his translation of *De Consolatione*, the superiority of Boethius's thoughts over his own, Drouart, while acknowledging that he translated "a Latin book," never "serves" the author of this book, but rather tries to present his *roman* as his own. All the important distinctions[17] between *De Amore* and *Li Livres d'Amours* can ultimately be traced and "excused" by the translator's appropriation of the work. As long as the translator (no matter how *de facto* faithful) remains a *remanieur* of an unacknowledged authority, he is his own "authority." And in such a situation, the faithfulness of his translation is not essential, but as in any *remaniement*, incidental, for the recasting cannot be really "faithful" by definition.

This typically medieval appropriation of a specific source-authority, and the subsequent establishment of the authority by the recaster / translator, helps us to understand the very nature of *Le Livre d'Enanchet*. What we find in this book is essentially Drouart's traits, so to speak, exaggerated. Written some forty years[18] before Drouart, Enanchet does not even acknowledge that he translates anything. Rather, he writes his own moral treatise, addressed to his son. The results of meditation upon many good readings[19] constitutes thus the subject matter of this treatise. This Franco-Italian version of *De Amore* is contained in the last three books of Enanchet's doctrinal, or *speculum*. Presented in the form of a dialogue between Enanchet the father (teacher) and his son and heir (pupil), Book 1 offers a disquisition of moral duties (*la dotrine*) of the different classes of people (children, different orders of clergy, working men, merchants, other artisans, doctors, judges, courtiers, slaves, knights, ladies, young men). Book II treats these different estates historically. Enanchet gives thus an explanation of the origin of human society.[20] The first two books need not occupy us here, except for the following two points: (1) although he paraphrases the Bible and "cribs" from some scholastic writers here and there, Enanchet does not seem to translate any specific texts in either of the first two books; (2) he has a "doctrine" of moral literature which he exposes at the outset of his book. It is worth quoting here, because, I believe, it excuses in advance any liberty that he takes with the text of *De Amore*:

> Enanchet por soi dit que trois choses portienent as autor. C'est matire, ententions et utilité. Matire est mere de la chouse, si com lo fer est dou cortel. Ententions est l'aovrement de l'oevre. Utilité est l'onor e-l preu de matire et et d'ententions. Mes en cest livre est matire, ententions et utilité. Matire est la dotrine. Ententions son aovrement. Utilité est conclusions de matire et d'ententions."
>   (p. 2)

> [Enanchet says himself that three things belong to authors: the subject matter, the intention, and the usefulness. The subject matter is the mother of the thing, just as the iron is the mother of the knife. The intention is the elaboration of the work. The usefulness is the honor and the profit of the subject matter and of the intention. In this book there are the subject matter, the intention, and the usefulness. The subject matter is the doctrine. The intention its elaboration. The usefulness is the combination of the subject matter and the intention.]

There is no doubt that Enanchet applied his theory faithfully to the translation-exploitation of Andreas's *tractatus*. His Book 3 is introduced by an apostrophe to the "doctrine of Love" in which, again, Enanchet hints at his own and his readers' *theoretical* independence from any model texts: "M'ame est exaucíe de sor les nues por les rechoises que vos m'avez donees. Don ge vos proi, la

doctrine d'amor, a ce que chascuns qui viaut enseignament, poise
trover en moi ce que il plus aime en dotrine" [p. 41, my punctuation;
My soul is exalted above the clouds by the riches that you have
given me. Thus I beg you, doctrine of love, that everyone who seeks
instruction could find in me what he loves the most in the doctrine].
Notice in passing the highly elevated and fundamentally religious
tone of this opening passage. Enanchet wishes his reader to find
what he loves most in the book that he begins to compose. He
doubtless had the same selective attitude towards Andreas's text.
But there must not have been much that he himself found "to love"
in the *dotrine* of *De Amore*, for he omits a great deal from it and, at
the same time, modifies it by adding his own materials as well as
materials that he found elsewhere.

Let us see some of the important omissions as well as other
significant modifications and additions that he introduced into the
text of *De Amore*. The introductory definition of love is replaced by
Enanchet's own very idealist, Christian concept:

> Amors est generablement pleement a la chouse delitable
> com destendemant a li. Mes les boens amor est fontaine
> et naissimant de tot bien; por ce qe-u douz sangnors [r.
> Sangnors] est amors, dilecion et charitez. Et il est
> fontainne et naissimant de toz bien. Autresi est amor
> leece d'ame et tribulacions de cors.   (p. 42)

> [Love is generally an inclination toward the delectable
> thing as if it were an extension of it. But the good love
> is the fountain and the birthplace of all good; because the
> sweet Lord is love, delight, and charity. And thus He is
> the fountain and the birthplace of all good. Similarly,
> love is the jubilation of the soul and the tribulation of the
> body.]

Note only faint echoes of Andreas's "medical" definition in the first
sentence.[21]   But note also that from the beginning, Enanchet
distinguishes between *love* and *good love*. Immediately after this, he
launches into the exposition of the origin of love by giving the story

of Adam and Eve.[22] The love described here is very like the love in Andreas's Book 3, "The Rejection of Love."   Like Drouart, Enanchet does not formally reproduce this book, but states here and there throughout his text the basically Christian, anti-fornication, and anti-adultery views.   Love defined in "Ondes vient amor" [Whence does love come] was instituted for procreation (but "sanz desir de char ni de sanc" [p. 46; without carnal or blood desire]; see Fiebig's comment on this line, p. 110), for mutual support, and for maintaining the sacrament of the Church.   Enanchet, like Drouart, omits the *lai*, culminating in the reception of the first set of love commandments.   (He also omits the second, Arthurian, *lai* with its second set of the rules of love.)   Introducing the first (and only) set of his rules, he simply says: "Donques chascuns qui viaut amer, covient savoir huit principax comandemanz d'amor" [p. 47; Thus any one who desires to love should know the eight principal commandments of love].   His eight rules can serve as an example of the extreme freedom with which he treats Andreas's subject matter, even in the passages that he obviously "translates," i.e., reproduces the ideas of the Latin model text which he has before him.   First of all, he reduces the twelve *regulae* in the *De Amore* to eight.   He omits the ninth, the tenth, and the twelfth rules of the *De Amore* (dealing with the proscription of malicious speech, secrecy of love, and respect of the desire of the lovers in practising love).   Only his 1, "cortoisie sanz aucune vilenie" [courtliness without any vile thought or action]; 2, "largece sanz avarice" [generosity without avarice]; and V, "non eschafer soi de celi que no covient a fame" [do not love a woman who would not fittingly be your wife], correspond (more or less) to Andreas's ninth, first, and fourth rules respectively. Enanchet's 6 and 7: "estre creenter d'amor" [be a protector of love] and "honorer les fames an totes gises" [honor the women in all possible ways] reflect Andreas's seventh rule.   But most importantly, Enanchet adds his own three rules: 4, "non amer fame de religion" [do not love a nun], echoes the injunction embodied in Andreas's Book 1, Chapter 7, "De amore monacharum" [the love of nuns].   But his rules 8, "ardimanz sanz coardise" [courage without cowardice], and 3, "non amer fame d'autrui" [do not love someone else's wife] do not have counterparts in Andreas.   The last goes against the very basis of the ideology on which *De Amore* is built.

There is no doubt, however, that Enanchet had the text of Andreas before him. After having very briefly defined three types of love (the third seems to be an echo of the *amor de lonh* [p. 49; love from afar], and declared the clergy ineligible for love service,[23] Enanchet begins to follow the text of Book I, Chapter V, "What persons are fit for love."[24] Let us glance at the source-text and its translation:

Est nunc videre, quae sint aptae personae ad amoris arma ferenda. Et scire debes, quod omnis compos mentis, qui aptus est ad Veneris opera peragenda, potest amoris pertingi aculeis, nisi aetas impediat vel caecitas vel nimia voluptatis abundantia. Aetas impedit, quia post sexagesimum annum in masculo et post quinquagesimum in femina, licet coire homo possit, eius tamen voluptas ad amorem deduci non potest. . . . (p. 11)

[We must now see what persons are fit to bear the arms of love. You should know that everyone of sound mind who is capable of doing the work of Venus may be wounded by one of Love's arrows, unless prevented by age, or blindness, or excess of passion. Age is a bar, because after the sixtieth year in a man and the fiftieth in a woman, although one may have intercourse, his passion cannot develop into love. . . .]

Donques est droit veoir as quex se convienent amor, a ce que ma dotrine i poise valoir. Chascuns home en puet joir second ce que il est, estier qe sa etez, ou le suen avoglemenz, ou le trop desir no l'encombre. Sa etez l'encombre puis setante anz, ou il voile ou non. Et la fame puis cinquante anz. Com il poissent geisir ensemble chaitivement, anpuis ni poient-il demener lor desirs ausi come covient a amor. . . . (pp. 49-50)

[It is thus proper to see for whom love is suitable, according to my doctrine. Any man can practice it as he is, provided that he is not barred from it by his age, his

blindness, or the excess of desire. His age bars him after
the seventieth year. And the woman after the fiftieth.
They still can lie together badly, however they cannot
carry out their desire as it fits love. . . .]

It is clear that Enanchet, despite his writing in prose, is even less
exact in reproducing Andreas's thoughts than Drouart (see his
rendering of the lines 465-81). There is even greater "down-to-
earth" simplification taking place here. Where the Latin author
speaks in a precise, technical language of "everyone of sound mind,"
our Franco-Italian translator simply generalizes "any man." When
the learned Andreas writes "to bear the arms of love," Enanchet
simply and prosaically translates "to love." Similarly the fancy
"doing the work of Venus" and "Love's arrows" are rendered by a
more pedestrian *en joir* (lit. to enjoy it). More important, however,
is the inserted phrase "a ce que ma dotrine i poise valoir" [according
to my doctrine, lit. so that my doctrine may be of value here]. Like
Drouart (who will write: "Et vous poez de moy tenir" [v. 468; and
you can take it from me], Enanchet insists, in this ideologically
crucial passage, on his own teaching. Neither of them "serves"
Andreas. Both expound what they wish us to think to be their own
dotrine.[25]

Enanchet follows more or less faithfully Andreas's text to the
end of Book 1, Chapter 6. But even here, he inserts his very own
passages (under the rubrics "Qe feit cortoisie en amor" [What is the
role of courtliness in love] and "Coment se doit parler as fames"
[How one should speak to women]) or the passages taken from other
sections of *De Amore* ("Por qe les fames ni otrient les voloir des
amant" [Why women refuse their lovers' wishes], "Les joiaux que se
covient as fames" [The jewels which befit women], and "Les joiaux
des chivaler" [Knights' jewels]), or the passages that he found
elsewhere. Thus the ideologically very significant sections (pp.
59-61): "Les signe d'amor" [The signs of love], "Qu'est endice"
[What is an indication], "Qu'est signes" [What is a sign], and
"Qu'est sospirs" [What is a sigh] are translated-elaborated from
another, unacknowledged Latin source: Magister Boncompagno's
Rota Veneris (composed before 1215).[26] One could write very well

on "Enanchet, translator of Boncompagno," but the term "translator" would be even more tenuous than in relationship with Andreas, and this simply on account of quantity, rather than quality of translation. More indirectly influenced by Boncompagno are the short passages which follow here introducing the dialogues ("La pistre de trametre a s'amie" [The letter to be sent to his beloved]--"La responsions" [The answer] pp. 63-65). They deal with the epistolary art, Boncompagno's specialty.[27]

As with anything else, Enanchet takes far greater liberties with the dialogues than Drouart. In fact, while incorporating certain thoughts, which Andreas placed in the dialogues, throughout his text, he reproduces explicitly only five dialogues: (1) "A man of the middle class speaks with a woman of the same class" is preceded by a somewhat misleading rubric, "Ci parole l'ome cola fame" [p. 67; Here the man speaks with the woman]. Its concluding section, "Ci respont la pucele esposee a l'amant" [p. 72; Here a married young woman answers her beloved] is "lifted" from another dialogue. (2) "A man of middle class speaks with a woman of higher nobility" is rendered, quite correctly, as "Ci parole un borgois a une contoise" [pp. 72-76; Here a bourgeois speaks with a countess]. (3) "A man of higher nobility speaks with a woman of the middle class" contains, like the next, a change in rank: "Ci parole uns vavesor a une borgese" [pp. 76-78; Here a noble vavassor speaks to a bourgeois woman]. (4) "A nobleman speaks with a woman of the middle class is rendered as "Ci parole li cuens a une borgoise" [pp. 78-85; Here a count speaks to a bourgeois woman]. Finally, (5) Enanchet's section "Ansi se parole a la fame desamoree [pp. 85-89; Thus one speaks to a woman who does not love] contains materials taken largely from "A nobleman speaks with a noblewoman." The treatment of the dialogues, which are after all the most important part of *De Amore*, is typical in this recasting / translation. Enanchet is apparently not interested in the finer shades of Andreas's "sociology" of love. Neither is he interested in the "symmetry" with which this "sociology" is presented.[28] Here, as elsewhere, he is concerned, as he said in his Introduction (p. 41), that "one who wishes to receive instruction may find what he loves most in the doctrine."

The following section "Coment se doit donegier en autrui pais" [pp. 89-91; How one must court women abroad] does not correspond to anything in *De Amore*. Likewise, "Le donegier des filles des laboreors" [pp. 91-92; Courting of peasants' daughters] does not contain any direct "borrowings" from Andreas's "The Love of Peasants," except that it treats a generally similar subject matter. After these two sections, Enanchet seems to be ready to end his treatise: "Filz, ge t'ai apris en amor, por que tu lo me querris, a ce que tu poisses satisfer a chascun en dotrine; et se plus viauz, demande seurement! car tu l'auras" [p. 92; Son, I have taught you about love, because you have asked me, and so that you might satisfy every one in teaching it; and if you wish more, ask surely and you will receive it]. The most obedient son thanks his father: "Benoiz soit li sermons de la vostre boche qui m'a dotrinez ausi sotilment!" [Blessed be the speech of your mouth which has taught me so subtly], asks indeed a question concerning buying of love, and demands some of love's *sentences*. This gives the father the chance to reproduce (pp. 92-94) Book 1, Chapter 9, "The Love of Prostitutes." As for the *sentences*, he warns his son against "fames luxuroises" and "vileins luxurios" [pp. 94-95; lascivious women and lascivious vile men], in the passages containing only faint echoes of Andreas.

The rest of *Le Livre d'Enanchet* consists of three short sections or chapters. They do not contain anything taken from Andreas and could be dismissed as not of direct interest to us here. But since they explain the sense not so much of translation but of the undeniable ideological coherence of his recasting, let us briefly touch upon them. These sections are doubtless an expression of the author's own ideology, which here goes against everything that Andreas said (except in his final *Rejection of Love*). But Enanchet's rejection of love is very different from Andreas's (and Drouart's). It contains no traces of misogyny. In its Christian idealism, it goes beyond anything that Andreas and Boncompagno have said. The first section, "La chastiement de son hoir" [p. 96; Instruction of his heir] is a short sermon on the theme "ge te proi que tu aimes amor, c'est lo douz segnor (r. Segnor). Et fui luxure! a ce que tu poises joir en cest monde et puis apres lui" [I beg you to love love, for it is the sweet Lord. And flee lust! so you may enjoy this world and the one after]. The second chapter, "Conclusion de ceste doctrine" [pp. 96-97; Conclusion of this doctrine] is largely a translation of the final lines of *Rota Amoris*.[29] Boncompagno wrote his own brief and rather perfunctory rejection of love stating that Solomon himself wrote the *Song of Songs*, where love is presented as Christ's relationship with his Church. Enanchet translates this faithfully and then develops this idea in a way which led Fiebig to call it "the sudden religious shift" (die plötzliche religiöse Umbiegung).[30] The development consists of the following passage which ends in a prayer:

> Don ge proi chascun qu'il retornent la ou ge ai escriz qe Dex est amor, et notent ce qu'il i troveront escriz. Apres sachent qui [*sic*] je ai mise la pucele et la dame en leu de la preciouse Virge seinte Marie, por qu'ele fu sovraine Pucele et Dame qui onques fust, ni que soit, ni qui sera. Pucele, ainz qui nasquist de [li] li douz Sangnor; Pucele et Dame puis sa naission, a ce qu'ele soit deproiee doucement por ses amanz. Don je la proi ausi com douce Dame et Roine de Paradis qu'ele est, et Port de tote pitié, qu'ele deproie son Creator, Pere et Fil, car, si ge ai mis aucune chouse por l'adornement de l'oevre, qu'il m'en face estre verrais penetant ou tot ce que ge li ai forfeit, si com mauvais serjanz que ge sui contre teu Sangnor, com il est. Et d'or avant moi conferme au suen servise, ausi qe-u Cors dou suen precious Fil promaingne en moi, ausi com il devroit de raison. Soit ausi! (p. 97)[31]

[Thus I ask all to go back to the place where I have written that God is love, and to note what they find there. They should know that I have put the young woman and the lady in place of the precious Virgin Saint Mary, because She was the most sovereign Virgin and Lady who ever was, who is and who shall be. Virgin She was before the sweet Lord was born of Her; Virgin and Lady after His birth, so that She might be besought on behalf of those who love Her. I beseech Her as the sweet Lady and Queen of Paradise that She is, and as the Port of all

> compassion, that She pray Her Creator, Father and Son,
> because, if I have written something to embellish my
> work, may He make me a true penitent in everything that
> I have sinned against Him, as a bad servant that I am of
> such a Lord that he is. And henceforth may I be
> confirmed in His service, so that the Body of His
> precious Son may remain with me, as it reasonably
> should. Amen!]

This could have been the real ending of Enanchet's book, but it is not. He continues the eternal dialogue between the fundamentally irreconcilable Christian and courtly ideologies[32] and turns again to his beloved *dame* in "Ceste epistre tramist Annanchet a la celerere de joie" [pp. 97-98; Annanchet sent this letter to the dispenser (lit. "cellar-keeper") of joy]. The lover-author blesses her as his "doucisme celerere de ma vie" [sweetest dispenser of my life][33] and then prays to God thanking Him for all the "splendors" that he received through his lady love. He begs her again to have him for her faithful lover. All this is couched in the fanciful language of a love epistle.

The only truly "sudden religious shift" in these final passages is the explicit identification of the beloved with the Virgin (no such development in Boncompagno). But it is not really "sudden." A careful reader of Enanchet should have been prepared for this development. The introductory passages (as Enanchet says it himself here) are certainly imbued with the God is love idea.

This religious framework permits us to seize not only the gist of Enanchet's ideology, which is staunchly orthodox Christian, but also to understand the real scope of his indebtedness to Andreas. *Grosso modo*, the beginning and the end are either Enanchet's or taken by him from elsewhere. The middle section of the treatise is a recasting / paraphrase / translation from Andreas. In this section, he either translates certain passages from *De Amore* (chiefly from its Book 1), respecting the order in which they are presented, or he gleans certain ideas (chiefly from Books 2 and 3), arranging them in his own structure. If, as Enanchet says, "matire est la dotrine," the subject matter of Enanchet comes largely from him, from the *Vita Adae et Evae* and from the *Rota Amoris*, but the "entention" and the elaboration ("aovrement") of the doctrine come largely from Andreas.

The two recastings / translations of *De Amore* tell us something important about the thirteenth-century French translations from Latin. Neither can be called a faithful translation, for they "hide," so to speak, the source-text. The difference between them is not one in kind, but rather in degree. If we discard the chronology, we can say that Enanchet exaggerated the main tendency of Drouart to make the translation his own book. Neither of the texts represents thus a "service translation," that is to say, a translation which "serves" the acknowledged *authority* of the Latin text. Neither of the texts distinguishes between the functions of compiler and translator: both introduced in their texts the matter found outside *De Amore*.[34]

There is no doubt in my mind that the acceptance of the idea of service translation, with its concomitant, albeit inexplicit, superiority of the source text over the target text was a *sine qua non* for the development of translation as we know it. Thus, in the final analysis, the nature of the text translated had a preponderant influence on the nature of the translation. The "truth" of sacred or secular history could doubtlessly find a "service translator" more easily than the opinions of learned treatises, not to speak of the "fables" of fiction. The problem of "truth" in writing was a very serious one (especially after 1200). Distinctions between the "truth" of what "really" happened, the "truth" of what could have happened, and the "lie" of fictional tales were deeply felt. Isidore of Seville, that fountainhead of medieval wisdom, stated this unambiguously, long before 1200: "Item inter historiam et argumentum et fabulam interesse. Nam historiae sunt res verae quae factae sunt; argumenta sunt quae etsi facta non sunt, fieri tamen possunt; fabulae vero sunt quae nec fieri possunt, quia contra naturam sunt"[35] [We must distinguish between history, argument, and fable. Histories are the real things which have happened; arguments are those which did not happen, but could have happened; fables are those which could not have happened, because they are against nature]. Our two recasters / translators did not, I am sure, suffer any qualms from hiding the identity of their source and taking all the liberties with it, for after all, what they translated was not the "truth." Andreas's text with all its sophistication and eloquence was apparently no more prestigious than their literary ambition. He was not an authority to be served (like those Latin historians served by the anonymous translator / compiler of *Li Fet des Romains*), but simply a body of opinion (of *argumenta*) to be made their own.

In the final analysis, the greatest importance of Enanchet and of Drouart lies in the fact that in their recasting (Enanchet) or pretended recasting (Drouart), they had a recourse to translation. Since medieval writing was (always in theory and often in practice) a rewriting, it is important that this rewriting could take the form of translation. It is particularly important in Drouart, because he explicitly said that his book, his (re)writing, was translated. Such uses of translation in compilations and recastings made the reading public used to the idea of translation, preparing thus the real "service translations" which would become more common not long after Drouart la Vache "rhymed" his *Livre d'Amours* for his lady love.

NOTES

1. *Viator* 17 (1986):255-66.

2. The treatise is also known as *Tractatus de Amore*, *Tractatus Amoris*, *Liber Amoris*, *De Arte honeste amandi*, etc. The text was edited by E. Trojel, *Andreae Capellani regii Francorum De Amore libri tres* (Copenhagen: Libraria Gadiana, 1892); henceforth cited as *De Amore*. English translations of Andreas's text supplied here come from John J. Perry, trans., *The Art of Courtly Love* (New York: W. W. Norton, 1969).

3. Werner Fiebig, ed., *Das "Livre d'Enanchet" nach der einzigen Handschrift der Wiener Nationalbibliothek*, Berliner Beiträge zur romanischen Philologie, 8, 3/4 (Jena: W. Gronau, 1938). The Book 3 of Enanchet was discovered and edited by Adolf Mussafia in "Über Bonvesin da Riva und eine altfranzösische Handschrift der K. K. Hofbibliothek," *Sitzungsberichte der kaiserlichen Akademie der Wissenschaften, philosophisch-historische Classe* 39 (Vienna: K. Gerold's Sohn, 1862), pp. 546-53. V. Putanec made known the existence of: "Un second manuscrit du *Livre d'Enanchet*," *Romania* 70 (1948):74-83. The concluding part of this manuscript is missing. In 1960, Fiebig announced his plans for a new edition, but as far as I could ascertain, they were not realized. See his "Das

'*Livre d'Enanchet.*' Zur Frage der Namensdeutung und zu seinen Quellen," *Zeitschrift für französische Sprache und Literatur* 70 (1960):198. A new edition would certainly be useful. Fiebig's use of capital letters makes the reading often difficult [see n. 33 below]: his punctuation is sometimes uncertain; most of the textual footnotes are unnecessary; many difficult passages are left unexplained; and his glossary is certainly insufficient, for it tries to add to the store of knowledge of Old French dictionaries rather than to elucidate difficult terms of the text.

4.   Robert Bossuart, ed., *Li Livres d'Amours de Drouart la Vache, texte établi d'après le manuscrit unique de la Bibliothèque de l'Arsenal* (Paris: Champion, 1926).

5.   *Drouart la Vache, traducteur d'André le Chapelain (1290)* (Paris: Champion, 1926); henceforth *Traducteur*.

6.   For some twelfth-century examples of such identification of prose with truth, taken from Nicolas de Senlis, translator of the *Pseudo-Turpin*, as well as two other anonymous translations of this text, and for Pierre de Beauvais, translator of *Physiologus*, see my "Learned Latin Treatises" [n. 1 above], p. 258. It is not easy to distinguish in these assertions the defense of the "truth" and the "excuse" for using prose. It is important to note here that such identification of prose with truth and, inversely, of verse with lie will continue to be one of the intellectual clichés in certain prosifications in the fourteenth and fifteenth centuries. (See Georges Doutrepont, *Les Mises en proses des romans chevaleresques du XIVe au XVe siècles*, Mémoires de l'Académie Royale de Belgique, Classe des lettres, 40 [Brussels: Palais des Académies, 1939], pp. 380-410.) There is no doubt in my mind that the history of prosification parallels that of translation.

7.   Drouart apparently did not know of Enanchet's book. There is a strange, modern parallelism in this. Fiebig (Enanchet's editor) does not mention Bossuat's edition of Drouart. Bossuat, in turn, does not make any reference to Fiebig's edition of Enanchet in his "André le Chapelain," *Dictionnaire des lettres françaises*, 1, *Le Moyen Age* (Paris: Fayard, 1964), p. 55. This (perhaps apparent) ignorance is not surprising if we realize that the two works examined here belong to quite different categories. Except for different degrees of the indebtedness to their common model, they have really little in common.

8. *Traducteur* [n. 5 above], pp. 33-71.

9. Doubtless very influential and certainly typical attitudes can be seen in the intemperate opinion emitted by the great Gaston Paris in his brief and denigrating mention of his discovery of Drouart's text, "Une Traduction d'André le Chapelain," *Romania* 13 (1884):403. Bossuat sums up very aptly the results of Paris's judgement. It "rejeta le poème de Drouart dans l'oubli, d'où il ne l'avait momentanément tiré que pour fonder sur lui d'irréalisables espoirs" [*Traducteur* (n. 5 above), p. vii; he threw back Drouart's poem into oblivion, from where he had recovered it, just long enough to place upon it unrealizable hopes]. For positivistic scholars of that epoch such as Adolf Mussafia [n. 3 above], for whom one of the chief objects of research was to unearth and identify the "sources" and "influences" in the work studied, the early Old French recastings / translations were disappointing. The sources and influences were both obvious (and like love in *De Amore*, too easily acquired, therefore unworthy) and deformed. Thus, he describes Enanchet's Book 3 as "grösstenteils nichts anders als ein Auszug, oft eine buchstäbliche Übersetzung aus dem bekannten 'Tractatus amoris' des Andreas Capellanus" [p. 547; mostly nothing else but an extract, often a literal translation, of the well-known "Treatise on Love" of Andreas Capellanus]. Pio Rajna was even more explicitly ill-disposed to Enanchet: ". . . questa parte ci si dà conoscere come una mal digesta mescolanza di roba cavata fuori dal tratato di Andrea, con pensieri propri o presi d'altronde" [. . . this part (=Book 3) reveals itself as a badly digested mixture of things pulled out of Andreas treatise, of his own ideas, or of ideas taken from elsewhere]. After stressing the divergencies between Andreas and Enanchet, Rajna finally finds the sole virtue in the latter's work: it testifies to the wide influence (*divulgazione*) of the former. ("Per Andrea Cappellano," *Studi di Filologia Romanza* 5 (1891):209. More recent literature on Enanchet and Drouart lays stress not so much on the problems of translation as on the *Rezeptionsgeschichte* of *De Amore*. Thus Alfred Karnein, *De Amore in volkssprachlicher Literatur*, Germanisch-Romanische Monatsschrift, Beiheft 4 (Heidelberg: C. Winter, 1985) studies the echo of Andreas's treatise in medieval France, Italy, and Germany. The work of Enanchet is analyzed briefly on pp. 179-84. In discussing Drouart (pp. 184-87), Karnein returns to the problem of the general tone of his *roman* (amused, laughing, smiling?) raised by Barbara Nelson Sargent in "Medieval Commentary of Andreas Capellanus," *Romania* 95 (1973):528-41.

10.   The main point concerning translation problems presented by Jeanette M. A. Beer in her excellent study of *Li Fet des Romains* (*A Medieval Caesar*), Etudes de Philologie et d'Histoire 30 (Geneva: Droz, 1976) is precisely this: the compiler-translator is capable of being "faithful," but he adapts the material to suit his own medium.

11.   In Drouart's poem the dialogues take up some 3100 verses, that is to say, less than 40% of his text.

12.   Drouart's translations of the *regulae amoris* reveal a common problem of Old French translators from Latin. Andreas presents the rules in a lapidary, epigrammatic fashion. The Latin economy of words cannot be reproduced in Old French. (See the discussion of rendering *veni, vidi, vici*, in *A Medieval Caesar* [n. 10 above], pp. 2-5.) He seems to have misunderstood rule 12: instead of stressing the monogamous character of love, as does Andreas, Drouart repeats the idea of rule 5: "Nus loiax amans n'est tentés / D'acomplirre ses volentés, / Contre la volenté s'amie" [lines 6519-21; No loyal lover is tempted to accomplish his desires against the desire of his beloved].

13.   One of the differences between *De Amore* and *Li Livres d'Amours* is caused by an external factor: the rubricator in the former divided the material clearly into three books. In Drouart's text, the system of rubrics (sometimes in French, sometimes in Latin) is entirely different: it stresses the unity of the work, rather than the tripartite, antithetic division. Thus the last part of the *Livre d'Amours* (corresponding approximately to Book 3 of Andreas) is entitled "Por quoi et comment Amours est reprovee" [Why and How is Love Rejected] and constitutes its Chapter 23 (lines 6573-7546).

14.   The last ninety verses are devoted to praising his book, written for clerks rather than for "les laies gens / Qui sont .i. peu nices et foles" [lines 7550-51; . . . for lay people who are a little ignorant and foolish] and to giving the date of the work and the name (DROUARS) and surname (LAVAHCE, *sic*) of the author in the form of an all too easily decipherable enigma.

15.   *Traducteur* [n. 5 above], pp. 63-64.

16.   See *A Medieval Caesar* [n. 10 above], pp. 31-35.

17.   For the other distinctions (suppressions, additions, inventions, and updatings), see *Traducteur* [n. 5 above], pp. 41-61. Although this phrase appears in a passage that Enanchet translates-paraphrases from the text of the *Rota Veneris* (ed. Friedrich Baethgen, Texte zur Kultur-geschichte des Mittelalters 1 [Rome: W. Regenberg, 1927]), the idea is his own.

18.   The date of Enanchet's composition is often given as 1287 (see *Traducteur* [n. 5 above], p. 23). This is the date of the manuscript. For the date of the composition (circa 1250), see Fiebig's Introduction [n. 3 above], p. xxxv.

19.   See, for example, "Don ge ai cerchee maintes ystoyres por soe membrance, es les queles ai trouvez que Salemons . . . escrist . . ." [p. 96; Thus I have perused many histories for an indication of it, among which I have found that Salomon . . . wrote. . .].

20.   In the manuscript, the division into three books is marked either by a large initial letter or by an empty space.

21.   Note also the concrete character of Enanchet's vocabulary; *pleement* means literally "bending" or "folding."

22.   Fiebig traces the source of this passage specifically to the *Vita Adae et Evae* (ed. Wilhelm Meyer, Abhandlungen der bayerischen Akademie der Wissenschaften, 3, Abteilung 14 [Munich: Akademie der Wissenschaften, 1878], pp. 192-228).

23.   Fiebig, faithful to his positivistic desire to discover any possible source of Enanchet's texts, offers in his footnotes the passages of *De Amore* which parallel or echo the ideas in the Franco-Italian text, confusing thus translated passages with those which merely reflect similar ideas. A good example of the latter is his citing of the passage from Book 1, Chapter 7, "The Love of the Clergy," which accompanies Enanchet's opinion on the subject: "Des clers ne voil-ge pas dire en cist livre, por q'il deivent sorestier a lor oreison, et no deivent pas metre son estude temporablement contre fame, por qu'il en perdront les gloires de paradis ou l'onor de cest

monde, et ele en sera ausi honie, que a grant peine recovera-ele mes honor"
[p. 49; I do not want to speak in this book about the clerics, because they
should remain at their prayers and should not direct their worldly efforts
toward a woman, because by it they will lose the glory of Paradise and the
honor in this world, and she (=the woman loved) will also be held in
contempt so much that she will recover her honor with great difficulties].
It is obvious to me that this opinion has very little to do with the more
nuanced and permissive attitude of Andreas. A casual perusal of Fiebig's
edition can certainly give the impression that Enanchet "translated"
Andreas far more than he in fact did.

24.   If there is no doubt in my mind that Enanchet had Andreas's text
before him, the same thing cannot be said about the rubricator. The section
in question is preceded by a misleading rubric: "Coment eté encombre
amor" [How age is an impediment to love]. We see this kind of misleading
rubric often in Enanchet. They do not contribute to our perception of the
coherence of the text. In comparison, the rubrics in Drouart follow rather
faithfully the text of *De Amore* (but see n. 13 above).

25.   The Franco-Italian text contains an actual error (not commented
on by the editor): *post sexagesimum annum* [after the sixtieth year]
becomes *puis setante anz* [after the seventieth year]. This error could very
well have been due to the (doubtless fifty-nine-year-old) scribe, but in any
event, it shows again the freedom with which Andreas, text is treated either
by the translator or by the copyist even in this obviously translated passage.

26.   See n. 17 above. Fiebig was not aware of this text-model when
he prepared his edition. It was pointed out by M. Forte, "L'*Enanchet* e la
Rota Veneris," *Archivum Romanicum* 22 (1938):392-98. Fiebig discusses it
in his 1960 article [n. 3 above]. The extent of the "borrowings" from the
Rota as well as other problems of Enanchet's text have been very aptly
appraised by Ernstpeter Ruhe, "Enanchet--'semplice compilatore'?,"
Neuphilologische Mitteilungen 71 (1970):1-28. For the passage concerning
the sighs, obviously translated from the *Rota*, see p. 24. Ruhe is not so
much interested in translation *per se* as in the problems of the compiler
who arranges what he has found elsewhere in a *coherent* text of his own.
He sees compilations as a serious (sub)genre of medieval literature, and he
is right.

27.   See Ruhe [n. 26 above], pp. 12-13.

28.   Note, however, that even in the text of *De Amore* this symmetry is flawed by the omission of a dialogue by a nobleman (*nobilis*) with a woman of higher nobility (*nobilior*), a most natural, realistic social situation, it seems to me, at the court of Marie de Champagne. I must confess that I do not know of any discussion of this omission by Andreas. Could he have considered such a particular dialogue as dangerous?

29.   See Ruhe [n. 26 above], pp. 8-9.

30.   Introduction [n. 3 above], p. xxx. As we know, Fiebig was unaware that the first part of this passage was taken from the *Rota Amoris*. The "sudden religious shift" applies also to Boncompagno's evocation of the *Song of Songs*.

31.   In order to facilitate the reading of this crucial passage, I capitalized the names of the Trinity, as well as the various allegorical appellations of the Virgin. (See n. 33 below.)

32.   *De Amore* (and its two Old French recastings / translations) testify perhaps better than other contemporary works to this irreconcilability. Cesare Segre (*Grundriss der romanischen Literaturen des Mittelalters*, vol. 6, 1 [Heidelberg: C. Winter, 1968], p. 116) is right when he reaffirms the "essenziale estraneità delle teoriche cortesi alla morale cristiana" [essential incompatibility of courtly theoretical positions with Christian morality].

33.   This sudden shift back to the courtliness was not noticed by certain commentators who simply took "la celerere de joie" [the dispenser of joy] as being yet another allegorical name for the Virgin. (See, e.g., Ferdinand Wolf, *Altfranzösischen Doctrinen und Allegorien von der Minne*, Denkschriften der kaiserlichen Akademie der Wissenschaften, philosophisch-historische Classe, 13, 1 [Vienna: K. Gerold's Sohn, 1864], p. 191.) Ruhe [n. 26 above], p. 7, shares Wolf's opinion and considers it as generally ("gemeinhin") held. He further criticizes Pio Rajna [see n. 9 above, p. 208] for not giving any reasons why he believed that the *celerere* is the author's lady love. Let me supply these reasons; they pertain to Christian cult: Enanchet begins his letter by a formal, trinitarian blessing:

"La grace de Deu Pere omnipotent et la gloire dou suen Fil Jesucrist et enspiramenz dou Saint Espriz sempres soit a vos, doucisme celerere de ma vie . . ." [p. 97, my capitalization; The grace of God the Father almighty, the glory of His Son Jesus Christ and the inspiration of the Holy Spirit be always with you, sweetest dispenser of my life. . .]. Since the Virgin is already blessed, such a blessing cannot be addressed to Her. The *celerere* cannot be the *Celerere*, it must be a human being. Note the importance of proper, modern French capitalization in the editing of Old French texts.

34. Drouart "borrows" many ideas from various sources, without, however, translating long passages from them, as Enanchet did. See *Traducteur* [n. 5 above], pp. 74-115.

35. *Etymologiae*, ed. W. M. Lindsay (Oxford: Oxford Univ. Press, 1911), 1.44.5 (I cite this passage from *A Medieval Caesar* [n. 10 above], p. 69). Although *argumentum* in Isidore means a "possible fiction," rather than more narrowly "learned opinions," his distinctions certainly apply to the two Old French translators of *De Amore*.

DIRECT SPEECH--A KEY
TO THE GERMAN ADAPTOR'S ART?

Karen Pratt

Passages of direct speech in Old French romances have a variety of functions. Around sections of dialogue are constructed what modern critics frequently designate as "scenes" (a term which usefully underlines the dramatic nature of much medieval narrative), while monologues and especially laments often serve as lyrical interludes in both epic and romance. Dialogue and soliloquy also provide a means of presenting character directly and dramatically (a person's words revealing his personality without the intervention of the narrator) as well as of conveying a character's momentary emotional state. They are thus useful tools for psychological investigation by the poet and are generally expected by the critic to meet criteria of realism or *vraisemblance*. However, some less plausible passages of speech can be included by the author in order to develop his own message and his moral conception of the material. Debate may be encouraged through the juxtaposition of conflicting views within dialogue or through the creation of oppositions within a monologue. Both types of utterance are then a vehicle for deliberative or persuasive rhetoric, thus revealing the schooling or *clergie* of the medieval poet. Furthermore, a work's general tone or ethos can be conveyed through direct discourse. *Courtoisie* or the lack of it are detectable in the protagonist's words, his use of salutations, and in the form of address he chooses. It has even been suggested that *oratio recta* plays an important role in the structuring of a whole work, the divisions of the narrative being more easily recognizable by an audience if they are marked by direct speech.[1]

The richness of function of direct speech was clearly recognized not only by the authors of French romances, but also by the German adaptors of these sources. Indeed, the translation of *oratio recta* provided the latter with a special challenge, to which they responded in a variety of ways. One of the conclusions of Michel Huby's study of adaptation in Germany in the late twelfth and early thirteenth centuries[2] is that direct speech in particular offered adaptors great scope for individual, independent treatment and extensive modification. Huby concentrates on changes from direct to indirect speech and vice versa, from monologue to dialogue and the reverse, and on alterations in the length or content of utterances. He also treats the omission or addition of speeches. Unfortunately, though, he is often content with mere numerical analysis, and many possible literary observations are left unmade. Though statistics compiled by Peter Wiehl will be included here, I prefer to concentrate on the literary effect of these modifications on the form, content, and ethos not only of isolated passages of speech, but of the adaptations as a whole.

The corpus of material from which my examples are taken spans some thirty years of adaptation in Germany. Veldeke's translation of the *Roman d'Enéas*, which also drew on Virgil's *Aeneid*, was completed by 1190 and marked, according to Gottfried von Strassburg in the literary excursus in his *Tristan*, the first grafting of French courtly culture onto the root-stock of German literature:

> er impete daz êrste rîs
> in tiutescher zungen;   (lines 4736-37)[3]
>
> [he grafted the first scion
> in the German tongue]

Hartmann's works (including his translations of Chrétien's *Erec et Enide* and *Yvain*, dated c. 1190 and 1200 respectively) represented in Gottfried's eyes an ideal: the epitome of clarity:

> wie lûter und wie reine
> sîn kristallîniu wortelîn
> beidiu sint und iemer müezen sîn!   (lines 4626-28)

[how limpid and how clear
his crystalline words
both are and always will be]

In the first decade of the thirteenth century Meister Otte wrote his adaptation of Gautier d'Arras's *Eracle*, a romance version of the life of the emperor Heraclius. In his concern for historicity and in his use of supplementary chronicle material, Otte's method is somewhat similar to that of Veldeke.[4] Konrad Fleck, in contrast, was greatly influenced by Hartmann; witness the many verbal parallels in the works of the two authors.[5] His reworking of the Old French romance *Floire et Blancheflor* (*version aristocratique*) was composed c. 1220 and can usefully be compared with the translation of the same model into Middle Dutch composed by Diederic van Assenede in Flanders around 1260. Little is known of the biographies or the poetic aspirations of the Germanic adaptors to be treated here.[6] Indeed none of them indulged in the sort of literary criticism practiced by Gottfried. Their attitude to the task of translation therefore has to be gleaned from their own practice, by comparing their adaptations with their Old French models.[7]

Since modification features strongly in the German translator's treatment of direct speech, it must first be ascertained whether or not changes were forced upon the Germans because of the difficulty of translating Old French grammar and syntax into Middle High German.[8] Clearly, there was also the problem of finding suitable pairs of rhymes in German, despite the fact that the metre of German courtly romance (with no fixed number of syllables per line) was more flexible than the Old French octosyllabic rhyming couplet. Furthermore, complete fidelity to the source involved the preservation not only of the content of a speech (lexical equivalents which covered the same semantic field and possessed the same associative and connotative values), but also its formal characteristics. These include the length and number of utterances (which can have a bearing on the importance of the speaker in the work and the persuasive force of his words), the inclusion or omission of *verba dicendi* (the omission creating a more dramatic effect, while the constant use of verbs of speaking draws the audience's attention to

215

the presence of the author / narrator), the use of stichomythia (which can reflect urgency or a troubled or excited state of mind and is often accompanied by the omission of *verba dicendi*), and the exploitation of *brisure du couplet* or *rîme brechen*. The effect of the latter within dialogue is to quicken the pace or to strengthen a question or challenge uttered in the first line of the couplet; if it occurs at the end of dialogue it creates an air of openendedness. *Rîme samenen* (ending a speech on the second line of the couplet), in contrast, makes a person's utterance sound final and definitive, leaving no room for objection or reply.[9]

Despite the complexity of function and effect of direct speech, adaptors were capable of rendering *oratio recta* in their model very accurately if they chose to do so--metrical, semantic, and formal obstacles could largely be overcome. A good illustration of this is Aeneas's conversation with his messengers on their arrival in Carthage. The stichomythia of the *Roman d'Enéas*, reflecting the hero's eagerness to learn news, is retained by Veldeke with minimal amplification, as the following extracts show:

> Contr'els ala et se lor dit: (*verbum dicendi*)
> "Qu'avez trové? - Nos bien. - Et coi?
> - Cartage. - Parlastes al roi?
> - Nenil. - Por coi? - N'i a seignor.
> - Coi donc? - Dido maintient l'enor.
> - Parlastes vos o li? - Oïl.
> - Menace nos? - Par foi, nenil.
> - Et que dist donc? - Promet nos bien,
> soiez segurs, mar crembroiz rien."   (lines 644-52)[10]

[He went to meet them and said to them,
"What did you find?" "Something to our
    advantage." "What was that?"
"Carthage." "Did you speak to the king?"
"No." "Why not?" "There is no lord there."
"What is there then?" "Dido holds sway there."
"Did you speak with her?" "Yes."
"Is she threatening us?" "By my faith, no."
"What did she say then?" "She promises us nothing but

good,
don't worry, there is no need to fear
anything."]

(The men then report Dido's message, ending on line 662 at the end
of the rhyming couplet.)

He sprac: "wat hât ir fonden?"	(*verbum dicendi*)
"allet goet." "ende wat?"	
"Kartâgô." "wat es dat?"	added
"et es ein borch hêre."	added
"dorch got, segget mêre:	added
es sî iet verre?" "nein, si es nâ."	added
"vondet ir den koninc dâ?"	
"da es koninges niet." "wie danne sô?"	
"da es di rîke frouwe Dîdô."	
"sprâket ir sî?" "jâ wir dâden."	
"wie vondet ir sî?" "wale berâden."	
"wat enbôt sî ons?" "allet goet."	
"meinet sî't sô?" "jâ sî doet"	(lines 608-20)[11]

[He said, "What did you find?"
"Nothing but good." "What else?"
"Carthage." "What is that?"
"It is a magnificent town."
"By God, tell me more.
Is it very far?" "No, it is nearby."
"Did you find the king there?"
"There is no king there." "How is that so?"
"Powerful Queen Dido is there."
"Did you speak with her?" "Yes, we did."
"How did you find her?" "Well disposed."
"What did she offer us?" "Nothing but good."
"Does she really mean it?" "Yes, she does."]

(Dido's message, which includes a reference to *êre*, a leitmotif in so
many German adaptations, continues in expanded form to line 639.
It ends on the first line of the couplet, but this is then completed by

217

the innovative comment "doe froude sich Enêas" [line 640; Aeneas was then very pleased].)

Veldeke's preservation of both form and content (including the same form of address *vous / ir*, the identical inclusion only once of the *verbum dicendi* and the same general tone of excitement and nervousness, with a touch of humor concerning Aeneas's sexist assumption about the kingdom's ruler) is not the result of a novice's lack of confidence to stray from his source. It represents, rather, a deliberate choice to translate faithfully on this occasion. Elsewhere he adapts more freely. Indeed, there is no evidence that novice adaptors produced literal translations. On the contrary, it has been noted, in particular by Huby, that Hartmann in the second of his two Arthurian romances, *Iwein*, tends to adhere more closely to his source than in *Erec*.[12] There is therefore no correlation between fidelity and inexperience; adaptors were in control of their art and preserved their models or adapted them freely at will.

Comparison of a passage from *Floire et Blancheflor* translated into two different Germanic languages by Fleck and Diederic bears out this view. When Floire returns from school to find his beloved Blancheflor missing, he inquires of her mother what has become of her:

> -"Dame, fait il, u est m'amie?"
> Cele respont: - "El n'i est mie."
> (B: "Sire, par foi, nen i est mie.")
> -"U est?" - "Ne sai."- "Vos l'apelés!"
> -"Ne sai quel part."- Vos me gabés.
> Celés la vos?"- "Sire, nonal."
> -"Par Diu, fait il, çou est *grant* mal!"   (B: gieu)
> (lines 677-82)[13]

> ["My lady," he says, "where is my beloved?"
> She replies, "She is definitely not here."
> ("My lord, by my faith, she is definitely not here.")
> "Where is she then?" "I don't know." "Call her."
> "I don't know where to call." "You are mocking me.
> Are you hiding her?" "No, my lord, I am not."
> "By God," he says, "this is a terrible thing."]

Although the Flemish adaptor has rearranged his source material somewhat and inserted narrative describing the woman's reaction at an earlier point than in the source (*Floire et Blancheflor*, lines 683-84; Diederic, lines 1064-66), he begins by translating very closely and preserves the three utterances in line 679 of his model (though the subject matter is different) as well as the question and answer within the rhyming couplet (*Floire et Blancheflor*, lines 677-78; Diederic, lines 1060-62):

> "Vrouwe," seit hi, "waer es Blancefloer,
> Mine amië, die ic hier liet?"
> "U amië, des en weet ic niet."
> "Ghi houd u sceren." "In doe." "Gi doet."
> (Three lines of narrative)
> "Roepse mi", seit hi, "haestelike!"
>
> (lines 1060-63; 1067)[14]

> [My lady," he said, "where is Blancefloer,
> my beloved, whom I left here?"
> "Your beloved, I don't know anything about it."
> "You're joking." I'm not." "Yes, you are."
> "Call her for me," he said, "quickly."]

Fleck also retains the *brisure du couplet* (lines 2149-50),[15] but creates a much slower pace in the dialogue by allowing Flôre to make statements as well as to ask questions. What the German adaptor loses in drama and psychological realism he attempts (with little success) to win back in pathos:

> Flôre güetlîch zuo ir sprach
> "wâ ist mîn friundinne?
> sagent, ist sî hinne?
> daz tuont mir kunt an dirre frist."
> "ich enweiz wâ sî ist."
> "die rede lânt" sprach er "durch got,
> zeim andern hânt iuwern spot,
> und lânt mich wizzen, wâ sî sî.
> ez sint wochen wol drî,
> daz ich sî nie gesach mit ougen." (lines 2146-55)

[Flore said to her kindly,
"Where is my beloved?
Tell me, is she here?
Tell me right now."
"I don't know where she is."
"Hold your tongue," he said, "by God
and keep your mockery for another.
Tell me where she is.
It has been a good three weeks
since I saw her with my own eyes."]

Given the similarities between Middle Dutch and Middle High German, it is unlikely that linguistic or metrical difficulties explain the differences between these two translations of the dialogue. It is more likely that they represent two individual attitudes towards translation in the Middle Ages. Diederic's work is throughout a rather close rendering of the source, preserving not only its subject-matter, but many of its stylistic features.[16] Konrad Fleck, in contrast, adapts freely, expanding his source substantially by a quotient of around 2.5.

Theoretical justification for his unwillingness to adhere to the letter of his source may be found in contemporary rhetorical teaching concerning the reworking of traditional material, though nowhere do the *artes poeticae* advocate the extensive reworking Fleck practices. Nevertheless, Geoffroi de Vinsauf's *Documentum de modo et arte dictandi et versificandi* (early thirteenth century) does suggest that an adaptor should not tarry over digressions or descriptions found in the model, but should pass rapidly on; nor should he be tied to his predecessor's pattern of words or their order: "non debemus ibidem immorari circa digressiones vel descriptiones, sed breviter locum illum materiae transilire" [We should not delay on digressions or descriptions, but quickly pass over that place in the material]; "ne sequamur vestigia verborum. . . . Ibi dicamus aliquid ubi dixerunt nihil, et ubi dixerunt aliquid, nos nihil" [Let us not follow the order of words. Let us say something where they said nothing and where they said something, let us say nothing].[17]

Indeed, Huby in 1968 argued that German poets may well have

considered themselves in competition with their sources and would change direct speech into indirect and vice versa simply to be different. Since, in the view of the French critic, the adaptor was merely reacting rather mechanically to his model, this practice did not upset Huby's main thesis, that the Germans were tied to their sources and had little freedom to innovate.[18] This opinion is shared by Carl Lofmark, who, having compared a large number of French and German narrative poems, concludes that the adaptor was not allowed (one assumes by patron or public, including rival poets) to modify the content of his source, only its form. He could alter the presentation of events or character but "he must not concoct a significance of his own."[19] Not everyone agrees with this restricted assessment of the translator's freedom based on a somewhat artificial distinction between *fond* and *forme*,[20] and I suggest (see below) that modifications to passages of direct speech indicate the German poet's conscious desire to produce something new. However, since Lofmark's conclusions rest on a corpus of vernacular adaptors' statements about their tasks, it is worth considering briefly whether he is right in his interpretation of what they understood by translation.

The avowed aim of German poets translating French courtly literature into their mother tongue, like that of their French predecessors who were often also translators (but from Latin), was to render their source intelligible to a new audience. They had inherited from the early Middle Ages two approaches to translation:[21] the word-for-word procedure recommended by St. Augustine for Bible translation and practiced by translators of sacred texts into Old High German; and Jerome's view (illustrated most clearly in his renderings of the Church Fathers) that the content alone was important and should be conveyed using one's own words ["non verbum de verbo, sed sensum exprimere de sensu"[22]]. In the same context a famous quotation from Horace's *Ars poetica* (lines 133-34) is used by the author of the Vulgate to support his advice against literal translation: "nec verbum verbo curabis reddere fidus interpres" [nor should you try to render your original word for word like a slavish translator]. Thus translation for the poets of the *Blütezeit* involved an element of interpretation--of making the innate meaning and significance of the original words clearer--and the term *diuten* (meaning both to explain and to translate) was frequently used by them to describe their task. This emphasis on the preservation of meaning and the frequent fidelity-to-the-source claims in vernacular prologues and epilogues led Lofmark to the conclusion that adaptors were indeed attempting to adhere faithfully to their models. Wishing rightly to judge medieval literature by the aesthetic values of the time, he nevertheless goes too far when he states: "Demnach müssen wir ihre Aussage ernst nehmen, dass sie den Inhalt ihrer Vorlage nicht wesentlich umgestalten" ["Der höfische Dichter," p. 43; For this reason we have to take (seriously) their statement that they do not substantially modify the content of their source].

In fact, Lofmark's investigations produce much evidence to belie the fidelity claim, and despite his ingenuity, he never succeeds in reconciling theory and practice. James Schultz, in his review of Lofmark's book, rightly argues that the latter has overlooked "the importance of the tension between the convention and its occasional violation . . . it is precisely by means of this tension that the MHG authors hint at the conflict between their obligations to the source and their independent creative vision."[23]

It seems, therefore, that, while acknowledging the authority of their source and while at times translating it very accurately, German adaptors often considered their task to include the modification of it, though they rarely admitted this. Medieval rhetoric, this time represented by Matthew of Vendôme's *Ars versificatoria* (c. 1175), gives the *remanieur* leave to eliminate from his model deficiencies in grammar, vocabulary, metre, and logic and to delete superfluous elements (4, 3f., Faral, pp. 180f.). Furthermore, the adaptor's avowed desire to bring out more obviously the meaning of his source justifies the many examples in the translations of explicitation, elaboration of key themes, and the clearer motivation of actions. Indeed, the very nature of translation involves a process akin to the *explication de texte*, and, as Jean Fourquet suggests,[24] the German adaptor naturally incorporates his commentary into his version of the story. However, many of the adaptors' modifications, omissions, and additions go beyond the limits outlined by rhetoric or dictated by the nature of translation itself, nor do they square with the adaptors' own theoretical pronouncements. They can only be explained by a concern to alter the overall meaning and ethos of a work and to rewrite it to suit different social, political, and cultural tastes. Modifications of this kind in the realm of direct speech will now be examined briefly under the following heads: characterization, ethos, theme / meaning, narrative technique and poetic effects, and structure.

Characterization

Oratio recta can contribute to two aspects of character portrayal: the revelation of temporary states of mind or of more permanent character traits. The former is exemplified by the passage from *Floire et Blancheflor* (lines 677-82) discussed above, where Floire's anxiety is conveyed dramatically by the stichomythia of the dialogue, while his distress at learning of his beloved's death is presented by means of a *planctus* (*Floire et Blancheflor*, lines 717-92; Fleck, lines 2241-2354; Diederic, lines 1131-1204), in which repetition, exclamation, and an apostrophe to death increase its emotive, sentimental force. However, while both adaptors preserve a complete lament--Fleck in particular giving it full rhetorical amplification--the German does sacrifice some of the heightened emotion of the preceding dialogue by lengthening the utterances and destroying the stichomythia.

In contrast to this, Hartmann in *Iwein* exploits stichomythia and an increase in the number of exchanges between speakers in order to convey Laudine's eagerness to see her lover and her concern to be alone with him. Compare the pace of the French passage with the shorter bursts of speech in the German translation:

> Et a sa dame a conseillié,
> Que revenuz est ses messages,
> Si a esploitié comé sages.
> "Comant?", fet ele, "Quant vandra
> Mes sire Yvains?" - "Ceanz est ja."
> "Ceanz est il? Vaigne donc tost
> Celeemant et an repost,

Demantres qu'avuec moi n'est nus.
Gardez que n'an i vaigne plus;
Car je harroie mout le quart."   (lines 1894-1903)[25]

[She has advised her lady
that her messenger has returned,
and has carried out the task successfully.
"What," she says, "when will
my lord Yvain come?" "He is already here."
"He's here? Then let him come immediately,
privily and in secret
while there is no one with me.
Make sure that no one else comes in,
for I would hate a fourth person to be present."]

sî sprach "gebet mir daz botenbrôt:
iuwer *garzûn* der ist komen."   (cf. *Yvain*, line 1827, *garçon*)
"waz mære hâstû vernomen?"
"guotiu mære." "sage doch, wie?"
"dâ ist ouch mîn her Îwein hie."
"wie mohter komen alsô vruo?"
"dâ treip in diu liebe darzuo."
"sage durch got, wer weiz ez doch?"
"vrouwe, ezn weiz niemen noch,
niuwan der garzûn unde wir."
"wan vüerstun danne her ze mir?
nû genc enwec, ich beites hie."   (lines 2204-15)[26]

[She said, "Give me the reward for the messenger;
your squire has arrived."
"What news have you heard?"
"Good news." "Tell me, what good news?"
"My lord Iwein is here too."
"How did he manage to come so soon?"
"He was spurred on by love."
"Tell me, by God, who knows about it?"
"My lady, no one knows except for the squire and us."
"Why don't you bring him here to me then?
Go now, I shall wait here."

Furthermore, the German adaptor transforms the indirect statement of the source (lines 1894-95) into *oratio recta* and adds the detail that Lunete's news makes her lady "von vreuden bleich unde rôt" [line 2203; turn pale and flushed with joy]. This leaves the audience in no doubt that Hartmann's heroine is in love, and contributes to his portrayal of her character.

Another good example of the use of direct speech to convey psychological turmoil is added to the narrative by Hartmann when Erec decides to leave "nâch âventiure wâne" [line 3111; in an aimless search for adventure]. In the source, Erec's reaction to the crisis is opaque (lines 2572f.)--he gives orders and arms himself, but nothing of what is going through his mind is disclosed. Hartmann presents his hero as equally inscrutable but changes Erec's public departure into a more secretive affair and tells us that his protagonist was cunning in his dissimulation [line 3070; "er tete alsam der karge sol"]. Next the adaptor invents a speech in which Erec criticizes the bad condition of his helmet:

> er sprach: "mîn helm enist niht wol.
> mirst liep daz ichz hân ersehen:
> und wære mir sîn nôt geschehen,
> sô wære ich gar geirret.
> ich sage iu waz im wirret:
> man sol in baz riemen."   (lines 3071-76)[27]

[He said, "There's something wrong with my helmet.
It is a good job I noticed it:
if it had turned out that I had needed it,
I would have been in real trouble.
I'll tell you what's wrong with it;
it needs better straps."]

Hartmann hints at the psychological significance of these words when he comments:

> dô enwas aber niemen
> der sich des mohte verstân
> wie sîn gemüete was getân.   (lines 3077-79)

225

[However, there was no one there
who could fathom
what was going on in his mind.]

Erec's implicit castigation of those responsible for his armor fits in well with his clever plan to disguise the real reason for his departure (he pretends to be riding out *ûz kurzwîlen*--for pleasure). Hartmann thus adds psychologically convincing detail to his source when he shows Erec venting on others the anger he feels because of his own *verligen*. Significantly, it is Erec's helmet, closely associated with the practice of knighthood, which becomes both the symbol of his failure and the catalyst for his rage.

In contrast, the object of the French Erec's wrath is Enide. This is demonstrated by the knight's far from courteous words when instructing his servant to fetch his wife:

> va, se li di
> que trop me fet demorer ci;
> trop a mis a li atorner;
> di li qu'el veigne tost monter,
> que ge l'atant. (lines 2663-67)[28]

[Go and tell her
that she is making me wait here too long.
She has taken too much time to get ready.
Tell her to come and mount her horse immediately,
for I am waiting for her.]

This speech, which smacks of an imperious husband who has been wronged by a less than obedient wife, has no counterpart in the adaptation, in which Erec is generally less brusque with his spouse than in the source. As we have seen above, Hartmann channels Erec's anger elsewhere.

More permanent character traits conveyed by means of dialogue can be seen in Hartmann's modified portrayals of Enide and Laudine. In the lecherous count episode (*Erec et Enide*, lines 3308-3406; *Erec*, lines 3753-3899), Enide's reaction to the count's overtures is at first haughty and dismissive:

> "Sire, de neant vos penez,"
> fet Enyde, "ce ne puet estre."   (lines 3326-27)

> ["My lord, you are wasting your time,"
> says Enide, "it cannot be."]

Then she says that she prefers to die rather than to commit treason against her husband, but, seeing the imminent danger to Erec, she finally pretends that she will enjoy being Galoain's wife. Enide's feigned erotic desires, which are reminiscent of a troubadour's aspirations ("Je vos voldroie ja santir / an un lit certes nu a nu" [lines 3390-91; I would rather feel your naked flesh / next to mine in bed]) could never be voiced by Hartmann's more modest heroine. The latter simply states at the end of the dialogue that she is ready to comply with the count's request. Furthermore, her initial rejection of him (lines 3797ff.) is more polite than in the source, the German woman affirming tactfully that she is of too humble origins to be a countess.

Enite is a gentler, more modest (in all senses of the word) woman than Enide; she is also more overtly God-fearing (invocations of God being generally more common in speeches of the adaptation). Her words thus convey Hartmann's softened view of her character. Equally, though, the adaptor exploits Enite's monologues and dialogue in order to praise his hero, whom the narrator frequently calls "der guote kneht" (lines 3112, 3345, etc.).

Laudine, whose portrayal by Chrétien is much influenced by the *belle dame sans merci* type,[29] is endowed with more compassion and humanized by Hartmann.[30] Evidence for this view is found in the "reconciliation scene," to which Hartmann adds a speech (lines 8122-29) in which Laudine recognizes Iwein's suffering on her account (she seems, though, to be acknowledging that his travail was on her account rather than admitting her own guilt) and asks for forgiveness. Furthermore, earlier in the adaptation, she had said to Lûnete, on hearing that she will have to be reconciled with Iwein, that she must therefore try to win from her husband greater love than he had shown to her before (lines 8094-96). These words, reflecting the softer side of Laudine's character, constitute an addition to the source. In Chrétien's version, Laudine's speech ends with her anger at being trapped and her extreme reluctance to take Yvain back (lines 6760-76). While Hartmann has not changed the plot to any significant degree, his additions and modifications to Laudine's utterances have made the happy outcome more plausible. At the same time, though, they have removed the ambivalence of Chrétien's final lines, thus reducing the subtle irony of the source.

A final example of character presentation through dialogue is to be found in Kay's conversation with Calogrenant and the queen at the beginning of *Yvain* (lines 71-104).[31] The epitome of the *homme anticourtois* in Chrétien's romance, Kay gives a clear demonstration of his bile in this dialogue, employing first irony and sarcasm against Calogrenant (lines 71-74), then accusing him outright of being stupid [line 76; "tant estes vos de san vuidiez"]. Guinevere is also the victim of Kay's tongue when he suggests that she has been taken in by Calogrenant's show of *courtoisie*. She, in her short defense of the more courtly knight (lines 86-91), does not mince her words when accusing Kay of being full of poison. His reply is equally direct and yet more insulting:

> "Dame! se nos ne gaeignons,"
> Fet Kes, "an vostre conpaignie,
> Gardez que nos n'i perdons mie!"   (lines 92-94)

> ["My lady, if we gain nothing,"
> says Kay, "from your company,
> at least make sure that we lose nothing by it."

Finally he disrespectfully tells her to drop the subject--[line 97; "teisiez vos an!"]--and to command Calogrenant to relate his tale (if she wants to be useful!).

Hartmann preserves the irony of Keiî's initial words (lines 113-35), reinforcing them with the over polite "her Kâlogrenant"[32] and emphasizing the folly of fellow-courtiers' illusions with the terms *wænet* and *dunket* (cf. *cuidiez, cuit*, which the queen perhaps deliberately and ironically echoes in *Yvain*; "au mien cuidier" [line 87; in my view]). However, Hartmann's Keiî avoids a direct attack on Kâlogrenant, and his queen is likewise more restrained in her reply (lines 137-58), nowhere insulting him with the equivalent of *vilain*. Although Hartmann tells us that Keiî is angry, his retort (lines 160-88) is more reasoned than in the source, and the lengthening of the utterances of all speakers tends not only to reduce the anger of the moment, but also to undermine somewhat our view of Kay as "ranposneus, fel et poignanz et afiteus" [lines 69-70; slanderous, bad-tempered, and sarcastic and insulting]. Interestingly, Hartmann does not translate very closely this character assessment by the French narrator, referring instead to Keiî's envy of another's honor and his desire to discredit honorable men whenever possible (lines 108-12).

Direct speech has a further role to play in guaranteeing the importance of individual characters, both major and minor, in the work as a whole. For example, an important secondary figure in Gautier d'Arras's *Eracle*, the seneschal, is given little to say and is treated more perfunctorily by Meister Otte. The latter has in fact exceptionally reduced his source overall,[33] and direct speech often falls victim to this *abbreviatio*. However, some speeches are nevertheless expanded, and characters such as the *entremetteuse* Morphêâ are given more to say at the expense of, among others, the seneschal. Since one of Gautier's patrons, Thibaut V of Blois, was seneschal of France at the time, it is not surprising that the incumbent of this office at the imperial court is portrayed fully and sympathetically in *Eracle*. Otte's reduction of his role, however, is not so easily explained (though by making his emperor behave less harshly towards the slave boy Heraclius, the German adaptor has decreased the necessity for Heraclius to have a sympathetic ally nearby). Whatever the reason, the fact remains that the suppression of dialogue has transformed the seneschal into an insignificant, minor figure.

Ethos

The term *adaptation courtoise* employed by Huby and others implies not only the translation of *courtly* romances, but also the transformation of them into something more courtly still.[34]   Jean Fourquet says of adaptation: "il faut tout redire dans une autre langue, aussi courtoisement, plus si possible" [p. 23; one has to retell everything in a different language, in just as courtly a manner, more so if possible].   Many critics have noticed that German poets give a more idealized picture of their heroes, emphasize courtly etiquette (salutations, the correct form of address), and remove coarser elements from their models.   Some of the modifications noted above in the portrayal of Erec, Enide, and Kay may indeed have been dictated by a desire to produce more seemly behavior and language.

Hartmann, for instance, appears to be conveying the ideals of courtly behavior when he modifies the treatment of Ider's dwarf at the beginning of *Erec*.[35]   In the source, the dwarf is presented as obviously evil and uncourtly, and Guinevere's *demoisele*, but especially Erec, treat him with the contempt he deserves:

> "Fui!" fet Erec, "nains enuieus,
> trop es fel et contralïeus;
> lesse m'aler."   (lines 213-15)

> ["Out of my way," says Erec, "vile dwarf,
> you are too treacherous and belligerent;
> let me pass."]

Line 215 echoes the girl's words: "Nains . . . lesse m'aler"; line 167.)   Hartmann's *juncvrouwe*, in contrast, greets the dwarf *mit zühten* (*zuht* being the usual term for *courtoisie* in many Middle High German romances) saying:

> "got grüeze iuch, geselle,
> und vernemet waz ich welle."   (lines 32-33)

["In God's name, greetings, friend,
and hear what I have come for."]

Then she mentions her lady's *zuht*, the greeting she sends to the dwarf and her desire to know about his lord. The *nain*'s two impolite speeches in the model are replaced by an indirect command (lines 45-47), which attenuates the violence of the evil creature's language. Similarly, the German Erec's reaction to the dwarf's ill-treatment of the maiden is to address him rather disparagingly as "ir wêniger" (line 76), but then to appeal calmly, rationally (and most inappropriately, as things turn out) to the ideal of *zuht* (line 79). The dwarf replies "lâ dîn klaffen sîn" [line 83; stop prattling] and strikes him.

Erec's restrained, exemplary conduct here even stretches to the use of *ir* for the dwarf, while the latter addresses the hero as *dû*. In the source, we find that the dwarf uses *vous*, while Erec employs the scornful *tu*. Thus the translator is probably exploiting the mode of address to suggest that his hero can remain polite even under provocation; the dwarf, however, does not have the grace to address a noble knight correctly.

The mode of address can become a very subtle stylistic device at the disposal of French poet and German adaptor alike.[36] However, since conventions in the use of *tu / vous* in Old French literature differ from those in Middle High German literature, translators often modify the form of address simply to comply with German traditions.[37] In assessing modifications of this kind it has to be borne in mind that the form chosen not only reflects the status of the addressee (whether a relative, enemy, inferior or superior, etc.), but can also reflect the lack of refinement of the speaker. Furthermore, a person normally addressed as *vous* may receive *tu* if the utterer is angry or disdainful, while the rather friendlier *dû* in German[38] is sometimes replaced by *ir* if the speaker wishes to convey coldness. For this reason the mode of address adopted by one character for another can vary within a piece of dialogue or during the course of the romance. As a rule, though, adaptors faced with the shifting use of *tu / vous* to convey differing emotions or attitudes usually modify their sources so that their characters are consistent in their choice of form of address for each individual addressee.

Theme / Meaning

Adaptors exploit passages of direct speech in order to elaborate upon themes they consider to be implicit in their sources and to develop others which are part of their own conception of their subject-matter. Konrad Fleck transforms a love story with its covert message about constancy and passive resistance into an overtly didactic, exemplary tale. The key themes that unify the adaptation are announced in the prologue: *rehte hôhiu minne, tugent, triuwe, stæte, kumber*, and *froude* (true love, virtue, fidelity and constancy, the pains and joys of love), and these are taken up by the protagonists in their own sometimes sententious utterances.

When the lovers are finally reconciled, Floire tells Blancheflor how much sadness and suffering he has experienced since their parting (*Floire et Blancheflor*, lines 2458-66), and she replies, referring to the treacherous actions of his father, pledging her love, and asking how he came to enter the tower (lines 2467-80). Diederic follows his French model closely and invents little (lines 3102-28). However, Fleck gives Flôre a forty-four-line speech (lines 5969-6012) in which he contrasts his former suffering with his present joy (an antithetical pair which the adaptor loves to exploit rhetorically: *fröuden / sorge, wünne / arbeit*) while attributing his present good fortune to God:

> got hât wol an mir getân,
> daz er mich hât gewert
> des ich dicke hân gegert.　　　　　　　(lines 5992-94)[39]

> [God has treated me well
> in granting to me
> what I have often wished for.]

Blanscheflur's reply (lines 6014-78) indicates that their recon-ciliation is in answer to her prayers and a sign of God's mercy and understanding of her innocent plight (lines 6034-47, 6050-53, 6068-78). This emphasis on the role of God is important for Fleck's overall attitude to his material. Blanscheflur is a Christian slave whose love for a pagan prince encourages him to convert to

232

Christianity. The idea is already present in the source, but in his version Fleck stresses the conversion theme, linking human love with love of God.

A strong religious element is also discernible in the supplementary dialogue composed by the German adaptor. Blanscheflur's lamenting, to which she refers in line 6035, is presented dramatically by Fleck (lines 1743-1858) and is preceded by a conversation with the emir. Both the monologue and the dialogue constitute additions to the model. In her *planctus*, the young heroine invokes God, refers to her *unsælde* (roughly equivalent to the workings of fortune's wheel mentioned elsewhere in *Floire et Blancheflor*), to her former joy and present suffering, to Flôre's *triuwe* and *stæte*, and gives an idealized physical portrait of her beloved. Here too, then, the familiar exordial themes are rehearsed.

Earlier, the adaptor had added two further scenes built around dialogue and involving Blanscheflur. The first consists of a conversation in the king's orchard (lines 777-801) during which the adolescents express their love in courtly terms. They address each other as *ir* (the usual form of address for a courtly couple); Blanscheflur is called *frou künginne* and *frouwe mîn*, while Flôre is *süezer âmîs*; there are references to *minne* and *triuwe* and to the famous paradox of the bitter-sweetness of love. Since the type of love in the source is more Ovidian and less sophisticated than this, it is clear that Fleck is again exploiting dialogue in order to modify one of the key themes inherited from the source.

The second new scene contains the farewell dialogue of the lovers prior to their parting (lines 1076-1341). Blanscheflur relates her dream prophesying disaster, and Flôre then announces that he must leave. The girl's subsequent lament on the theme "better not to have loved than to have loved and lost" again contains the leitmotifs of *sælde* and *unsælde* (the *annominatio* is impressive, especially in lines 1180-91), which she considers are meted out by God. Eventually she attempts suicide with a writing stylus, the very same object Flore will later use in his similarly abortive attempt on his life.

These passages of dialogue invented by Fleck not only enable him to introduce a didactic element into the utterances of his protagonists in order to thrust home his own message. They also direct the audience's attention towards the role of the heroine, which is more significant in the adaptation and closely linked with the Christian moral of the text.

Dialogue is again used to develop leitmotifs and to convey meaning in Hartmann's *Erec*. This adaptation lacks a prologue, but the epilogue mentions the key theme in this work: *êre*. Erec's honor (along with his *sælde*[40]) features strongly (lines 8543, 8548, 8556, 8560, 8562, 8568) in words spoken by the hero to Ivrein just before the *joie de la cort* adventure (lines 8520-75). There is no clear equivalent in the source, and Hartmann's own composition here strengthens his portrayal of the hero as a man "en devenir."[41] For Erec considers this adventure to be reserved for him alone, so that he might give irrefutable and definitive proof of his knightly prowess and might win a fine reputation after the ignominy of his *verligen*.

As Kellermann has rightly said, "Hartmann a centré son roman sur le personnage d'Erec" (p. 513), while "Chrétien a voulu écrire le roman d'un couple" [p. 514; Hartmann has centered his romance on the figure of Erec. . . . Chrétien wished to write a romance about a couple]. For Chrétien, it is not only Erec's *recréantise*, but also Enide's *parole* that provide the motivating force behind most of the action. Hartmann, though, attenuates Enite's responsibility for the crisis and refuses to reproduce this "roman de la parole." It is fitting that the new conception of the subject-matter, in which speaking out does not play such a vital role, should be achieved largely by means of modifications in direct speech.

How does Hartmann dismantle this "roman de la parole?" First, it is significant that we not hear the French Enide speak until the day of her fateful utterance. The adaptor, by inserting one rather banal sentence spoken by Enite in line 322, obscures this subtle interpretative detail. Second, the episode of the *parole* is much more developed in the source (lines 2492-2606). It includes Enide's lament beginning "con mar fui" and ending "con mar fus" (the equality and intertwined destinies of man and wife expressed through syntactical parallels), her revelation of the rumors to her husband, and her lengthy monologue in which she regrets her *parole* and castigates herself for her *folie* and *orguel* (lines 2585-2606). Whether or not

Chrétien himself believed that Enide was so much to blame for the marital crisis[42] (both as the object and instigator of Erec's passion and as the one who dared to voice criticism of him), the fact remains that both hero and heroine act and, more importantly, speak as if she should never have spoken out. In particular, the following extract smacks of some presumption on Enide's part, and a medieval audience may well have considered that advice of this kind was not appropriate coming from a wife:

> Or vos an estuet consoil prandre,
> que vos puissiez ce blasme estaindre
> et vostre premier los ataindre,
> car trop vos ai oï blasmer.   (lines 2562-65)

> [Now you must decide
> how to quell this reproach
> and win back your former good reputation,
> for I have heard you criticized too much.]

Whereas the moment of crisis in the French romance is marked by extended dialogue and monologue, its German counterpart is more closely integrated into the narrative proper and fails to qualify as a dramatic scene. Hartmann develops somewhat his account of the criticism of Erec by his men, reduces the lament which causes the crisis from twelve to four lines (3029-32), and simply reports that Enite at Erec's bidding reveals *diu rede* to him (line 3051). Furthermore, there is no monologue of self-castigation by Enite. Since in the adaptation we do not actually witness the heroine's speaking out, the term *rede* loses much of its verbal force, signifying "matter or affair" rather than "speech." Thus Hartmann, in translating the term *parole* (a leitmotif and interpretative key in the model) by *rede*, has altered the meaning of Chrétien's Erec romance.

Significantly, the French hero eventually forgives Enide her crime of repeating the criticism levelled at her husband:

> et se vos rien m'avez *mesdit*,
> je le vos pardoing tot et quit

del forfet et de la *parole*.   (lines 4891-93; emphasis added)

[And if you have ever *spoken ill* of me,
I forgive you completely and utterly,
both for the offense and for the *word*]

Hartmann's hero at the same point in the action asks his wife (in *oratio obliqua!*) to forgive him for the suffering he has caused her (lines 6795-99).   Thus speech in the two episodes of crisis and reconciliation offers the key to the adaptor's new conception of his material.   As Kellermann notes, Hartmann has replaced the "double culpabilité" (*recréantise* of Erec and *parole* of Enide) of Chrétien's romance with "une motivation beaucoup plus simple et beaucoup plus claire" [p. 519; a much simpler and clearer plot motivation], i.e., Erec's *verligen* alone.   However, as the German critic rightly observes, clarity is won at the expense of complexity and subtlety. Indeed ambiguity, vital to the rich texture of romance, is often forfeited when an adaptor's analytical skills are brought to bear on his source.[43]

Narrative Technique and Poetic Effects

Modifications in passages of direct discourse can produce a range of poetic effects which elicit different responses from the reader / listener.   For example, the addition or expansion of *oratio recta*, or a change from indirect to direct speech; produces dramatic immediacy and gives the audience the illusion that it is witnessing directly (without the mediation of a narrator) events and actions. Dramatic narrative features strongly in Chrétien's *Erec et Enide* and *Yvain*, which boast 37% and 46.9% direct speech respectively (cf. *Roman d'Enéas*, 41.5%; *Eneit*, 36.8%).   Hartmann has reduced the proportion of direct speech in his *Erec* (31%), but increased it substantially in *Iwein* (52.3%).[44]   However, Wiehl has shown that much of the added *oratio recta* in *Iwein* comes from an increase in the average length of utterances (from 9.5 lines in the model to 14.2 in the adaptation) and that only monologues and half-dialogues (where a speaker expects a reply but this is absent, or at least not reproduced in *oratio recta*), but not dialogues proper, have increased in number in the two adaptations. These modifications lead to a heightened lyrical effect where monologues predominate, but also to what Wiehl (p. 79) calls an *Entdramatisierung* or *Episierung*, especially when only one of the two speakers present in the source is allowed to speak, the reply being suppressed, given as an indirect statement, or merely hinted at in the narrative itself. Furthermore, the lengthening of dialogue and utterances within it (which allows for more rational argument and didacticism) can also reduce its lively, dramatic effect.

The tendency, which Wiehl has noted in Hartmann, to produce "eine epische Dichtung," i.e., narrative in which the controlling hand of the poet is always discernible and his presence clearly felt,[45] is compatible with features of *adaptation courtoise* identified by Lofmark--namely the adaptor's preference for past tenses rather than the historic present common in Old French romances and his treatment of the source material in a slightly detached manner as if it were history, rather than attempting to recreate events before his audience's very eyes, which is the impression produced by Chrétien's narrative technique.

Structure

Wiehl's main aim in his book is to show that Hartmann, in omitting, developing, or adding direct speech, has modified the structure of his source so as to produce groups of *Redeszenen* which fall into pleasing numerical patterns. For example, he finds that Hartmann's *Iwein* divides into two sections of 3878 and 3896 lines plus a short coda of 386 lines[46] and that these divisions (*Werkstruktur*) correspond almost exactly to blocks of scenes based on direct speech (*Szenenstruktur*). The first half of *Iwein* is made up of scenes arranged into symmetrical groups of eight alternating with individual scenes (with monologues, often added by Hartmann, playing a vital role in this numerical composition), while the second half of *Iwein* has the number seven as its guiding principle.

Although I accept Wiehl's contention that a listening audience would have been capable of recognizing narrative patterns created by scenes built around direct speech and that the *Redeszenen* are therefore a better potential guide to the structure of romances than Linke's theory of divisions marked by manuscript initials (the position of which can vary from codex to codex),[47] his identification of numerical patterns and symmetry is less convincing. Even if one does accept that poets deliberately strove for this kind of numerical harmony in their works, it is difficult to imagine a medieval audience counting *Redeszenen* on its fingers and attempting to spot significant patterns while listening to a gripping romance.

What *is* important in Wiehl's study is his recognition that the adaptor could modify the structure of his model through "Doppelungen, Wiederholungen, Parallelszenen, Kontrastbildungen, Steigerungen, Rahmungen, Verklammerungen, Verschachtelungen" [p. 300; doubling, repetition, parallel scenes, contrasts, gradation, framing, linking, interlacing]. Parallelism and repetition have already been noted in Fleck's *Flore und Blanscheflur*, in which Blanscheflur's *planctus* and attempted suicide form a pleasing diptych to Flôre's similar behavior. Apart from the thematic possibilities outlined above, Fleck may also have invented this scene for aesthetic, structural purposes.

Another example of supplementary dialogue composed for the purpose of symmetry is to be found in Otte's *Eraclius*, lines 1541-74.[48] In the source, Eracle goes to market twice to buy first a precious stone, then a horse for the emperor. Both times he pays far too much for the goods but is criticized by his lord's *serjans* only on the first occasion in the source (*Eracle*, lines 887-96).[49] Otte not only preserves this utterance, placing it in the mouths of Fôcas's chamberlains (lines 1088-1140), he produces a similar speech for the *kamerære* when the foal is likewise purchased at an exorbitant price later. Thus, despite Otte's overall reduction of his model, he is still keen to highlight parallels not fully exploited by his predecessor.

Conclusion

In this study of the German adaptor's approach to the translation of passages of direct speech I have shown that German poets were capable of rendering both form and content of their models quite accurately if they so desired, but that they frequently modified their source in order to produce new meaning or new poetic effects. Some of the changes carried out by later adaptors may well have been made in an attempt to conform to developing German literary traditions. It seems that Veldeke[50] and then Hartmann exercised some influence on their successors, and thirteenth-century adaptors no doubt found their fidelity to their sources compromised by the poetic fashions of their own culture. An analysis of direct speech alone cannot cover all aspects of the adaptor / translator's art. However, dialogue and monologue, because of the complexity of their nature and function, represented a special challenge to the translator and offered special possibilities for innovation to the gifted German adaptor.[51]

NOTES

1. See Peter Wiehl, *Die Redeszene als episches Strukturelement in den Erec- und Iwein-Dichtungen Hartmanns von Aue und Chrestiens de Troyes* (Munich: Wilhelm Fink, 1974). This view will be examined critically later.

2. Michel Huby, *L'Adaptation des romans courtois en Allemagne au XIIᵉ et au XIIIᵉ siècle* (Paris: Klincksieck, 1968).

3. Quotations from Gottfried von Strassburg, *Tristan*, ed. Peter Ganz, 2 vols. (Wiesbaden: Brockhaus, 1978).

4. Illustrative material from Meister Otte, *Eraclius. Deutsches Gedicht des dreizehnten Jahrhunderts,* ed. Harald Graef, Quellen und Forschungen, 50 (Strassburg: Karl Trübner, 1883) will be used sparingly in this chapter. For a fuller discussion of his adaptation see Karen Pratt, *Meister Otte's "Eraclius" as an Adaptation of "Eracle" by Gautier d'Arras*, Göppinger Arbeiten zur Germanistik, No. 932 (Göppingen: Kümmerle, 1987).

5. See Carl Rischen's list of quotations of Hartmann by Fleck in *Bruchstücke von Konrad Flecks "Floire und Blanscheflur" nach den Handschriften F und P unter Heranziehung von BH*, ed. Carl Rischen, Germanische Bibliothek, part 3, vol. 4 (Heidelberg: Carl Winter, 1913), pp. 101-28.

6.   For biographical details and information about possible patrons see Joachim Bumke, *Mäzene im Mittelalter: die Gönner und Auftraggeber der höfischen Literatur in Deutschland 1150-1300* (Munich: Beck, 1979).

7.   Since German poets were working from a manuscript copy of their source which may have contained readings not present in the original French work or in the texts prepared by modern editors, it is important to take into account all manuscript variants before drawing conclusions about the adaptor's dependence on or independence of his model.

8.   Jeanette Beer mentions the problem of translating accurately from Latin into Old French in *A Medieval Caesar* (Geneva: Droz, 1976). Paul Salmon shows in *The Works of Hartmann von Aue in the Light of Medieval Poetics*, Ph.D. diss., London 1957, that it is impossible to transpose certain rhetorical devices from Latin into Middle High German.

9.   *Brisure du couplet* is exploited in particular in the Old French drama, where changes of speaker within the couplet became the norm by the middle of the thirteenth century.

10.   Quotations from *Le Roman d'Enéas*, ed. J.-J. Salverda de Grave, C.F.M.A., 2 vols. (Paris: Champion, 1925 and 1929).

11.   Quotations from Heinrich von Veldeke's *Eneide*, ed. Otto Behaghel (Heilbronn: Gebr. Henninger, 1882).

12.   However, Hartmann's approach to individual passages in *Iwein* can vary from fidelity to the complete rewriting of the model; see Hartmann von Aue, *Iwein*, ed. G. F. Benecke, K. Lachmann, and Ludwig Wolff (Berlin: De Gruyter, 1974).

13.   Normally I quote from manuscript A in the synoptic edition by Jean-Luc Leclanche: *Floire et Blancheflor*, ed Jean-Luc Leclanche, in *Contribution à l'étude de la transmission des plus anciennes oeuvres romanesques françaises. Un cas privilégié: "Floire et Blancheflor"*, 2 vols., Ph.D. diss., Paris 4, 1977 (Lille: Service de reproduction des thèses, Université de Lille 3, 1980). Since both Fleck and Diederic appear to have used a manuscript belonging to the B̲ family, though not containing all the innovations identified in the extant B̲ manuscript, variants from the B̲ tradition will be noted where relevant.

14.   Quotations from J. J. Mak, ed., *Floris ende Blancefloer van Diederic van Assenede uitgegeven met inleiding en aantekeningen*, Klassieken uit de Nederlandse letterkunde, 13 (Zwolle: W. E. J. Tjeenk Willink, 1964).

15.   Quotations from Konrad Fleck, *Flore und Blanscheflur: eine Erzählung von Konrad Fleck*, ed. Emil Sommer, Bibliothek der gesammten deutschen National-Literatur, 1st Series, no. 12 (Quedlinburg and Leipzig: G. Basse, 1846) and from Carl Rischen [n. 5 above] for the passages he has re-edited.

16.   For a fuller discussion of Diederic and Fleck as adaptors see my article "The Rhetoric of Adaptation: The Middle Dutch and Middle High German Versions of *Floire et Blancheflor*" forthcoming in the selected proceedings of the fifth triennial congress of the International Courtly Literature Society, Utrecht, August 1986.   See also Roland Lane, "A Critical Review of the Major Studies of the Relationship Between the Old French *Floire et Blancheflor* and its Germanic Adaptations," *Nottingham Medieval Studies* 30 (1986):1-19.

17.   *Documentum* 2, 3, items 133-34, quoted from Edmond Faral, *Les Arts poétiques du XIIe et du XIIIe siècle: Recherches et documents sur la technique littéraire du moyen âge*, Bibliothèque de L'Ecole des Hautes Etudes, no. 238 (Paris: Champion, 1924), p. 309.

18.   Huby has published many works over the last fifteen years, never really modifying this thesis.   See his "L'Adaptation courtoise, position des problèmes," in *Le Moyen Age et littérature comparée. Actes du 7eme Congrès national de la Société française de littérature comparée, Poitiers, 1965* (Paris: Didier, 1967), pp. 16-27; "L'Approfondissement psychologique dans *Erec* de Hartmann," *Etudes Germaniques* 22 (1967):13-26; "Untersuchungen über den Aufbau höfischer Werke," Ph.D. diss., Paris, Sorbonne, 1968; "Le Rôle de la structure dans l'étude de l'adaptation courtoise," B.B.S.I.A. 20 (1968):136-47; "Veldekes Bedeutung für die Entwicklung der Bearbeitung der französischen höfischen Romane," *Heinric van Veldeken Symposion Gent* (Antwerp, Utrecht: De Nederlandsche Boekhandel, 1971), pp. 160-79; "Adaptation courtoise et société ou 'la réalité dépasse la fiction'," *Etudes Germaniques* 29 (1974):289-301; "Hat Hartmann von Aue im *Erec* das Eheproblem neu gedeutet?," *Recherches Germaniques* 6 (1976):3-17; "L'Interprétation des romans courtois de Hartmann von Aue," *Cahiers de civilisation médiévale* 22

(1979):23-38; with Alois Wolf, "Streitgespräch," *Germanisch-Romanische Monatsschrift* 33 (1983):301 324; and n. 2 above.

19. Carl Lofmark, *The Authority of the Source in Middle High German Narrative Poetry*, Bithell Series of Dissertations (London: Institute of Germanic Studies, 1981), p. 73.

20. Notably Tony Hunt, "Beginnings, Middles, and Ends. Some Interpretative Problems in Chrétien's *Yvain* and its Medieval Adaptations," in *The Craft of Fiction. Essays in Medieval Poetics*, ed. Leigh Arrathoon (Rochester, MI: Solaris Press, 1984), pp. 83-117; Wilhelm Kellermann, "L'Adaptation du roman d'*Erec et Enide* de Chrestien de Troyes par Hartmann von Aue," *Mélanges Frappier* (Geneva: Droz, 1970), vol. 1, pp. 509-22; Ojars Kratins, *The Dream of Chivalry. A Study of Chrétien de Troyes's 'Yvain' and Hartmann von Aue's 'Iwein'* (Washington: Univ. Press of America, 1982); René Pérennec, "'Adaptation et société,' L'adaptation par Hartmann von Aue du roman de Chrétien *Erec et Enide*," *Etudes Germaniques* 28 (1973):289-303; and Pratt [nn. 4, 16 above].

21. See Carl Lofmark, "Der höfische Dichter als Übersetzer," in *Probleme mittelhochdeutscher Erzählformen, Marburger Colloquium 1969*, ed. Peter Ganz and Werner Schröder (Berlin: Schmidt, 1972), pp. 40-62; hereafter "Der höfische Dichter." See also L. G. Kelly, *The True Interpreter: A History of Translation Practice and Theory in the West* (Oxford: B. Blackwell, 1979).

22. Jerome, 'Epistola,' 57, *Ad Pammachium*, ed. Migne, *Patrologia Latina*, 22, col. 571.

23. *Germanic Review* 57 (1982):164-66, here p. 166. The subtlety with which the convention of source fidelity is employed by German adaptors is similar to the use of the truth topos as examined by Jeanette Beer in *Narrative Conventions of Truth in the Middle Ages* (Geneva: Droz, 1981). Neither convention should necessarily be taken at face value.

24. Jean Fourquet, *Hartmann d'Aue, Erec Iwein. Extraits accompagnés des textes correspondants de Chrétien de Troyes avec Introduction, Notes et Glossaires*, Bibliothèque de Philologie Germanique, 5 (Paris: Aubier, 1944).

25.   Quotations from Chrétien de Troyes, *Yvain (Le Chevalier au Lion): The Critical Text of Wendelin Foerster with Introduction, Notes and Glossary by T. B. W. Reid* (Manchester: Manchester Univ. Press, 1942, rpt. 1948, 1952, 1961, 1967, 1974, 1984).

26.   Quotations from Hartmann von Aue, *Iwein* [n. 12 above].

27.   Quotations from Hartmann von Aue, *Erec*, ed. Albert Leitzmann, 3rd ed. Ludwig Wolff, Altdeutsche Textbibliothek, 39 (Tübingen: Niemeyer, 1963).

28.   Quotations from Chrétien de Troyes, *Erec et Enide*, ed. Mario Roques, C.F.M.A. (Paris: Champion, 1973).

29.   See A. R. Press, "Chrétien de Troyes' Laudine: A Belle Dame Sans Mercy?," *Forum for Modern Language Studies* 19 (1983):158-71.

30.   See Hunt [n. 20 above]. He also argues convincingly for the importance of intertextual allusion in the interpretation of Chrétien's romance.

31.   I have analyzed only half of this conversation which illustrates Chrétien's masterly gift for producing dialogue. In reality, this is an example of what Wiehl calls *Polylog* consisting of a series of "duologues." What is striking is the way that the person addressed is not always the one to reply, nor does the speaker always receive a response. For example, Chrétien shows Guinevere leaping to Calogrenant's defense (lines 86-91), then Calogrenant to the queen's (lines 105-23); Kay then snubs Calogrenant, and Guinevere does likewise to him, by preferring to speak to another member of the trio. The adaptor preserves many of the formal characteristics of this conversation, including the same number of utterances, though there is no *brisure du couplet* in the German romance.

32.   The use of the title may however equally be Hartmann's way of toning down Keiî's insult.

33.   Herbort von Fritzlar, in his *Liet von Troye*, is the only other German adaptor to shorten his model.

34.   See Pratt [n. 4 above], chapter 10, where I conclude that Meister
Otte, despite his concern for realism, does suppress some of the uncourtly
elements in *Eracle*, but is less prudish and more risqué than his predecessor
in his treatment of the erotic episodes.

35.   A further striking feature of the adaptation is that while the
French Erec waits until Guinevere tells him to approach the dwarf, the
German Erec offers his services before being asked (lines 70-72).   There is
thus no possible doubt about Erec's chivalry at this point in Hartmann's
version.

36.   For a discussion of the manner of address see Julia Woledge,
"The Use of 'Tu' and 'Vous' in Medieval French Verse Romances from
1160-1230," Ph.D. diss.,   London 1976, and Gustav Ehrismann, "Duzen
und Ihrzen im Mittelalter," *Zeitschrift für deutsche Wortforschung* 1, 2, 4,
5, here vol. 5 (1903-04), pp. 127-220, "Das höfische Epos."

37.   Guinevere probably uses *dû* for Keiî in *Iwein* (lines 137f.)
because he is a seneschal and as such would be addressed as *dû* in German
romance.   See Ehrismann [n. 36 above], vol. 5, p. 159.

38.   French *tu* and German *dû* were by no means equivalent in the
Middle Ages, the latter not having the harsh connotations which the former
could acquire.

39.   For further references to God see Fleck, lines 5978 and 6008.

40.   See F. P. Pickering, "The 'Fortune of Hartmann's Erec'," in
Essays in Medieval German Literature and Iconography (Cambridge:
Cambridge Univ. Press, 1980), pp. 110-29.

41.   See Wilhelm Kellermann's excellent comparison of the two
versions of *Erec* in "L'Adaptation du roman d'*Erec et Enide* de Chrestien
de Troyes par Hartmann von Aue" [n. 20 above], p. 512.

42.   When the narrator announces that the *parole* will be the result of
bad luck or ill fortune (*mescheance*, line 2482), and that Enide will
consider it *folie* ("une parole, dom ele se tint puis por fole," lines 2483-84),
and when he compares the lamenting Enide to a goat which scratches

around until it cannot lie down comfortably ("tant grate chievre que mal gist," line 2584), we wonder if Chrétien might not be more sympathetic towards Enide than she is to herself. Erec does, after all, admit that he deserves criticism for his *recréantise* (lines 2572-73).

43.   The plethora of studies on *Erec et Enide* treating the possible faults of the couple and Erec's motives for setting out with his wife bear witness to the ambiguities and complexities of Chrétien's romance.

44.   Statistics are taken from Wiehl [n. 1 above], p. 67. In terms of the number of lines devoted to direct speech and narrative respectively the figures are: *Erec et Enide*, 2578 and 4380; *Yvain*, 3202 and 3620; *Erec*, 3164 and 7028; *Iwein*, 4270 and 3890.

45.   Hartmann's interventions as poet and his imaginary conversations with his audience are a striking illustration of this.

46.   Chrétien's romance, on the other hand, is divided into three more equal sections of 2419, 2287, and 2116 lines.

47.   Hansjürgen Linke, *Epische Strukturen in der Dichtung Hartmanns von Aue. Untersuchungen zur Formkritik, Werkstruktur und Vortragsgliederung* (Munich: Fink, 1968).

48.   Line numbers refer to Meister Otte, *Eraclius*. [n. 4 above].

49.   Line numbers refer to Gautier d'Arras, *Eracle*, ed. Guy Raynaud de Lage, C.F.M.A. (Paris: Champion, 1976).

50.   The frequency of the monologue form in Veldeke's *Eneit* (reflecting its extensive use in the *Roman d'Enéas*) may well explain Hartmann's predilection for monologue in his Arthurian romances. See Wiehl [n. 1 above], p. 75.

51.   I am aware that the distinction between translation and adaptation is largely a modern one, which the medieval *interpres* would probably not have recognized. However, the fact that the advantages and disadvantages of literal translation were debated throughout the Middle Ages indicates that the concept of verbal closeness to the original suggested

by the opposition translation / adaptation was not foreign to medieval poets.

ADDITIONAL REFERENCES

Fourquet, Jean. "Hartmann d'Aue et l'adaptation courtoise. Histoire d'une invention de détail." *Etudes Germaniques* 27 (1972):333-40.

_____. "Les Adaptations allemandes des romans chevaleresques français." *Etudes Germaniques* 32 (1977):97-107.

Freytag, Wiebke. "Zu Hartmanns Methode der Adaptation im *Erec*." *Euphorion* 72 (1978):227-39.

Hilka, Alfons. *Die direkte Rede als stilistisches Kunstmittel in den Romanen des Kristian von Troyes.* Halle: Niemeyer, 1903.

Wolf, Alois. "Die 'Adaptation courtoise.' Kritische Anmerkungen zu einem neuen Dogma." *Germanisch-Romanische Monatsschrift* 27 (1977):257-83.

THE ENGLISHING OF
THE COMIC TECHNIQUE IN
HUE DE ROTELANDE'S *IPOMEDON*

Brenda Hosington

The Anglo-Norman *Ipomedon*, a courtly romance composed by Hue de Rotelande shortly after 1180, must have had both an endearing and an enduring quality since it was translated into English three times between the last quarter of the fourteenth century and the middle of the fifteenth, and into forms as diverse as tail-rhyme stanzas, rhyming couplets, and prose. The present study is concerned with the 8890-line, tail-rhyme version written in a North Midlands dialect in the late fourteenth century. It is preserved in the Chetham MS Mun. A. 6. 31 (8009) and was labeled *Ipomadon A* by Kölbing in his 1889 edition of it.[1]

It is Kölbing who first examined in detail the various translating techniques employed by the author of *Ipomadon A* (pp. xxxvi ff.). He was able, thanks to his accurate and thorough analysis, to establish that the author was working from a written source and not from memory, as had previously been believed. Moreover, by setting the French and English texts side by side, he identified the following five translation techniques: very close, word for word; free adaptation; transferral, or shifting of a passage from its place in the source text to another in the target text; the addition, omission, or abridgement of a passage; and repetition of a phrase or passage not repeated in the original. Despite this valuable analysis, Kölbing's commentary contains no detailed assessment of the quality of the translation, pointing out simply that it is "very close" and "of dubious literary worth," nor does it discuss the character of the English poem as compared with its original.

Writers since Kölbing[2] have agreed with him on the closeness of

247

the translation, which extends even to the borrowing of words and preservation of French rhyme-words and rhyme-pairs.   Holden, *Ipomedon's* most recent editor, turns on more than one occasion to the English text for elucidation of the French.   Such fidelity, some claim, is unusual in the Middle English romances and makes *Ipomadon* A something of an "oddity."[3]   Regarding the style of Hue's poem and its imitation in the English version, comments have been few.   Hibbard complains that it does not preserve the "special excellencies of Hue's humorous and leisurely romance" (p. 225); Mehl comments that "the tone of the source has been changed in many ways" (p. 54); Trounce, while praising the poem as a "capital performance--one of the peaks of Middle English literature," (p. 43), says it has little of the original's chivalric spirit despite its chivalric paraphernalia (pp. 107-08).   Pearsall, however, characterizes it as "courtly, witty, smooth, enormously leisurely, and technically highly gifted."[4]   In their introduction to selections from *Ipomadon A,*[5] Schmidt and Jacobs note that the poet's manner "conveys little suggestion of the refined sensuality of his original."   More specifically, they criticize the translator's neglect of almost all of Hue's humorous comments and the resulting "somewhat routine or neutral tone common in most romances."

The humor in *Ipomedon* has in fact long been recognized as one of the poem's salient features.[6]   Telling the story of a young knight's conquest of an "orgueilleuse d'amour," the Duchess of Calabria known only by her nickname of La Fiere, the romance presents an ambivalent view of aristocratic society.   At times rather idealistic in its didactic portrayal of chivalry and feudal values, the poem nevertheless repeatedly undercuts both with brief ironic asides and sometimes cynical commentary on characters and events in the narrative.   The same ambivalence characterizes Hue's treatment of literary conventions.   *Ipomedon* is cast in the form of a courtly romance, exploiting traditional themes and motifs found in works like the *Roman de Thèbes*, the Anglo-Norman *Tristan*, *Cligès*, and *Partonopeu de Blois*.   Yet again Hue challenges convention, undercutting the "courtliness" of romance by mocking his characters, using inappropriate language, introducing fabliau elements, and mixing the exotic with the familiar.   The effect is to create an unusually strong sense of author-audience complicity. The exact identity of that audience is not known, but it presumably was aristocratic, Anglo-Norman, and resided in the Hereford region where Hue was living at the time of composition, given the number of local allusions in the poem.

Preserving the style of a work bearing such a strong authorial stamp and written two centuries earlier for a very different type of audience must not have been easy. Nothing is actually known of the anonymous translator's audience.[7] We can surmise that it was well-to-do and possibly drawn from the local gentry. Although perhaps fairly familiar with some courtly romances, its members would have been less well-read than their Anglo-Norman predecessors and, of course, less knowledgeable about feudal values and social conventions. They almost certainly would not have understood the topical allusions of the source. In assessing the fidelity with which the translator renders the tone of the original, these points must be kept in mind. Above all, it is important to discover whether the changes occur consistently, forming patterns that transform the very nature of the English poem. Are certain of Hue's favorite rhetorical figures--amplification, hyperbole, anti-climax, for example--frequently or only sporadically omitted? How is the strong and often humorous narratorial voice handled? Is the irony that characterizes the original as pervasive in the translation? Are the many distancing techniques contributing to that overall irony reproduced? The effect of rigorously deleting references to illicit love, greatly reducing the number of humorous sexual comments or toning many of them down, would be to make the risqué nature of many passages more serious and moral. Persistent omission of Hue's cynical remarks would result in a more idealistic presentation of a chivalric milieu that for a fourteenth-century non-aristocratic audience must have been rather remote. As for Hue's references to himself and to local people and places, which help to establish the author-audience complicity that provides much of the poem's humor, they could be included, with or without gloss, deleted, or updated. Inclusion, like deletion, inevitably results in a loss: allusions to the unfamiliar and humor that needs explaining are no longer funny; but replacing Hue's references with local ones known to the audience would preserve much of the comic tone.[8]   Thus the translator was free to exercise a number of choices in his handling of humorous materials.[9] This article will examine his choices and their effect in four crucial areas: literary hoaxes, sexual comment, broad comedy, and proverbs.

Hue's *Ipomedon* begins and ends with a literary hoax.   After telling his audience that good may be learned from old stories, the narrator deplores the fact that his story could not be understood in the Latin original--no one can read Latin any longer.   The story must therefore be put into "romanz" (French) and be translated quickly, ignoring questions of case and tense and keeping only its "verrour." "Ki grant ovre voet translater / Brefment l'estuet outre passer" [lines 43-44; The person wanting to translate a great work / Must go through it quickly].   No Latin original in fact existed. The prologue is intended to deride the "learned" preambles of the time.

The English poet ignores the prologue of the French source.[10] He offers instead two stanzas of his own in which he recognizes the joys and pains of love and announces he will give lovers hope by presenting them with the example of a lover who "of his love was lothe to lese" (line 14) and who to this end pursued prowess, albeit incognito. No one will have heard of a more secretive knight (lines 20-24).   Thus the English introduction states the story concisely, emphasizes the subject of love and hints at its vagaries, addresses the audience directly, and concludes on an amusing note.   However, it ignores all the comic effects of the original: the reference to a non-existent Latin source, Hue de Rotelande's excuses in the third person for ignoring the grammatical niceties of the original, his mockery of the "learned" clerks who, surprisingly, have ignored this Latin text, and his explanation that the translation's "brevity"--only 10,580 lines--is intended to avoid boredom in his audience. These omissions were presumably calculated.   The translator astutely realized the inappropriateness of Hue's prologue. A hoax about an imaginary foreign source is less effective in a romance translated from a foreign source. Mockery of an unfamiliar convention is ineffectual, and the translator's audience was less sophisticated than the French author's. Hue's pretended concern for the "brevity" and "veracity" of the translation is therefore omitted consistently by the translator whenever it is articulated. Remarks on the truth of the tale were comic only within the context of a hoax.

Similar treatment is given to Hue's extravagant claim, occurring at the poem's close, that *Le Roman de Thèbes* was inspired by the story of Ipomedon (lines 10541-42). This is ignored by the English poet, who nevertheless uses the Thebes reference for narrative expansion. To Hue's comment "A Thebes fut Ipomedon" and his command that the audience instruct themselves because "Hue s'en test e se repose" [line 10552; Hue is now silent, and is resting] is added the information that Ipomedon died at Thebes, after which his wife, the Fere, refused to eat or drink, and "for pure love dyed" (lines 8860-63). Comedy is this time replaced by the romanticism of a heroine's inconsolable love-sickness.

Hue's reference to Thebes occasions further parody. Lovers are sent a message from Ipomedon in an epilogue that Holden calls "scabreux" (p. 51), "une parodie directe" of Thomas d'Angleterre's farewell to his "fins amants" in *Tristan*. Lovers are instructed by the God of Love to love loyally "sens tricherie e senz fauser" [without cheating and without deceiving], for he will excommunicate those who abstain from love. Abstainers are free to find pleasure where they can, and the most successful will be absolved (lines 10562-70). In the final lines Hue personally invites the women of the region to the "chartre . . . de l'absoluciun" in his house at Credenhill. Those who do not believe him will be punished. He concludes crudely that "ço n'ert pas trop grant damages / Se li seaus il pent as nages" [lines 10579-80; it will not do too much harm if the seal (of the charter) hangs down from her behind].

The English translator borrows the motif of Ipomedon's message to lovers: "His messyngere makythe he me" (lines 8876-78). Hue's personal message is however omitted:

> He commaundythe on goddis behalue,
> To lovys wounde ye lay no salue,
> But poynttis of grette pette.
> Where right loue was in herte brought,
> That for a littill lette ye noughte:
> Sertes, no more dyd hee.   (lines 8879-84)

Thus the translator echoes the sentiments of his introductory stanzas concerning the pains of love and the need for courage and stead-fastness. He transforms Hue's "deu d'amur" into "God" and ends with a Christian invocation:

> That good lorde bringe vs to his blis,
> That bought vs on the rode tre!
> And that ye shall for louers *pray*
> To hym, that made bothe nyght and day. (lines 8886-89)

This shift from Hue's comic ending is in conformity with the translator's overall treatment of Hue's literary parody.

Another source of Hue's comedy is his narrator's attitude towards sexuality, which ranges from the frankly obscene to the risqué and from parodic to satiric. The translator omits all occurrences of "fotre" and "jouster" for the love act. (The former, found at lines 8648 and 10516, occurs only in one manuscript, in fact, having been already changed in the others by "prudish scribes," according to Holden.[11]) At line 8648 ("Dehez ait il, se il ne la fut!" [curse him if he doesn't fuck her!]) it is the only omission from an otherwise closely translated passage. The line "il se entrefoutent tute jur" [line 10516; they fucked all day], which parodies the happy ending of romances, occurs among multiple jokes about sexual inexperience and virginity. Here the whole section is replaced by a rather repetitious twenty-line passage praising the perfect harmony that united the lovers throughout life (lines 8816-36). Similarly, "juster enz el lit" [jousting in bed] is always omitted, although its surrounding context is carefully rendered. And Hue's naming of his heroine's private parts, her "cunet" (line 2269), in an otherwise conventional catalogue of feminine charms is conspicuously absent from the English version.

The translator's rendering of Hue's remarks about homo-sexuality is noteworthy. Sir Dryas criticizes the choice of the King of Spain's son, a homosexual, for La Fiere: "Ja ne verrez un sul herite, / Ki en ses garçons se delite . . . Ffemme ennurrer" [lines 2367-70; Never will you see a single homosexual who takes delight in his boys, that can honor a woman]. The perils of marrying homosexuals are described in some detail. Local evidence is cited of known victims and is followed by the hackneyed observation that women are insatiable. The translator transforms this passage into Sir Dryas's exclamation:

> "For I am no eratyke,
> I meyne for my ladye. . . .
> There shall neu*er* eretyke, as I haue roo,
> Worshipe to no woman doo"   (lines 2104ff.)

The French "herite" has therefore been interpreted as "heretic," a word that in Middle English had no homosexual connotations.[12] The translator may, of course, be punning on the word's two possible meanings, "heretic" and "rascal," the former applicable to the King of Spain's son, the latter to Sir Dryas. The line "ki en ses garcons se delite" is rendered as "For lev*er* theu had*de* w*ith* lassis to loure, / Than to joye w*yth* byrd*es* in bowre" (lines 2112-13).[13]

Hue's poem also contains dubious jokes about women and love. For example, in a comic description of Ipomedon's night wanderings he matches the hero's fervor for hunting (lines 4475-4500) with the court women's fervor for sex (lines 4501-10), concluding with the women's complaint to the queen that they should be left to sleep in the morning: "Aukes ad plus süef dedut / Les deit l'um esveiller la nuit" [For the sweetest pleasure, a man must wake them at night]. This comic juxtaposition of hunting and sexual fervor is replaced by the translator's own brand of humor. The court women mockingly tell the queen that for her, "grett strok*es* will he [Ipomadon] geve / In forest vnder an *a*ke" (lines 3615-16). The hero's supposed lack of prowess is lamented by the queen in the following stanza: "Syne he is so fayre all wyce, / That no prowes on hym lysse" (lines 3620-21). Thus Hue's sly humor is replaced by a more serious attitude. Two other passages containing risqué humor are omitted in their entirety.[14]

Hue's narrative also contains satiric comments about women and love, again parodying the sentiments of contemporary romances.[15] Woman's deviousness is exemplified by La Fiere,[16] who will always find a way to send a message to a man (lines 830-32). Ismeine's behavior is judged typical of a woman's "engign." Hue concludes that women "pur rien sachent nul mal faire, / Se n'est en un sul jur mil paire" [lines 1911-24; cannot commit *one* bad deed--they commit a thousand in a day]. But the translator always renders the narrative without its anti-feminist commentary. Inconstancy, another feminine trait, is illustrated by La Fiere's changing reactions at the three-day tournament--she admires first the white knight, then the red, and finally the black. The English heroine is less fickle. Desiring news of the white and red knights, she changes color at the sight of Ipomedon and forgets the other two. Hue's final aphorism "Ja ne verrez femme si sage / Ke akune feiz ne chant curage" [lines 5447-48; Never will you see a woman so sensible that she won't change her mind] is omitted. Fickleness, impetuosity, and contrariness are allied in women. According to Hue's narrator, women love most the men they have hated the most and quickly become hostile towards those that would serve them, as he himself can testify: "Jo en sai le veir, pur ço le di" [lines 8657-66; I know this is true, that's why I'm saying it]. The English narrator, however, says a woman is "bothe warre and wyse" and has much to teach men. Women change their minds not because they are unstable but because they prefer men who do not pursue them too eagerly. The personal intervention in the French becomes a gentle (if somewhat patronizing) "God*es* dere blessyng and myne / Muste they have therefore!" (lines 7088-96). Woman's impatience, illustrated in La Fiere (lines 6937-40), is faithfully rendered:

> As wome*n*, what þey will haue wrought,
> To do ther lykyng, lett they noughte,
> Come aft*er*, what sum maye."   (lines 5328-30)

And the translator's sympathy towards "the feyre" does not prevent him from rendering Hue's parody of a suffering courtly heroine. Her sighing "vahalet" and Ismeine's pretended incomprehension (lines 1495-1519) lose none of their comedy in the translation's "v-alete" scene (lines 1439-71).

Like the subject of women, the theme of love's universal power is sometimes treated with irony. This too is toned down in the

English poem. One such passage (lines 9095-9110) opens with the courtly-sounding "Mut ad grant valur amur fine" [*Fine amor* has great power] but immediately continues with a catalogue of biblical men tricked by women, overcome by love, and robbed of all virtue. The translator omits the humorous juxtaposition, stating simply that love overpowers men of all social situations, and ends tritely: "Love may save, love may spille" and "turne all vp and downe" (lines 7346-54). A similar comic procedure occurs when a description of the classic conflict between love and prowess is followed by the suggestion that the hero should have feigned sickness and stayed with his lady (lines 6711-24). Again, the juxtaposition is lost by the omission of the narrator's comment, no doubt a conscious one because Hue's comment undercuts both the chivalric and moral tone of the passage (lines 5092-5100).

In scenes of broad comedy Hue's humor depends upon exaggeration, repetition, and caricature. The hero's noisy comings and goings when in hunter's disguise are described by the translator in six passages, of which five retain their original comedy. The final hunting scene (lines 4729-38), however, is rendered more realistic than humorous by the conversion of the English ladies' mirth to wrath. Other scenes of broad comedy--the hero's arrival at court dressed as a fool and his nights with Ismeine in a similar disguise--reproduce the overall comedy of the original and even at times heighten Hue's comic tone. For example, the figures of speech the translator uses to describe Ipomadon and Imayne, despite their superficial appearance of tags or line-fillers, are humorous because totally inappropriate: Ipomadon "lep vp as bryme, as any bore" (line 7405) although he knows his assailant is only Imayne; she, having sighed and suffered throughout the scene, is called "that byrde so bryght" (line 7414). The translator's caricaturist portrait of Leonine actually surpasses the original both in length and hyperbolic detail:

Mut est grant e mut hisdus,	A fowler man ther may non be
Le chef ad cresp e neir rus,	Ne more vncomely thying:
Le vis ad neir e teint e pers,	Hys hed ys row w*yth* feltred here,
La gule beë en travers,	Blake bryste*l*d as a bore,
Les denz lunges, hors de la bouche,	His browys full they hynge

255

Le nes lunc, deske as denz li tuche;   W*yth* longe tethe, I warand yow,
A desmesure est corporuz,   Eu*ery* lype, I dare avowe,
Unc si grant hum ne fut veüz   Hyngyth lyke a blode puddynge!
Ne si tres fors hom par semblant,
Petit i faut ke il n'est geant.   This dare I sau*erly* make a sethe,
        (lines 7703-12)   His nose towchys on his tethe,
    His mothe wrythis all way,
    Blake as any *p*eche hys face,
    As two dobelers eu*ery* eye he hathe,
    W*yth* gorget gret and gray;
    His berde as pyche ys blake,
    His body hathe an euyll smake,
    The vesnamy fovle, I saye,
    Neke as an ape, nebe as an owle:
    In all this worlde ys none so fovle,
    This dare I sau*erly say*!
        (lines 6145-64)

An important element in Hue's comic technique is his use of proverbs.[17] As interjections in direct speech, comments embedded in the narrative, or audience-directed digressions, they establish a direct relationship between author and audience. For example, when King Darius offers his daughter to Ipomedon, whose heart as the audience knows belongs to La Fiere, the narrator comments: "Mes teus pot batre les bussuns / Dunt autre en porte les muissuns" (lines 7587-88). The same complicity is achieved in the exactly equivalent English proverb, "on the bushe bett*es* one, / A nothere man hathe the b*r*yde" (lines 6021-22), although less deftly on account of the preceding explanatory comment (lines 6009-10). Essentially comic in their effect, Hue's proverbs also contribute to the poem's "distance ironique par rapport à la conception courtoise" [ironic distancing of itself from the courtly tradition] because many are inappropriate to courtly romance.[18] Moreover, they are often introduced by formulas that emphasize that inappropriateness. Others still are used for parodic effect.

Proverb translation, like any other, presents a number of choices--literal translation, paraphrase, substitution of an equivalent, or omission--while at the same time imposing certain constraints.

Proverbs are set, codified statements whose form and meaning are fixed in both source and target languages. The translation methods adopted to render Hue's proverbs demonstrate the same freedom and variety as was seen in the translator's other comic techniques.

Of Hue's sixty-one proverbs, barely one-third are retained, to which are added three of the translator's own. Some are very closely translated in both form and content: "Mal est batu qe plurer n'ose" (line 1218) becomes "Sore is he bett, that darre not wepe" (line 1175). A few are modified in function or in formulaic content: "E asez li unt dit suvent: / Maulveise atente ad cil ki pent!" (lines 1852-53) is an interjection in direct speech. However, in the English it is a flat statement: "In our*e* longe tareynge / Comes greves monyefold!" (lines 1800-01). Others occur in passages that humorously accumulate a series of proverbs and mockingly present them according to the models provided in the rhetoric handbooks. The English closely reproduces La Fiere's lament over her pride (lines 4587-4614), paraphrasing the first proverb on pride (lines 3680-81) and its application (lines 3683-84) and giving the same exemplum of Lucifer (lines 3693-94) and its application (lines 3695-96). The effect of the two proverbs following immediately upon each other, however, is lost, for only one is rendered, albeit in a phrase with a decidedly proverbial ring.[19] Only once does the translator imitate this procedure by adding a proverb of his own, when he successfully achieves the same effect as his French model (lines 211-22).

In handling Hue's often ironic introductory formulas, the translator exhibits a similar range of translating techniques: omission, paraphrase, and addition. Of the two dozen different formulas, only five are translated. For "li vilains" (line 3497) is substituted "in olde sawe" (line 3018), for "saive gent" (line 4607), "Wyse men" (line 3686). A passive verb, "It hathe byn sayd" (line 941) replaces "cil dit bien," (line 971) while another, "ofte ys sayd in old sawe," (line 1385) substitutes poorly for a direct question, "L'um reprove, savez vus quei?" (line 1445). The general "Mut ai oï dire suvent" (line 8561) is made more specific, "I se full well there bye" (line 6965). The translator adds a formula of his own to a proverb he has translated quite closely: "But ofte is sayd be me*n* of skole" (line 6436). The first three English renderings are close in form and spirit to their source, as is the translator's own original offering. The remaining two are less successful. The omission of the over-whelming majority of introductory formulas, however, inevitably reduces the comic tone in many passages.

One passage in which proverbs are frequent, Ipomedon's rather self-important "instruction" to his master Tholomeu, is illustrative of the translator's handling of long proverbial passages. Hue's accumulation of generalities is ironic, humorously distant by its impersonal form. The English version is directed more specifically to love and lovers, and its personal quality is reinforced by the introductory formulas "Thynkes mee" and "I trowe" and the shifting of the comment on the wand of courtesy into the first person. The comic tone is reinforced by Hue's mix of *curteisie* and *folur*, a parody of a similar passage in *Perceval* (lines 1646-54), and by the abrupt, anti-climactic change of tone in the final lines.[20] Neither of these comic procedures appears in the English:

Mestre, sovent fet cil qe sage	For eu*er* more, mayst*er*, thynk*es* mee,
Ki set ben cuvrir sun curage,	That lovers shold *well leynand* be,
Meint home en tel liu se descovre	For mekyll I pre*y*se that wande,
Ke meulz li vaudreit celer sa ovre;	
Meins valt trop dire ke celer,	That brek*es* not and will well bowe;
Ki s'i savreit amesurer;	Righte so it farythe be them, I trowe,
Cil ki mut parole sovent	That lovys and well can layne;
Ne se pot astenir neent	In few word*es* ys curtesye:
Ke aukune feiz folur ne die,	Lette his ded*es* bere wittenes, why
Le bel teisir est curteisie;	He shuld be louyde agayne!
Le fous, se il parole tut tens,	In suche place, me*n* may hym dyscure,
Aukune feiz ahurte a sens.	Hym were better, to hold hym sure,
Ne voil si, mestre, arester mes,	For ofte that poynte dothe payne;
Asez ai chevaus e herneis.	In fele wordis be reson ys lyes,
(lines 2621-34)	And ay the moste man of price
	The leyste of them selff wille sa*y*ne!
	(lines 2333-47)

The same is true for other extended proverbial passages in *Ipomedon*. Changes and the omission of two-thirds of the proverbs effect a shift away from the burlesque of the original, even when

258

author-audience complicity is maintained.

In his version of *Ipomedon*, the English translator shows himself capable of striking a balance between preserving the substance of his French original and creating a poem that can be enjoyed in its own right on account of its lively style, successful handling of the difficult tail-rhyme stanza, and wittiness. As we have seen, the last of these virtues manifests itself in ways often different from those of its source. Using a variety of translating methods from literal translation to paraphrase and fairly close rendering to adaptation, to which he adds humorous passages of his own, the author of *Ipomedon A* has produced a composition that, if not as incisively witty and parodic as the original, is nevertheless indisputably humorous. He has sacrificed much of the sarcastic comedy and parody, a salient feature of Hue's poem, by replacing the literary hoaxes with framing stanzas on the power of love or serious statements like that about Thebes, by either omitting or changing the many comments on love, women, and the protagonists, and by reducing the number and impact of the proverbs. Hue's more daring forays into the realm of sexual comedy are either omitted or replaced by a different type of humor, both gentler and more genteel. The cynical comments on women in particular are toned down, and the English narrator does not reflect his French model's callousness. Together with the stammering scene, the episodes most faithfully reproduced in letter and spirit are those depending on broad comedy. It is with this type of humor that the English poet seems most at home, often even outdoing his source. At this point, it is inevitable to evoke audience-response explanations. A more socially mixed but less educated group than Hue's aristocratic Anglo-Norman circle would respond less readily to an ironic treatment of courtly characters and themes and a parodic flouting of literary conventions, and more readily to the direct, broad humor of slapstick, caricature, and hyperbole. The deletion or toning down of the dirty, very cynical jokes might also be attributable to differing audience responses, or, perhaps, could quite simply represent the response of a rather prudish translator.

As Holden cautions in his discussion of the nature of *Ipomedon*, "déterminer avec exactitude la tonalité d'une œuvre médiévale n'est pas chose facile" [p. 52; it is not easy to decide what exactly the tone of a medieval work is]. Nevertheless it is safe to say that a clearly perceptible modulation of tone occurs in the English work. In his "Englishing" of Hue's poem, the *Ipomadon A* translator largely replaces parody and satire by a gentler wit. At the same time, he shares many a joke. By retaining some of Hue's comic techniques, he has maintained a certain degree of what George Steiner calls "mediation" between the original and his version;[21] at the same time, by rejecting others, he has produced not a "miroir fidèle" such as modern translators strive for, but a humorous and entertaining "trahison fidèle," a worthy representative of the age in which it was written and a fine English romance.

NOTES

1. *Ipomedon in drei englischen bearbeitungen*, ed. Eugen Kölbing (Breslau: Ernsdorf, 1889). All quotations will be from this edition unless otherwise stated. Quotations from the French poem are all from *Ipomedon*, ed. A. J. Holden (Paris: Klincksieck, 1979). References to Kölbing's and Holden's editorial comments will be given in the text in parentheses.

2. Among these are Laura Hibbard, *Medieval Romance in England*, new edition (New York: Benjamin Franklin, 1960), p. 225; J. Burke Severs, *A Manual of the Writings in Middle English, 1050-1500*, vol. 1, *Romances* (New Haven, CT: The Connecticut Academy of Arts and Sciences, 1967), p. 154; Flora Ross Amos, *Early Theories of Translation* (New York: Columbia Univ. Press, 1920), p. 21; Dieter Mehl, *The Middle English Romances of the Thirteenth and Fourteenth Centuries* (London: Routledge, 1968), who adds that it is more akin to the "Anglo-Norman courtly tradition than to the English romances" (p. 67); and Albert C. Baugh, "The Middle English Romance: Some Questions of Creation, Presentation, and Preservation," *Speculum* 42 (1967):1-13.

3. A. McI. Trounce, "The English Tail-Rhyme Romances," *Medium Aevum* 1 (1932):87-108 and 3 (1934):30-50.

4. Derek Pearsall, "The Development of the Middle English Romance," *Medieval Studies* 27 (1965):91-117.

5.   A. V. C. Schmidt and Nicholas Jacobs, eds., *Medieval English Romances*, 2 vols. (London: Hodder & Stoughton, 1980), 2:40-49.

6.   M. Dominica Legge (*Anglo-Norman Literature and its Background* [Oxford: Clarendon Press, 1963], pp. 85-96) goes so far as to call it "almost a parody of the courtly romance." In *The Individual in Twelfth-Century Romance* (New Haven, CT: Yale Univ. Press, 1977), pp. 123-35, Robert W. Hanning recognizes the comic elements and ironical treatment of chivalry and adds that *Ipomedon* is more than simply a satire or burlesque, for chivalry is also given an educative function in the poem. Philippe Ménard in *Le Rire et le sourire dans le roman courtois en France au moyen âge: (1150-1250)* (Geneva: Droz, 1969), pp. 336-53, while recognizing the humor in *Ipomedon* denies any overall parodic intent. Schmidt and Jacobs [n. 5 above] for their part deny any cynicism and rather questionably prefer to call Hue's brand of humor "realistic worldly wisdom, which in some ways anticipates Chaucer."

7.   In an interesting article on the three English *Ipomedons*, Carol Meale discusses the audiences and owners of the extant manuscripts. After examining the composition of the Chetham MS in which *Ipomadon A* is found, she concludes that *Ipomadon A* and *Ipomydon B* (called by critics the "courtly" and "popular" versions) were in fact "being read at the same time, almost certainly in the same city [London] and probably by members of the same class [merchant]"; see Carol Meale, "The Middle English Romance of *Ipomedon*: A Late Medieval 'Mirror' for Princes and Merchants," *Reading Medieval Studies* 10 (1984):136-91.

8.   The translator in fact chooses to omit all the references to Hue by name and all the allusions to his contemporaries (Walter Map, Huge de Hungrie, Rhys ap Gruffydd) and surroundings (Hereford, Credenhill, Gloucester, Shrewsbury, Worcester). Most of these appear in all the extant French manuscripts (Map and Credenhill appear in only one; one reference to Hereford is in all the manuscripts, the other missing in two). It is fairly safe, therefore, to assume that they were omitted from the translation on purpose. Moreover, the translator chose not to replace them with contemporary allusions.

9.   For a general discussion of this subject, see Roger Ellis, "The Choices of the Translator in the Late Middle English Period," in *The*

Medieval Mystic Tradition in England (Exeter: Univ. of Exeter Press, 1982), pp. 18-46.

10.   Contrary to what Mehl [n. 2 above] says (p. 59).

11.   Holden [n. 1 above], p. 564.

12.   Kölbing [n. 1 above] points out (p. 396) that an association was sometimes made between Saracens and homosexuals and that Spain was called "paynim" in later English romances.

13.   Kölbing suggests two readings for "lassis": young members of either sex or women of ill repute. He based the first on Skeat's similar reading of "gerles" in Chaucer's Prologue to *The Canterbury Tales*, but I find this unconvincing, especially since no such meaning is documented. There is, however, ample evidence for the second meaning in both northern and Scottish dialects. Moreover, the reading is supported by the contrast set up, not between homosexual and heterosexual love but between illicit and honorable love and reinforced by the verbs "loure" and "joye" and the nouns "lassis" and "byrdes."

14.   Hue's use of medical terminology to describe Ipomedon's kiss bestowed upon the queen (lines 5512-19), a passage otherwise closely translated (lines 4161-66), and his reference to the young couple's virginity and loss thereof (lines 10503-13).

15.   As Holden [n. 1 above] points out (p. 53), anti-feminine remarks are almost always present in the romances, even the most idealistic and courtly, but in *Ipomedon* they are uncommonly frequent and harsh (p. 55). This would suggest they are being used by Hue to flout the literary conventions of the time.

16.   For a comparative study of La Fiere and the heroines in the three English versions, see Brenda [Hosington] Thaon, "La Fiere: The Career of Hue de Rotelande's Heroine in England," *Reading Medieval Studies* 9 (1983):56-69.

17.   Although the proverbs in *Ipomedon A* have been discussed by B. J. Whiting in "Proverbs in Certain Middle English Romances in Relation to

their French Sources," *Harvard Studies and Notes in Philology and Literature* 15 (1933):75-126, the subject can bear a second scrutiny, partly because his article contains a number of errors but more important, because his intent was to identify the proverbs and assess their originality, not to study the translating methods used or the overall effect of the proverbs on the poem. In studying the proverbs in *Ipomedon* and *Ipomadon A*, the following reference works were used: Joseph Morawski, *Proverbes français antérieurs au XVe siècle* (Paris: Champion, 1925) and "Proverbes français inédits tirés de trois recueils anglo-normands," *Zeitschrift für romanische Philologie* 56 (1936):419-39; Samuel Singer, *Sprichwörter des Mittelalters*, 3 vols. (Berne: Verlaag Herbert Lang & Cie., 1944-47); B. J. Whiting, *Proverbs, Sentences and Proverbial Phrases from English Writings Mainly Before 1500* (Cambridge, MA: Harvard Univ. Press, 1968); M. P. Tilley, *A Dictionary of the Proverbs in England in the Sixteenth and Seventeenth Centuries* (Ann Arbor, MI: Univ. of Michigan Press, 1950). Also consulted were the various modern dictionaries of proverbs and the usual general dictionairies.

18. Elisabeth Schulze-Busacker, *Proverbes et expressions proverbiales dans la littérature narrative au Moyen-Age français: Recueil et analyse* (Paris: Champion, 1985), pp. 75-82.

19. The French proverb, "Ki munte trop haut / Tost pot descendre a mauveis saut" (lines 4609-10), is rendered as "Who hes them selff, þat beli*v*e is las" (line 3687). This is perhaps a variation on "Who mounts higher than he should falls lower than he would," whose first recorded use is ascribed to Caxton in 1484. It appears in both Whiting's *Proverbs, Sentences and Proverbial Phrases* [n. 17 above] and Tilley's *Dictionary of Proverbs* [n. 17 above].

20. Schulze-Busacker [n. 18 above], p. 79.

21. George Steiner, *After Babel: Aspects of Language and Translation* (London: Oxford Univ. Press, 1975), p. 267.

ADDITIONAL REFERENCE

Crotch, W. J. B., ed. *The Prologues and Epilogues of William Caxton.* E. Early English Text Society, O. S. 176. London, 1928.

THE *FIORE* AND THE *ROMAN DE LA ROSE*

Earl Jeffrey Richards

E ver since its publication in 1881, the Italian translation of the *Roman de la Rose*, called the *Fiore* by its original editor Ferdinand Castets, has occasioned scholarly controversy. Repeated attempts have been made to assign the work's authorship to Dante,[1] and the dispute over attribution has diverted attention from the *Fiore*'s literary merits. Since commentary has been prejudiced by the assumption that the *Fiore* must somehow fit into the evolution of Dante's career, I shall not presuppose Dante's authorship but instead refer to "the *Fiore* poet" in an attempt to escape the circularity of much *Fiore* scholarship.

The date of the translation has prompted much speculation: Bernhard Langheinrich argued for a composition during the 1280s since the *Fiore*'s language appears more archaic than Dante's;[2] Giuseppe Petrocchi suggested 1286-87;[3] Gianfranco Contini, in his recent critical edition of the *Fiore*, follows Petrocchi;[4] and Joseph A. Barber has presented statistical evidence which suggests a much later date.[5] The *Fiore*'s sonnets (some 3,245 surviving hendeca-syllabic lines) radically recast the some 21,750 lines of the original, and many of the *Rose*'s most conspicuous features are missing in the Italian. The dream format and the corresponding *dédoublement* of narrator and protagonist are gone; the poem's action has been shifted from May to January; the role of Reason is significantly abbreviated; the speeches of Nature and Genius are omitted entirely; and focus has been redirected to the sections of the original devoted to Ami, La Vieille, and Faux-Semblant. Of the *Rose*'s sources, Juvenal has taken a more prominent place than Ovid, and all references to Vergil in the *Rose*[6] have been deleted from the *Fiore*.

265

Examining the craft with which the *Fiore* poet molded his work is a two-step process. First, it is important to derive and apply historically valid criteria for evaluating the *Fiore* as a translation in the narrow sense; second, it is useful to derive and apply historically valid criteria for evaluating it as a literary work in its own right. Throughout the evaluation it is indispensable to avoid anachronism. It would, for example, be tempting to take Quintilian's observations on the freedom of translation (*Inst. Orat.*, 10, 5, 3) as a basis for discussing medieval translations; however, Quintilian was largely unknown to the Middle Ages until Poggio rediscovered his works in 1415. While Quintilian is of little use, Horace is all the more valuable. His *Ars poetica* was widely read and commented upon during the period in question, and his disparaging comments on the *fidus interpres* provide the general context for any consideration of medieval translation. One cannot criticize the *Fiore* for not being a faithful translation because fidelity *per se* was not cultivated. As Louis G. Kelly noted:

> As a technical term, fidelity begins under a cloud, equated with the literal translation: *fidus interpres* is the slighting term Horace applies to the translator in *Ars Poetica* 133. . . . It is Horace who best sums up the duty of a translator: in *Ars poetica* 131-5, he forbids the poet to venture where "modesty forbids or the laws governing the work" (*operis lex*). As the central point of discussion, *operis lex* means two things: the first, always taken for granted, is communicative purpose, that is the author's balance between symbol, symptom and signal. Only in light of this can the second element in the *operis lex*, relationship between matter and form, have any significance.[7]

Considering the lack of scholarly consensus in interpreting the *Rose*, determining its *operis lex* may seem doomed at the outset. Nevertheless, whether one interprets the *Rose* as a work of Augustinian irony or as a vernacular narrative heavily indebted to Chartrian philosophical epic with a more "biological" or "naturalistic" emphasis, or as a work espousing a particular creed of poetry,[8] one can point to some characteristics of the French work on which all observers agree: Guillaume's portion contains descriptions cast in a more "courtly" diction than that found in the more "scholastic" parts of Jean's section, and the *Rose*, considered as a whole, presents a wide spectrum of views concerning love. The *Fiore* poet has followed the *operis lex* of the *Rose* in somewhat idiosyncratic fashion. Raison's presence is sharply reduced (the entire discussion on *coilles* and obscene language is omitted). Ami, La Vieille, and Faux-Semblant receive disproportionate attention, and Nature and Genius are wholly absent. Perhaps these omitted portions of the *Rose*, with their "biological" emphasis, struck the *Fiore* poet as immodest in the Horatian sense. These changes, however, do not explain the omission of the dream format, the narrative *dédoublement*, the description of the *jardin de Deduit*, or the substitution of a sonnet cycle for narrative verse. Thus, it is clearly wrong to claim, as does John Took, that

> this generous cycle of sonnets represents by any standard
> a diligent reading of the original text; it is faithful both
> to its narrative as a whole and to its various comic
> psychological subtleties. . . . [Dante] omits altogther
> [the] naturalistic element from his own version of the
> *Rose* and in doing so . . . he effectively redefines the
> terms of the problem. For now, in the *Fiore*, it is Reason
> rather than Nature who determines the perspective of the
> poet's argument.[9]

The diminished role of Ragione in the *Fiore* as compared to Raison in the *Rose* argues for the contrary. The *Fiore* poet was deliberately selective, and his radical recasting may be illustrated by a switch from macroscopic analysis to a microscopic comparison of the translation with the original.

Two sonnets from the *Fiore*, (numbers 12 and 180), exhibit a close correspondence to the original, based on the exhaustive list of such correspondences provided in the apparatus to Contini's edition of the *Fiore*.[10] (In the examples below, numbers in the parentheses printed to the left of the Italian text refer to the corresponding lines in Lecoy's edition of the *Rose*.[11])

12
L'Amante

(3135)	Tutto pien d'umilità verso 'l giardino
(3130)	Torna' mi, *com'* Amico avea parlato,
(3139)	Ed i' guardai, e sì eb[b]i avisato
(3141)	Lo Schifo, con un gran baston di pino
	Ch'andava riturando ogne cammino
	Che dentro a forza non vi fosse 'ntrato;
	Si ch'io mi trassi a lui, e salutato
(3142)	Umilemente l'eb[b]i a capo chino,
(3144)	E sì gli dissi: "Schifo, ag[g]ie merzede
	Di me, se 'nverso te feci alcun fallo,
	Chéd i, sì son venuto a pura fede
(3147)	A tua merzede, e presto d'amendarlo."
	Que' mi riguarda, e tuttor si provede
(3209)	Ched i' non dica ciò per ingan[n]arlo.

Tant parla Amis et tant dis	3130
qu'il m'a auques reconforté.	
. . . .	
A Dangier sui venuz honteus,	3135
de ma pais fere covoiteus;	
mes la haie ne passai pas,	
por ce qu'il m'ot veé le pas.	
Je le trovai en piez drecié,	
fel par samblant et corocié,	3140
en sa main un baston d'espine.	
Je tins vers li la teste encline	
et li dis: "Sire, or sui ici	
venuz por vos crier merci.	
Mout me poise s'il peüst estre	3145
dont je vos fis onc irié estre.	
Mes or sui pres de l'amender	

268

si con vos savroiz comander. . . ."
[speech continues until line 3172]

. . . .

Dangier se prent garde sovent   3209
se ge li tien bien son covant.

12
[The Lover

All filled with humility, toward the garden
I turned, when Friend had stopped speaking,
And I looked and espied
Repugnance [=Danger], with a large staff of pine
      who was going around closing every path
So that I could not have entered in there by force;
So that I drew myself up to him and greeted him
Humbly, with head bowed,
      And so I said to him, "Repugnance, have mercy
On me; if I have committed some fault toward you
[Know] that I have come in good faith
      [To ask for] your mercy, ready to make up for it."
He looked at me, but still was cautious
      That I was not saying this to deceive him.]

[Friend spoke and said so much
that he comforted me a little.

. . . .

I went to Danger ashamed,
and eager to make my peace;
but I could not cross the hedge
because he had forbidden me entrance.
I found him standing,
Looking unmerciful and angered,
in his hand a staff of pine.
I held my head bowed toward him
and said to him: "Lord, now I have
come here to ask your mercy.

269

It weighs heavily upon me if it could be
that I have ever offended you.
But now I am here to make up for it
just as you might command."

. . . .

Danger frequently took care
that I upheld his commands well.]

180
La Vecchia

(13,765)	"Sî dé la donna, s'ell' è ben sentita,
(13,769)	Quando ricever dovrà quell'amante,
(13,766)	Mostralli di paura gran sembiante,
	E ch'ella dotta troppo es[s]er udita,
(13,761)	E che si mette a rischio de la vita.
(13,768)	Allor dé esser tutta tremolante,
(13,777)	Dir ch'ivi non puot' es[s]er dimorante:
(13,780)	Poï stea, che llor gioia sia compita.
(13,781)	Ancor convien ched ella si' acorta
(13,784)	Di far ch'e' v'entri per qualche spiraglio,
(13,785)	Ben potess' egli entrarvi per la porta:
	Ché tutte cose c[h]'uom' à con travaglio,
	Par c[h]'uon le pregi più, e le diporta;
	Quel che non costa, l'uon non pregia un aglio."

"Si doit fame, s'el n'est musarde,
fere samblant d'estre couarde,
de trembler, d'estre pooreuse,
d'estre destraite et angoisseuse
quant son ami doit recevoir,
et li face antendre de voir   13,770
qu'an trop grant perill le reçoit
quant son mari por lui deçoit,
ou ses gardes, ou ses paranz;
et que, se la chose iert paranz
qu'ele veust fere en repoutaille,   13,775

270

morte seroit sanz nule faille;
et jurt qu'il ne peut demourer,
s'il la devoit vive acourer;
puis demeurt a sa volanté,
quant el l'avra bien anchanté.   13,780
Si li redoit bien souvenir,
quant ses amis devra venir,
s'ele voit que nus ne l'aperçoive,
par la fenestre le reçoive,
tout puisse ele mieuz par la porte. . . ." 13,785

180
[*The Old Woman*

"Therefore the lady must, if she is truly sincere,
when she is to receive this lover,
put on a great show of fear --
that she is terribly afraid of being overheard,
          and that she is risking her life.
Then she must tremble with all her body,
and say that she cannot stay there:
Then let her stay until their joy is complete.
          Then she must be clever
to have him enter by some small opening,
even if he could enter through the door:
          since every thing which one gains with effort
seems to be worth more and bring more pleasure;
Whatever costs nothing is not worth a fig"
  (lit., a garlic-clove).

"So a woman, if she isn't thoughtless,
must pretend to be a coward,
to tremble and to be afraid,
to be distraught and fearful
when she is supposed to receive her lover,
and let her make him see
that she is receiving him at great peril
when she deceives her husband for him,

271

> or her guards or her relatives,
> and that, if the affair came out in the open
> which she had wanted to keep private,
> she would die without fail;
> and she must swear that he cannot stay,
> unless he means to kill her.
> Then he will stay at her will
> after she has enchanted him well.
>
> She must also remember well
> when her lover is to come
> if she sees that no one should perceive him,
> let her receive him through the window,
> even if she could just as well receive him by the door."]

These two sonnets are indicative of the stark reduction of the *Rose* throughout the *Fiore*; for example, Amant's original speech of thirty lines (3143-72) is cut to three and a half in Sonnet 12, a disproportionate abbreviation.[12] The condensed speech emphasizes above all L'Amante's humility: "honteus" becomes "tutto pien d'umilità" and "umilemente" is added; the one occurrence of "merci" is repeated twice in the Italian. Amant's humility is, of course, important in the original, but the Italian version presents it with considerably more intensity. The comfort afforded to Amant by Ami seems hardly present in the translation. In other words, where the translation has gained psychological intensity, it has lost psychological subtlety, a transformation which would be expected from the abridgement of the original and from the change in poetic format: the discursiveness of the French narrative is sacrificed in favor of the lyrical intensity afforded by the sonnet form itself. Similarly, the highly compressed form of the translation is apparent in its two-line conclusion, which makes the dramatic situation of the original much more explicit.

This process of compression and condensation, whereby the expansive narrative flow of the French is distilled into sonnets, is also evident in Sonnet 180. The first three lines of this sonnet are a close, almost literal, translation of three lines in the French, an example of fidelity that is unusual for the *Fiore*. The literalness of these three lines does not show evidence of syntactical, grammatical, or lexical calques, an important fact which bears on the consideration of the many Gallicisms scattered throughout the translation. The *Fiore* poet was perfectly capable, when he so desired, of translating literally into a non-Gallicized idiom. This capability would suggest that the lexically conspicuous Gallicisms of the *Fiore* correspond to a deliberate stylistic strategy whose effectiveness is open to question. In any event, Sonnet 180, like Sonnet 12, intensifies the situation portrayed in the original by honing down the dramatic situation to its bare essentials and by transforming the discursiveness of the French in the process. The translation of line 13,780, "quant el l'avra bien anchanté" as "Poï stea, che llor gioia sia compita" is more intense and more explicit than the French, showing that the Horatian injunction against immodesty was not always followed. The more courtly, diplomatic, attitude of the *Fiore* poet is seen in his positive transformation of "s'el n'est musarde" into "s'ell' è ben sentita."

This last change is an obvious addition to the text: in fact, only a third of the entire text of the *Fiore* bears a close textual resemblance to the original. The remainder summarizes and condenses the source. Moreover, there are relatively few examples in the *Fiore* where the translator rendered continuous passages from the *Rose*. Instead, he exercised enormous freedom in rearranging the original at will. Also, there are a few significant additions which conform to the overall patterns of shifting emphasis in the *Fiore*. The most important occurs early in the poem, when l'Amante pledges his loyalty and obedience to Lo Dio d'Amore. In the French version, Love's commandments are spelled out in lines 2073a-2221 (ed. Lecoy). The Italian version omits the commandments. In their place Lo Dio d'Amore proclaims, in language somewhat reminiscent of the First Commandment in the Old Testament:

> E quelli allor mi disse: "Amico meo,
> I' ò da te miglior pegno che carte:
> Fa che m'adori, ched i' son tu' deo;
>   Ed ogn' altra credenza metti a parte,
> Né non creder né Luca né Matteo
> Né Marco né Giovanni." Allor si parte.   (5, 9-14)

[And he then said to me: "My friend,
I have from you a better token of faith than charters.
Be sure to adore me, for I am your God;
   And put aside every other belief,
Don't believe Luke, nor Matthew,
Nor Mark, nor John." Then he left.]

This addition may be ironic, as John Took suggests,[13] but the irony is, at best, heavy handed. Certainly the addition focuses attention on the "religion of love" within the poem, regardless of the interpretation one cares to assign to such rhetorical intensity. One can tentatively conclude that the *Fiore* eliminates the didactic portions of the *Rose* and reduces the narrative to a bare minimum in an effort to "lyricize" the work. The choice of a sonnet cycle rather than *canzoni* or *settenari a rima bacciata* (the form of Brunetto Latini's *Tesoretto*) is essential to this lyrical recasting of lyric / narrative, dreams / truth, and Reason / Nature.

The transformation of a verse narrative into a sonnet cycle does not explain the removal of the dream format, a change which may be crucial to the intent of the *Fiore*. It must be recalled that many vernacularizations of Latin texts explicitly justify themselves as being more truthful than other versions. The prologues of numerous verse romances from the twelfth and thirteenth centuries repeatedly bring up the issue of truthfulness, and, as Jeanette Beer has shown, the conventions surrounding truthfulness were extremely important in many prose works.[14] In verse romances such as Benoît de Sainte-Maure's *Roman de Troie* or the anonymous *Histoire ancienne jusqu'à César*--works circulating in Italy prior to the *Fiore*'s composition and thus relevant to the cultural context in which Old French works were received in northern Italy[15]--the author invariably stressed the fidelity and the truthfulness of his so-called "translation." While it would be imprudent to generalize from these two works alone, a pattern emerges: the translator, while claiming to be faithful and true, amplifies extensively on his original, a fact which must be kept in mind when evaluating the truly radical abbreviation which the *Fiore* poet undertook. Benoît, in a celebrated passage, links fidelity to his original with a corresponding amplification:

Ci vueil l'estoire comencier
Le latin sivrai e la letre,
Nule autre rien n'i voudrai metre,
S'ensi non com jol truis escrit.
Ne di mie qu'aucun bon dit
N'i mete, se faire le sai,
Mais la matire en ensivrai.   (lines 138-44, ed. Constans)

[Here I want to begin the story: I will follow the Latin
version and its letter, nor do I intend to put anything else
in unless it is just as I have found it written. I am not
saying that I will not put in some well turned phrase, if I
know how to do so, but I will follow the subject matter.]

His claim linking fidelity and amplifications corresponds quite
accurately to his actual practice. For Benoît, the radical departure
from Dares's original in the form of extensive amplifications is a
means of serving the truth which he, Benoît, finds implied in the text
he is translating. That Benoît's ideal of translation was perhaps
widespread is attested by the parallel between it and Gottfried von
Strassburg's practice in his *Tristan*. While Gottfried's work has no
direct historical connection to the *Fiore*, it does serve as a clear
illustration of medieval practice which in general may have influenced the *Fiore* poet.

Gottfried's prologue provides one of the clearest formulations of
what might be called the "my-translation-is-more-truthful-AND-
more-artistic-than-the-others" *topos*, with the implication that truth
and art, if not interchangeable, are at least inseparable. Gottfried's
criticism of his vernacular predecessors is categoric: they have not
read the original correctly [daz sî niht rehte haben gelesen, line 147].
Gottfried claims as his ideal a "correct" translation:

die rihte unde die wârheit
begunde ich sêre suochen
in beider hande buochen
walschen und latînen
und begunde mich des pînen
daz ich in sîner rihte
rihte dise tihte.   (lines 155-61)

[I began thoroughly to search for the right and the truth
in both sorts of books, Romance and Latin, and I began
to take great pains that I correctly compose this poem.]

Of course, no medieval version of the Tristan story takes such
artistic liberties with its subject matter--*amplificatio*--as does
Gottfried's, and all of this transformation occurs in the name of
serving the truth.

The abbreviation of the original in the *Fiore*, while contrary to
the implicitly expected amplification, should also be viewed in light
of the goal of truthfulness. The highly complicated discussion of
dreams in the *Rose* provided the *Fiore* poet with a perfect authoriza-
tion for abbreviating the original and for eliminating the dream
format itself. If dreams are truly, as some say, only fables and lies,
then, in order to preserve the "truth" of the *Rose* in translation, the
dream format must be eliminated.

If this elimination represents a radical intervention in the text, it
is nevertheless consistent with the implicit concern for truth and for
poetic artistry on the part of the *Fiore* poet. (Significantly, Brunetto
Latini's own Italian "translation" of his *Livres dou Tresor*, the
Tesoretto, carries out a similarly radical abbreviation of its original
and, like the *Fiore*, omits the didactic and philosophical passages of
its original.) For a consideration of the *Fiore* in its own right, the
historically relevant poetic treatises include Geoffroi de Vinsauf's
Documentum de modo et arte dictandi et versificandi and Dante's
De vulgari eloquentia, whose respective dates of composition fall
before and after the generally accepted dating of the *Fiore*. Geoffroi
de Vinsauf's works were well known in northern Italy, and Dante's
treatise is an important record of literary critical reflection for the
period prior to the composition of the *Commedia*. Geoffroi de
Vinsauf, following the general Chartrian practice,[16] listed the *vitia
stylorum* (2, 3, 146) whereby "style" refers primarily to diction. A
poet's language can be criticized for being *turgidum*, *inflatum*,
dissolutum, *fluctans*, *aridum*, and *exsangue* [turgid, swollen,
careless, vascillating, dry, and lifeless]. These criteria, while meant
for Latin school compositions and not for vernacular translations,
give some sense of contemporary standards for judging poetic

diction. Many of these defects are present in the *Fiore*. The striking use of five syllable words might be seen as "turgid." The excessive loading of the text with words of French origin and the frequent placement of Gallicisms in rhyming positions, as if to accentuate them stylistically rather than contextually, might be judged as "careless" in that they seem poorly motivated. Gallicisms in the *Fiore* rarely stem from literal translations of the original, despite scattered examples of "direct Gallicisms,"[17] but generally reflect an attempt to use French terms even where comparable Italian ones were available,[18] and even to assign them prominence in the rhyming position.[19]

For example, the *Fiore* poet uses *saramento*, "oath," twelve times and never uses the Italian *giuramento*. Similarly, he uses *dottare*, "to fear," twenty-two times rather than the normal term *temere*. By always appearing in place of the expected Italian term, the Gallicism loses whatever *specific* contextual motivation it could potentially have had. Dante's carefully motivated use of Gallicisms, already studied by T. E. Hope and this writer,[20] supplies a significant contrast to the *Fiore*. Three passages from the *Commedia*, among others, exemplify Dante's practice: *Pur.* 11.80-81, "quell'arte / ch'alluminar chiamata è in Parisi" [that art which is called illumination in Paris]; *Pur.* 16.125-26, "e Guido da Castel, che mei si noma / francescamente il semplice Lombardo" [and Guido da Castel, who is better called / in the French way the 'simple' Lombard]; and *Par.* 33.57, "e cede la memoria a tanto oltraggio" [and memory yields to such an outrage]. The first case, often cited by art historians, has been explained by Charles Singleton: "It is significant that Dante designated the art by a word that was current in France in both Latin and French (*enluminer*) in the thirteenth century, but not in Italy, as early commentators were at pains to point out."[21] Dante clearly marks the word as a borrowing by noting that it is called "illumination in Paris." The second case, as explicitly marked a borrowing from French as the first, uses the positive connotation of "simple" in French. Dante's Gallicisms, as T. E. Hope remarked,[22] were often rare words which early commentators failed to understand. If early commentators had difficulty understanding Dante's Gallicisms, which are often marked as linguistic borrowings, early readers of the *Fiore* must have experienced much more trouble in deciphering the Gallicisms there. Dante's linguistic borrowings can usually be explained with specific reference to the context in which they occur. For example, in the third example given above, Dante uses the rare word "oltraggio" [outrage, excess] which occurs only in the *Fiore* and in the *Commedia* among early Italian works and is based on the French *outrages*. The specific contextual motivation of this Gallicism lies, as I have argued elsewhere,[23] in the implicit parallel being drawn between the plucking of the Rose in the *Rose*, called *outrages* there, and Dante's vision of the Celestial Rose in Paradise. The Gallicisms found in the *Fiore* lack such specific contextual motivation. From Geoffroi de Vinsauf's perspective, they appear above all to be somewhat undisciplined or careless, *dissolutum*.

The translator's intent may have been a conscious mixing of the two languages, which goes beyond an attempt to follow the *Rose* faithfully, as Luigi Peirone has noted.[24] If one considers, however, that many of the Gallicisms in the *Fiore* are *hapax legomena* (Luigi Vanossi's census of some 350 words of French provenance revealed fifty-some examples[25]), one can conclude that the artificiality of the *Fiore*'s diction fails to reproduce "linguistic reality." In other words, the *Fiore*'s diction may be viewed as highly artistic, but its artificiality would point to its "lifeless" quality. These evaluations of the *Fiore* in light of Geoffroi de Vinsauf are offered tentatively. The "orgy" of Gallicisms in the *Fiore*, to use Contini's phrase, could be attributed to verbal inventiveness. Their quantitative prominence and very excessiveness might be explained sympathetically as symptomatic of the striving of the *Fiore* poet to be innovative and pioneering, to forge a new kind of verse narrative. Many features of the *Fiore* bespeak precisely this intention: the radical recasting of the *Fiore* as discussed above can most easily be explained as arising from a desire to be innovative.

The *Fiore* poet's intention, however one may choose to reconstruct it, should not divert attention from the manner in which the poem, in all likelihood, was read. I would suggest that early readers of the *Fiore* would have been puzzled by its use of sonnets, of the hendecasyllabic line, and of stanzaic enjambement as well as by its

Gallicisms. This observation is based on a number of general remarks made by Dante in *De vulgari eloquentia*. If Dante were reading the *Fiore* around 1305, when he wrote his treatise, he would have been surprised by the *Fiore*'s use of the sonnet form rather than the *canzone*, a form he characterized as "most excellent" when compared to ballads, sonnets, and irregular forms (2, 3, 2-3). The use of hendecasyllables to treat the mundane subject matter of the *Rose* would have further puzzled Dante, for he associated this verse line with the tragic style (2, 12, 2 and 6). Without wishing to privilege Dante's own remarks, one must note that Contini's suggestion that the *Fiore* can be characterized as Dante's "primo poema 'comico'"[26] [first 'comic' poem] contradicts Dante's own observations. Dante's preference for the *canzone* over the sonnet was based on the *canzone*'s well-defined stanzaic construction and division (what he called its *conjugatio stantiarum* and *partium habitudo* [12, 9, 1], respectively). The *Fiore* when evaluated by this standard exhibits, by contrast, an inconsistent use of stanzaic divisions within the sonnet (4 / 4 / 3 / 3) for purposes of setting off one speaker from another. Consider, for example, the following random sampling: Ragione's speech to L'Amante in Sonnet 35 goes from lines 5-14; in Sonnet 68, L'Amante s speech to Amico extends from lines 3-12, in Sonnet 70 from lines 1-11; in Sonnet 75, Richezza speaks to L'Amante from lines 4-14; and in Sonnet 77, Lo Dio d'Amore addresses L'Amante from lines 8-10. Joseph A. Barber recently published a statistical analysis of both the language and the prosody of the *Fiore* compared to many contemporary works. His analysis of stanzaic divisions demonstrates clearly that the *Fiore*'s failure to respect stanzaic divisions represents a significant departure from the norm.[27]

Barber's study also reveals a far higher percentage of polysyllabic words in the *Fiore* than in Dante's *Commedia* and *Rime*, and in selected works of Pucci, Fulgore, and others.[28] In *De vulgari eloquentia* Dante lays particular stress on the careful combination of words in a line of verse (*regulata compago dictionum*, 2, 6, 2) and provides eleven model lines drawn from Provençal and Italian works. In these examples no word is longer than four syllables, which may at first seem prosodically extraneous. But in a hendecasyllabic line, it should be remembered, any word longer than four syllables would be metrically clumsy. Thus it is striking that the *Fiore* poet uses so many five syllable words. At the same time, the common verbs *avere* and *fare* occur far more frequently in the *Fiore* than they do in contemporary works, a phenomenon which may in fact show that the *Fiore* poet was often forced to paraphrase when unable to find a proper equivalent. These prosodic and lexical aspects would point to a certain lack of stylistic sophistication on the part of the *Fiore* poet. In fact, Barber's characterization of the *Fiore*'s language bears repeating. He found: (1) an abundance of long words of four or five syllables; (2) a comparatively infrequent use of prepositions, particularly of "da"; (3) an excessive use of *avere* and *fare*; (4) the absence of *poi* [then] in favor of *allora*; (5) an extremely limited use of *sempre* [always]; (6) an idiosyncratic conception of the syntactic structure of the sonnet. Barber calls these features the "fingerprints" of the *Fiore* poet; they demonstrate clearly how far the *Fiore* diverged from contemporary works and provide independent substantiation for the observation that the *Fiore* must have puzzled its first readers.

This analysis tends to show how the *Fiore* combines a striving for poetic innovation with a certain careless handling of diction and prosody. One cannot forget that the very notion of translating the *Rose* was in itself an ambitious undertaking which required from the outset a high level of literary culture. Judged by the rhetorical standards of both Geoffroi de Vinsauf and of Dante, the *Fiore* is a defective and puzzling work. It highlights its Gallicisms by placing them in prominent rhyming positions, overusing many of them so that they lose specific contextual motivation. It substitutes for the discursive and didactic passages of the *Rose* a lyrical intensity of its own. Its language departs drastically, however, from the stylistic norms of contemporary works, as these can be reconstructed statistically. The literary and historical uniqueness of the *Fiore* guaranteed that it would have virtually no impact on other Italian writers. Its highly individual, idiosyncratic, nature makes it an extreme example of the freedom of the medieval translator.

NOTES

1. The most important works dealing with attribution are by Gianfranco Contini and Luigi Vanossi: Gianfranco Contini, "La questione del *Fiore*," *Cultura e scuola* 13-14 (1965):768-73; "Un'interpretazione di Dante," *Paragone* (letteratura) 16 (n.s. 8) (1965):3-42; "Un nodo della cultura medievale: la serie *Roman de la Rose--Fiore--Divina Commedia*," *Lettere italiane* 25 (1973):162-89; Luigi Vanossi, *Dante e il "Roman de la Rose:" Saggio sul "Fiore"* (Florence: Olschki, 1979). The best *bibliographie raisonnée* on the *Fiore* is Contini's *Il Fiore e il Detto d'Amore, attribuilio a Dante Alighieri* (*Le Opere di Dante Alighieri*, Edizione Nationale a cura della Società Dantesca Italiana, vol. 8) (Milan: Mondadori Editore, 1984), pp. xxiii, xlix, with 1983 as the cut-off date.

2. Berhard Langheinrich, "Sprachliche Untersuchung zur Frage der Verfasserschaft Dantes am *Fiore*," *Deutsches Dante-Jahrbuch* 19 (n.F. l0) (1937):190.

3. Giuseppe Petrocchi, in the *Enciclopedia Dantesca*, v. 6 (Appendice) (1978), 8-9, 21, 35.

4. Contini [n. 1 above] (1984), cix-cxiii.

5. Joseph A. Barber, "Prospettive per un'analisi statistica del *Fiore*," *Revue des études italiennes* N.S. 31 (1985):5-24.

6. Vergil is mentioned explicitly in the *Rose* on lines 8978ff., 16295, 18697, 19139, and 21299.

7. Louis G. Kelly, *The True Interpreter, A History of Translation Theory and Practice in the West* (Oxford: Blackwell, 1979), pp. 205, 207.

8. Karl August Ott in *Der Rosenroman* (Erträge der Forschung, 145) (Darmstadt: Wissenschaftliche Buchgesellschaft, 1980) provides the best survey of scholarly interpretations on the *Rose* currently available.

9. John Took, "Dante and the *Roman de la Rose*," *Italian Studies* 37 (1982):4-5.

10. The following representative survey will show how much variation in textual correspondence is present in the *Fiore*. In the first twenty sonnets, Contini's critical apparatus lists correspondences for 73 of 280 lines (=26%); for the next twenty, 103 of 280 (=36%); and for Sonnets 100-120, 133 of 280 (=47.5%), giving an average of 36.8% or roughly one-third on the average. The two sonnets selected fall considerably above this statistical norm.

11. Guillaume de Lorris and Jean de Meun, *Le Roman de la Rose*, 3 vols., ed. Felix Lecoy (CFMA: Paris, 1965-70).

12. The point must be stressed that the abbreviation of the *Rose* is by no means uniform or consistent throughout the *Fiore*: for example, the ratio between the lengths of the two works is 3245:21750 or 14.9%. Considering, however, that the *Fiore* poet did not actually translate the first 1500 or the last 5000 lines of the *Rose*, the real ratio between the two works is 3245:15150 or 21.4%. Using this ratio, the reduction of Amant's thirty-line speech to three and half lines would have produced a speech in the Italian translation twice as long or six lines, if the translation were attempting to preserve more or less the same emphasis of the passages which are actually translated.

13. John Took, "Towards an Interpretation of the *Fiore*," *Speculum* 54 (1979):500-27.

14. Jeanette M. A. Beer, *Narrative Conventions of Truth in the Middle Ages* (Geneva: Droz, 1981).

15. Earl Jeffrey Richards, *Dante and the "Roman de la Rose," An Investigation into the Vernacular Context of the "Commedia,"* Beihefte zur Zeitschrift für romanische Philologie, 184 (Tübingen: Max Niemeyer Verlag, 1981), pp. 46ff.

16. Franz Quadlbauer, *Die antike Theorie der genera dicendi im lateinischen Mittelalter* (Öst. Akademie der Wiss., Phil.-Hist. Kl., Sitzungsber. Bd. 241) (Vienna: Böhlau, 1962), pp. 94ff.

17. Contini [n. 1 above] (1984), pp. xcvii-ciii.br. 18.

18.   Giuseppe Petronio, "Introduzione al *Fiore*," *Cultura neolatina* 8 (1948):58.

19.   Ignazio Baldelli, *Enciclopedia Dantesca*, v. 6 (Appendice) (1978), 63.

20.   T. E. Hope, "Gallicisms in Dante's *Divina Commedia:* A Stylistic Problem?," in *Studies in Medieval Literature and Languages in Memory of Frederick Whitehead*, ed. W. Rothwell et al. (Manchester: Manchester Univ. Press, 1973), pp. 153-72; and Richards [n. 1 above], pp. 9f., 18, 23f.

21.   Charles S. Singleton, in Peter Brieger, Millard Meiss and Charles S. Singleton, *Illuminated Manuscripts of the Divine Comedy* (Princeton: Princeton Univ. Press, 1969), vol. l, p. 36.

22.   T. E. Hope [n. 19 above], p. 168.

23.   Richards [n. 14 above], pp. 98-103.

24.   Luigi Peirone, *Tra Dante e "Il Fiore," Lingua e Parola* (Genoa: Tilgher, 1982), p. 52.

25.   Vanossi [n. 1 above], p. 236.

26.   Barber [n. 5 above], p. 21.

27.   Ibid., p. 15.

28.   Ibid., p. 23.

LE BESTIAIRE D'AMOUR EN VERS

Jeanette Beer

The translation of verse into prose was not unusual in the Middle Ages. Individual works and, in some decades, whole genres (notably romance) were formally transformed in this way. The reasons that dictated a verse to prose conversion were various: popular vogue, the anticipated reactions of a given audience, the instructions of an influential patron, and perhaps the translator's own disinterest in the formal metrics of his source. The reverse process, prose to verse, was more unusual. Its isolated occurrences therefore deserve particular attention in any study of medieval attitudes towards translation.

A conversion of Richard de Fournival's *Le Bestiaire d'amour* to rhyming octosyllabic couplets has survived on folios 89-92 of the B.N. Ms. 25.545 (anc. fonds Notre-Dame 274 bis).[1] The manuscript dates from the fourteenth century, but the fragment, now entitled *Le Bestiaire d'amour en vers*, states in both title and text that it is Richard's own translation:

> MAISTRES RICHARS DE FORNIVAL.
> Maistres Richars ha, por miex plaire,
> Mis en rime le Bestiaire. . . .

> [Master Richard, to give more pleasure, has put the *Bestiary* in rhyme. . . .]

Le Bestiaire d'amour en vers would then have been composed between 1255 and 1260, perhaps in the last year of Richard's life.

His motivation for reworking the original prose bestiary is not immediately clear, and the modern reader must sympathize with Paul

Meyer's bewilderment:

> Cette rédaction en prose, qui parait être l'original, a été
> très souvent copiée. . . . Mais on ne voit pas pourquoi
> Richard de Fournival, ayant d'abord rédigé son ouvrage
> en prose, l'aurait plus tard repris en vers, et sous une
> forme un peu plus longue.[2]

> [This prose redaction, which appears to be the original,
> has been very frequently copied. But it is not apparent
> why Richard de Fournival, who originally composed his
> work in prose, would later have redone it into verse *and*
> at slightly greater length.]

Its editor, Arthur Långfors, cautiously suggested that the Richard de
Fournival of the verse translation need not necessarily be the
Richard de Fournival who authored *Le Bestaire d'amour*: "Il
faudrait examiner si toutes les mentions d'un Richard de Fournival
se rapportent réellement à un seul et même personnage"[3] [It would
be advisable to examine whether every mention of a Richard de
Fournival really refers to one and the same person.] The reason for
this hesitation on the part of eminent bestiary scholars is
undoubtedly the pedestrian quality of the verse translation, which
has lost all the cynical ambiguities of the original by its platitudinous over-statement. Richard's switch to verse was furthermore
an abrupt volte-face. The prologue to *Le Bestiaire d'amour* had
renounced lyricism; and it had satirized Richard's performance as a
poet-lover with images of impotent futility: a crowing rooster,
braying ass, summer cricket, dying swan, and vomiting dog.

Reasons for the production of a new version of *Le Bestiaire
d'amour* can, however, be found if one examines the intellectual
climate of the fifties. *Le Bestiaire d'amour* was written in the early
fifties,[4] around the time when the University of Paris withdrew its
proscription of Aristotle's scientific treatises and prescribed the
whole Aristotelian corpus for the faculty of Arts. Significantly,
Richard began his bestiary with a translated dictum from Aristotle's
Metaphysics I, 1: "Toutes gens desirent par nature a savoir" [All

men naturally desire knowledge].[5] That introduction was at best paradoxical. Reason was, according to Aristotle, man's proper characteristic which distinguished him from beasts. *Le Bestiaire d'amour* showed love--and woman--to be inimical to reason and deployed a series of animal similes as models of "amor naturalis."

Meanwhile, acceptance of Aristotelian ideas and techniques had not been achieved merely by the removal of all ecclesiastical let and hindrance. Conflict marked the decade of 1255-65 (and beyond!). That conflict had its effect upon the reception of *Le Bestiaire d'amour*, which soon acquired a *Response* from Richard's (anonymous) lady. *Her* initial dictum was that a man of sense and discretion ["hom qui sens et discretion a en soi"] should not by word or deed perpetrate anything that might harm any man or any woman ["nus ne nule"]. Clearly the Platonic conventionalities of the love lyric would have been preferred over Aristotelian ambiguities!

Richard's decision to attempt a metric version of *Le Bestiaire d'amour* represents just one more stage in this early "querelle de la rose," *his* response to the *Response*. His introduction to *Le Bestiaire d'amour en vers* is, in my view, a topical comment, tinged perhaps with bitterness, about his audience and its preferences:

> Maistres Richars ha, por miex plaire,
> Mis en rime le Bestiaire,
> Por ce que on en ait un peu,
> 4 Puis en rost et puis en esceu;
> Si praingn'on le quel c'on vaurra
> Et qui a oïr miex plaira.
> Bien sera chascuns escoutez,
> 8 Car je vos di, c'est veritez,
> Toutes gens a savoir desirrent
> Les fais que li encien escrirent.

> [Master Richard, to give more pleasure,
> Has put the *Bestiary* into rhyme,
> So that it may be sampled now
> First as a roast, then boiled;
> Thus one may take one's preference,
> Whichever one wants to hear.

287

Each will have a good audience
Because, I tell you truly,
Everyone wants to know
The writings of the ancients.]

Le Bestiaire d'amour en vers courts those of Richard's contemporaries who prefer the entertainment of love literature to
Aristotelian *exposés*. In imagery that is curiously modern Richard
compares his bestiary to a consumer product ["meat"!] whose
presentation is a variable. His main concern is, of course, the
content, which cannot fail to please when its different packaging
caters to all tastes. Thus the determining factor in all formal aspects
of the work is the translator's public. The fact that prose had been
the medium of the *Metaphysics*, of the *Physiologus*, and of at least
one recent bestiary,[6] was without immediate relevance. Richard now
wishes to address "por miex plaire" a public that enjoyed the
octosyllabic couplet of romance. Medieval translation, even self-
translation, had its own necessities of which the principal was
audience appropriateness.

That audience is now addressed with a platitude about the
universality of the ancients (lines 9-10 above). The new dictum is a
retreat from the magisterial "Toutes gens desirent par nature a
savoir." Aristotle's introduction has been circumscribed and
rendered innocuous, and his *Metaphysics* has lost ground to the
Physiologus, which more properly qualifies as "les *fais* [facts / feats]
que li ancien escrirent." The equally platitudinous truth assertion of
line 8, used in essentially non-intellectual contexts,[7] confirms the
suitability of the material for a non-Aristotelian public.

The next two lines are also explanatory additions:

Par nature et par les .v. sens
Peut on apenre mout de sens.

[From Nature and the five senses
One can learn a lot of sense.]

This new stress upon didacticism rather than knowledge provides a rebuttal of the *Response*'s criticism that *Le Bestiaire d'amour* was potentially harmful. The homophonic end-rhyme "sens"-"sens" emphasizes Richard's awareness of his duties as "hom qui *sens* et discretion a en soi" (*Response*, line 1). The brief eight-line prologue has thus promised both instructional and entertainment value to the audience. The subject-matter of the original begins at line 9:

Toutes gens desirent par nature
a savoir. Et pour chu ke nus
ne puet tout savoir, ja soit che
ke cascune cose puist estre seüe,
si covient il ke sacuns sache aucune cose, et che ke li uns ne
set mie, ke li autres le sache; si
ke tout est seü en tel maniere
qu'il n'est seü de nullui a par
lui, ains est seü de tous ensamble.
Mail il est ensi ke toutes gens
ne vivent mie ensamble, ains sont
li un mort avant ke li autre
naissent, et cil ki ont esté cha
en ariere ont seü tel cose ke nus
ki ore endroit vive ne le con-
querroit de son sens, ne ne seroit
seü, s'on ne le savoit par les
anchiiens.
[All men naturally desire knowledge. And inasmuch as no one
has the capacity to know everything (although everything has
the capacity to be known), it
behooves everyone to know something, then what one man does
not know another will. Thus
everything is known in such a
manner that it is not known by
one man for himself, but rather
it is known by all in common.
But all men do not coexist to-

Toutes gens a savoir desirrent
Les fais que li encien escrirent.
Par nature et par les .v. sens
12 Peut on apenre mout de sens.
Et por ce que nus hon qui soit
Par lui savoir tout ne porroit,
Ja soit que puist estre seüe
16 Chascune chose et conneüe,
Si convient que aucune rien
Sache chascuns ou mal ou bien,
Et se que li uns ne set mie,
20 Qu'au savoir l'autre s'estudie;
Si que tout est aperceü
En itel meniere et seü,
Si qu'il n'est seü de nului,
24 Ce sachiez bien, tout a par lui,
Ains est seü de tous ensamble.
Mail il est einsi, ce me samble,
Que toutes gens ne vivent pas
28 Ensamble ne a un compas,
Ains sont li un mort et finé
Ains que li autre soient né,
Et cil qui ont esté jadis
32 Tel chose ont seü, ce m'est vis,
Que nus hon qui soit orendroit
De son sens ne le troveroit
Ne ne seroit seü por riens,
36 Se n'estoit par les enciens.

289

gether. Some die and others
then are born. Our forebears
knew what no one now alive
could find out by his own intel-
ligence, and it would not be
known unless it were known
from the ancients.]

The most obvious difference between the versions is that of
length: 124 words in the original as against 167 in the metric (and,
overall, 1438 as against 1641). The expansion derives almost
entirely from repetitive emphasis and *chevilles*, while the substantive
material is preserved to a remarkable degree, as might be expected
from the author himself. The translation unit, as was customary in
literary translation, is the sentence rather than the individual word.
Since the translation unit and the metric unit (the octosyllable) rarely
mesh, expansional phrases frequently serve to bring the octosyllable
to closure, for example, in the above passage "et conneüe" (line 16);
"ou mal ou bien" (line 18); "et finé" (line 29); "ce m'est vis" (line
32); and "por riens" (line 35).

A further difference between the versions is that of emphasis
within the translation unit. Metric translation necessarily imposes
different foci, notably at the end-rhyme, as a comparison of the
second sentence of the original with its metric translation (lines
14-25) will demonstrate. The original prose sentence was a
synthetic fugue which elaborated upon the Aristotelian theme of
"savoir" after its exposition in the initial *sententia* "Toutes gens
desirent par nature a *savoir*." Richard had symbolized the different
phases of human knowledge through the forms "savoir," "savoir,"
"estre seü," "sache," "set," "sache," "est seü," (and in the next
sentence "n'est seü," and "savoit"). The metric translation, needing
no such means of emphasis, disperses the device, first by a *cheville*
"nus hon qui soit," then by the positioning of "porroit" rather than
"savoir" at the end-rhyme, and finally by the extension of meaning
of "est seü" in the synonymic binomial "seü et conneü." The use of
different stylistic devices for prose and verse is not in itself
surprising. Interestingly, in Richard's two bestiaries the prose

version has acquired poetic resonance from *annominatio*'s variations upon a theme, while the metric version has balanced its poetic rhythms with the colloquialisms of prose.

Some of the expansions could be judged unfortunate if the criterion were appropriateness to content. Magisterial assertions have been attenuated by such tentative phrases as "ce me samble," "ce m'est vis," or "ou mal ou bien." In the exposition of the auditory and visual accesses to memory (lines 37-70) the superfluity continues:

Et pour chu Diex, ki tant aime
l'omme qu'il le velt porveoir
de quent ke mestiers lui est,
a donné a homme une vertu de   40
force d'ame ki a non memoire.
[Wherefore God, who so loves
man that He wants to provide
for his every need, has given   44
him a particular faculty of
mind called Memory.]

Et por ce Dex, qui tant aimme homme
Que il le veut a la parsomme
Porveoir si que il li prest
Trestout ce que mestiers li est,
Dex donne a homme une vertu
De force d'ame, et revestu
L'en a, ce devons nos tuit croire;
La vertus a a voir[8] memoire.

In the above, the adverbial phrase "a la parsomme" has little theological significance. There is meaningless bifurcation of the verb "a donné" into both "prest" [lends] and "donne" [gives]. An added metaphor "a revestu" [has clothed] sheds no possible light on memory function. Aristotelian science is not clarified by the assertions that (a) God-given memory is a matter of belief: "ce devons nos tuit croire"; (b) it is known by all instinctively: "si les set chascuns par nature," line 49; (c) it is observable if one gives attention to it: "c'est bien apparent, s'en i garde," line 57; and (d) memory function is analogous to the wind: "on peut . . . a memoire . . . repairier, si tost con vens vole," lines 53-55. The weather simile can have little relevance to Aristotle's graphic view of memory as the recapture of a series of visual images!

Not all the *chevilles* are inappropriate to context. A substantial increase of truth affirmations in the passages declaring love ("sans mençonge retraire," "voire," "sachiez," "ce sachiez," and "sachiez bien") contributes to the message. Frequent *chevilles* serve overall to stress the uncontroversial nature of the new bestiary for Richard's public.

That public is defined unambiguously now by two small additions. The prose bestiary had spoken generically about the reconstructive power of imagery: "Quant on voit painte une estoire ou de Troies ou d'autre, on voit les fais des preudommes ki cha en ariere furent, ausi com s'il fussent present" [p. 5, lines 3-5; When one sees the depiction of a history of Troy or of some other place, one sees the deeds of those past heroes as if they were present.] Richard now adds the specification of *where* his public saw those romances *viz.* on their walls and on their ceilings: "Quant on voit / Paint une hystoire *en la paroit* / Ou de Troie ou d'autre *en dais*" (lines 66-67).

Perhaps that same public's taste for falconry has induced also an otherwise incomprehensible change in the description of a bestiary: "Cis escris est de tel sentence k'il painture desire. Car il est de nature de bestes et d'oisiaus ke miex sont connissables paintes que dites." [This composition is of such a nature as to need pictures, for animals and birds are naturally more recognizable when depicted than when described.] becomes:

> Cis escris qui est en present
> D'itel sentence est, par saint Sire,
> Que il la peinture desire,
> Qu'il est de natures d'*oisiax*
> *Et de pluseurs bestes ysniax*:
> Paintes sont mout miex connuisables
> Que dites, *et mout miex veables*.
>
> (lines 122-28, emphasis added)

Significantly, however, the new prologue makes no change in Richard's renunciation of lyric poetry (for example, in lines 148-49, 196-97, 220-21, and 276-80). Clearly Richard conceives of his new metric version as non-lyric narrative: "Cis escris ici en chantant / N'est mie fait, mais en contant" [lines 259-60; This composition is not made in lyric form but as a narrative]; "Me veil je de chanter retraire" [line 303; I wish to desist from singing]. The present tenses of "est" and "veil" confirm the relevance of these statements of intent to the metric version of *Le Bestiaire d'amour* as well as to its source. There is, in fact, little resemblance between Richard's early *chansons* and *Le Bestiaire d'amour en vers*, and the construction of a poetic profile for him would be difficult with such variable evidence.

His twenty-one *chansons* reveal a preference for five strophes (in twelve out of twenty-one), for a *unissonans* rhyme-scheme (in thirteen out of twenty-one), and for strophes of fewer than ten lines (in seventeen out of twenty-one). Most important of all, a crystalline brevity characterizes Richard's often hermetic lyrics, while hermeticism is hardly relevant to expository popularization. Thus the only common quality of all Richard's verse writings is their preference for masculine rhyme. Masculine rhymes outnumber feminine by about 72% to 28% in the *chansons*.[9] In *Le Bestiaire d'amour en vers* there are 116 masculine as against 64 feminine rhymes.[10] It is important to avoid value judgements implied by the modern rhyme hierarchies of "pauvre," "riche," "léonine," etc., which have most relevance in a printed context that serves both eye and ear. The observation may, however, be made that Richard's frequent homophonic rhymes are rarely used to full potential in *Le Bestiaire d'amour en vers* since they do not always emphasize the focal points of individual sense-units (see, for example, "garde"-"garde" in lines 57-58, "on"-"on" in lines 63-64, and "fait"-"fait" in lines 75-76, but compare "sens"-"sens" discussed above).

An occasional enjambement eases the transition from prose to verse. "Ceste memoire si a .ij. portes, veïr et oïr, et a cascune de ces portes si a un cemin" (p. 4, lines 3-5) is restructured as:

> Le vertus a a voir memoire.
> .II. portes ceste vertus a:
> Veoir, oïr, et chascune a
> Un chemin, a briement parler.   (lines 44-47)

The linkage "a / Un" cleverly moves the homophonically rhyming couplet in a new direction, while symbolizing the uninterrupted pathways which lead to memory.

Word order is exploited more as the bestiary progresses. For example, "L'amour dont on n'a del tout esperance ne del tout desesperance" [p. 9, lines 5-6; the love where one has neither complete confidence nor complete despair] becomes "L'amour de coi en esperance / N'a del tout ne desesperance" (lines 183-84). The reordering is successful in that it has positioned the two key-words of the sense-unit at the end-rhyme, thus giving them emphasis. Equally successful is the reordering of "Car le canter doi jou bien avoir perdu" [p. 10, line 9; For I am bound to have lost my singing] to "Car je le chanter avoir doi / Perdu (lines 223-24). Its fragmentation symbolizes stylistically the halting failure of the poet's song. There is little doubt that Richard's renunciation of past lyricism continues into *Le Bestiaire d'amour en vers*.

It is important not to overlook the specific target audience of Richard's anonymous lady as a possible influence upon his stylistic choices. If it was to counter her criticisms that Richard now stressed the edifying nature of his bestiary, then even its *chevilles* acquire new significance. The seemingly otiose "par Saint Sire" of line 123 (see above) may be genuinely useful, mimicking her frequent invocations of the Deity in the *Response*. And his repetitive "car sachent bien *toutes et tuit*" (line 169) may be a parody of her insistence that "man" not automatically embrace "woman" (cf. her "nus ne nule" quoted above).

Similarly, *Le Bestiaire d'amour en vers* adds several new adjectives to the phrases by which Richard addresses his lady. The original "bele tres douce amie" (p. 5, line 11) had been blandly formulaic. It appears in its appropriate place (line 81) in the metric version, but is supplemented by "biax tres dous cuers frans" (line 129), "douce debonnaire" (line 146), and "biaus dous cuers savourous et dous" (line 165). The appropriateness of "frans" to the free-spirited author of the *Response* cannot be disputed, and the designation "savourous" is undeniably piquant. Neither occurred in the original, suggesting an evolving situation or, at least, debate. Even the apparent "fill-in" phrases "sans rancune" and "sans mespresure" in "Car je vous envoi *sans rancune* / En cest escrist, *sens mespresure*" (lines 99-100, emphasis added) become meaningful if *Le Bestiaire d'amour en vers* is a specific response to the vehemently anti-clerical, anti-Richard sentiments of the lady's *Response*! And are Richard's newly tentative qualifications such as "si senefie, *se me samble*" (line 182, emphasis added) mere line-fillers, or do they reflect a psychological realignment after attack?

Ultimately, then, *Le Bestiaire d'amour en vers* still contains ambiguities. Substantively its fidelity to its original is absolute; stylistic alterations occur primarily through repetitive expansion; and no new lexical choices displace the source-vocabulary. Yet shifts toward a new public have created new problems. Was Richard's expressed desire to please a romance-loving public genuine? In that case, it could be the reason for the fragment's brevity. Ovidian misogyny was not calculated "por miex plaire," and the fragment appears to have been terminated just before Richard's crucial characterization of women as lubricious, fickle, and false. There is another possibility, however: that the prologue was motivated not by a real desire to please but by bitter irony. The phrase "un peu" in "por ce que on en ait un peu / Puis en rost puis en esceu" would then be literally true and not a mere *cheville*. The fragment was intended to be fragmentary, a demonstration of disrespect for a certain public or, of course, a certain person. If that is true, Richard's metaphoric description of his bestiary as roasted or boiled meat and his lady as "savourous" is profoundly complex; the prologue is to be interpreted *per contrarium*; and a recipe now exists for the naturalistic treatise which would be written some years later--by Jean de Meun.

NOTES

1. "*Le Bestiaire d'amour en vers* par Richard de Fournival," ed. A. Långfors, *Mémoires de la Société néophilologique de Helsingfors* 7 (1924): 291-317.

2. Paul Meyer, "Les Bestiaires," *Histoire littéraire de la France* 34:632.

3. Långfors [n. 1 above], p. 297.

4.   Precise dating of its composition is difficult. I have discussed this problem in "The New Naturalism of *Le Bestiaire d'amour*," *Reinardus* I, 1 (Grave: Alfa, 1988), p. 14, and in my article "Richard de Fournival's Anonymous Lady: The Character of the *Response* to *Le Bestiaire d'amour* (forthcoming in *Romance Philology*).

5.   The best edition of *Le Bestiaire d'amour* is *Li Bestiaires d'Amours di Maistre Richart de Fornival e li Response du Bestiaire*, ed. C. Segre (Milan and Naples: Riccardo Ricciardi, 1957).   English translations are taken from *Master Richard's Bestiary of Love and Response*, trans. Jeanette Beer (Berkeley and Los Angeles: Univ. of California Press, 1986).

6.   *Bestiaire en prose de Pierre le Picard*, ed. C. Cahier and A. Martin, *Mélanges d'archéologie, d'histoire et de littérature* 2 (1851): 85-100, 106-232; 3 (1853):203-88; 4 (1856):55-87; and also *Le Bestiaire de Pierre de Beauvais*, ed. Guy Mermier (Paris: A. G. Nizet, 1977).

7.   See Jeanette Beer, *Narrative Conventions of Truth in the Middle Ages* (Geneva: Droz, 1981).

8.   The substitution of "voir" for "non" was presumably made by the copyist rather than the translator. See Lângfors [n. 1 above], p. 304, n. to line 44, and p. 317 (Glossary) under "voir."

9.   See *L'Œuvre lyrique de Richard de Fournival*, ed. Y. Lepage (Ottawa: Editions de l'Université d'Ottawa, 1981), p. 27.

10.   Lângfors [n. 1 above], p. 294.

A CASE STUDY IN
MEDIEVAL NONLITERARY TRANSLATION:
SCIENTIFIC TEXTS FROM LATIN TO FRENCH

Lys Ann Shore

Introduction

The late thirteenth century marks, as far as can be determined, the first appearance in French of scientific and technical works which until this time had been written in Latin. This phenomenon entailed a broader view, on the part of writers and their audiences, of the vernacular as an appropriate and adequate medium for presenting complex technical concepts and information. Over the next two hundred years, dozens out of the hundreds of scientific treatises in Latin were translated into French. It is the purpose of this paper to examine the flow of technical information and knowledge from Latin into French, using as a case study the "science of the stars" (Lat. *scientia stellarum*; Fr. *science des estoilles*)--astronomy and astrology. It may thus be possible to find at least the suggestions of answers to such questions as: what texts were translated, when, by whom, and for what purpose? In addition, an examination of several translations reveals some of the techniques used to resolve the problems peculiar to the translation of technical works.

During the period under consideration, from the late thirteenth century to the end of the fifteenth, astronomy reigned as the queen of the sciences. The science of the stars encompassed both quantitative and qualitative aspects. On the one hand, it included the study and measurement of the positions of heavenly bodies (astronomy); on the other, the interpretation of the significance of these positions for individuals and nations (astrology).

Medieval astronomy dealt with the motions of the seven "planets"--the moon, Mercury, Venus, the sun, Mars, Jupiter, and

Saturn--through the sky, and their changing positions relative to each other and to the starry background against which they move, as well as the motion of the fixed, or background, stars about the celestial pole. Astronomy included the calculation and prediction of eclipses, planetary conjunctions, and oppositions.

Astrology took up where astronomy left off, using the measurements of celestial positions to assess their effects on terrestrial creatures (especially man) and events (both natural and political). Heavenly bodies were considered to produce their effects through "influence" (Lat. *influentia*; Fr. *influence*), which can be visualized most conveniently as flowing outwards and downwards from them like rays of light.

The foundation of astrology as a science had been laid by the great astronomer of the second century, Claudius Ptolomaeus, or Ptolemy. In his *Tetrabiblos* (Lat. *Quadripartitum*)--the textbook of astrology that followed his celebrated treatise on astronomy, the *Almagest*--Ptolemy began with the obvious terrestrial effects caused by the sun and moon. From this, he reasoned that all heavenly bodies must produce physical effects on earth. By observing carefully the terrestrial effects that accompanied various configurations of the heavenly bodies, he believed it would be possible to build up a system of recognized causes and effects, which would then enable astrologers to make accurate predictions. For example, if it were once established that famine followed each lunar eclipse, then--since lunar eclipses could be predicted--it should be possible to predict the occurrence of famine as well.

Throughout the Middle Ages this reasoning was accepted as valid. Because of the general belief in the predictive nature of astrology, interest in and respect for the science of the stars ran high throughout the later Middle Ages. As one of the seven liberal arts, astronomy held a recognized place in the medieval university curriculum, as did astrology (at least in Paris) after the middle of the fourteenth century. Both were widely studied by practitioners (astrologers and physician / astrologers) and their patrons, who relied on astrological predictions as an aid in decision making.[1]

The Context of Translation

Tracing the flow of astronomical and astrological knowledge from Latin into French is a historical enterprise that depends largely on the accidents of the survival, acquisition, and cataloguing of manuscripts. It is impossible to know what fraction of the total volume of this flow is represented by the manuscripts known today. Likewise, it is not possible to determine to what extent the surviving works are representative of the kinds of texts that were translated and the types of translation that were made.

In some cases, the evidence of surviving manuscripts can be supplemented by information drawn from other sources, such as medieval library catalogues and book bequests. But the evidence remains patchy at best, allowing only an approximate reconstruction of the flow of Latin astronomical texts into French. For example, modern catalogues of manuscript collections often list the contents of manuscripts only briefly. But an astrological work might circulate in several versions, more or less complete, with or without commentary. It might be attributed to different authors or known under different names. In these circumstances, a brief listing may be frustratingly uninformative

Complicating this problem is the unfortunate fact that many cataloguers in the past considered astrological texts unimportant or uninteresting (as compared with, say, works of literature or philosophy). As a result, the contents of a manuscript that contains several astronomical or astrological works might be described simply as "varia astronomica" or "quaedam astrologica." Where incipits are given, of course, the historian's task is eased considerably, thanks to the pioneering bibliographical efforts of such scholars as Thorndike and Carmody.[2]

From medieval and modern library catalogues, it is possible to list at least fifty manuscripts that contain astronomical and astrological texts in French.[3] These manuscripts range in date from the late thirteenth to the late fifteenth century. Tracing the identity of the texts they contain, however, and determining whether they are translations, compilations, or original treatises, is precarious business, especially in the later period. For example, different texts may be combined in translation, so that one is, in effect, "hidden" within the other. This is the case with one of the works in an early fourteenth-century manuscript (Paris, B.N. fr. 613), which includes a translation of Leopold of Austria's *Compilatio de astrorum scientia* (c. 1271). Included without a break at the end of the eighth book of the *Compilatio* and labeled "Ninth Treatise" is a partial translation of a completely different work, the *De Judiciis astrorum* of 'Ali ibn Abi' l-Rijāl (Haly Abenragel, fl. c. 1040).[4]

The distinction between translation and compilation is particularly fine, since a work compiled from several sources may reproduce portions of its sources word for word. This situation occurs, for example, in the anonymous fifteenth-century *Petit traictié de la signification des comettes*, a compilation that consists largely of passages translated from two other works.[5] Further, a translator may draw on one or more additional works--such as commentaries--to supplement the information given in the text. For example, the thirteenth-century translation of Aristotle's *Meteorologica* by Mahieu le Vilain (see below) draws heavily on the commentary on the *Meteorologica* by Alexander of Aphrodisias (late second century and early third century). To take another example, Paris B.N. fr. 1353, a thirteenth-century manuscript dedicated to Baldwin of Courtenay (Emperor Baldwin II of Constantinople, d. 1273), contains (fols. 7-66) an *Introduction to Astronomy*. One might expect this to be the *Introductorium maius* of Abū Ma'shar (Albumasar, d. 885), one of the best-known of Arabic astronomical texts. In fact, as Richard Lemay recognized, it is a compilation based in part on Abū Ma'shar's *Introductorium* (probably in the Latin translation of Hermann of Carinthia), but also drawing on the works of several other authors.[6]

The secondary literature about a text can also create confusion. For example, a late thirteenth-century manuscript (Paris, Bibliothèque de l'Arsenal 534) is said by several sources to contain (fols. 91-107) a Latin astronomical text, the *Calendarium* of William of Saint-Cloud (late thirteenth century). But one scholar who had personally examined the manuscript maintained that it held the French translation of this text, *Le Calendrier la royne*.[7]

Existing translations cover a wide variety of astronomical and astrological texts, including the works of ancient authors, Arabic and Jewish writers, and "moderns," as well as anonymous works and those attributed to legendary sages, such as Hermes Trismegistus. French translations exist, for example, of Aristotle's cosmological treatise *De caelo et mundo* and *Meteorologica*. Ptolemy's *Quadripartitum* was translated; so was the set of one hundred astrological maxims known as the *Centiloquium* that circulated under his name throughout the Middle Ages. Among the Arabic authors, translations were made of works by Abū Ma'shar, Māshā'Allāh (Messehala, before 800), 'Ali ibn Abi'l-Rijā l, and al-Qabīsī (Alcabitius, d. 967), among others. "Modern" authors translated include such names as Leopold of Austria, Guido Bonatti (thirteenth century), and Peter Philomena (fl. 1290-1300). In their content, the works translated ranged from general introductions to the science of the stars to technical treatises on measuring and interpreting celestial positions, as well as collections of astrological maxims, notes on the use of astronomical instruments, and discussions of various types of astrological predictions.

In fact, among all the astronomical and astrological texts that passed from Latin into French during the thirteenth, fourteenth, and fifteenth centuries, only two are conspicuous by their absence. These are the *De sphera* of Johannes de Sacrobosco (John of Holywood, early thirteenth century) and the various works that went by the generic title of *theoricae planetarum* (descriptions and explanations of the motions of the planets).[8] Together, the *De sphera* and a *theorica planetarum*, such as the one attributed to Gerard of Cremona (d. 1187), made up the core of the standard university curriculum in astronomy from the thirteenth century onward. Although they gradually came to be supplemented with treatises on instruments (such as the quadrant and the astrolabe) and mathematics (the *computus*), these two texts remained central to the organized study of astronomy.

Despite--or, perhaps, because of--the unique importance of these texts, they appear not to have been translated into French until the very end of the Middle Ages. The only evidence of a *theorica planetarum* in French is an anonymous work contained in a single fifteenth-century manuscript.[9] As for the *De sphera* of Sacrobosco, it has been suggested that Nicole Oresme's *Traitié de l'espere* in French, composed about 1368, was a translation of Sacrobosco's work. It appears, however, that Oresme's work is really an independent composition that draws on Sacrobosco as a source.[10] A direct translation of *De sphera* seems to have been published only in 1504, in an abridged form as part of a composite work called *Le Cuer de philosophie.*[11]

Thus, the treatises on the science of the stars that were selected for translation into French, although many and various, were not generally those of the university curriculum in astronomy. Astrological treatises, works by popular and respected writers--especially Arabic--and practical treatises on instruments and technique were all translated, but the available evidence indicates that university students learned astronomy in Latin.

Translators and Translations

The Thirteenth Century

The flow of astronomical knowledge from Latin into French appears to have begun with individuals working independently in different locations, for different reasons, and with different goals in mind. The first who has left some trace of his activities is one Mahieu le Vilain of Neufchâtel-en-Bray, who about 1270 made a French translation of portions of Aristotle's *Meteorologica*, based on the Latin version of William of Moerbeke.[12]

Mahieu explained in his preface that he had often heard his patron, the Count of Eu,[13] who "took delight in the perfections of the sciences," despair at ever being able to understand what Aristotle says in his *Meteorologica*. For this reason, Mahieu said, he decided to translate the work for him, word for word, into French. As a prudent man, however, he undertook at first to translate only an "extract"; if that pleased his patron, he would then translate the rest.[14]

What has survived, in a single manuscript, is an elaborated translation of Book 1 through Book 3, Chapter 4, of the four books of the *Meteorologica*.[15] Despite Mahieu's statement of his inten-

302

tions, his translation is by no means a simple "word for word" rendering: it is stuffed with citations of the commentary on the *Meteorologica* by Alexander of Aphrodisias. This commentary had also been translated into Latin by William of Moerbeke. In addition, *Les Metheores* contains passages that appear to be additions original with Mahieu. One of the latter, for example, is a naturalistic explanation of the supposed astrological effects of comets, appended to Aristotle's discussion of comets in Book 1, Chapter 7.[16] It is interesting to note that William of Moerbeke's Latin version of the *Meteorologica* was completed in 1260, so that Mahieu chose a new and authoritative version of Aristotle's text on which to base his translation.[17]

At about the same time that Mahieu was translating Aristotle's *Meteorologica*, a group of scholars in the Belgian town of Malines (Mechlin) were collaborating on a translation of an astrological treatise, the *Livre du commencement de sapience* of the Jewish scholar Abraham Ibn Ezra (mid-twelfth century). They recorded the circumstances of their project in a colophon:

> The Book of the Beginning of Wisdom that Abraham Ibn Ezra made . . . which Hagin the Jew translated from Hebrew into Romance, and Obert de Montdidier wrote the Romance, and it was made at Malines, in the house of Lord Henry Bate, and was finished the year of grace 1273, the day after the feast day of St. Thomas the Apostle [i.e., Dec. 22].[18]

It is difficult to determine from this brief note the role played by each of the three individuals mentioned in translating the *Livre du commencement de sapience* (and in all probability the four works that accompany it in the manuscripts).[19] Was Hagin the translator, and Obert merely the scribe? Was Henry Bate simply the patron, or did he take a more active part in the project than just providing living and working quarters? Bate, after all, was himself a well-known astronomer, who later (in 1281 and 1292) made Latin translations of several treatises by Ibn Ezra, including *The Beginning of Wisdom*. It seems likely that the collaboration was arranged by

Bate, who may have felt the need in his own scientific work of ready access to works of Ibn Ezra.[20] A translation into French by a Jew who knew both Hebrew and the vernacular might have promised faster and more accurate results than a translation into Latin via the vernacular.[21]

Thus, even the earliest examples of French translations of astrological works plunge us *in medias res*: into ambitious projects deliberately undertaken and systematically pursued. Likewise, these projects indicate the wide scope of scientific translation throughout this period. Mahieu translated a Greek authority, Hagin and his colleagues a Jewish scholar, and at the same time others were undertaking translations of Arabic astrological works.

Translations of several Arabic works are found in a thirteenth-century manuscript (Paris B.N. fr. 1353) that bears a dedication to Baldwin of Courtenay.[22] Following the *Introduction to Astronomy* discussed above, the manuscript contains the *Livre des nativitez des enfenz* of Abû 'Ali (Albohali, mid-ninth century), the *Epistle es choses de l'eclipse* of Māshā'Allāh and the *Flores* of Abū Ma'shar. These texts could well have been selected by the translator or compiler to provide an introduction to astronomy and astrology suitable for a noble patron. The translations were made from Latin versions of the Arabic texts. It is worth noting that the texts included in this manuscript are those of the Arabic writers whose works achieved the greatest popularity in the vernacular. Judging by the number of their works translated and the number of surviving manuscripts containing the translation, it seems clear that Māshā 'Allāh and Abū Ma'shar were among the most popular authorities on astrology.[23]

Just as Mahieu le Vilain based his translation on a recent version of Aristotle's *Meteorologica*, the translator Nicolas de la Horbe in 1327 chose to translate a recent and widely known Latin work, an introductory astrological text called *Astrologia judiciaria* by Guido Bonatti (d. before 1300).[24] Bonatti's massive work (occupying 359 single-column folios in one nearly complete version) was widely known and might well have seemed an obvious choice if Nicolas de la Horbe wanted to make available in the vernacular a comprehensive introduction to astrology. Unfortunately, nothing is known of the background or profession of this enterprising translator.[25]

In the final years of the thirteenth century and the opening years of the fourteenth, the French royal court began to take an active interest in the translation of works on the science of the stars. Evidence for this comes from the varied projects of the astronomer William of Saint-Cloud, who was active in the final decades of the thirteenth century.[26] An observational astronomer who seems to have taken no interest in astrology, he was on a good footing at the court of Philip IV (Philip the Fair, d. 1314).

William composed an astronomical calendar (with a base year of 1292) for Marie de Brabant, widow of Philip III (d. 1285); after her death he himself translated the calendar into French at the request of Jeanne de Navarre (d. 1305), wife of Philip IV. It may also have been for Jeanne de Navarre that William translated into French another of his astronomical works, *Directorium* (*L'Adrescoir*), the text of which begins, "Most noble lady. . . ."

One of the manuscripts containing William's French version of his *Calendarium*, *Le Calendrier la royne*, bears the date 1303.[27] Since Jeanne de Navarre, for whom the translation of the *Calendarium* was made, was still alive in that year, it is tempting to speculate that the manuscript may have been compiled for her. If this were true, the contents of the manuscript would present an instructive example of the kinds of texts that appealed to this royal patroness. In any case, however, the manuscript contents shed light on the flow of astronomical knowledge from Latin into French.

The lengthy manuscript (538 folios, written in three columns) contains a miscellany of texts--all of them in French. Biblical books (the Book of Job), religious poetry (poems on the Virgin Mary by Gautier de Coincy), and philosophical works (Boethius's *De consolatione philosophiae* in the translation of Jean de Meun, made for Philip IV), among others, coexist from folio 43 onward. The opening folios, however, contain astronomical texts. First is *La Lettre a savoir le vrai cours de la lune par le qualendrier mestre Pierre de Dace, dit Rosignol* (Peter Philomena) (fols. 1^v-8), followed by William's calendar and tables. Folios 41^v-43 contain the *Almanach* of Ibn Tibbon (Profatius Judaeus).

Peter Philomena and Ibn Tibbon were writing at the end of the thirteenth and the beginning of the fourteenth century; Ibn Tibbon died in 1283, while Peter Philomena flourished about 1290-1300.[28] The inclusion of such recent works indicates an interest in contemporary scientific developments not often associated with the tastes of late medieval literary patrons.[29] It is possible that William of Saint-Cloud might himself have translated the *Lettre* of Peter Philomena and the *Almanach* of Ibn Tibbon in addition to his calendar, which they accompany.

Another translation connected with the court of Philip IV is a French version of Abū Ma'shar's *Electiones* made by Arnoul de Quinquempoix (d. after 1329), a physician at the royal court. Arnoul's name first appears in documents in 1304, at which time he had already been serving the court for a long time as physician to Philip III and his sons.[30] His is the first name known in the series of physician / astrologer / translators. He is an even more interesting figure for having made translations from French into Latin as well as from Latin into the vernacular.

Arnoul may have been unaware of the Latin translation that Pietro d'Abano (d. c. 1315) had made of Hagin's French version of astrological works of Abraham Ibn Ezra. Arnoul translated two of these into Latin.[31] He may also have known Hebrew and have made a translation from Hebrew into French. That, at least, is the impression given by the description (from an inventory taken in 1373) of a now-lost manuscript that belonged to Charles V: "Alkindus, *De imbribus et pluviis*, in Latin, together with *La Redemption des fils d'Israel*, in a volume bound in parchment, which Master Arnoul de Quiquampoit [*sic*] caused to be translated from Hebrew into French, at Paris."[32]

One of the two manuscripts containing Arnoul's translation of Abū Ma'shar's text was compiled sometime before 1324. This manuscript (Paris B.N. fr. 613, mentioned above) has been called "the most important single collection of scientific works in French."[33] Its 149 folios are filled with a collection of astronomical and astrological works in French, the work of several translators.[34] Authors represented in the collection include Leopold of Austria, 'Ali ibn Abi'l-Rijāl, and "Robert Grosseteste" (apparently a false attribution), as well as several anonymous texts. In Carmody's opinion, the manuscript "was intended as an omnibus on astrology and astronomy for some prospective client or for some rich collector." Overall, the compilation presents a mix of translations of "modern," Arabic, and legendary authors. It is interesting to note that the ever-popular Māshā'Allāh is not represented in the collection, although several otherwise unknown texts are included. (This manuscript is the sole source known for at least four of the texts included.)

The Court of Charles V

Royal interest in the science of the stars--and in French translation--reached its height under Charles V (Charles the Wise, 1338-80), who ascended the throne in 1364. Charles was a great literary patron who commissioned French translations of many kinds of works, including several works of Aristotle. Astrology was a lifelong special interest of his. The astrologer Symon de Phares, writing a century later, was (for once) probably not exaggerating when he described Charles as one who

> loved the science of astrology so much that he caused to
> be translated all the books he could find about the
> science of the stars, and, among others, he caused the
> *Quadripartitum* of Ptolemy, the *Centiloquium*, Abraham
> Ibn Ezra, Guido Bonatti, Haly Abenragel, and many
> others to be translated from Latin into French.[35]

Similarly, the translator whom Charles commissioned to translate Ptolemy's *Quadripartitum* said of the king that

> once he had Holy Scripture in his own tongue, he desired
> also to have books in French concerning the most noble
> science in the world, that is true astrology without
> superstition, and especially what noteworthy and
> approved philosophers have written about it.[36]

307

Inventories of Charles's library in the Louvre record more than thirty manuscripts of astronomical and astrological texts in French, encompassing a wide variety of authors and titles.[37] This figure can be contrasted with the two books on astronomy that Duke John the Fearless of Burgundy inherited in 1404 from his father Duke Philip I (Philip the Bold), and the three that he in turn bequeathed to his son, Duke Philip II (Philip the Good), in 1419.[38] John, Duke of Berry (d. 1416), brother of Charles V, numbered some eight books on astrology in his large library.[39]

Charles began to commission translations of scientific works while still a young man, several years before his accession to the throne. As early as 1359-62, he employed two of the professional astrologers in his service to translate astrological works into French. Robert Godefroy, master of arts, translated the anonymous *Livre des neuf anciens juges de astrologie* (*Liber novem judicum*); Pèlerin de Prusse translated the *Liber introductorius* of al-Qabīsī and in addition either translated or composed a work on astrology in three parts and a treatise on the use of the astrolabe.[40] During this period, Charles also sponsored translations of astrological works of Māshā 'Allāh and Sahl (Zael, d. c. 822-850). As dauphin, Charles took up residence in the Hôtel Saint-Pol in Paris, and at least one translator, Pèlerin de Prusse, records living at the hôtel while working on his translations.[41]

Charles's principal translator, however, was the scholar and bishop Nicole Oresme (c. 1320-82).[42] In the 1370s, Charles entrusted Oresme with the translation into French of Aristotle's *Ethica*, *Politica*, *Economica* and *De caelo et mundo*.[43] In addition, Oresme was the author of numerous works on a variety of scientific, theological, and economic topics in Latin and French. Knowledgeable in astronomy, he was a vigorous opponent of astrology. His *Tractatus contra iudiciarios astronomos*, written in Latin, was later translated into French;[44] Oresme himself then composed a similar work in French, *Le Livre de divinacions*.[45] Oresme was also the author of a work on mathematical astronomy, *Traitié de l'espere*.

Charles V employed Nicole Oresme's brother, Guillaume, to translate into French the *Quadripartitum* of Ptolemy. This project, completed about 1362-63, is the earliest French translation known of

Ptolemy's astrological work.[46] Until recently, it was believed that
Nicole Oresme was the translator of another astrological work that
circulated under Ptolemy's name, the *Centiloquium*. However, the
date of the manuscript containing that translation (Paris, B.N. fr.
1349) has in recent years been revised to c. 1300. Too early for
Oresme, the revised date makes this translation an early one in the
history of astronomical and astrological works in French.[47]

Charles V has been described as a king who "seldom acted
against the advice of his court astrologers."[48] He kept a staff of
several astrologers (including Robert Godefroy and Pèlerin de
Prusse) and physician / astrologers (among them, Thomas of Pisano,
father of the poet Christine de Pisan). He also maintained near him,
and relied upon the advice of, a group of learned men and clerics, of
whom Nicole Oresme was one. Many of these theologians also
served Charles as translators of Latin historical and theological
texts.[49] That there was some overlap, perhaps extensive, between
the two groups seems clear, at least to judge by the various roles
filled by Oresme. Menut described the theologians as "intimate
colleagues," who read and commented upon each other's translations.[50] They were also in the privileged position of suggesting to
Charles books they felt were appropriate for translation into the
vernacular.[51] It is probable that Charles's astrologers likewise
advised him on the selection of astrological and astronomical works
for French translation.

Menut's vivid picture of a group of theologians and scholars
reading, criticizing, and appreciating each other's work as translators
almost certainly reflects the practice of Charles's astrological
advisers as well. That impression comes from the frequent comments by translators like Robert Godefroy and Pèlerin de Prusse, as
well as Oresme, on their goals, techniques, and problems of translation. According to Menut, Oresme in his translation of Aristotle's
Economica "often . . . complains in his glosses that his originals are
corrupt and defy intelligent interpretation." Menut calls Oresme's
product "one of the earliest examples of textual criticism in a
modern language."[52] Yet, while Oresme's talents were superior to
those of Charles's other scientific translators, and his comments and
commentary on his Latin sources more detailed and perceptive, his

methods were in the end essentially the same as theirs. For example, at the end of his translation of the *Livre des neuf anciens juges de astrologie*, Robert Godefroy commented:

> If in this book . . . there is anything unclear or rather obscure, it is due to the Latin original which is quite obscure and unusual and perplexing beyond measure in its language, which is not like the manner of speech used by authors of astrology, but is rather completely different, and it is full of images and incorrect ways of speaking, which is not very useful in such a science. And also all the books that we have seen of this text are defective, incorrect, and corrupt throughout. And so, if in this book there are some things which are insufficient or too obscure, let it not be imputed to the translator before the reader has looked at the original.[53]

The comments made by Pèlerin de Prusse at the end of each of his works indicate a careful overall plan for his translation. Of his astrological treatise in three parts, he explains, "I have put this general rule at the end of this part of this book of universal elections of the twelve houses, in order that it may be the key to all the others, and the lock."[54] He explains at the end of his treatise on the use of the astrolabe:

> I have . . . completed the benefits and chapters of the practice of the astrolabe briefly and simply, [dealing] only with the use of the astrolabe without mingling extraneous tasks in the form of calculations, so that the lessons would be simple and comprehensible to all.[55]

It was thus under the patronage of Charles V that scientific translation first began to take place in an organized manner, as the product of a school, rather than individuals and small groups working independently on special projects. While previous translations appear to have resulted from a patron's interest or a specialist's needs, for the first time under Charles V a patron's serious interest was united with the financial and intellectual resources that only a great court could command.

The Fifteenth Century

After the death of Charles V, there is only occasional and sporadic evidence for royal patronage of astrological translations or compositions. For example, in 1479, Jehan de Beauvau, bishop of Angers, dedicated to Louis XI (1423-83, ruled 1461-83) his work called *La Figure et image du monde*.[56] And in an autograph manuscript dated 1481 there survives a French astrological text called *Influencia celi*, the work of "Robert du Herlin, secretaire du roy [Louis XI]."[57] Neither of these works has been identified as a translation; they may be compilations or even original compositions.

Numerous indications link fifteenth-century astrological translations with medical students and practitioners. Although Latin was at this time still the language of medical schools--and students--some may have found French translations useful, either as a crib or as a supplement to Latin texts. For example, a fifteenth-century manuscript (Dijon, Bib. mun. 449) was at least partly compiled by a medical student who identified himself in a colophon as "Pierre Pevidic at the University of Dole, unworthy master of arts and student of medicine, 1459."[58] In this manuscript, a series of Latin astrological and medical texts is followed by two French works: a translation (dated 1301 in the explicit) of the *Abbreviationes Alcabitii* of John of Saxony (a commentary on the *Isagogus* of al-Qabisi̅) and a translation of the *Centiloquium*. It is reasonable to see in Pierre a medical student transcribing for his own use texts, whether in Latin or French, that might prove useful to him in his studies.

Fifteenth-century astrological translations were more modest in scope than the ambitious projects undertaken previously, and few appear to have enjoyed a wide circulation. Few names of translators and compilers are recorded.

One fifteenth-century writer on the science of the stars whose name and biography are better known than most is Jean Fusoris (c. 1365-1436). This physician, astrologer, and instrument maker composed several works in French on astronomical instruments, including a *Pratique de l'astrolabe* dedicated to Pierre de Navarre, Count of Mortain.[59] Fusoris's *Pratique* may have served, not long after its composition, as the model for a similar but more elaborate work. The astrologer Symon de Phares reported for the year 1435:

> At this time, my lord Jehan de Bregy was at the court of the king. He was a notable knight and great astrologer. He was instructed and brought up in the house of Burgundy. He composed, for King René of Sicily, the practice of the astrolabe in French, and he included several examples and fixed stars that master Jehan Furoris [*sic*] had not included.[60]

More typical, however, are the three astrological treatises on comets that survive in three late fifteenth-century manuscripts.[61] Two of the treatises are translations of thirteenth-century Latin works; the third is a short compilation called the *Petit traictié de la significacion des comettes*. All three appear to be the work of a single individual--about whom absolutely nothing is known.

This rapid overview of the process by which Latin treatises on the science of the stars were assimilated into the vernacular reveals the action of many minds and hands, working independently at first, then in the second half of the fourteenth century benefiting from the intellectual stimulation and cross-fertilization found in the literary and scientific circle about a great monarch. In the fifteenth century, the activity is once again that of individuals, including students and professionals mostly anonymous but part of the numerous university-trained intelligentsia of fifteenth-century France.

Techniques of Translation

Neither the medieval translators nor their modern editors say much about the techniques developed and used by those who undertook the challenging task of translating technical works. Modern editions of these texts have traditionally focused primarily on philological concerns, examining the grammar, syntax, and vocabulary of the translation and only cursorily, if at all, comparing it to the original to reveal the translator's practices. An excellent example is Edgren's edition of Mahieu le Vilain's translation of

312

Aristotle's *Meteorologica*.[62] Edgren devotes some eighty pages of his introduction to an exemplary linguistic study, while summarizing Mahieu's techniques of translation in a short three pages. Edgren's edition also exemplifies what might be called the "judgmental tradition" of the edition of medieval French texts. That is, like the majority of editors before him and many since, he takes pains to evaluate Mahieu's work in order to assign it to its proper place in the French literary pantheon: "The work of Mahieu le Vilain is worthy of our respect and . . . deserves an honorable place in the history of French scientific literature."[63]

These editorial traditions mean that, even for critically edited and published translations, the translator's treatment of his original generally remains to be analyzed through a detailed comparison of translation and original. Another difficulty arises in determining the exact original on which a medieval translator based his work. In the case of Nicole Oresme's translation of Aristotle's *De caelo*, for example, it is clear that Oresme used William of Moerbeke's Latin version translated from the Greek, rather than a Latin version based on an Arabic original.[64] It is by no means equally clear, however, what manuscript Oresme used, and what other, related works it may have contained in addition to Moerbeke's text--factors that could have an important bearing on a detailed study of his techniques of translation.

In the absence of detailed comparisons of translations with originals, general observations on the techniques used must be based on the sparse comments of the modern editors of such translations. Nonetheless, when editors' comments are examined, some common elements appear. For example, two techniques popular with many of the translators mentioned in this article are the use of *doublets* and the use or creation of *latinisms*.

Doublets: The use of paired synonyms to render a single Latin word has been called "a common affectation" in fourteenth-century translations.[65] Even in translations of technical works, this device appears to be more a matter of style than an effort to attain greater precision. Thus, for example, the translator of Leopold of Austria's *Compilatio de astrorum scientia* uses "solides et fermes" to translate Latin "solidus."[66] The anonymous late fifteenth-century translator of Giles of Lessines's *De essentia, motu, et significatione comet-arum* frequently used two pairs of doublets within a single sentence, such as "seoir et durer" to translate "sedeat" and "non certain et vague" for "incerto."[67] In neither of these representative examples does the addition of a second term add to the precision of the translation.

Nonetheless, the use of doublets has been viewed by at least one scholar as part of a trend toward greater explicitness seen in the circle of translators at the court of Charles V. According to this view, translators' *additions* to the original are another manifestation of the same trend.[68] In fact, many translators (not only those at Charles V's court) added short explanations or definitions of technical terms used in their originals. Thus, for example, the translator of *De essentia* twice explained the term "dyaphanum" ("transparency"): "en dyaphane c'est a dire en transparent"; "par dyaphane c'est a dire par corps transparent."[69] Carmody notes that the translator of Leopold of Austria's *Compilatio* was so consistent in his practice of providing definitions that "if a learned or technical word is introduced without such comment, it may be assumed, given the translator's general practice, that the word was already known or at least comprehensible."[70] It is reasonable to see this common practice as an effort by translators to ensure that readers would understand their work.

Latinisms: Translators of technical works frequently found that the vernacular lacked exact equivalents for technical terms common in Latin. Many, like Oresme, adopted the expedient of "turning the Latin into French by dropping a case ending or by altering a verb tense to conform to the French system."[71] Both Edgren and Carmody, for example, note the predilection for latinisms on the part of Mahieu and the translator of Leopold of Austria respectively.[72] Thus, for example, "equatio" would become "equacion"; "latitudo," "latitude." In their edition of Oresme's *Livre du ciel et du monde*, Menut and Denomy refer to these latinisms, or calques, as neolog-isms, and append a list of some of the several hundred terms coined by Oresme on the basis of his Latin original. That many of these have survived to the present day gives added interest to the editors' listing.[73]

Translators frequently retained latinisms in their translations for ordinary, nontechnical words and phrases as well as technical terms--a practice that could be attributed to haste, laziness, caution, or preference. The translator of *De essentia*, for example, frequently retained the word order as well as the vocabulary of his original, translating "quarum nomina et effectus quidam astrologi scripserunt" by "des quelles les noms et les effectz aucuns astrologiens ont mis par escript."[74]

In addition to specific stylistic devices, the translations mentioned in this article reveal other interesting characteristics. One of these is the contrast between extremely literal translations and those so free as to constitute paraphrases or which incorporate so much additional material that they become commentaries or glosses as well as translations. A good example of the latter, as seen in the previous section, is Mahieu le Vilain's *Les Metheores*. Another is Oresme's *Livre du ciel et du monde*. In both cases, the translators' comments about their work prepare the reader for a literal translation; both, however, are free translations that incorporate commentary as well. Oresme's editors state that "his translations are indeed so free that they may be considered as paraphrases."[75] Edgren describes Mahieu's translation as "very free and very expanded, even though he claims to be translating word for word."[76]

At the opposite extreme stand such works as the anonymous late fifteenth-century translation of an anonymous comet tract, the *Livre de la signification des cometes*. Comparison of the translation with the original "reveals chapter after chapter of painstakingly literal, often word-for-word, translation." The minor changes made by the translator "pale into insignificance against the translator's overwhelming tendency to translate his original as faithfully as possible."[77]

The translations considered in this article also reveal a contrast between systematic errors and carefulness in translation. Several examples of errors on the part of the translator are noted by Carmody in his edition of the translation of Leopold of Austria's *Compilatio*; these include "several occurrences of *equacion* for *equator*, *orient* once for *horizon*, and frequent confusion of *lieu* and *cours* for *motus*, of *espere*, *orbe*, and *cercle* indifferently for

315

circulus, orbis, and *sphera.*"[78]   Similarly, the *Livre de la signification des cometes* repeatedly and consistently, although
incorrectly, translates "complexio" by "conjonction."[79]   Interestingly, however, the same work reveals great care on the part of the
translator, who left blank spaces for words that were unclear in the
original as well as for material missing from the original.

To some extent, these contrasts and seeming inconsistencies can
be understood by considering the problems peculiar to translations
of technical works.   Translators, who might themselves be "indiffer-
ent latinists," were faced with technical terms in both Latin and
Arabic that frequently had no exact equivalent in the vernacular.[80]
In addition, and perhaps as a consequence, translators often failed to
distinguish between terms for similar or related concepts. (This can
be seen in the interchangeable use, mentioned above, of "espere,"
"orbe," and "cercle" for Latin "circulus," "orbis," and "sphera" in
the translation of Leopold of Austria.)

Stone provides a fascinating list of French medical terms from a
late thirteenth-century translation along with the various Latin terms
they are used for; he finds that a single word such as "raseur"
(modern French "rasoir") stands for not only "rasorius" and
"novacula" (razor) but also "incisorius" (knife, and probably scalpel)
and "radius" (rod).[81]   In astronomical and astrological translations,
especially, the confusion of terms can be seen in the interchangeable
use of Latin and French names for the signs of the zodiac (such as
"Aries" and "Mouton"), or the retention of Arabic names and terms,
often in garbled form.

This confusion of terms may have been one reason why
translators of technical works so frequently added material--whether
short definitions or longer commentaries--to their translations.   As
Dembowski pointed out, for Oresme "tr[anslation] and gloss are . . .
two complementary facets of a single undertaking, whose main
object is not merely to render A[ristotle] into French, but to make
the work readily assimilable for the intelligent youth of his day."[82]

The best description of a translator tackling a technical work is
given by Stone:

> In his struggle to find expression for the terminology of
> the Latin model, the translator tried or experimented with

a variety of devices: now he uses a folk-term, now he paraphrases in simple French; again he leaves the term intact, alone or with an explanation, a comment, or a French approximation.[83]

Faced with a difficult job, translators of technical works on the science of the stars in the thirteenth to fifteenth centuries adopted a variety of practices to accomplish their task. While some of these, such as the use of doublets, likely represented stylistic preferences of the time, others--such as the use of latinisms and the addition of definitions and explanations--reflect the difficulty of translating technical concepts into a nontechnical vernacular.

Conclusion

The science of the stars thus provides an example and illustration of the more general process of the transfer of technical knowledge into vernacular languages in the Middle Ages.

By conducting and collecting similar studies for other fields of technical knowledge and other European vernaculars, it will eventually be possible to synthesize an overview of the gradual transformation of European technical knowledge from an elite preserve to a pool of information available to all who could read in their native language.

NOTES

1. Two useful general surveys of medieval astrology are Theodore O. Wedel, *The Mediaeval Attitude Toward Astrology, Particularly in England*, Yale Studies in English 60 (New Haven, CT: Yale Univ. Press, 1920) and A. J. Meadows, *The High Firmament: A Survey of Astronomy in English Literature* (Leicester: Leicester Univ. Press, 1969). In addition, see Lynn Thorndike, "The True Place of Astrology in the History of Science," *Isis* 46 (1955):273-78.

2. Lynn Thorndike and Pearl Kibre, *A Catalogue of Incipits of Mediaeval Scientific Writings in Latin*, The Mediaeval Academy of America Publication no. 29, rev. ed. (Cambridge, MA: The Medieval

Academy of America, 1963); Francis J. Carmody, *Arabic Astronomical and Astrological Sciences in Latin Translation: A Critical Bibliography* (Berkeley and Los Angeles: Univ. of California Press, 1956).

3. For an annotated list of these manuscripts and their contents, see Lys Ann T. Shore, "Three Treatises on Comets in Middle French: A Study in the Development of a Vernacular Scientific Tradition" (Ph.D. diss., University of Toronto, 1984).

4. Leopold of Austria, *Li Compilacions de le science des estoilles*, ed. Francis J. Carmody, University of California Publications in Modern Philology 33, no. 2 (Berkeley and Los Angeles: Univ. of California Press, 1947). Incorporating portions of one work into another, without title or attribution, was not an uncommon practice during this period. For example, the fourteenth-century French writer Philippe de Mézières reproduced large portions of Nicole Oresme's *Livre de divinacions* in Book Two of his *Le Songe du vieil pelerin*. See Philippe de Mézières, *Le Songe du vieil pelerin*, ed. G. W. Coopland, 2 vols. (Cambridge: Cambridge Univ. Press, 1969).

5. Shore [n. 3 above], pp. 87-103.

6. Richard Lemay (30 September 1978, private communication) concluded that in all probability "this is not a straight translation from a (Latin) text of Abū Ma'shar, but a kind of compilation, principally of these two authors: Zael and Abū Ma'shar."

7. Emmanuel Poulle, "William of Saint-Cloud," *Dictionary of Scientific Biography* (1970-80), states that MS Arsenal 534 contains the Latin *Calendarium*. Antoine Thomas, "Notices succinctes . . . Maitre Etienne Arblant, astronome," *Histoire littéraire de la France* 35 (Paris, 1921), p. 628n., noted that the French *Calendrier la royne* "is contained in MS 534 of the Arsenal . . . where nothing leads one to suspect the fact, which we point out based on direct examination of the manuscript" (my translation). Recently, at my request, Claire R. Sherman perused the MS; she found it to contain only the Latin text of the *Calendarium*, beginning on fol. 91 (29 November 1982, private communication).

8. See Lynn Thorndike, *The Sphere of Sacrobosco and Its Com-*

mentators (Chicago: Univ. of Chicago Press, 1949) and Olaf Pedersen, "The Theorica Planetarum-Literature of the Middle Ages," *Classica et Mediaevalia* 23 (1962):225-32.

9.   Paris, B.N. fr. 2078-2079 (anc. 7945 and 7945[2]). See description in *Catalogue des manuscrits français: Bibliothèque impériale*, 1 (Paris: Firmin Didot, 1868), p. 355.

10.   Lillian M. McCarthy, ed., "Maistre Nicole Oresme, Traitié de l'espere" (Ph.d. diss., University of Toronto, 1943, pp. 33-34).

11.   Published at Paris by Antoine Vérard in 1504, the work includes as its first part a text called *Placides et Timeo*; the second is the abridgment of *De sphera*; the third is a *computus*. See Ernest Renan, "Le Livre des secrets aux philosophes ou Dialogue de Placide et Timeo," *Histoire littéraire de la France* 30 (Paris, 1888), pp. 567-95.

12.   Mahieu le Vilain, *Les Metheores d'Aristote*, ed. Rolf Edgren (Uppsala: Almqvist & Wiksells Boktryckeri AB, 1945).

13.   This may have been Alphonse (d. 1270), Count of Eu and son of King John of Jerusalem, or possibly his son, John of Brienne, Count of Eu (d. 1294). See Edgren [n. 12 above], pp. vii-xvi, and Shore [n. 3 above], p. 43.   John of Brienne commissioned a French translation of Vegetius's *De re militari* from the poet and translator Jean de Meun in 1284.

14.   Edgren [n. 12 above], p. 1.

15.   Brussels, Bib. roy. de Belgique 2903, fourteenth century.   This MS may have been copied by the scribes of Charles V.   At least two other MSS of Mahieu's translation are known to have existed, one in the fifteenth century, the other in the first half of the fourteenth.   See Edgren [n. 12 above], pp. i-ii.

16.   Edgren [n. 12 above], pp. 42-43.

17.   This statement assumes the accuracy of Edgren's suggested date (1260-70) for Mahieu's translation.   I have suggested elsewhere that a more conservative dating would be 1260-94.   See Shore [n. 3 above], p. 43.

18. "Li Livres du commencement de sapience que fist Abraham Even Azre . . . que translata Hagins li Juis, de ebrieu en romans, et Obers de Mondidier escrivoit le romans, et fu fait a Malines, en la meson Sire Henri Bate, et fu finés l'an de grace 1273, l'endemein de la seint Thomas l'apostre" (MS Paris, B.N. fr. 24276, fol. 66), quoted in Henri Omont, *Bibliothèque nationale, Catalogue général des manuscrits français (Ancien petit-fonds français, 2: Nos. 22885-25696 du fonds français)* (Paris, 1902), p. 300. The translation has been edited: Abraham Ibn Ezra, *The Beginning of Wisdom*, ed. Raphael Levy, The Johns Hopkins Studies in Romance Literatures and Languages, extra vol. 14 (Baltimore: Johns Hopkins Univ. Press, 1939). See also Raphael Levy, *The Astrological Works of Abraham Ibn Ezra, A Literary and Linguistic Study*, The Johns Hopkins Studies in Romance Literatures and Languages, 8 (Baltimore: Johns Hopkins Univ. Press, 1928).

19. The *Livre des jugements*, *Livre des elections*, and *Livre des interrogations* of Ibn Ezra, and the *Livre des revolutions* of Abū Ma'shar. David C. Lindberg, "The Transmission of Greek and Arabic Learning to the West," in *Science in the Middle Ages*, ed. David C. Lindberg (Chicago: Univ. of Chicago Press, 1978), pp. 32-90, incorrectly states (p. 68) that more than fifty works on astrology by Ibn Ezra were translated by Hagin. See also Paulin Paris, "Hagins le juif, traducteur français de plusieurs livres d'astronomie," *Histoire littéraire de la France* 21 (Paris, 1847), pp. 499-503.

20. Emmanuel Poulle, "Henry Bate of Malines," *Dictionary of Scientific Biography* (1970-80), states that Hagin translated from Hebrew into Latin, while Obert de Montdidier rendered the Latin into French. On the basis of the MS colophon, this statement is incorrect. Poulle believes that Bate "certainly had a more responsible role in this matter than providing lodging for his authors." He notes that the five texts in the manuscript are all "too similar in style not to have been the result of the same collaboration" (p. 272). Bate's knowledge of Hebrew may have been minimal in spite of his translation into Latin of works by Ibn Ezra. Poulle speculates (ibid.) that Hagin may have assisted Bate in these later efforts as well.

21. This seemingly cumbersome method of translation was used more than once in the Middle Ages. For example, Ibn Sina's (Avicenna)

De anima was translated (c. 1151-66) from Arabic into Latin via Castilian by a learned Jew, Avendauth, working with the translator Gundisalvi; see James A. Weisheipl, "Albertus Magnus and Universal Hylomorphism," *Southwest Journal of Philosophy* 10 (1980):247. Lindberg [n. 19 above], p. 70, discusses translations made at the court of Alfonso X of Castile (1252-84). Arabic works were translated into Castilian by Jewish translators, and then retranslated into Latin.

22. See description in *Catalogue des manuscrits français, Bibliothèque impériale*, 1 [n. 9 above], pp. 216-17.

23. Shore [n. 3 above], pp. 213-32.

24. The translation, entitled *Livre nommé introductoire*, is found in two fifteenth-century MSS: Paris, Bib. de l'Arsenal 2911 and Valenciennes, Bib. de la ville 348 (355). The translator's name with the date, 1327, occurs in the explicit of part two of the work (fol. 156^v of the Arsenal MS). See Charles Langlois, "Notices succinctes . . . Nicolas de La Horbe, traducteur," *Histoire littéraire de la France* 35 (Paris, 1921), pp. 629-30.

25. See the brief biographical note in the *Dictionnaire des lettres françaises: Moyen âge*, ed. Robert Bossuat, Louis Pichard, Guy Raynaud de Lage (Paris: Fayard, 1964) and Langlois [n. 24 above].

26. The earliest recorded date of William's activity is December 28, 1285, when he observed a conjunction of Jupiter and Saturn. See Emmanuel Poulle [n. 7 above]. An earlier biographical notice is that by Emile Littré, "Guillaume de Saint-Cloud, astronome," *Histoire littéraire de la France* 25 (Paris, 1849), pp. 63-74.

27. Rennes, Bib. mun. 593, fol. 170rb. See *Catalogue général des manuscrits des bibliothèques publiques de France--Départements*, 24 (Paris: Plon, 1894), pp. 238-48.

28. Juan Vernet, "Ibn Tibbon, Moses Ben Samuel," *Dictionary of Scientific Biography* (1970-80); Olaf Pedersen, "Peter Philomena of Dacia," ibid.

29. C. E. Pickford, "A Fifteenth-Century Copyist and His Patron," in

Medieval Miscellany presented to Eugène Vinaver, ed. Frederick Whitehead, A. H. Diverres, and F. E. Sutcliffe (New York: Barnes and Noble, 1965), pp. 259-60.

30.   Antoine Thomas, "Notices succinctes . . . Arnoul de Quinquempoix, médecin et astrologue," *Histoire littéraire de la France* 35 (Paris, 1921), p. 631.   The most recent source of biographical information on Arnoul is Danielle Jacquart, *Ernest Wickersheimer, Dictionnaire biographique des médecins en France au moyen âge: Supplément*, Centre de recherches d'histoire et de philologie 5: Hautes études médiévales et modernes 35 (Geneva: Droz, 1979).

31.   Raphael Levy [n. 18 above].

32.   "Alkindus de imbribus et pluviis en latin, et avec la Redemption des fils d'Israel, en un volume couvert de parchemin, que fist translater de ebrieu en francois, a Paris, maistre Arnoul de Quiquampoit," quoted in Léopold V. Delisle, *Recherches sur la librairie de Charles V*, vol. 2 (Paris, 1907; rpt. Amsterdam: van Heusden, 1967), p. 127 (no. 777).

33.   The epithet is that of Francis J. Carmody [n. 4 above], p. 47. Carmody gives a complete list of the MS contents on pp. 48-51.

34.   Ibid.

35.   "Cestui ayma tant la science de astrologie qu'il fist translater tous les livres qu'il peut finer et trouver de la science des estoilles et, entre autres, fist translater de latin en francois le *Quadri partiti Ptholomei, le Centilloque*, Abraham Avennerre, Guido Bonatti, Hali Abenragel et plusieurs autres." Symon de Phares, *Recueil des plus celebres astrologues et quelques hommes doctes*, ed. Ernest Wickersheimer (Paris: Champion, 1929), p. 228.

36.   "Après ce que il a eu en son language l'escripture divine, il veut aussi avoir des livres en francois de la plus noble science de cest siecle, c'est vraie astrologie sans superstecion et par especial ce que en ont composé les philosophes excellens et approuvés." Quoted in R. Delachenal, "Note sur un manuscrit de la Bibliothèque de Charles V," *Bibliothèque de l'Ecole des Chartes* 71 (1910):33-38, esp. 38.

37. L. Delisle [n. 32 above], 2:95-120.

38. Georges Doutrepont, *La Littérature française à la cour des ducs de Bourgogne* (Paris: Champion, 1909), pp. 281-82.

39. Delisle [n. 32 above], 2:248-52. It is noteworthy in this context that the unique example in an illuminated manuscript of the "anatomical man" or "astrological man" (a figure showing the relations of the zodiacal signs to the various organs of the human body) is found in a MS made for John of Berry. See *The Très Riches Heures of Jean, Duke of Berry: Musée Condé, Chantilly*, ed. Jean Longnon and Raymond Cazelles (New York: Braziller, 1969), pl. 14 and commentary. The editors point out, "An extension of the calendar, to which it was added in the form of an inset page, the present example is a remarkable exception explained by Charles V's passionate interest in astrology, shared by his brothers."

40. Robert Godefroy's translation of the *Liber novem judicum* is found in a fourteenth-century MS: Paris, Bib. de l'Arsenal 2872, fols. 85-309. MS description in H. Martin, *Catalogue général des manuscrits de la Bibliothèque de l'Arsenal*, 3 vols. (Paris: Plon, 1897), 3:134-38. Pèlerin de Prusse's translations are contained in a fourteenth-century MS, Oxford, St. John's College 164, fols. 33-111 (the treatise on astrology in three parts), fols. 111-19 (treatise on the use of the astrolabe), and fols. 119-58 (al-Qabisi). MS descriptions in H. Coxe, *Catalogus codicum manuscriptorum qui in collegiis aulisque Oxon hodie adservantur*, 1 (Oxford, 1852), pp. 51-52; G. W. Coopland, *Nicole Oresme and the Astrologers: A Study of His 'Livre de divinacions'* (Cambridge, MA: Harvard Univ. Press, 1952), pp. 184n-185n; Léopold Delisle, *Le Cabinet des manuscrits*, 4 vols. (1868-81; rpt. New York: Burt Franklin, 1973), 3:336-37.

41. Coxe, ibid.

42. Recent biographical sketches of Oresme are Marshall Clagett, "Oresme, Nicole," *Dictionary of Scientific Biography* (1970-80), and *Maistre Nicole Oresme: Le Livre de Politiques d'Aristote*, ed. Albert D. Menut, Transactions of the American Philosophical Society, N.S. 60, pt. 6 (Philadelphia: American Philosophical Society, 1970), pp. 13-22.

43. Menut, ibid., p. 19.

44. Coopland [n. 40 above], p. 10.

45. Coopland maintains that the *Livre* is "clearly not a translation of the earlier work," although the purpose of the two is the same (ibid., p. 20).

46. *Le Livre quadriperti* is contained in a fifteenth-century manuscript (Paris: B.N. fr. 1348). The translator is named in a prologue as "G. Oresme"; the prologue is transcribed in R. Delachenal [n. 36 above], pp. 37-38. There has long been disagreement over whether this translation should properly be assigned to Guillaume or to Nicole Oresme. The most balanced view is that expressed by Menut [n. 42 above], p. 19: "Several historians have maintained that the *Quadripartitum* was actually translated by Nicole--that Guillaume, a shadowy figure, is an error for Nicole. However, there was quite definitely a Guillaume Oresme and, until further evidence, it would be premature to deny him the attribution of the *Quadripertit Ptholomee*." For the attribution to Nicole Oresme, see R. Delachenal [n. 36 above]. Coopland [n. 40 above], p. 181n, notes that "[Nicole] Oresme, who often refers to Haly's commentary [on the *Quadripartitum*], makes no mention of having translated it." This commentary, in French, accompanies the translation of the *Quadripartitum* attributed to Guillaume Oresme.

47. The revised date has been suggested by François Avril of the Bibliothèque Nationale, Paris; it was communicated to me by Bert Hansen (8 November 1982, private communication). Several other manuscripts contain French versions of the *Centiloquium*; see Shore [n. 3 above], pp. 213-32.

48. *Maistre Nicole Oresme: Le Livre de yconomique d'Aristote*, ed. Albert D. Menut, Transactions of the American Philosophical Society, N.S. 47, pt. 5 (Philadelphia: American Philosophical Society, 1957), p. 790.

49. Charles's friendly relations with the scholars who served as his translators are emphasized by Claire R. Sherman, "Representations of Charles V of France (1338-1380) as a Wise Ruler," *Mediaevalia et Humanistica*, N.S. 2 (1971):83-96. Sherman analyzes several MS portraits of Charles, including those found in astrological works.

50.   Menut [n. 42 above], p. 30.

51.   Menut [n. 48 above], p. 789.

52.   Ibid., p. 788.

53.   "Et se en ce livre . . . sunt aucunes choses mains claires et trop obscures, c'est pour la cause de l'original en latin qui est merveilleusement obscur et de language estrange et outrageusement suspensif, qui n'est past semblabe [*sic*], mais est aussi comme du tout estrange de la maniere de parler des autres acteurs d'astrologie, et y a tout plain de methaforez et inpropres manieres de parler, qui n'est pas mont expedient en tele science. Et aussi touz les livres que nous avons de ce veuz sunt deffectueus, incoretz et corrumpuz aussi comme partout. Et pour ce, se en ce livre sunt aucunes choses meins suffisantes ou trop obscures, ne soit pas impute au translateur, devant que l'en ait veu l'original" (MS Paris, Bib. de l'Arsenal 2872, fol. 309). Quoted in Henri Martin [n. 40 above], pp. 134-38.

54.   "Et ceste ruile generale ai je mis au bout de ceste partie de cest livree des elections universeles de 12 maisons, a fin quelle soit la clef de toutes autres et fermaire" (MS Oxford, St. John's College 164). Quoted in Coxe [n. 40 above], p. 51.

55.   "Et ainssi ay je . . . accompli les proffiz et chapitres de la practique de astralabe briefment et simplement tant seulement par usage de astralabe sans meller ouvrages et besoignes estrainges par guise de calculacion, afin que les ouvrages soient simples et de chascune personne entendables." Quoted in Coxe, ibid., p. 52.

56.   Found in MS Paris, B.N. fr. 612, fols. 1-162. See Carmody [n. 4 above], p. 50.

57.   MS Paris, B.N. fr. 2080, described in *Catalogue des manuscrits français, Bibliothèque impériale* [n. 9 above], p. 355. Another, nonastrological, translation by Robert du Herlin is *Le Débat du faucon et du levrier;* see *Dictionnaire des lettres françaises* [n. 25 above], "Herlin, Robert de."

58.   "Moy Pierre Pevidic, en l'Universite de Dole, maistre ès ars indigne, estudient en medecine, l'an M CCCC LIX . . . ," quoted in

Catalogue général des manuscrits des bibliothèques publiques de France--Départements, 5 (Paris: Plon, 1859), pp. 109-10. See also E. Wickersheimer, *Dictionnaire biographique des médecins en France au moyen âge* (Paris, 1936; rpt. Geneva: Droz, 1979), "Pierre Pevidic."

59. Emmanuel Poulle, *Un Constructeur d'instruments astronomiques au XVᵉ siècle: Jean Fusoris* (Paris: Champion, 1963).

60. "En ce temps estoit à la court du roy messire Jehan de Bregy, notable chevalier et grant astrologien. Cestui fut principié et erudit en la maison de Bourgongne. Cestui composa pour le roy René de Sicille la pratique de l'astrolabe en françois et y mist plusieurs exemples et estoilles fixes que maistre Jehan Furoris [*sic*] n'y avoit pas mises." Symon de Phares, *Recueil,* ed. Wickersheimer [n. 35 above], pp. 254-55.

61. MSS Paris, B.N. fr. 12289 (anc. suppl. fr. 2467, suppl. fr. 324); Paris, B.N. fr. 2071 (anc. 7942); and Vatican City, Bib. Apost. Vat., Reg. Lat. 1330. See detailed analysis of texts and manuscripts in Shore [n. 3 above].

62. *Mahieu le Vilain, Les Metheores d'Aristote* [n. 12 above].

63. Ibid., p. xxi (my translation).

64. *Nicole Oresme, Le Livre du ciel et du monde*, ed. A. D. Menut and A. J. Denomy (Madison: Univ. of Wisconsin Press, 1968), p. 10.

65. Ch. Brucker, "Quelques aspects du style de Denis Foulechat, traducteur de Charles V," *Zeitschrift für französische Sprache und Literatur* 80 (1970):97-101, esp. 101.

66. Carmody [n. 4 above], p. 45.

67. Shore [n. 3 above], p. 84.

68. Brucker [n. 65 above], 102.

69. Shore [n. 3 above], p. 84.

70. Carmody [n. 4 above], p. 45.

71. Menut and Denomy [n. 64 above], p. 13.

72. Edgren [n. 12 above], p. xxi; Carmody [n. 4 above], p. 45.

73. Menut and Denomy [n. 64 above], p. 763.

74. Shore [n. 3 above], p. 82.

75. Menut and Denomy [n. 64 above], p. 11.

76. Edgren [n. 12 above], p. xxiii (my translation).

77. Shore [n. 3 above], pp. 75-76.

78. Carmody [n. 4 above], p. 45.

79. Shore [n. 3 above], p. 86.

80. The phrase is Howard Stone's, "Puzzling Translations in the Thirteenth Century Multiple Equivalents in Early French Medical Terminology," *Romance Notes* 9 (1967):174-79, esp. 178.

81. Ibid., 176-78.

82. Peter Dembowski, "Nicole Oresme's *Le Livre du ciel et du monde*: A Philological View," *Romance Philology* 22 (1969):614-20, esp. 615.

83. Stone [n. 80 above], p. 175.

RAOUL DE PRESLES'S TRANSLATION OF SAINT AUGUSTINE'S *DE CIVITATE DEI*

Charity Cannon Willard

In the midst of the many troubles which beset France in the middle of the fourteenth century, the brief reign of Charles V (1365-80) stands out as a period of respite. Not only did he rebuild and enhance Paris and win back French territory lost to the English after the defeat at Poitiers in 1356 and the Treaty of Brétigny in 1360, he also established a royal library in one tower of the Louvre. He did this partly for his own pleasure--he was an avid reader and a man who enjoyed the company of scholars from the University of Paris.   He was also concerned with the diffusion of knowledge, apparently wanting to bridge to some extent the intellectual gap between the scholars he admired and his less learned relatives and courtiers. To achieve this, he commissioned a series of translations of the Latin books, whether Christian or pagan, that he considered especially significant, particularly those having bearing on the political and moral conduct of government. His ultimate, although probably not his sole aim, was the strengthening of the bases of his own monarchy.   Christine de Pizan comments in her biography of the king, the *Les Fais et bonnes meurs du sage roy Charles V*:

> Because of the great love he had for his successors who would reign in a future time, he wished to provide them with instruction and knowledge promoting all virtues, and for that reason he had translated from Latin into French by distinguished scholars, knowledgeable in all sciences and arts, all the most important books. . . .[1]

In the *Livre de la Paix*, she comments further:

He showed well that he was himself scholarly, for he
loved books above all else and had a marvelously large
number of all sorts of them . . . nevertheless, so that his
brothers and those who would follow him, and also other
lay people, might have the advantage of knowing the
contents of these books, he had translated by very
capable clerks, Masters in Theology, all the most
important of these books. . . . Among them, the great
book of Saint Augustine, *The City of God*.[2]

The king's interest in Saint Augustine's great work was undoubtedly inspired at least in part by his knowing that it was one of
Charlemagne's favorite books, a circumstance which is mentioned in
the prologue of the translation. The king was ever eager to point to
a link between his own reign and that of his famous predecessor to
underscore its legitimacy, contested not only by the King of England, Edward III, but also by his own brother-in-law, the King of
Navarre, (Charles the Bad). The claims of both having a certain
merit, Charles V was always careful to demonstrate the superior
legitimacy of his own claim to the crown. He also felt the need to
enhance the prestige of the crown after the French defeats at Crécy
and Poitiers, and his father's subsequent captivity in England.

The translator he chose for Saint Augustine's text was Raoul de
Presles, a member of the royal household and the recipient of many
royal favors. A lawyer by training, Raoul de Presles was known for
his own admiration of Saint Augustine and his interest in antiquity.
He had already written works which were much to the king's taste,
for they undertook to show how the lessons to be learned from the
past could be useful in finding solutions for contemporary problems.
The first of these was a *Compendium morale de republica*, finished
in 1363, which combined a discussion of the eternal conflict between
virtues and vices in society, a struggle he saw as an essential
element in the human drama, with an examination of the history of
certain antique empires, giving particular attention to their cults of
pagan gods and to the role of Fortune in their affairs. He was
especially interested in comparing the troubles of France to those of
Rome. He would appear to have shared the conviction of his

contemporary, Petrarch, that history is philosophy teaching by example in which the past, if correctly understood, informs and instructs the present.[3]

A second work, entitled *Musa*,[4] was dedicated to the king around 1365. This recounts a series of imaginary adventures which take place in famous sites of the Greek and Roman past, where the author looks for the roots of certain of the ills besetting fourteenth-century France. The quest proving fruitless, he returns to Paris, where a better result is obtained from consulting the French patron saint, Saint Denis. Although the work exalts the memory of the latter, extensive use is also made of Saint Augustine's teachings. Understandably it was the appearance of *Musa* that suggested to Charles V the suitability of Raoul de Presles as a translator of Saint Augustine's *De Civitate Dei*.

It is evident that both of the earlier works contributed to the translation which Raoul de Presles undertook in 1371 and completed at the beginning of September 1375, for they formed the basis of his understanding of antiquity and his enthusiasm for many aspects of it. They were also the principal source for the commentary which accompanied the actual translation and which was typical of the translations commissioned by the king. These commentaries were presumably inspired by the university practice of teaching chosen texts, whether classical, scientific, or theological, through commentaries. Such commentaries were not limited to mere expositions, but were rather a means of offering criticism and proposing original interpretations and conclusions.[5] It is not surprising, then, that Raoul de Presles should have reinforced his own knowledge of antiquity with three earlier commentaries on Saint Augustine's text. The commentary of Nicolas Trevet (c. 1260-1334), a professor at Oxford University, was probably written before 1332. A commentary by the Welshman, Thomas Waleys (d. 1364) was completed in 1332 and was well known on the Continent. Thomas was more interested in the historical background of the work than his predecessor and, indeed, was more interested in history and mythology than in Saint Augustine's theological doctrines. The third commentator was François de Meyronnes (d. 1328), a Franciscan educated at the University of Paris. His *Flores Augustini*, gave

331

particular attention to Augustinian doctrine, often using it as the basis for discussions of contemporary religious issues.[6] Because he used these commentaries extensively in preparing his own, Raoul de Presles has on occasion been accused of lacking originality, which was scarcely an issue at the time he was writing.[7] It is more important to remember that he was making some of the ideas developed in these earlier commentaries available to readers whose Latin was at best probably limited. Furthermore, it was Raoul's method to discuss and compare these commentaries as he used them, showing how they illuminated Saint Augustine's text for contemporary lay readers, who could not be expected to read the Latin commentaries for themselves. There is no doubt that Raoul de Presles's commentary added greatly to the popularity of the text, providing annotations to the myths and historical events mentioned. As he was careful to cite his sources, it also produced a sort of encyclopedia of Rome and the culture of antiquity. His commentary was not, of course, intended for a learned audience, but rather for readers who were not informed on the matters discussed by Saint Augustine, and who were, furthermore, attracted by the digressions on Greek and Roman history drawn from Valerius Maximus and other sources not yet readily available. In consideration of the needs and capabilities of these contemporary readers and in response to the king's ambition to educate his subjects, Raoul de Presles set forth the following method of translation in his prologue:

> Et se je n'en suy en ceste translacion les propres mos du texte et que je y voise aucunesfois par une maniere de circumlocucion ou autrement il me sera pardonné, pour ce que vous m'avez commandé pour la matiere esclarcir que je ensuive la vraie, simple et clere sentence et le vray entendement sans ensuivre proprement les mos du tiexte. Si y a plusieurs mos qui ne peuent pas bonnement translater en françois sans addicion ou declaracion, car si comme dessus est dit, ce livre est compilé de diverses et hautes matieres et de hault stile et d'ancienne gramaire chargié de grans sentences suspensives en brieves paroles, plusieurs et diverses histoires abregees de divers

et anciens aucteurs dont les originaulx ne peuent
bonnement estre trouvéz en cest pays pour y avoir
recours es pas et es termes qui desirent declaracion.
Toutesvoies est mon entencion d'y mettre aucunes
declaracions et exposicions pour donner declaracion au
tiexte es parties et par ou il aura doubte ou obscurté.

(B.N. ms. fr. 23, fol. 2v^6)

[And if I do not follow in this translation the exact words
of the text, and if I proceed sometimes by circumlocution
or some other such method, may I be excused, for you
have ordered me to make use of true, simple and
comprehensible sentences giving the true sense, without
necessarily following the exact words of the text, in
order to clarify the meaning. There are indeed certain
words which cannot be translated adequately into french
without additions or explanations for, as has already
been said, this book is composed of diverse and elevated
matter and in an elegant style and antique grammar
heavy with long, perplexing sentences as well as
numerous and varied stories taken from certain ancient
authors of which the originals cannot easily be found in
this country so that it is impossible to verify passages
and exressions which require explanation. Furthermore,
it is my intention to include some explanations and
elaborations for the purpose of clarifying the text in
places where it may seem difficult or unintelligible.]

Beyond the commentary, the text was to be made additionally
clear and attractive by a remarkable series of illustrations, beginning
with Charles V's own copy and continuing, with certain variations
by individual artists, through the first printing of the text in 1486.
They thus became an integral part of the translation for more than a
century. Before the translation, there had been only four known
illustrated copies of St. Augustine's text, but by the beginning of the
sixteenth century there were fifty-seven, forty-five of which were
copies of Raoul de Presles's translation. Regrettably, until the
present day the text of that translation has received less attention

than its illustrations.[8]

The copy which was presented to Charles V (Paris, B. N. ms. fr. 22912), the first of the series, is naturally of considerable interest, particularly for the dedication page at the beginning. The king is portrayed seated on a low stool in a Gothic architectural frame, against a background of fleurs-de-lys. He peers intently at the volume held out to him by the translator who kneels before him. Behind him angels hold back a drapery which reveals the fleurs-de-lys. To the right of this group is Saint Augustine, a surprisingly youthful figure, who presents the translator to the king in the manner of a patron saint presenting a donor to a holy personage in a religious painting. Especially striking is the representation of a personal communication between the king and Raoul de Presles. This type of dedication miniature was not unusual in the translations commissioned by Charles V, and was an obvious allusion to the king's scholarly tastes and personal involvement with the translation.[9]

This is reinforced by the prologue which reveals the king's concern for the legitimacy of his reign. Raoul de Presles begins with a description of the eagle, king of birds because it can look directly into the sun. Saint Augustine is compared to the eagle. The greatest doctor of the primitive church, the saint was able to penetrate the mysteries of the faith as the eagle looks into the sun, and had confounded heretics hostile to Christian dogmas. Raoul next compares Charles V to the eagle. The king possesses special powers through his heritage as the son of a French king and through his anointing at Rheims with that same holy oil that had once been brought by a dove to Saint Remi for King Clovis's consecration. Consequently the king performs miracles, and the "king's touch" enables him to cure scrofula. Further, the king bears on his arms three fleurs-de-lys, symbol of the Trinity, which God had sent to Clovis through an angel after the king's victory over the Saracen king Candat. The lilies were to replace the three crescents which had formerly marked the king's arms, hence also the dedication miniature's angels which draw back a curtain to reveal the fleurs-de-lys. Reference is also made here to the oriflamme, the sword and banner borne by the French king in battle, but otherwise kept at the Abbey of Saint Denis. Raoul de Presles had already written a *Traité de l'oriflamme* in 1369,[10] the period when Charles V was about to abrogate the Treaty of Brétigny. His theme in the *Traité* was the people's obedience to the king and the king's allegiance to God in undertaking a war whose cause must be just. This theme is further developed in the prologue to the *Cité de Dieu*.

Charles V is praised also by Raoul de Presles for the fact that he honors learning and has himself studied as continuously as his duties have permitted, both for his own pleasure and for the benefit of his subjects. This interest of the king's is so frequently repeated that one can scarcely doubt its veracity, but one should also understand that the king liked to have it mentioned.

It appears that the king was less interested in a literal translation of the original text than one which would be readily understandable to those who were not scholars. The aim of the translation is to simplify the elevated, complicated style of the original. The translator expresses the hope that he will be able to clarify difficulties and to explain terms which are not readily understood. At the same time, he complains of the difficulty of having to explain and to identify quotations from certain authors whose works are not available in France.

He then outlines the plan of Saint Augustine's book, pointing out that the first ten books or divisions are devoted to the destruction of certain pagan errors, particularly those arising from idolatry. They constitute, in fact, a detailed study by St. Augustine of pagan culture in the fourth century. The second half of the work--twelve books--is more theological in nature. It is devoted to the discussion of the City of Evil and the confirmation of the Heavenly City, the City of God. It was to the commentary on the first ten books that Raoul de Presles turned with particular enthusiasm, for he made no claim of being competent to discuss the theological questions treated in the second part. These should be discussed only by theologians in more suitable circumstances. He is writing for lay persons who are perhaps ignorant of such questions as the ones presented in these later books, and he does not want to risk leading them into error.[11] For some of the chapters in the second part, then, there is little or no commentary. In some cases there is merely an identification of the source of the ideas developed by Saint Augustine, especially those from Plato, whose *Timaeus* was of particular importance to *De Civitate Dei*. And frequently Raoul de Presles leans heavily on the commentary of François de Meyronnes. The result is that the commentary on the first ten books is far more interesting than that on the second part.

It should be understood that in the commentary, Raoul de Presles does not make unlimited use of the earlier commentators, but calls upon the erudition of his own earlier works. Although some of his sources are second-hand, he demonstrates an impressive knowledge of medieval as well as of ancient literature, quoting from Alain de Lille and John of Salisbury, Boethius and Ovid.

His first prologue, dedicated to the king, is followed by a second, addressed to all potential readers of the translation. It explains the two parts of the book and the further divisions within these parts. The divisions into chapters apparently presented the translator with particular problems. He claims to have consulted some thirty manuscripts. Some contained no chapter divisions, and in other cases divisions were variable from manuscript to manuscript. Raoul therefore organized his own system, frequently discussing the alternative chapter divisions he found elsewhere and noting disagreement with the chapter divisions in the commentaries of Nicolas Trevet and Thomas Waleys. He says, for instance, in his commentary on Book 5, Chap. 13:

> We say this in particular for those who might see other books than the one from which we have made our translation, where they will find the chapters noted differently, as we saw them in several other books which we saw along with our principal one, though we never saw any more perfect, for in certain ones there are no rubrics either at the beginning of the Books nor for individual chapters.[12]

A particular concern of the translator was the occurrence in the text of certain terms that the reader could not be expected to understand. An example of this problem has to do with material of which the antique gods were made, for according to the literal translation, Saint Augustine seems to have said: "Ilz sont de arain et n'ont pas de sang." Raoul de Presles points out that some of the manuscripts he has consulted give *erei* (arain) while others have *aerei* (air), whereupon he recalls the idea of Apulius, based on Plato, that the gods and the devils were creatures of air without visible bodies. He then recalls another passage (Book 8, Chap. 16) where Saint Augustine says that these airy creatures can take any form they like when they choose to become visible, but states that he does not care to pursue the subject any further, as he considers it too subtle and dangerous to discuss.

After explaining the wisdom of the sibyls through their virginity, he provides the etymological comment that *sibyl* derives from *theosbule: theos* meaning God and *bule* meaning word or sermon. Sibyls can thus be understood to represent the word of God. In a later commentary, he recalls the Erythaean sibyl's prophecy concerning the coming of Christ (Book 18, Chap. 23). That prediction, made by a sibyl to the Emperor Augustus, was to become a favorite subject for illustration around the end of the fourteenth century, not only in such manuscripts as the Duke of Berry's so-called Brussels Hours (Bibliothèque Royale MS 11060-61), but in two carvings in the Church of the Celestines in Metz.[13]

One of the most important and extensive explanations, however, is devoted to the *scena* of early dramatic festivals. The definition given is based on Isidore of Seville's *Etymologiae* and corresponds to the one given by Trevet, but Raoul de Presles's explanations are worthy of comment. Saint Augustine's remarks about the Roman theatre had been brief and disapproving. In Book 1, Chap. 31, he refers to plays as "those spectacles of uncleanness, those licentious vanities," explaining that they were first instituted to appease the gods during a time of pestilence. Returning to the subject in the course of Book 4, Chap. 26, he asks why learned Romans should have written and presented such base things, which were even approved by the Roman senate.

The commentary and many of the illustrations transmit a somewhat different view of these "jeux sceniques." Raoul de Presles describes the *scena* as

> a small house in the middle of the theatre in which there
> was a lectern from which the tragedies and comedies of
> the poets were read, and where there were people in
> disguise who represented those who were the subjects of
> songs and diversions, just as they perform today in plays
> and charivaris.[14]

He speaks of other performers who played on various instruments,
but goes beyond his sources in his description of theatres surrounded
by seats mounting in tiers "just as they still appear in ancient
theatres."

Where Saint Augustine speaks of gladiatorial contests (Book 2,
Chap. 14), the commentator takes the opportunity to speak further of
theatres, pointing out how theatres, amphitheatres, and circuses
differ from one another. He mentions combats between men and
beasts which sometimes took place in the sand which covered the
floor of an amphitheatre or arena, as it was called ("les araines").
Such *araines* were still to be seen in the city of Nîmes. He points
out that such arenas, or amphitheatres, were round, whereas the
theatres were semi-circular.

This distinction was not always observed by the illustrators, for
in several manuscripts the *scena* where a play is being read is in the
center of a circle, reflecting, perhaps, that medieval plays were
sometimes performed in existing amphitheatres. In one manuscript[15]
a poet is seen reading from a sort of pulpit in a round theatre, where
trumpeters are present but no actors are visible. The audience is
seated below rather than above the poet as if listening to a sermon.
Although little attention is usually given to Saint Augustine's
condemnation of the theatre, an exception is to be found in Arsenal
MS 5060, which shows two authors reading their plays from scrolls,
supervised by the two Roman censors mentioned in the commentary.
These are surrounded by couples who are embracing, while in the
foreground a man holds a mask before a woman who is beginning to
undress. The mask, apparently intended as the masks used in
classical theatres and in mystery cults, underscored the idea of
evil.[16] Raoul de Presles includes Livy's statement that the moral
values in Roman plays had deteriorated with time.

Raoul's enthusiasm for classical literature is nevertheless evident in his commentary on Book 2, Chap. 8, where the mention of poetic fictions in the drama inspires him to explain three types: where only the poet speaks (for example, Virgil's *Georgics*), where the poet does not speak directly but expresses himself through the characters he presents (tragedies and Terence's comedies), and where both the poet and his characters speak (Virgil's *Aeneid*). He refers learnedly to these three modes as *didascalicum, dragmaticum,* and *hermeneuticum,*[17] directing the reader to John Balbus of Genoa's thirteenth-century Latin grammar and dictionary, the *Catholicon,* for further information.

Raoul's reference to Terence is an indication of his role in the revival of interest in that dramatist. The *Comedies* were not illustrated during the thirteenth and fourteenth centuries, but two early fifteenth-century manuscripts of the comedies were products of the same Parisian workshops which produced copies of the translation of the *Cité de Dieu.*[18]

Raoul de Presles diverges from Saint Augustine again in his commentary on Fortune versus Divine Providence. Saint Augustine, in common with other early Church fathers, was opposed to the pagan concept of Fortune as a goddess, insisting (Book 4, Chap. 18) that Fortune and Human Felicity could not be two separate goddesses, and that Fortune could scarcely be a goddess at all because of her unfavorable aspects. He thus undertook to disprove her existence, maintaining that those who believe in God should be content with Virtue and Felicity. In the commentary, Raoul de Presles does not seem to be prepared to go so far. He is obviously attracted by the traditional image of Fortune with her wheel, adding to his description of her the tradition of her face which is half bright and half dark. He supports this concept by citing the twelfth-century *Anticlaudianus* by Alain de Lille as well as Jean de Meun's use of the same image in the *Roman de la Rose.* He ends his discussion by referring to the *De Consolatione* of Boethius (Book 2) where the pagan goddess coexists with the Christian God, although the explanation of how this is possible is somewhat vague.[19] The role of Fortune in human affairs had a particular interest in the second half of the fourteenth century, and Petrarch's *De remediis utriusque*

Fortunae was translated into French at Charles V's request by Jean Daudin. Indeed, the oration which the Italian humanist had delivered at the French court in 1361 in celebration of the king's return from English captivity attributed Jean II's tribulations to Fortune.

The discussion of Fortune continues in the commentary on the first chapter of Book 5, which in certain manuscripts is introduced by an illustration of Fortune with her wheel. In B.N. MS fr. 25, however, a philosopher discourses between Fortune on the one hand and God, representing Divine Providence, on the other. The chapter in the original text was devoted to evidence that neither the Roman Empire nor any other kingdom owed its prosperity to Fortune or to astrology.[20] The commentary discusses whether Fate should be understood as an aspect of Fortune or of Divine Providence. After citing both Seneca and Boethius, Raoul de Presles arrives at the conclusion that Fate is the aspect of Providence which binds the universe together and, in a sense, permits free will. He then introduces the poetic concept of the Fates, Clotho who carries a spindle, Lachesis who spins, and Atropos who breaks the thread. Throughout Raoul's long explanation, theology and mythology combine, providing a possible source for the appearance of Atropos as a representation of Death in certain manuscripts produced in Paris around 1400.[21]

Parallels between past and present were frequent in the first ten books. The best known of these is Raoul's account of the foundation of Paris by Francion and by other exiled Trojans (suggested by Saint Augustine's discussion of the favors shown by God to Constantine as he was building Constantinople, Book 5, Chap. 25).[22] Raoul de Presles cited the opinion of a series of authorities concerning the Trojan origins of Paris, but his description of the primitive city is significant also for the topographical information it supplies concerning the early development of the city Charles V was now so proudly rebuilding and refurbishing. This passage ends with a reference to Geoffroy of Monmouth's version of the history of King Lear, in which an early French king, Aganippus, married to one of Lear's daughters, eventually restores the old king to his throne.[23]

Of more immediate concern to Charles V and his subjects was the discussion of the *lex vocoma* (Book 3, Chap. 21) which Raoul de

Presles, a lawyer by training, saw as the equivalent of Salic law.[24] Both prohibited the inheritance of property by women, even daughters when there was no male heir. Saint Augustine's view of the law was that it was barbarous and unjust, an opinion which posed a problem for a reign whose legitimacy depended on the application of Salic law. This inspired Raoul de Presles to insist that Saint Augustine was speaking of private inheritance rather than the transfer of royal power, calling to witness the views of both Thomas Waleys and François de Meyronnes, as well as of Aulus Gellius in his *Noctes Atticae*. He insisted that the Salic Law was formulated by those who originally devised laws for France because they felt that the realm could be better defended by a man. than a woman. This was, of course, a pure invention because there had been little, if any, interest in the question before 1328, when Charles IV died without leaving an heir to the throne.

Digressions need not serve current issues. Saint Augustine's distinction between the desire for glory and the desire for power allows narration of the depravities of Nero (Book 5, Chap. 19). The commentary quotes Orosius's description of the burning of Rome, Suetonius's account of Nero's many vices, with mention of his pleasure in the harp and in his singing, and John of Salisbury's account of Nero's preference for jongleurs over philosophers.[25]

It is impossible now to determine which readers were attracted by Saint Augustine's text itself, and which valued it for the commentary, an encyclopedia of Roman culture. Courtiers in Paris and later in the Burgundian court acquired an impressive number of copies for their libraries. Charles V's brother, Duke John of Berry, had at least three copies, and the most important collectors of two or more generations also owned luxurious copies. With the notable exception of the Bishop Chevrot's manuscript (Brussels, Bibl. Roy. MS 1155), nearly all manuscripts belonged to laymen. Further, the translation was printed with illustrations at Abbeville in 1486, and in Paris as late as 1531. It even served as the basis for a further translation into Catalan.[26] Its influence was inevitably extensive and was surely important in moving Saint Augustine's work and thought into new, more secular circles. As the translation remains unavailable in a modern edition, it is difficult to judge the extent and nature of its influence on late medieval writers. A case in point is Christine de Pizan, a number of whose works were copied and illustrated in a workshop which also produced several copies of Raoul de Presles's translation. Her interest in the sibyls and in the role of Fortune in human affairs suggests possible influence from this translation, which she indeed mentions three times. It is evident that Philippe de Commynes read it, for he owned a copy (now divided between Nantes, Bibl. Mun. MS 8 and The Hague, Meermann-Westreenien Museum 11-1478). It would seem, therefore, that Robert Bossuat is unduly severe when he says that the translation has nothing new or original to offer.[27] Part of that large body of moral literature produced by humanists and popularizers, Raoul de Presles's *La Cité de Dieu* provides documentary evidence of Saint Augustine's evolving influence upon the European Middle Ages.

NOTES

1. "Pour la grant amour qu'il avoit a ses successeurs qui, au temps a venir, les voult pourveoir d'enseignemens et sciences introduisibles a toutes vertus, dont, pour celle cause, fist par solemnelz maistres, souffisans en toutes sciences et ars, translater de latin en françois les plus notables livres. . . ." *Les Fais et bonnes meurs du sage roy Charles* V, ed. S. Solente, vol. 2 (Paris: Champion, 1940), p. 43; see also *Le Livre du Chemin de Long Estude*, ed. R. Puschell (Berlin: Damböhler and Paris: Le Soudier, 1881; rpt. 1974), pp. 213-14, vv. 5009-30.

2. "Et qu'il fust clerc, bien le demonstroit, car souverainement amoit livres, dont il avoit a merveilles grant quantité, et de toutes manieres . . . neantmoins, afin que ses freres et ceulx qui, le temps a venir, le succederoient et tous autres gens laiz peussent avoir le bien d'entendre ce que les livres contiennent, fist translater par tres suffisans clers, maistres en theologie, tous les plus notables livres. . . . Item, le grant livre de Saint Augustin *De la Cité de Dieu.*" *Le Livre de la Paix*, ed. C. C. Willard (The Hague: Mouton, 1958), p. 142.

3. Paris, B.N. MS lat. 15690 and nouv acq. lat. 1821, summarized by Robert Bossuat in his article on Raoul de Presles in the *Histoire Littéraire de la France*, 40 (1974):142-54; for Petrarch's view of history, see Myron

P. Gilmore, "The Renaissance Conception of the Lessons of History" in *Humanists and Jurists* (Cambridge, MA: Harvard Univ. Press, 1963), p. 18.

4. B.N. MS lat. 3233; Oxford, Balliol College, MS 274, fols. 238-53; summarized by Bossuat [n. 3 above], pp. 142-54.

5. See, for instance, A. J. Crombie, *From Augustine to Galileo*, vol. 2 (Cambridge, MA: Harvard Univ. Press, 1979), p. 18.

6. On Trevet and Waleys, see Beryl Smalley, *English Friars* (Oxford: Blackwell, 1960), pp. 58-65, 75-108, 309-10; also her article "Thomas Waleys O.P.," *Archivum Fratrum Praedicatorum* 24 (1954): 50-107; for François de Meyronnes, C. V. Langlois, "François de Meyronnes, Frére Mineur," *Histoire littéraire de la France* 26 (1927): 305-42.

7. See Bossuat [n. 3 above], pp. 184-86.

8. Notably A. de Laborde, *Les Manuscrits à Peintures de la Cité de Dieu de Saint Augustine*, 3 vols. (Paris: Ed. Rahir, pour la Société des Bibliophiles française, 1909); Sharon Off Dunlop Smith, "Illustrations of Raoul de Presles' Translation of St Augustine's *City of God* between 1375 and 1420," Ph.D. diss., New York University, 1974 a typescript of which is deposited in the J. Pierpont Morgan Library, New York).

9. Claire R. Sherman, *The Portraits of Charles* V *of France* (New York: New York Univ. Press, 1969), p. 23.

10. A seventeenth-century copy exists in B.N. Collection Duchesne 65, fols. 38-45.

11. B.N. MS fr. 24, fol. 1: "Combien que au commencement de ceste translacion et exposicion en nostre prologue nous aions promis a mettre declaracions et exposioions es pas et es lieux qui desirent declaracion, toutevoies nostre entencion ne fu oncques de mettre ces paroles principalment fors en ce qui seroit de histoire ou de poetrie, et non pas de touchier a ce qui regarde la theologie, car telz choses ne cheent pas en exposicion quant a nous. Mais cheent a desputer et arguer en la chayere et a determiner a ceulz a qui il est permis, c'est assavoir a ceulx par qui la foy catholique est soubstenue."

[Although at the beginning of this translation and commentary, in our Prologue, we promised to include clarifications and expositions in the passages and places which require clarifications, at the same time it was never our intention to add these except where it was a question of history or of poetry, and not to touch on anything which has to do with theology, for such things do not fall within our competence, but are meant to be disputed and discussed in the pulpit, and to be decided by those assigned to this, that is to say by those who sustain the Catholic faith.]

12.   B.N. MS fr. 23, fol. 99: "Et cecy disons nous notablement pour ceulx qui pourront veoir autres livres que celuy sur lequel nous avons faicte nostre translacion esquelz ilz trouveront les chappitres autrement notéz, si comme nous mesmes le veysmes en autres livres plusieurs que nous avions avecques nostre principal, duquel nous ne en veismes oncques nul plus parfait, car es aucuns ne se trouvoyent aucunes rebriches ne au commancement des livres ne sur chacun chappitre."

13.   Millard Meiss, *French Painting in the Time of Jean de Berry: The Limbourgs and their Contemporaries* (New York: Braziller, 1974), p. 140.

14.   B.N. MS fr. 23, fol. 28^v: "La sena . . . est une petite maison ou milieu de theastre, en laquelle avoit un letryn ou l'en lisoit les tragédies et comedies des poetes, et y avoit gens desguisees qui faisoient les contenances de ceulx por les queulx l'on chantoit et faisoit les jeux, aussi comme tu voiz que l'on fait aujourd'hui les jeux de personnages et charivaris."

15.   Brussels, Bibl. Roy. MS 9294, fol. 330^v; Meiss [n. 13 above], pp. 53-54.

16.   Meiss [n. 13 above], pp. 50-54.

17.   B.N. MS 23, fol. 33^v (*Cité de Dieu*, Book 2, Chap. 8): "Et n'est pas encore a delaissier que les poetes ont .iii. manieres de stiles de proceder en leurs besognes: l'un est ou le poete tant seulement parle si comme Virgile en Georgiques, l'autre ou le poete ne parle nulle fors si comme es comedies et es tragedies et ce se appelle dragmatique pour ce que il le fait entre .ii. personnages, c'est assavoir entre l'interrogant et le respondant si comme en Terence, selon ce que dit Huguce et Papie si acorde. Le tiers est

ou aucune fois le poete parle aucune fois ces personnes introduites si comme en Virgille Eneydos. Et se tu veuls veoir quele difference il a entre ces .iii. manieres de parler, c'est assavoir *didascalicum, dragmaticum,* et *hermeneuticum,* voy *Catholicon* sur le mot *hermeneuticus.*"

18. B.N. MS lat. 7907A; Arsenal MS 664; Meiss [n. 13 above], pp. 41-45.

19. B. N. MS fr. 23, fol. 136.

20. B.N. MS fr. 23, fol. 150^v: "Que la cause de l'empire de Romme et de tous les royaumes n'est point en estat par Fortune ne par la posicion ou constellacion des estoilles."

21. See especially Christine de Pizan's *Epître d'Othéa* in B.N. MS fr. 606, fol. 17 and Meiss [n. 13 above], pp. 30-31.

22. This description was published by A. Le Roux de Lincy and L. M. Tisserand, *Paris et ses historiens aux XIV et au XVe siècles* (Paris: Imprimerie Impériale, 1867), pp. 83-115.

23. Ibid., p. 115, retold after *Le Roman de Brut de Wace,* ed. Ivor Arnold, 2 vols. (Paris, SATF, 1938-40), lines 1697-2114.

24. B.N. MS fr. 23, fol. 101.

25. B.N. MS fr. 23, fol. 170^v.

26. Bossuat [n. 3 above], pp. 173-74; Martin de Riquer, *L'Humanisme Català* (Barcelona: Ed. Barcino, 1934) and Joan Ruiz i Calonja, *Historia de la Literatura Catalana* (Barcelona: Ed. Teide, 1954), p. 192.

27. Bossuat [n. 3 above], p. 186.

ADDITIONAL REFERENCES

Chadwick, Henry. *Augustine.* Oxford: Oxford Univ. Press, 1986, p. 118.

Kristeller, Paul Oskar. "Augustine and the Early Renaissance." *Review of Religion*, 8 (1944), 339-58. Rpt. in *Studies in Renaissance Thought and Letters*. Rome: Storia e Letterature, 1956.

_____. *Renaissance Thought II: Papers on Humanism and the Arts* (New York: Harper Torchbooks, 1956), p. 28.

Lancelot, A. "Mémoires sur la vie et les ouvrages de Raoul de Presles." *Mémoires de littérature tiréz des registres de l'Académie des Inscriptions* 13 (1740):607-13; 617-55.

Martin, André. *Le Livre Illustré en France au XV Siècle*. Paris: F. Alcan, 1931.

Saint Augustine. *La Cité de Dieu*. Trans. Raoul de Presles. Paris, B.N. Ms. fr. 23-24, c. 1405.

Saint Augustine. *La Cité de Dieu*. B.N. Ms. fr. 22921-13. (Copy presented to Charles V, 1375).

Saint Augustine. *La Cité de Dieu*. Abbeville, Pierre Gérard, and Jehan du Pré. 1486-87. 2 vols. in-fol.

Saint Augustine. *The City of God*. Trans. John Healy. 2 vols. London: J. M. Dent, 1954.

Saint Augustine. *The City of God Against the Pagans*. Latin text and English. Trans. George E. McCracken. 7 vols. Cambridge, MA: Harvard Univ. Press and London: W. Heineman, 1977.

HUMANIST DEBATE
AND THE "TRANSLATIVE DILEMMA"
IN RENAISSANCE FRANCE

K. Lloyd-Jones

There can be few more revealing--or, for that matter, more dramatic--illustrations of the variety of problems subsumed under the notion of translation in Renaissance France than the case of the philologist, translator, and printer Etienne Dolet. In his early years he was hailed as one of the most distinguished latinists of his time; later he was celebrated by the most influential of his successors[1] as one of the champions of the vernacular. Some of the issues raised by his work include: the social, political, and ideological functions of the translator; the methodologies appropriate to the realization of those functions; the conceptual, formal, and artistic differences between original and translation; and the rhetorical shifts implied in moving from source language to target language. Had it been granted him to do so, he would surely have brought the fullest theoretical development to such questions as these in his projected *Orateur Françoys*, announced in 1540 but unfinished, or at least unpublished, at the time of his execution for blasphemy in 1546.[2] To posterity's impoverishment, when Dolet's corpse was consigned to the pyre, a large number of forbidden texts and papers seized from his printing house in Lyon were also thrown onto the flames, and all that now remains of the grand design of the *Orateur Françoys* is a brief text entitled *La maniere de bien traduire d'une langue en aultre*, now considered to be the first translation manual written in French.[3]

My purpose here is not to analyze this text in detail,[4] but rather to focus on the impact of certain Humanist concerns on the relationship between Latin and French as exemplified by various

347

aspects of Dolet's own translations. Before doing so, however, it is appropriate to remind ourselves of the five guidelines which he includes in his little manual. They provide not so much a standard against which to evaluate his own translations as the theoretical context for his approach to the process:

> En premier lieu, il fault que le traducteur entende parfaictement le sens et matiere de l'autheur qu'il traduict; car par ceste intelligence il ne sera iamais obscur en sa traduction. . . . La seconde chose qui est requise en traduction, c'est que le traducteur ait parfaicte congnoissance de la langue de l'autheur qu'il traduict; et soit pareillement excellent en la langue en laquelle il se mect à traduire. . . . Le tiers poinct est qu'en traduisant il ne se fault pas asseruir iusques la que l'on rende mot pour mot. . . . La quatriesme reigle que ie veulx bailler en cest endroict, est plus à obseruer en langues non reduictes en art, qu'en autres. I'appelle langues non reduictes encores en art certain et repceu: comme est la Françoyse . . . et autres vulgaires. S'il aduient doncques que tu traduises quelque liure Latin en icelles . . . il te fault garder d'vsurper mots trop approchans du Latin . . . contente toy du commun, sans innouer aucunes dictions follement, et par curiosité reprehensible. . . . Venons maintenant à la cinquiesme reigle . . . laquelle est de si grand'vertu, que sans elle toute composition est lourde et mal plaisante. Mais qu'est-ce qu'elle contient? rien autre chose que l'obseruation des nombres oratoires; c'est asscavoir vne liaison et assemblement des dictions auec telle doulceur, que non seulement l'ame s'en contente, mais aussi les oreilles en sont toutes rauies; . . . d'yceulx nombres oratoires ie parle plus copieusement en mon orateur: par quoy n'en feray icy plus long discours.
>
> (pp. 13-18)

> [In the first place, the translator must understand perfectly the meaning and subject matter of the author he is translating, for such understanding will prevent him from ever being obscure in his translation. . . . The

second thing that is required in translation is that the
translator have perfect knowledge of the language of the
author he is translating, and that he have an equally
excellent grasp of the language into which he is about to
translate. . . . The third point is that, when translating,
we must not enslave ourselves to a word for word
rendition. . . . The fourth rule that I wish to establish
here applies more to those languages still awaiting
artistic development, than to others. By languages still
awaiting complete and universally recognized artistic
development, I have in mind such languages as French . .
. and the other modern languages. If it should happen,
that you are translating some Latin book into one of
these languages . . . you must guard against using words
that are too close to Latin. . . . Content yourself with
everyday usage, and do not, out of reprehensible
affectation, invent insane and newfangled forms of
expression. . . . Let us now come to the fifth rule, which
is so important that, without it, all writing is heavy and
displeasing. What does this rule involve? No more than
fidelity to the flow and rhythms of classical oratory: that
is to say, linking and putting together what is being said
with such harmony as not only to gratify the spirit but
also to delight the ear. . . . I will deal at greater length
with this question in my *French Orator*, and so will say
no more about it here.]

It is at once apparent that what is granted unequivocal priority here
is the importance of the translator's *linguistic* competence, without
which only imperfect communication can be attained. While the
first rule posits the need for a complete understanding (i.e., a
faultless conceptual or intellectual grasp) of the resonances and
contextual frames of reference of the original, this understanding can
only be communicated to others by the fullest mastery of the target
language, and in particular of its rhetorical resources, in the absence
of which all writing is deemed "lourde et mal plaisante." It is this
last, tantalizingly undeveloped homage to a certain concept of
rhetoric and thereby to a certain understanding of what happens to

ideas as a function of the manner of their communication, that will serve as the starting point here.

Dolet had sprung into prominence a decade or so before his death with the publication of his *De Imitatione Ciceroniana*,[5] a bitingly satirical and merciless *ad hominem* attack on Erasmus's views concerning the appropriateness of Ciceronian Latin, which (although not published until 1535) was no doubt begun as early as 1528, the year in which the latter's *Ciceronianus, sive De Optimo Genere Dicendi* came out in Bâle.[6] Briefly stated, Erasmus argues that the earlier Humanists' attempts to restore the Latin language to the purity and elegance it had enjoyed under Cicero have, by the 1520s, led to two far-reaching sets of difficulties. The first of these may be characterized as essentially "esthetic" or "stylistic" in nature: just as ways of thinking are reflections of their time, so are the ways of expressing such thinking, and it would be as foolish to ape the linguistic mannerisms, stylistic idiosyncracies, and conceptual assumptions of Cicero and his contemporaries as it would now be to walk the streets wearing a toga. To open a discourse with the words "Quanquam" or "Etsi" simply because Cicero does so on occasion, to cultivate a convoluted syntax in order to be able to use Cretic *clausulae* like "esse videatur," is to value form over substance, to dishonor one's model, and to reveal one's own intellectual inadequacies:

> Quid autem magis ridiculum, ac Ciceroni dissimilius esse possit, quam nihil habere Ciceronis, praeter tales uoculas in orationis exordio? De quibus si quis percontetur Ciceronem, quur ab iis uocibus sit orsus, respondebit, opinor, quod in insulis fortunatis Luciano respondit Homerus, roganti quur primam Iliadis dictionem uoluerit esse Μῆνιν nam haec quaestio multis seculis torserat grammaticos, "illud," inquit "tum forte uenit in men-tem."   (ed. Gambaro, p. 90)

> [What could be more ridiculous and less like Cicero than to have nothing of Cicero's except some paltry words of this sort right at the beginning of a speech? If anyone were to ask Cicero why he began with these words in

350

particular, I imagine he would give the same answer as
Homer gave to Lucian in the Islands of the Blest, when
he asked why he had decided to make the first word of
the *Iliad* "Μῆνιν" (wrath)--a question which had vexed
grammarians for centuries. "It was the first word," he
said, "that happened to come into my head."]

(tr. Knott p. 371)

The second set of problems seen by Erasmus as facing those
whose misguided veneration of Ciceronian Latin leads them to
mindless imitation follows directly from the first and may be
considered as "ideological" or "doctrinal" in nature: as such, it must
be taken far more seriously. Writing a scant decade after Luther's
break with the Church and haunted by the ever-growing spectacle of
Christian disunity, Erasmus re-invokes the accusation made against
St. Jerome almost twelve centuries earlier: "Ciceronianus es, non es
Christianus." Language cannot be separated from thought, and to
use the very syntax and vocabulary of those to whom, no matter how
great their virtue and merit, God has in His infinite wisdom denied
the revelation of His truth is unavoidably to think and speak as one
of them--as a pagan. Ever faithful to his mission to attract, to
persuade, and to convert, Erasmus lightheartedly evokes the
quagmire that the aping of Ciceronian Latin can lead to:

> Quid faciet? quo se uertet hic ille superstitiose cicer-
> onianus? An pro patre Christi dicet "Iuppiter Optimus
> Maximus," pro filio dicet "Apollinem" aut "Aescul-
> .apium"; pro uirginum regina dicet "Dianam"; pro
> ecclesia "sacram concionem," aut "ciuitatem" aut
> "rempublicam"; pro ethnico "perduellem"; pro haeresi
> "factionem"; pro schismate "seditionem"; pro fide
> christiana "christianam persuasionem" . . .? Quid hic
> faciet ciceronianiae phraseos candidatus? Utrum'ne
> tacebit, an ad hunc modum immutabit recepta Christianis
> uocabula? (ed. Gambaro, pp. 140-42)

[What shall our meticulous Ciceronian do? Where shall
he turn? Shall he for Father of Christ say "Jupiter

Optimus Maximus," for the Son "Apollo" or "Aescul-
apius"? Shall he for Queen of Virgins say "Diana," for
church "sacred assembly" or "state" or "republic"; for
pagan "foeman"; for heresy "faction"; for schism
"sedition"; for the Christian faith "the Christian
persuasion . . ."? What is our aspirant after the Ciceronian turn of phrase going to do here? Is he going to say
nothing, or is he going to make the kind of substitution
I've suggested for established Christian vocabulary?]

(tr. Knott, pp. 388-89)

But the eventual answer, in the context of the religious turmoil of
the early Reformation, has nothing lighthearted about it:

> At non ille dicit ciceroniane, qui christianus apud
> Christianos ad re christiana loquitur, quemadmodum
> olim ethnicus apud ethnicos de rebus prophanis loquutus
> est Cicero. . . . Paganitas est, mihi crede . . . , paganitas
> est quae ista persuadet auribus atque animis nostris.

(ed. Gambaro, pp. 150, 156)

> [I won't have it that a man is speaking in a Ciceronian
> manner, if, being a Christian, he speaks to Christians on
> a Christian subject in the way that Cicero, being a pagan,
> once spoke to pagans on non-Christian subjects. . . . It's
> paganism, believe me . . . , sheer paganism that makes
> our ears and minds accept such an idea.

(tr. Knott, pp. 392, 394)

While close inspection of the two writers' positions shows that, in
some areas, they are more in agreement than either of them found it
convenient to believe at the time, it is of course Dolet's perception
of what divided them that matters here. It is nevertheless worth
remembering that Erasmus's contention that we should not imitate
blindly, for example, will be fully echoed in Dolet's *Oratio secunda*
(see n. 8), and that both authors argue that the ability to choose
among the varying qualities of the proposed model is essential. The
principle of selectivity is thus fundamental to the theory of imitation

espoused by both Erasmus and Dolet, and this is so essentially because their understanding of the persuasive function of rhetorical discourse is the same: when Erasmus's protagonist swears, as a guarantor of his seriousness of purpose, "Ita me bene amet nostra Πειθὼ, rem seriam ago" [For the love of our Peitho, I am in earnest; ed. Gambaro, pp. 144; tr. Knott, p. 389], he is invoking not only the goddess of Rhetoric herself, but the very deity to whom Dolet would later implicitly consecrate the culmination of his *Art de bien traduire*, with its call for the cultivation of the "nombres oratoires."[7]

Dolet, educated in Padua by one of the very Ciceronians that Erasmus singles out for derision, Simon de Villeneuve (Villanovanus), and certainly ambitious to make a name for himself by engaging in a polemic with the most famous scholar in Europe, is stung into a two-fold response. While a student at the University of Toulouse, he is given the opportunity to make two public speeches in Latin in late 1533; the published version of these discourses[8] will seek to be a practical demonstration of all the brilliance and power of Ciceronian eloquence, whereas the *Erasmianus* of 1535 will endeavor to engage Erasmus in a more directly theoretical, and even ideological, combat.

Dolet's rebuttal of Erasmus is essentially anchored in the canons of good style and good taste:[9] it makes no sense to copy any other than the best model available to us, and it is stylistically inappropriate to use syntax and vocabulary not to be found in the works of the best model. Lashing out at the tolerance for anachronism and neologism that he believes vitiates the style of writers such as Erasmus, Dolet attacks the Dutch humanist for what he considers his intellectual arrogance in encouraging the development of a personal style, for his insistence on blurring philosophy with theology rather than allying it to eloquence, and for seeking to legislate the forms of faith rather than leaving such questions in the privacy of the believer's heart. The essence of their dispute, in its stylistic dimensions at least, lies in the fundamental question of the author's place in his work. Although referring to Erasmus, T. Cave's words apply, in an exactly opposite sense, to Dolet's position: "Erasmus's Folly, from the beginning of her demonstrative exercise, will repeatedly reject rhetorical planning in favour of extempore speech;

immediacy, in her view, is a sign of nature and consequently a guarantee of authenticity."[10] Erasmian authenticity flows from the personal, original quality of the text, where the author's self is the controlling authority: Dolet's authenticity stems from a more objective sense of what constitutes, in all senses of the term, the guarantor of the *auctoritas* of his text. For Erasmus, it is a matter of speaking "from the heart," instinctively and naturally:

> . . . the issue of extempore speech is decisive in determining the opposition between a written (Ciceronian) and a spoken (Erasmian) model of discourse. . . . The project of Ciceronian imitation is enclosed within the space of the written; its commitment to the past, to isolation and absence, excludes it from life, presence, the accident of the moment.   (Cave, p. 139)

Dolet promotes, in contrast, an ideal drawn from the mind rather than from the heart, validated by the best minds of the past and drawing on our *virtus* and our *humanitas*--those features which distinguish us from the beasts and define our claim on posterity, and which call for the skill, learning, technique, and discipline that we must bring to the task of artistic creation. For Erasmus, artistic originality means self-realization; for Dolet it is a matter of surpassing the natural limits of the self. As C. Longeon has argued:

> L'une des critiques les plus vives qu'il adresse à Erasme est d'avoir choisi une certaine "mediocritas" et de s'être abandonné aux facilités de sa nature. . . . Si, comme il le croit, le sort "hic et nunc" de chacun dépend de soi-même, il faut se fixer un idéal rigoureux et mettre ses efforts inlassablement à l'atteindre.[11]

> [One of his sharpest criticisms of Erasmus is that he elected to pursue a certain "mediocritas" and to yield to the pliancy of his own nature. . . . If indeed, as Dolet believes, our fate, here and now, depends on ourselves alone, then we must set a stern ideal for ourselves, and tirelessly devote all our efforts to attaining it.]

But the issue at hand is not only a matter of world-view or personal philosophy of life. The Ciceronian dispute also, of necessity, implicates our understanding of what G. Norton refers to as "the translative dilemma." The widening rifts among the Humanist community and the perceived challenges to orthodoxy in all its forms in the France of the 1530s were such that it could hardly have been otherwise: ". . . the question of what constitutes replicability of discourse and, more to the point, how *res* / *sententia* are made immanent through *verba* becomes the harbinger for issues of rhetorical translation" (*Ideology*, p. 187).

It is precisely in the domain of such complex tensions as these, tensions which at once link and separate creator and imitator, original and copy, source and target, that both the theory and practice of Dolet's own notion of translation become particularly interesting. A significant number of his writings engage our reflection on what happens to ideas--themselves the products of rhetorical strategies and conceptual assumptions inseparable from the manner of their articulation--when they are subjected to semantic shift, and that is a matter of far-reaching ramification in the France of the 1530s and 40s. Here again, Norton pinpoints the problem:

> The translative dilemma . . . is that of allegiance to the letter. The problem is summarized effectively in the celebrated complaint brought by the Sorbonne theologians on January 10, 1534 against the newly created Royal Readers. Appointed by Francis I in 1530 at the encouragement of Guillaume Budé, the "lecteurs royaux" were authorized to "multiplier les lettres humaines" through instruction in Latin, Greek and Hebrew. But as they began to engage more and more in the practice of textual interpretation along with translation proper, it became clear that their interests placed them on a collision course with those of the Sorbonne theologians, if only because of the inherent ambiguity between the acts of interpretation and translation. This ambiguity . . . may indeed explain the consternation of the Sorbonne plaintiffs when they read the posted course announcements of the Royal Readers. A typical bulletin used as

> evidence against the defendants in an injunction of the
> Parlement early in 1533 refers, as a consequence, to
> Franciscus Vatablus's continued "interpretationem
> Psalmorum." Interlingual transfer or textual commentary:
> quite clearly both domains of analysis are blurred in the
> charges against the defendants. (pp. 59-60)

The inseparability of translation and interpretation, and all the attendant problems of such synonymity, could not be more starkly stated, and both the centrality of Dolet's writings to such questions as these and the extreme danger to which this centrality exposed him, may now be more fully appreciated: he not only authored the first translation manual written in French, he also translated a number of works into French--two of his own, two by Cicero, and two thought at the time to be by Plato.[12]

Initially, the problem of Dolet's self-translations--his epic poem on the reign of Francis I, the *Gallorum Regis Fata*, which he published under his own imprint at Lyon in 1539, and a poem written on the occasion of the birth of his son, the *Genethliacum Claudii Doleti* (also 1539)--arises in a particularly acute way in the context of my earlier remarks concerning the Ciceronian dispute.[13] If we remember that Dolet was executed in 1546, ostensibly for having translated part of the *Axiochus* in such a manner as to deny the immortality of the soul,[14] and if we remind ourselves that, in the religious controversies of the time, the positions adopted on such questions as free will and predestination, Fate and Fortune (as symbols of either a determined or of an accidental universe), and the consequent views of man's relationship to God, were literally matters of capital importance, then Dolet's self-translations make for essential reading. It is not possible here to compare his Latin originals to his French translations in close detail,[15] but a few examples will suffice to demonstrate the kinds of shifts Dolet is obliged (or elects?) to make as he moves from Latin to French and thereby confronts the "translative dilemma" in all its complexity.

The *Avant-naissance*, for instance, urges the new-born Claude to seek faith and wisdom in the humble pursuit of Christ's clemency and to strive to perfect his immortal soul, but these perfectly orthodox "Praeceptes Necessaires à la Vie commune" are frequently absent from the Latin original, or else present but in perhaps less orthodox ways. The references to the immortality of the soul and the prayers for divine forgiveness are not to be found in the *Genethliacum*. On the other hand, where the original speaks of the pursuit of knowledge as necessary to the acquisition of wisdom,

> His notis securus ages, nec territus ullo
> Portento, credes generari cuncta sagacis
> Naturae vi praestante, imperioque stupendo:
> Naturaeque eiusdem dissolvi omnia iussu . . .   (p. 10)

> [Knowing this, you will feel secure in your doings and, intimidated by nothing unnatural, you will consider all things brought into being by the preeminent power and astonishing sovereignty of wise Nature: likewise [you will consider] all things brought to their outcome through the prescription of Nature . . .][16]

the translation seems to alter its focus from wisdom to virtue and adds a parenthesis of potentially far-reaching importance:

> Par tel sçavoir tousjours constant seras;
> De monstre aulcun tu ne t'esmouveras:
> Mais tu croiras le tout faict par Nature
> (Mere de tout, de Dieu puissance pure)
> Et par icelle a sa fin tout venir. . . .   (p. 12)

> [Through such knowledge, you will ever act with constancy; you will be dismayed by nothing unnatural, but you will believe all things accomplished by Nature (mother of us all, pure might of God), and that everything comes to its end through her. . . .]

Such distinctions are even more striking in a later passage, where Dolet instructs his son on the attitude to adopt in the face of Death. The *Genethliacum* urges:

> . . . cum Mors pallens aetate peracta,
> Instabit, non aegro animo communia perfer
> fata: nihil nobis damni Mors invehit atrox,
> Sed mala cuncta aufert miseris, et sydera pandit.   (p. 19)

[When pale Death approaches, your years being completed, do not bear this universal destiny with an embittered spirit; severe Death brings us nothing harmful, but removes all bad things from the wretched, and opens up the heavens.]

But the *Avant-Naissance* seems to replace this fundamentally Stoic 'απάθεια with a lesson in Christian humility:[17]

> . . . [quand] fauldra le passage
> Commun à tous (j'entends la mort tant dure)
> Passer, à Dieu obëis, ne murmure.
> La mort est bonne et nous prive du mal,
> La mort est bonne, et nous oste du val
> Calamiteux. . . .   (p. 32)

[When the time comes for that journey we must all undertake--I mean death in all its severity--obey God, do not complain. Death is good, and shields us from harm. Death is good, and leads us out of this vale of tears. . . .]

If we turn to some examples from the *Fata* and the *Gestes*, we are struck by a similar set of differences. The Latin original starts in heroic manner:

> Fata cano Regis Galli, fata aspera fata;
> Sed quae invicto animo tandem cessere domantis
> Omnia consilio, virtute et mente virili.   (p. 9)

[I sing the destiny of the French king, the destiny, the harsh destiny: this finally yielded, nevertheless, to the unconquered spirit, the resolve, the virtue, and the manly spirit of the victor.]

The translation of this passage appears, however, to substitute *apologia* for epic endeavor and curbs the heroic power of *virtus* by the acknowledgement of our human limitations:

> Ce qui m'a induict d'intituler ce present Oeuvre en Latin FATA, qui en nostre langue veult aultant adire, des-tinées, est, que par sus tout ordre, et pouvoir humain, ay veu advenir au Roy tout ce qu'il a souffert d'infortune en aulcunes entreprises de ses guerres. Quant à l'ordre, nul ne doubte, qu'elle ne provienne de prudence et bonne execution. En ces choses le Roy Françoys n'est deffaillant. (p. 13)

> [What has led me to entitle the Latin version of this work "FATA" (which in our language means "things des-tined") is the fact that I have observed everything that has befallen the king, beyond all sense of arrangement and human control, in the course of his various military undertakings. There can be no doubt that an orderly existence stems from prudence and careful execution, and King Francis is not lacking in these qualities.]

Similarly, we may contrast the following from the *Fata*

> Est fatum divina propago Iovis, bona quaeque,
> Vel mala concilians, pro sollicitante Deorum
> Imperio. Humani haec subeunt, tolerantque; coacti
> Ordine perpetuo rerum; quo nomine recto
> Fata voces. Fatum est rerum immutabilis ordo:
> Cui licet accedat Virtus, tamen usque priores
> Fert fatum parteis in re quacunque gerenda . . .
> (pp. 9-10)

> [Fate is the divine offspring of Jove, bringing about good things or bad at the vexatious command of the Gods. Human beings undergo these things, and put up with them, forced to do so by the eternal order of things, by what by its rightful name we call Fate. Fate is the immutable ordering of all things. Virtue might be a

characteristic of any man: Fate nevertheless continuously plays the primary role in the management of whatever happens . . .]

with its counterpart in the *Gestes*:

> Le tout gist en ceste Destinée: de la quelle je baille telle diffinition. Destinée est une fille de Dieu omnipotent, laquelle suivant le vouloir, et commandement de son pere, nous cause, et pourchasse, tout ce que nous appellons bien et mal. Et ces deux choses, les Humains recoipvent par ung infaillible vouloir de Dieu: lequel droictement s'appelle Destinée, car Destinée n'est rien aultre, qu'ung ordre eternel des choses. Et combien qu'a icelle se puisse joindre quelque prudence, ou vertu humaine, toutesfois c'est elle qui regne, et ha tout pouvoir en noz actes.   (pp. 14-15)

> [Everything lies in the hands of this Destiny, which I define in the following way: Destiny is a daughter of God the omnipotent, who, obedient to the desire and commands of her father, causes and brings upon us everything we call good and ill. And these two things come to humankind through the infallible will of God, to which it is right to give the name "Destiny," for Destiny is no other than the eternal arrangement of things. And although some degree of prudence, or of human virtue, can be brought to bear on Destiny, it is nevertheless she who reigns and has complete control over our doings.]

Are we dealing here with stylistic differences occasioned by Dolet's rejection of anachronistic terminology, and therefore having more to do with semantic code than with doctrinal conviction? Or are we dealing with a Ciceronian whose linguistic usage forces his thinking toward the paganization warned against by Erasmus? Or even with a free-thinker deliberately exploiting the linguistic ambiguities to propagate unorthodox views in one language that will be proffered in less exceptionable tones in the other? Dolet's dreadful fate on the gallows of the Place Maubert leaves no doubt as to the way in which the Faculté de Théologie answered such questions, but it has ultimately to be conceded that, based as much on these particular texts as on the balance of his writings, we will probably never know for sure.

In the context of the present study, however, perhaps the questions are more important than the answers. Although directly biographical in their immediate reference, they lead us back to the broader question of the "translative dilemma" as it affected contemporary Humanist composition and translation. Interwoven with those aspects, whether stylistic or conceptual, of the Ciceronian debate that have been discussed so far are a number of questions of what we may term rhetorical strategy, and it is again to Dolet that I shall turn as a case in point. As V. J. Worth has pointed out,[18] Dolet's Ciceronianism did not prevent him from turning to other sources, and it is clear from the opening lines of the *Fata* quoted earlier, "Fata cano Regis Galli . . ." that the shadow of Vergil falls over this text at least as much as that of Cicero. Arguing that "an analysis of the principles [Dolet] follows in translating passages inspired by Vergil into French will raise a question fundamental to our understanding of the assimilation of classical literary influences within the vernacular tradition . . ." (p. 424), Worth compares the Latin opening with its French counterpart ("Fata cano . . ." and "Ce qui m'a induict . . ."), for example, in ways that yield quite different, although certainly complementary, results from those suggested earlier:

> The language [of the *Gestes*] reflects the process of logical thought necessary to the translator and chronicler, rather than the inspiration of the epic poet. . . . Further substantial differences . . . occur almost exclusively in narrative sections, where Dolet chooses to add details. . . . Had [these] occurred in the epic poem, they would have distracted the focus away from the hero, but they are consistent with the conventions of a prose chronicle.
>
> (pp. 424-25)

361

It is not simply that a writer inflamed by some divinely inspired "fureur poétique" uses different rhetorical registers from those practiced by the historian who claims credibility through the orderly presentation of events and a plausible explanation of their causes; a neo-Latin epic poem obviously supposes one kind of reader, while a prose chronicle in French posits a quite different target, and in transforming his text Dolet has clearly been brought to ponder "the transformed reader" he must now address himself to. This is further evidenced by Dolet's treatment of what Worth identifies as an element of the *Aeneid* presenting a different kind of problem, "the skilful Vergilian balance between the role of the heroes and that of the gods" (p. 425). It was suggested earlier that one difference between the Latin and the French might lie in Dolet's desire to offend orthodoxy as little as possible. However, since a partial reason for undertaking the translation was surely to gain the king's favor, it is also no doubt the case that

> it . . . suited both Dolet's personal ambition and the epic structure of his work that he chose to regard the defeat of the French at Pavia as the result of Fate, a force which, he emphasised at the start of the book, is beyond human control. Francis I is therefore presented as the victim of Fate, exonerated from any share of responsibility in his own capture and defeat. . . . (p. 426)

In this perspective, references in Latin epic poetry explaining the downfall of heroes in terms of their struggles with the gods clearly call for different treatment in French prose that seeks to explain what happened to His Most Christian Majesty Francis I.[19] Translation, when beset with the kind of ideological tensions alluded to in my remarks on Dolet's dispute with Erasmus, and when further compounded by the kinds of shift in rhetorical focus brought out by Worth, clearly becomes a transformative act in which the ties that link author and text are recalibrated as a function of the ties between text and reader. This is, of course, the case whether we speak of readers who experience the text in its original language, or of those who read in translation: but, *a fortiori*, it is even more the case when we consider the question of self-translation, and that is what gives particular interest to Dolet's efforts in the present context. To say as much, at this stage of the twentieth century, is perhaps to say nothing very new: but to raise such matters in a review of Dolet's activities is, surely, to warrant speaking of him as a pioneer.

A final question to be incorporated into the topic under review lies in the exploration, in the context of Dolet's Humanist activity, of the criteria governing the choice of texts to be translated. Here again, Worth provides us with valuable insights into some slightly different aspects of the "translative dilemma."[20] Given the earlier discussion of the recalibration brought about by the shift in focus between original and translation, and relating this to commercial as well as to more properly authorial concerns (Dolet was of course a printer and bookseller as well as a writer), Worth observes:

> La traduction offrait, certes, un marché tout prêt, mais en plus elle lui permettait d'apporter à une langue, à une culture en évolution les richesses de sa science d'humaniste. Il convient donc d'examiner chaque texte sous les deux aspects qui ont pu intéresser le traducteur: dans un premier temps, son contenu, et dans un deuxième temps, sa qualité littéraire. En précisant jusqu'à quel point il a respecté la forme et le style du texte original, nous serons à même d'établir ses priorités.   (pp. 51-52)

> [Translating certainly provided him with a ready made market, but it also enabled him to bring to a language and to a culture still in evolution all the wealth of his humanism. It is therefore appropriate to examine each text from the double viewpoint of its interest to the translator: first for its content, and then for its literary quality. By specifying how closely he has respected the form and the style of his original, we can identify his priorities.]

Thus, comparing elements of the *Genethliacum* to their counterparts in the *Avant-Naissance*, the latter text being expressly promoted as an "Oeuvre tresutile et necessaire à la vie commune: contenant,

comme l'homme se doibt gouverner en ce monde" [a most useful
and necessary Work for everyday life, including how man must
govern himself in this world] (hardly the purpose of the Latin
original, intended for an erudite and cosmopolitan readership),
Worth goes on to show how the formulaic and ceremonial aspects of
a conventional "pièce de circonstance" in the Latin poem emerge as
a plain-spoken declaration of pedagogical and utilitarian intent in the
translation: "à la différence des hexamètres latins, destinés à un
public savant, les vers français s'addressent à des lecteurs attirés par
le sujet plutôt que le style" [p. 53; unlike the Latin hexameters,
intended for a learned public, the French verse is addressed to
readers more attracted to the subject matter than to the style]. A
passage such as:

> Vive Deo fidens: stabilis fiducia Divum
> Tristitia vitae immunem te reddet ab omni . . .   (p. 9)

> [Live believing in God: the steadfast trustworthiness of the
> Gods will make you immune to every sorrow in life . . .]

is thus rendered as:

> En premier lieu, ta foy ce poinct tiendra
> Qu'il est ung Dieu tout puissant et unicque
> En ses effects. . . .   (pp. 10-11)

> [Before all else, it will be a tenet of your faith that there
> is one God, all powerful and without compare in all He
> does. . . .]

Such a transformation is not only explainable in terms of the stylistic
concessions necessary to the shift from Ciceronian Latin to an
unexceptionably orthodox French, but also, as Worth rightly
observes, in terms of the declaration of practical purpose at the head
of the translation. Carefully building her case on Dolet's translations of his own *Fata*, Cicero's *Familiares* and *Tusculanae*
(undertaken when Dolet was being mercilessly harassed by the

authorities), and the pseudo-Platonic dialogues that were to furnish the specific instruments of his indictment, Worth then goes on to show how the very choice of texts to translate reveals an evolving Dolet, coming to terms with the civic responsibilities of his craft and transforming the act of translation into an act of advocacy for both personal survival and the promotion of Humanist values:

> Dans un premier temps, il visait surtout à atteindre un nouveau public en leur proposant des oeuvres utiles. . . . Dans un deuxième temps, sûr de lui-même, il concevait la traduction comme moyen privilégié d'illustrer le français, tout en apportant une importante contribution pédagogique. Dans un troisième temps, il espérait que ses traductions attireraient l'attention sur les circonstances où il se trouvait, et défendraient ses projets pour l'avenir. (p. 61)

> [He was initially aiming at a new public, to whom he was offering texts that were practical in nature. . . . Secondly, sure of himself, he conceived of translation as a privileged means of glorifying the French language, while also making a significant pedagogical contribution. Thirdly, he hoped that his translations would focus attention on the circumstances in which he found himself, and would provide a bulwark for his future plans.]

It was in the midst of publishing these translations, in 1540, that Dolet brought out his *Maniere de bien traduire d'une langue en aultre*, and it is, I believe, in the context of what we have seen of Dolet's efforts to cope with the translative dilemma, to achieve an appropriate level of rhetorical register in his efforts to communicate ideas, that his five rules take on their fullest resonance. His awareness of the issues involved, not only succinctly revealed in his manual but also validated by his actual practice, reveals both his adhesion to and enhancement of a rhetorical tradition that places him squarely at the portals of a large part of modern translation theory.[21] Following his detailed and highly theoretical discussion of Dolet's five rules in the context of prior Humanist thought and practice, G. Norton concludes (and, most conveniently for our purposes here, draws together much of what we have been alluding to) in the following manner:

> Etienne Dolet's *Maniere de bien traduire* should not be judged (as, indeed, too frequently it has been) as a practicum for the translator. Its imperfections in design and elaboration make it too fragile a document for drawing up a plan of translative execution. . . . Dolet presents not a technique for translation as such, but an intellectual siting of the problem. He defines the itinerary of motions within which translation can occur, its points of initiation and achievement, its localization within a universal program of rhetoric. . . . That Dolet was the first to conceptualize for the vernacular a plan of total translation, inspired by rhetorical tradition, seems to far outweigh his work's structural weakness. . . . Dolet [established] translation as an event of enrichment for the unevolved vernacular.   (*Ideology*, pp. 205-16)

One cannot read much of Dolet, or much of Humanist writing for that matter, without being struck by that all-pervading anxiety over the annihilating power of Time which fosters as its counterpart the vigorous conviction that we can be said to have mattered only when Posterity knows of us. Dolet speaks for much of Renaissance Humanism when he writes, in the preface to his *Erasmianus*: "In hoc totus sum, ut me non solum uixisse, quod nobis cum brutis commune est, sed uirtutis studiosum uixisse, posteritas intelligat" [p. 5; Let posterity understand that I am fully defined within these words: I have not only lived--for that is something we share with the brute beasts--but I have lived with devotion to virtue]. We outwit Time when we speak to each other across the boundaries--whether temporal, spatial, or linguistic--that set us apart: only the cultivation of Letters, in the attempt to communicate with one another, can defeat Time's propensity to be silent about us.[22] There is something touching, even reassuring, in this sense of translation as being not so much a service to a monumentalized original, a homage to the past

366

and a concession to our dependency on it, but rather a service to the present, an affirmation and consolidation of our own capacity for self-reliance and our ability to speak and to mean in ways that are at once like and unlike those of our forebears. It not only exemplifies Dolet's response to what Norton calls that poignant

> nostalgia for method in French Renaissance notions of translation [which] would always remain precisely that, an implied hope that translation is in fact absolutely assimilable from a mastered program of rhetoric and metalanguage, and in the last resort, the chastening awareness that translation takes place in the interpretive activity of our thought . . . , *(Ideology*, p. 14)

it also affords insight into one of the ways in which humankind has sought not only to resolve the translative dilemma, but to fend off the ultimate Silence. That, of course, is why Renaissance Humanism so valorized the translator's skill and art: in all of Creation, as Cicero reminds us,[23] we alone are endowed with a wisdom that is only wise when it can be stated and conveyed and shared.

NOTES

1.   J. Du Bellay, *La Deffence et illustration de la langue françoyse* (Paris, 1549), ed. H. Chamard (Paris: Didier, 1948), pp. 85-86, for example, calls him "[un] homme de bon jugement en notre vulgaire" [a man of good judgment in our national language].

2.   The best biographical study continues to be R. C. Christie's *Etienne Dolet: The Martyr of the Renaissance*, rev. ed. (London: Macmillan, 1899), supplemented by the editorial material in those texts I shall be referring to; see also C. Longeon, "Etienne Dolet: Années d'enfance et de jeunesse," *Réforme et Humanisme* (Montpellier: Université de Montpellier, 1977), pp. 37-61, and his *Bibliographie des Oeuvres d'Etienne Dolet, écrivain, éditeur et imprimeur* (Geneva: Droz, 1980).

3.   *La Maniere de bien traduire d'une langue en aultre. D'advantage de la punctuation de la langue françoyse, plus des accents d'ycelle* (Lyon,

1540 [Paris: Techener, 1830]).

4. This has recently been done in G. Norton's *The Ideology and Language of Translation in Renaissance France, and their Humanist Antecedents* (Geneva: Droz, 1984), p. 187. No further discussion of the question of Renaissance translation is possible without reference to this immensely rich study: its bibliography alone will serve as the necessary starting point for any of the historical or theoretical issues arising from this present *excursus*. See also Norton's "Le Dessein rhétorique de la *Maniere de bien traduire d'une langue en aultre*," *Etienne Dolet (1509-1546), (Cahiers V. L. Saulnier, n°3)*, (Paris: ENSJF, 1986), pp. 93-103.

5. See *L'Erasmianus sive Ciceronianus d'Etienne Dolet*, facsimile of the original, with introduction and commentary by E. V. Telle (Geneva: Droz, 1974).

6. See A. Gambaro's bilingual edition (Brescia: La Scuola Editrice, 1965) and B. I. Knott's annotated translation in *The Collected Works of Erasmus*, vol. 28 (Toronto: Univ. of Toronto Press, 1986), pp. 323-603.

7. For further discussion of these matters, see J. Chomarat, *Grammaire et Rhétorique chez Erasme* (Paris: Les Belles Lettres, 1981), pp. 822 ff., and his "Dolet et Erasme," *Etienne Dolet (1509-1546)* [n. 4 above], pp. 21-36.

8. *Orationes Duae in Tholosam* (Lyon: [Gryphe], 1534); see K. Lloyd-Jones, "Dolet et la Rhétorique: *les Orationes in Tholosam*," *Etienne Dolet (1509-1546)* [n. 4 above], pp. 79-92; an edition and French translation of these *Orationes* are planned for publication soon.

9. See Telle's introduction and notes to his edition of the *Erasmianus* for a definitive analysis of Dolet's arguments.

10. T. Cave, *The Cornucopian Text: Problems of Writing in the French Renaissance* (Oxford: Clarendon Press, 1979), p. 127.

11. C. Longeon, "Cohérences d'Etienne Dolet," *Acta Conventus Neo-Latini Sanctandreani*, ed. I. D. McFarlane (Binghamton, NY: SUNY Press, 1986), p. 365.

12.   For Dolet's own works, see n. 13 below. His partial translation of the *Familiares* (*Les Epistres familieres*) was published in Lyon in 1542, his translation of the *Tusculanae* (*Les Questions tusculanes*) the following year. His *Deulx Dialogues de Platon* (the pseudo-Platonic *Axiochus* and *Hipparchus*) came out in 1544.

13.   Dolet later translated the *Genethliacum* as *L'Avant-Naissance de Claude Dolet* (Lyon, 1539) and the *Fata* as *Les Gestes de Françoys de valoys, Roy de France* (Lyon, 1540). The translation of the *Genethliacum* is not explicitly acknowledged as having been done by Dolet and is thus subject to some degree of doubt; see U. Köppen, "Etienne Dolet vaniteux traducteur de lui-même?," *Bibliothèque d'Humanisme et Renaissance* 34 (1972):505-09, arguing *contra*, and K. Lloyd-Jones, "Etienne Dolet, fidèle traducteur de lui-même?," *Bibliothèque d'Humanisme et Renaissance* 35 (1973):315-22, arguing *pro* its attribution to Dolet. Modern critical opinion generally supports the latter position; see C. Longeon, *Les Préfaces françaises d'Etienne Dolet* (Geneva: Droz, 1979), p. 60.

14.   Dolet was condemned for having translated too emphatically a phrase describing Death's inability to affect the wise man:

> Pour ce qu'il est certain que la mort n'est point aux vivants: et quant aux defuncts, ilz ne sont plus: doncques la mort les attouche encores moins. Parquoy elle ne peult rien sur toy, car tu n'es pas encores prest à deceder; et quand tu seras decedé, elle n'y pourra rien aussi, attendu que tu ne seras plus *rien du tout*.
>
> [It is therefore certain that death is not a condition of the living; and as for the dead, they no longer exist, and thus death affects them even less. That is why death has no hold over you, for you are not yet at the point of dying; and once you have died, death will still be powerless against you, since you will no longer be *anything at all*.]

It was the "addition" of these last three words (emphasis added) that sealed his fate; see Christie, pp. 461 ff. (It seems clear that Dolet was in fact translating from Marsilio Ficino's Latin version of the *Platonis Opera*, an edition of which had been published by Badius in Paris in 1533.)

15.   For a more detailed discussion of the doctrinal implications of the positions adopted by Dolet in the course of his "Ciceronian quarrel"

with Erasmus, based on a systematic textual comparison of the *Fata* and the *Genethliacum* with their translations, see K. Lloyd-Jones, "Orthodoxy and Language: Dolet and the Question of Ciceronianism in the Early Reformation," *Classical and Modern Literature* 2 (1982):213-30. Some of the quotations discussed there are reproduced in the present study.

16. Clearly, no English translation can fully bring out the conceptual implications of the Latin and French originals.

17. The overall impact of Dolet's studies in Padua (under teachers formed by the great Aristotelian, Pomponazzi) and in Venice, where he studied the *De Officiis* in ways that he would refer to more than once over the years to come, remains to be fully assessed, as does in consequence the place of Stoicism on his thinking. It will be remembered in this regard that, later in the century, the appropriateness of a Stoic approach to suffering was to become a major subject of religious debate, particularly among the Jesuits and their opponents.

18. V. J. Worth, "Etienne Dolet: From a Neo-Latin Epic Poem to a Chronicle in French Prose," *Acta Conventus Neo-Latini Sanctandreani*, [n. 11 above], pp. 423-29.

19. A similar confluence of pressures no doubt governs Dolet's introduction of mythology into the *Fata*, where Jupiter decides that Francis must lose the battle of Pavia so that mere mankind will always be reminded of its limitations--and, equally, his suppression of this "explanation" in the *Gestes*; see Worth [n. 18 above], p. 426.

20. V. J. Worth, "Etienne Dolet: le choix des textes à traduire" in *Etienne Dolet (1509-1546)* [n. 4 above], pp. 51-61.

21. Cf. G. Mounin, *Les Problèmes théoriques de la traduction* (Paris: Gallimard, 1963) and G. Steiner, *After Babel: Aspects of Language and Translation* (London: Oxford Univ. Press, 1975), *passim*.

22. Given its extent and variety, Humanist reflection on the relationships between Latin and the vernacular calls for a far more detailed treatment than can be provided here. Du Bellay's self-translations, for example, show a sense in which his cultivation of Latin appears to be a

means of preserving, both conceptually and linguistically, those values that Time destroys and which the French language, so far untried and imperfect, cannot yet protect: see K. Lloyd-Jones, "L'Originalité de la vision romaine chez Du Bellay," *Humanisme, Réforme et Renaissance* 12 (1981):13-21 and "Du Bellay's Journey from *Roma Vetus* to *La Rome Neufve*," *Rome in the Renaissance: the City and the Myth*, ed. P. A. Ramsey (Binghamton, NY: SUNY Press, 1982), pp. 301-19. For yet another highly fruitful line of inquiry, dealing with translation from Latin to the vernacular and then back into Latin, see E. S. Ginsberg, "Peregrinations of the Kiss: Thematic Relationships between Neo-Latin and French Poetry in the Sixteenth Century," *Acta Conventus Neo-Latini Sanctandreani* [n. 11 above], pp. 331-42.

23.   See *De Inventione*, 1.1-5.

BIBLIOGRAPHY

Items of particular relevance to medieval translation have been marked with an asterisk.

Abraham, Nicolas, and Torok, Maria. "The Shell and the Kernel." *Diacritics* 9 (1979):16-28.

*Adams, R. M. *Proteus, His Lies, His Truth: Discussions of Literary Translation.* New York, 1973.

Adkinson, B. W. "The Role of Translation in the Dissemination of Scientific Information." In *Ten Years of Translation.* Edited by I. J. Citroen. Oxford, 1967, pp. 91-103.

Aginsky, B. W. and E. G. "The Importance of Language Universals." *Word* 4 (1948):168-72.

*Amos, F. R. *Early Theories of Translation.* New York, 1920.

Andreyev, N. D. "Linguistic Aspects of Translation." In *Proceedings of the Ninth International Congress of Linguists.* The Hague, 1964, pp. 625-38.

Antolkolskij, P. "Quelques observations sur la traduction." In *Ten Years of Translation.* Edited by I. J. Citroen. Oxford, 1967, pp. 83-88.

Arnaud, Paul. "La traducteur technique de l'avenir: Le documentaliste linguiste." In *Ten Years of Translation.* Edited by I. J. Citroen. Oxford, 1967, pp. 109-17.

Arnold, Matthew. "On Translating Homer." In *On the Study of Celtic Literature and On Translating Homer*. New York, 1906, pp. 141-300.

Arnold, T. W., and Guillaume, A. *The Legacy of Islam*. London, 1931.

Arrowsmith, W. "The Lively Conventions of Translation." In *The Craft and Context of Translation*. Edited by W. Arrowsmith and R. Shattuck. New York, 1964, pp. 187-213.

*Arrowsmith, W., and Shattuck, R. *The Craft and Context of Translation*. New York, 1964.

Astre, F. "Aperçus critiques sur les traductions et les traducteurs." In *Mémoires de l'Académie des Sciences de Toulouse*. Vol. 2. Toulouse, 1870, pp. 135-50.

Atzert, K. *De Cicerone interprete graecorum*. Göttingen, 1908.

Saint Augustine. *Enarrationes in psalmos*. *Patrologia Latina*. Vols. 36/37, pp. 68-1960.

_____. *Epistola 28*. *Patrologia Latina*. Vol. 33, pp. 111-14.

_____. *Epistola 71*. *Patrologia Latina*. Vol. 33, pp. 241-43.

_____. *De doctrina christiana*. *Patrologia Latina*. Vol. 34, pp. 15-122.

Aulus Gellius. *Noctes atticae*. Edited by C. Hosius. Leipzig, 1903.

Austin, J. L. *How To Do Things With Words*. Cambridge, MA, 1975.

Bacon, Roger. *Grammatices graecae*. Edited by E. Nolan and B. A. Hirsch. Cambridge, 1902.

Bakhtin, M. M. *The Dialogic Imagination.* Edited by Michael Holquist. Translated by Caryl Emerson and Michael Holquist. Austin, TX, 1981.

Bakhtin, M. M., and Medvedev, P. M. *The Formal Method in Literary Scholarship: A Critical Introduction to Sociological Poetics.* Translated by Albert J. Wehrle. Cambridge, MA, 1985.

Bakhtin, M. M., and Voloshinov, V. N. *Marxism and the Philosophy of Language.* Translated by L. Matejka and R. Titunik. New York, 1973.

Bally, C. "Stylistique et linguistique générale." *Archiv für das Studium der neueren Sprachen* 128 (1912):87-126.

_____. *Traité de stylistique française.* 2d ed. 2 vols. Paris and Heidelberg, 1937.

_____. "La pensée et la langue." *Bulletin de la Société de Linguistique de Paris* 23 (1922):117-37.

_____. *Linguistique générale et linguistique française.* 4th ed. Berne, 1965.

Bardy, G. "Traducteurs et adapteurs au quatrième siécle." *Recherches de science religieuse* 30 (1940):257-306.

Bates, E. S. *Modern Translation.* London, 1936.

Barthes, Roland. *Image, Music, Text.* New York, 1977.

_____. *Mythologies.* New York, 1972.

Bassnett-McGuire, Susan. *Translation Studies.* London and New York, 1980.

Batts, M. S. *Translation* and *Interpretation, a Symposium.* Vancouver, 1975.

Bausch, K. R. "Die Transposition, Versuch einer neuen Klassification." *Linguistica Antverpiensia* 2 (1968):29-50.

_____. "Qualité en traduction et linguistique dite différentielle." *Babel* 16 (1970):13-21.

Bausch, K. R., and Gauger, H. M., eds. *Interlinguistica: Sprachvergleich und Übersetzung. Festschrift zum 60 Geburtstag von Mario Wandruszka.* Tübingen, 1971.

de Beaugrande, Robert. *Factors in a Theory of Poetic Translating.* Amsterdam, 1978.

Bédorat, H. "Les premières traductions tolédanes de philosophie--œuvres d'Alfarabi." *Revue néoscolastique de philosophie* 41 (1938):80-97.

*Beer, Jeanette M. A. *A Medieval Caesar.* Geneva, 1976.

*_____. *Narrative Conventions of Truth in the Middle Ages.* Geneva, 1981.

Bellanger, J. *Histoire de la traduction en France.* Paris, 1892.

Belloc, Hilaire. "On Translation." *London Mercury* 10:150-56.

_____. *On Translation. Taylorian Lecture.* London, 1931.

Benjamin, W. "Die Aufgabe des Übersetzens." In *Das Problem des Übersetzens.* Edited by H. J. Störig. Stuttgart, 1963, pp. 182-95.

_____. "The Task of the Translator." In *Illuminations.* Edited by Hannah Arendt. Translated by Harry Zohn. New York, 1969, pp. 69-82.

Benson, A. C. "Verse Translation." *Cornhill Magazine* 57 (1924): 586-98.

*Berger, S. *La bible française au moyen âge*. 1884. Reprint Geneva, 1967.

Bertelli, L. A. "A Glimpse at the History of Translation in Italy." *Babel* 11 (1965):76-78.

Berthelot, M. *La chimie au moyen âge*. 1893. Reprint Osnabrück, 1967.

Blatt, F. "Remarques sur l'histoire des traductions latines." *Classica et medievalia* 1 (1938):217-42.

Bloomfield, L. *Language*. New York, 1933.

Boas, M. *The Scientific Renaissance, 1450-1630*. New York, 1962.

Boethius. *In isagogen Porphyrii*. Edited by S. Brant. Corpus scriptorum ecclesiaticorum latinorum. Vol. 48. Vienna and Leipzig, 1906.

Bogenschneider, H. J. "Technischer Übersetzer und Technische Bibliothek." *Babel* 5 (1959):200-06.

Bolinger, D. "Transformation; Structural Translation." *Acta linguistica hafniensia* 9 (1966):130-44.

Bonnard, J. *Les traductions de la bible en vers français au moyen âge*. 1888. Reprint Geneva, 1967.

Booth, Wayne. Introduction to *Problems of Dostoevsky's Poetics*, by M. M. Bakhtin. Minneapois, 1984.

Bossuat, R. "Anciennes traductions françaises du *De Officiis* de Cicéron." *Bibliothèque de l'Ecole des chartes*, 96 (1935): 246 ff.

Bossuat, R. "Traductions françaises des *Commentaires de César* à la fin du 15ᵉ siècle." *Bibliothèque d'humanisme et Renaissance* 3 (1943):253-411.

Bourdieu, Pierre. *Outline of a Theory of Practice.* Translated by Richard Nice. New York, 1977.

Bovie, S. P. "Translation as a Form of Criticism." In *The Craft and Context of Translation.* Edited by W. Arrowsmith and R. Shattuck. New York, 1964, pp. 51-75.

Brislin, R. W., ed. *Translation: Applications and Research.* New York, 1976.

van de Broeck, R. "The Concept of Equivalence in Translation Theory." In *Literature and Translation.* Edited by J. Holmes, J. Lambert, and R. van den Broeck. Leuven, 1978, pp. 29-47.

Brower, R. A. *Mirror on Mirror: Translation, Imitation, Parody.* Cambridge, MA, 1974.

*_____, ed. *On Translation.* Cambridge, MA, 1959.

Brown, R. *Words and Things.* New York, 1958.

Bruce, F. F. *The English Bible, a History of Translations.* New York, 1970.

Bruni Aretino, Leonardo. "De interpretatione recta." In *Humanistische philosophische Schriften.* Edited by H. Baron. Berlin, 1928, pp. 81-96.

Bruss, E. *Beautiful Theories: The Spectacle of Discourse in Contemporary Criticism.* Baltimore, 1982.

Bryant, W. "A Comparison of Translation Styles." *META* (University of Montreal) 17 (1972):160-64.

*Buridant, Claude. "'Translatio medievalis': Théorie et pratique de la traduction médiévale." *Travaux de linguistique et de littérature* 21 (1983):81-136.

Burke, K. *A Grammar of Motives.* New York, 1952.

Calverley, C. S. "On Metrical Translation." *Works of C. S. Calverley.* London, 1901, pp. 496-503.

Campbell, George. *The Philosophy of Rhetoric.* 2d ed. New York, 1850.

_____. *A Translation of the Four Gospels with Notes.* 2 vols. London, 1789.

Carmignani, G. A. F. *Dissertazione critica sulle traduzioni.* Florence, 1808.

Carne-Ross, D. S. "Structural Translation: Notes on Logue's *Patrokleia.*" *Arion* 1 (1962):27-38.

_____. "Translation and Transposition." In *The Craft and Context of Translation.* Edited by W. Arrowsmith and R. Shattuck, New York, 1964, pp. 3-28.

Cary, E. "Défense et illustration de l'art de traduire." *La nouvelle critique* (June, 1949):82-93.

_____. *La traduction dans le monde moderne.* Geneva, 1956.

_____. "La traduction totale." *Babel* 6 (1960):110-15.

_____. "Pour une théorie de traduction." *Journal des traducteurs / Translators' Journal* 7 (1962):118-27; 8 (1963):3-11.

Cary, E., and Jumpelt, R. W., eds. *Quality in Translation: Proceedings of the Third Congress of the International Federation of Translators.* New York, 1963.

Casagrande, J. B. "The Ends of Translation." *International Journal of Applied Linguistics* 20 (1954):335-40.

Cassiodorus. *Cassiodori senatoris institutiones.* Edited by R. A. B. Mynors. Oxford, 1937.

Catford, J. C. *A Linguistic Theory of Translation.* London, 1965.

Cauer, P. *Die Kunst des Übersetzens.* Berlin, 1914.

Cermák, J. "La traduction du point de vue de l'interprétation." In *The Nature of Translation.* Edited by J. S. Holmes. The Hague and Paris, 1970, pp. 23-42.

Chapman, S. *A Theory of Meter.* The Hague, 1965.

Chase, C. "Paragon, Parergon: Baudelaire Translates Rousseau." In *Difference in Translation.* Edited by J. F. Graham. Ithaca, NY, 1985, pp. 63-80.

Chase, S. Foreword to *Language, Thought, and Reality* by B. L. Whorf. Cambridge, 1956, pp. v-x.

*Chaytor, H. J. *From Script to Print.* Cambridge, 1945.

Chomsky, N. *Aspects of the Theory of Syntax.* Cambridge, MA, 1969.

Cicero, Marcus Tullius. "De optimo genere oratorum." In *Ciceronis Rhetorica.* Vol. 2. Edited by A. S. Wilkins. Oxford, 1957.

_____. *De finibus bonorum et malorum libri IV.* Edited by W. L. Hutchinson. London, 1909.

Citroen, I. J. "The Translation of Texts Dealing with Applied Science." *Babel* 5 (1959):30-33.

Citroen, I. J. "Specialisation in Technical and Scientific Translation." *Babel* 8 (1962):66-71.

_____. "The Myth of Two Professions: Literary and Non-literary Translation." *Babel* 12 (1966):181-88.

_____, ed. *Ten Years of Translation*. Oxford, 1967.

*Clanchy, M. T. *From Memory to Written Record: England 1066-1307*. London, 1979.

Clark, E. "Locationals: Existential, Locative, and Possessive Constructions." In *Universals of Human Language*. Edited by J. H. Greenberg. Vol. 4. Stanford, 1978, pp. 85-126.

Clausen, A. *Augustinus sacrae scripturae interpres*. Copenhagen, 1827.

Costa Lima, L. "Mimesis and Social Representation." *New Literary History* 16 (1985):447-66.

Coste, J. "La première expérience de traduction biblique." *Maison-Dieu* 53 (1958):56-88.

Courcelle, P. *Les lettres grecques en occident de Macrobe à Cassiodore*. Paris, 1943.

Craddock, J. T. "The Translator's Tools." In *Technical Translator's Manual*. Edited by J. B. Sykes. London, 1971, pp. 64-87.

Crombie, A. C. *Medieval and Early Modern Science*. 2 vols. Cambridge, MA, 1967.

Cromer, E. B. "Translation and Paraphrase." *Edinburgh Review* 218 (1913):102-14.

BIBLIOGRAPHY

Crothers, J. "Typology and Universals of Vowel Systems." In *Universals of Human Language.* Edited by J. H. Greenberg. Vol. 2. Stanford, 1978, pp. 93-152.

Culler, J. *On Deconstruction: Theory and Criticism after Structuralism.* Ithaca, NY, 1982.

*Curtius, E. R. *European Literature and the Latin Middle Ages.* Translated by W. R. Trask. New York, 1953.

Dante Alighieri. *Il convivio.* Edited by M. Simonelli. Bologna, 1966.

_____. *La Commedia secondo l'antica vulgata.* Edited by Giorgio Petrocchi. Edizione Nazionale a cura della Società Dantesca Italiana. 4 vols. Milan: Arnaldo Mondadori Editore, 1966-67.

Darbelnet, J. "La transposition." *French Review* 23 (1949-50):115-18.

_____. "Traduction littérale ou traduction libre?" *META* 15 (1970):88-94.

_____. "Dictionnaires bilingues et lexicologie différentielle." *Langages* 19 (1970):92-102.

_____. "Accent de phrase et dialectique en anglais et français." In *Interlinguistica: Sprachvergleich und Übersetzung.* Edited by K. R. Bausch and H. M. Gauger. Tübingen, 1971, pp. 416-24.

Day Lewis, C. "On Translating Poetry." In *Essays by Divers' Hands.* Edited by J. Richardson. London, 1963, pp. 18-36.

Deanesley, M. *The Lollard Bible.* 1920. Reprint Cambridge, 1966 and New York, 1978.

de Bruyne, D. "*L'Itala* de Saint Augustin." *Revue bénédictine* 30 (1913):294-314.

de Certeau, M. "On the Oppositional Practices of Everyday Life." *Social Text* 3 (1980):3-43.

de Grandcombe (Boillot), F. "Réflexions sur la traduction." *French Studies* 3 (1949):345-50; 5 (1951):253-63.

De Man, P. *Blindness and Insight: Essays on the Rhetoric of Contemporary Criticism.* New York, 1971.

_____. *The Resistance to Theory.* Minneapolis, 1986.

*Dembowski, P. "Learned Latin Treatises in French: Inspiration, Plagiarism, and Translation." *Viator* 17 (1986):255-69.

Derrida, J. *The Ear of the Other: Otobiography, Transference, Translation.* Edited by C. V. McDonald. Translated by P. Kamuf. New York, 1985.

_____. "Les Tours de Babel." In *Difference in Translation.* Edited by J. F. Graham. Ithaca, NY, 1985, pp. 165-207.

_____. "Me-Psychoanalysis: An Introduction to the Translation of 'The Shell and the Kernel' by Nicholas Abraham." *Diacritics* 9 (1979):4-12.

_____. *Of Grammatology.* Translated by G. C. Spivak. Baltimore, 1976.

_____. "Plato's Pharmacy." *Dissemination.* Translated by B. Johnson. Chicago, 1981, pp. 63-171.

_____. *Positions.* Translated by A. Bass. Chicago, 1981.

_____. "The Principle of Reason." *Diacritics* 13 (1983):3-20.

Derrida, J. "Signature Event Context." *Glyph* 1 (1977):172-97.

_____. *Speech and Phenomena and Other Essays on Husserl's Theory of Signs*. Translated by D. B. Allison. Evanston, IL, 1973.

_____. "White Mythology." *New Literary History* 6 (1974): 5-74.

_____. *Writing and Difference*. Translated by A. Bass. Chicago, 1978.

de Vaux. "La première entrée d'Averroes chez les Latins." *Revue des sciences philosophiques et théologiques* 22 (1933):193-245.

Dickinson, G. L. "On Translation." *Nation and Athenaeum* 46 (1929):282-83.

Dionysius Exiguus. "Epistola ad Eugipium presbyterum." *Patrologia Latina.* Vol. 67, pp. 345-46.

Dostert, L. E. "Problems of Translation." *Monographs on Linguistics and Language Teaching* 8 (1955).

Douglas, K. "Problems in Literary Translation." *Georgetown Monographs* 8 (1955):80-86.

*Doutrepont, G. *Les mises en prose des épopées et des romans chevaleresques du XIVe au XVIe siècle*. Brussels, 1939.

Dragonetti, Roger. "Specchi d'Amore: *Il Romanzo della Rosa* e *Il Fiore*." *Paragone* (letteratura) 32 (no. 374) (1981):3-22.

Dubsky, J. "The Prague Conception of Functional Style." In *The Prague School of Linguistics and Language Teaching*. Edited by V. Fried. London, 1972, pp. 112-27.

Dunlop, D. M. "The Work of Translation at Toledo." *Babel* 6 (1960):55-59.

Ebeling, G. *Introduction to a Theological Theory of Language.* Translated by K. A. Wilson. London, 1973.

Eco, U. "Metaphor, Dictionary, and Encyclopaedia." *New Literary History* 15 (1984):255-71.

Ervin, S., and Bower, R. T. "Translation Problems in International Surveys." *Public Opinion Quarterly* 16 (1952-53):595-604.

Etkind, E. "La stylistique comparée, base de l'art de traduire." *Babel* 13 (1967):23-30.

Evans, O. E. *On Translating the Bible.* London, 1976.

Fang, Achilles. "Some Reflections on the Difficulty of Translation." In *On Translation.* Edited by R. A. Brower. New York, 1966, pp. 111-13.

*Faral, E. *Les arts poétiques du 12ᵉ et du 13ᵉ siècle.* Paris, 1962.

Ferry de Saint Constant, J. *Rudimens de la traduction.* 2 vols. Paris, 1808-11.

Finlay, I. F. "The Translation of Technical and Literary Material-- Science versus Art?" *Babel* 8 (1962):57-61.

Firbas, J. "On Defining the Theme in Functional Sentence Analysis." *Travaux linguistiques de Prague.* Vol. 1, pp. 267-80. Prague.

Firth, J. R. "Linguistics and Translation." In *Selected Papers of J. R. Firth.* Edited by F. R. Palmer. London, 1968, pp. 84-95.

_____. "Linguistic Analysis and Translation." In *Selected Papers of J. R. Firth.* Edited by F. R. Palmer. London, 1968, pp. 74-83.

Fish, S. *Is There a Text in this Class?* Cambridge, MA, 1980.

Fishman, J. "The Sociology of Language: Yesterday, Today, and Tomorrow." In *Current Issues in Linguistic Theory.* Edited by R. W. Cole. Bloomington, IN, 1979.

_____. "A Systematization of the Whorfian Hypothesis." *Behavioral Science* 5 (1960):323-79.

FitzMaurice-Kelly, J. "Translation." In *Encyclopedia Britannica.* 11th ed. Vol. 27. Cambridge, 1911, pp. 183-88.

*Folena, Gianfranco. "'Volgarizzare' e 'Tradurre': Idea et terminologia della traduzione dal Medio Evo italiano e romanzo all'umanesimo europeo." In *La Traduzione, Saggi e Studi.* Trieste, 1973, pp. 59-120.

Forster, L. "Translation, an Introduction." In *Aspects of Translation.* Edited by A. H. Smith. London, 1958, pp. 1-28.

Frawley, W. "Prolegomenon to a Theory of Translation." In *Translation: Literary, Linguistic, and Philosophical Perspectives.* Edited by W. Frawley. London, 1984.

Freudenthal, H. W. L. "The Problem of Translating." *Modern Language Journal* 26 (1942):62-65.

Fried, V., ed. *The Prague School of Linguistics and Language Teaching.* London, 1972.

Fromaigent, E. *Die Technik der praktischen Übersetzung: Deutsch-Französisch.* Zurich, 1955.

Furley, D. J. "Translating from Greek Philosophy." In *Aspects of Translation.* Edited by A. H. Smith. London, 1958, pp. 52-64.

Gachechiladze, G. R. "Realism and Dialectics in the Art of Translation." *Babel* 13 (1967):87-91.

Garnier, G. "Time and Tense in French and English: Some Translation Problems." In *Studies in English Grammer*. Edited by A. Joly and T. Fraser. Lille, 1975, pp. 163-84.

Garvin, P. "Syntactic Retrieval." In *Proceedings of the National Symposium on Machine Translation*. Edited by H. P. Edmundson. Englewood Cliffs, NJ, 1961, pp. 286-92.

Giglioli, P. P., ed. *Language and Social Context*. Harmondsworth, 1972.

Gingold, K. "A Guide to Better Translations for Industry." *Babel* 12 (1966):142-45.

Girard, R. *Violence and the Sacred*. Baltimore, 1977.

Goddard, K. A. "Translation and Bilingualism." *Babel* 18 (1972): 18-23.

Godzich, W. Introduction to *Mikhail Bakhtin: The Dialogical Principle* by Tzvetan Todorov. Minneapolis, 1984, pp. ix-xiii.

_____. "The Semiotics of Semiotics." In *On Signs*. Edited by M. Blonsky. Baltimore, 1985, pp. 421-47.

Goffin, R. "La terminologie multilingue et la syntagmatique comparée au service de la traduction technique." *Babel* 14 (1968):132-41.

Govaert, M. "Critères de la traduction." In *Interlinguistica: Sprachvergleich und Übersetzung*. Edited by K. R. Bausch and H. M. Gauger. Tübingen, 1971, pp. 425-37.

Graham, J. F., ed. *Difference in Translation*. Ithaca, NY, 1985.

Grasset, B. "Traduction et traducteurs." *Revue des deux mondes* (1938):459-66.

Greenberg, J. H., ed. *Universals of Human Language.* 4 vols. Stanford, 1978.

Gregory the Great. *Epistola XXXIX ad Aristobulum. Patrologia Latina.* Vol. 77, p. 482.

_____. *Epistola ad Narsum Religiosum.* In *Monumenta Germaniae Historiae.* Edited by P. Ewald and L. Hartmann. Berlin, 1881, ep. 1, p. 474.

Göttinger, F. *Zielsprache: Theorie und Technik des Übersetzens.* Zurich, 1963.

Haas, W. "The Theory of Translation." *Philosophy* 37 (1962): 208-28.

Halliday, M. A. K. "Linguistics and Machine Translation." In *Patterns of Language: Papers in General and Applied Linguistics.* Edited by M. A. K. Halliday and A. M. MacIntosh. Bloomington, IN, 1966, pp. 134-50.

Hardbottle, R. "Practical Translating and Its Techniques." In *Technical Translator's Manual.* Edited by J. B. Sykes. London, 1971, pp. 1-21.

*Haskins, C. H. *The Renaissance of the Twelfth Century.* Cambridge, MA, 1927.

*_____. *Studies in the History of Medieval Science.* Cambridge, MA, 1924.

*Hattenhauer, H. "Zum Übersetzungsproblem im hohen Mittelalter." *Zeitschrift der Savigny-Stiftung für Rechtsgeschichte* (Germ. Abt.) 81 (1964):341 ff.

Hébert, A., and Scott, F. *Dialogue sur la traduction.* Montreal, 1970.

*Heck, P. *Übersetzungsprobleme im frühen Mittelalter.* Tübingen, 1931.

Heffzallah, I. M. "The Art of Translation." *Babel* 16 (1970): 180-87.

Heiddegger, M. *On the Way to Language,* Translated by P. D. Hertz. New York and London, 1959. Reprint 1971.

Heilmann, L. "De officio arteque vertendi." In *To Honor Roman Jakobson, Essays on the Occasion of his Seventieth Birthday.* 3 vols. The Hague, 1967. Vol. 2, pp. 901-09.

Herbert, J. *Manuel de l'interprète.* Geneva, 1964.

Hilduinus. *Rescriptum Hilduini Abbatis ad serenissimum imperatorem, dominum Ludovicum.* In *Patrologia Latina.* Vol. 106, pp. 13-22.

Hockett, C. F. "Translation via Immediate Continuents." *International Journal of Applied Linguistics* 20 (1954):313-15.

Hollander, J. "Versions, Interpretations, and Performances." In *On Translation.* Edited by R. A. Brower. Cambridge, MA, 1959, pp. 173-95.

Holmes, J. S., ed. *The Nature of Translation.* The Hague and Paris, 1970.

_____. "Forms of Verse Translation and Translation of Verse Form." In *The Nature of Translation.* Edited by J. S. Holmes. The Hague and Paris, 1970, pp. 91-105.

Holmes, J., Lambert, J., and van den Broeck, R., eds. *Literature and Translation.* Leuven, 1978.

Holmstrom, J. E. "How Translators Can Contribute to Improving Scientific Terminology." *Babel* 1 (1955):73-79.

Holmstrom, J. E., ed. *Scientific and Technical Translation and Other Aspects of the Language Problem.* Paris, 1957.

Holquist, M. Introduction to *The Dialogic Imagination,* by M. M. Bakhtin. New York, 1973, pp. xvi-xxxiv.

Horguelin, P. A. "La traduction technique." *META* 11 (1966): 15-25.

House, J. *A Model for Translation Quality Assessment.* Tübingen, 1977.

Houziaux, M.-O. "Pour une autonomie des recherches en traduction automatique." *Babel* 11 (1965):118-21.

Howard, R. "A Professional Translator's Trade Alphabet." In *The Craft and Context of Translation.* Edited by W. Arrowsmith and R. Shattuck. New York, 1964, pp. 247-59.

Howerton, P. W. "Technical Translations: Their Initiation, Production and Use." *Special Libraries* 53 (1962):21-25.

Humbertus de Romanis. "Discourse at the Council of Lyons." In *Sacrorum conciliorum nova collectio.* Edited by J. D. Mansi. Vol. 24. Venice, 1780, pp. 128-29.

Hutcheon, L. *A Theory of Parody: The Teachings of Twentieth-Century Art Forms.* New York, 1985.

Iannucci, J. E. "Explanatory Matter in Bilingual Dictionaries." *Babel* 5 (1959):195-99.

Ilek, B. "On Translating Images." In *The Nature of Translation.* Edited by J. S. Holmes. The Hague and Paris, 1970, pp. 135-38.

Ingberg, A. C. "The Enigma of the Translator: A Poststructuralist Reading of Theories of Translation." Ph.D. diss., Purdue University, 1986.

390

*Jacobsen, Eric. *Translation: A Traditional Craft.* Copenhagen, 1958.

Jacobson, R. "On Linguistic Aspects of Translation." In *On Translation.* Edited by R. A. Brower. New York, 1966, pp. 232-39.

Jameson, Fredric. "Postmodernism, or The Cultural Logic of Late Capitalism." *New Left Review* (1984):53-92.

Jankowsky, K. R. "Lexicology and its Potential Contribution to the Theory of Translation." *Babel* 16 (1970):135-42.

Jechová, H. "La Perspective de la représentation littéraire et le problème de la traduction." In *The Nature of Translation.* Edited by J. S. Holmes. The Hague and Paris, 1970, pp. 43-46.

Johnson, Barbara. *The Critical Difference: Essays in the Contemporary Rhetoric of Reading.* Baltimore, 1980.

_____. Translator's Introduction to *Dissemination* by Jacques Derrida. Chicago, 1981, pp. vii-xxxiii.

Jumpelt, R. W. "Fachsprachen--Fachwörter--als Problem der Dokumentation und Übersetzung." *Sprachforum* 3 (1958):1-13.

_____. *Die Übersetzung naturwissenschaftlicher und technischer Literatur.* Berlin-Schöneberg, 1961.

_____. "Methodological Approaches to Science Translation." In *Quality in Translation: Proceedings of the Third Congress of the International Federation of Translators.* Edited by E. Cary and R. W. Jumpelt. New York, 1963, pp. 267-81.

Kahn, F. "Traduction et linguistique." *Cahiers Ferdinand de Saussure* 27 (1971-72):21-42.

Kattan, N. "Problèmes particuliers de la traduction de textes littéraires." In *Translation and Interpretation, a Symposium.* Edited by M. S. Batts. Vancouver, 1975, pp. 72-82.

Keen, D. "Les mots intraduisables." *Vie et langage* 61 (1957): 178-82.

Kehrein, J. *Kirchen- und religiöse Lieder aus dem zwölften bis fünfzehnten Jahrhundert.* Hildesheim, 1969.

*Kelly, D. "'Translatio studii': Translation, Adaptation and Allegory in Medieval French Literature." *Philological Quarterly* 57 (1978):287-310.

Kelly, L. G. "*Contaminatio* in *Lycidas*; an Example of Vergilian Poetics." *Revue de l'université d'Ottawa* 38 (1968):587-98.

_____. "Linguistics and Translation in Saint Augustine." *The Bible Translator* 24 (1973):134-39.

_____. "Saint Augustine and Saussurean Linguistics." *Augustinian Studies* 6 (1975):45-64.

*_____. *The True Interpreter: A History of Translation Theory and Practice in the West.* Oxford and New York, 1979.

Kemp, F. *Kunst und Vernügen des Übersetzens.* Pfullingen, 1965.

Kennedy, E. "The Scribe as Editor." In *Mélanges de langue et de littérature du moyen âge et de la Renaissance offerts à Jean Frappiers.* 2 vols. Geneva, 1970, 2:523-31.

Kirk, R. "Translation and Indeterminacy." *Mind* 78 (1969):321-41.

*Kloepfer, R. *Die Theorie der literarischen Übersetzung.* Munich, 1967.

Knight, D. "Translation: The Augustan Mode." In *On Translation*. Edited by R. A. Brower. New York, 1966, pp. 196-204.

Knox, R. A. *Trials of a Translator*. New York, 1949.

_____. *On English Translation*. Folcroft, 1957.

Koessler, M. and Derocquigny, J. *Les Faux Amis ou les trahisons du vocabulaire*. Paris, 1928.

Koschmeider, E. "Das Problem der Übersetzung." In *Corolla linguistica, Festschrift F. Sommer*. Wiesbaden, 1955, pp. 120-28.

Krzesowski, T. P. "Equivalence, Congruence and Deep Structure." In *Papers in Contrastive Linguistics*. Edited by G. Nickel. Cambridge, 1971.

Kutzleb, H. "Übersetzen." *Monatsschrift für das deutsche Geistesleben* (Nov. 1941):340-45.

LaCapra, Dominick. *Rethinking Intellectual History: Texts, Contexts, Language*. Ithaca, NY, 1983.

Lamb, S. M. "Machine Translation Research at the University of California, Berkeley." In *Proceedings of the National Symposium on Machine Translation*. Englewood Cliffs, NJ, 1961, pp. 140-54.

_____. "Segmentation." In *Proceedings of the National Symposium on Machine Translation*. Englewood Cliffs, NJ, 1961, pp. 335-42.

Larbaud, V. *Sous l'invocation de Saint Jerôme*. Paris, 1946.

Lefevre, Andre. "Beyond the Process: Literary Translation in Literature and Literary Theory. In *Translation Spectrum:*

Essays in Theory and Practice. Edited by Marilyn Gaddis Rose. Albany, 1981, pp. 52-59.

Lefevre, Andre. *Translating Poetry: Seven Strategies and a Blueprint.* Assen and Amsterdam, 1975.

_____. "Translation: The Focus and the Growth of Literary Knowledge." In *Literature and Translation.* Edited by J. Holmes, J. Lambert, and R. van den Broeck. Leuven, 1978, pp. 7-28.

_____. "The Translation of Literature: An Approach." *Babel* 16 (1970):75-80.

Levik, V. V. "La traduction et création littéraires." In *The Nature of Translation.* Edited by J. S. Holmes. The Hague and Paris, 1970, pp. 163-69.

*Levy, J. "Translation as a Decision Process." In *To Honor Roman Jakobson: Essays on the Occasion of his Seventieth Birthday.* Vol. 2. The Hague, 1967, pp. 1171-82.

*Levy, M. L. "As Myn Auctour Seyth." *Medium Aevum* 12 (1943): 25-39.

Lewis, Philip E. "The Measure of Translation Effects." In *Difference in Translation.* Edited by J. F. Graham. Ithaca, NY, 1985, pp. 31-62.

_____. *Die literarische Übersetzung: Theorie einer Kunstgattung.* Frankfurt and Bonn, 1969.

L'Isle, W. *A Saxon Treatise Concerning the Old and New Testament.* London, 1623.

Littré, E. "La poésie homérique et l'ancienne poésie française." *Revue des deux mondes* 19 (1847):109-61.

Longacre, R. E. "Items in Context, Their Bearing on Translation Theory." *Language* 34 (1958):482-91.

*Lucas, R. H. "Mediaeval French Translations of the Latin Classics to 1500." *Speculum* 45 (1970):225-53.

Lupan, R. "Sur l'esprit moderne dans l'art de traduire." In *The Nature of Translation*. Edited by J. S. Holmes. The Hague and Paris, 1970, pp. 150-56.

Lyotard, Jean-François. "The Differend, The Referent, and the Proper Name." *Diacritics* 14 (1984):4-14.

_____. *The Postmodern Condition: A Report on Knowledge*. Minneapolis, 1984.

Maillot, J. *La traduction scientifique et technique*. Paris, 1970.

Malblanc, A. *Vers une stylistique comparée du français et de l'allemand*. Paris, 1944.

_____. *Stylistique comparée du français et de l'allemand*. Paris, 1968.

Manchester, P. T. "Verse Translation as an Interpretive Art." *Hispania* 34 (1951):68-73.

*Margot, J.-C. *Traduire sans trahir*. Lausanne, 1979.

Marouzeau, J. "La traduction et l'ordre des mots." *Revue des études latines* 2 (1924):189-95.

_____. *La traduction du latin*. 4th ed. Paris, 1951.

_____. *Traité de stylistique appliquée au latin*. Paris, 1935.

Marrou, H. I. *Saint Augustin et la fin de la culture antique*. Paris, 1949.

Marti, H. *Übersetzer der Augustin-Zeit: Interpretation von Selbst-zeugnissen.* Munich, 1974.

Matejka, L., and Titunik, R. Translators' Introduction to *Marxism and the Philosophy of Language*, by M. M. Bakhtin and V. N. Voloshinov. New York, 1973, pp. 1-6.

May, J. L. "Concerning Translation." *Edinburgh Review* 245 (1927):108-10.

McFarlane, J. "Modes of Translation." *Durham University Journal* 45 (1953):77-93.

Melville, Stephen W. *Philosophy Beside Itself: On Deconstruction and Modernism.* Minneapolis, 1986.

Miko, F. "La théorie de l'expression et de la traduction." In *The Nature of Translation.* Edited by J. S. Holmes. The Hague and Paris, 1970, pp. 61-77.

Milligan, E. E. "Some Principles and Techniques of Translation." *Modern Language Journal* 41 (1957):66-71.

Minnis, A. J. *Medieval Theory of Authorship: Scholastic Literary Attitudes in the Later Middle Ages.* London, 1984.

*Monfrin, J. "Humanisme et traductions au moyen âge." In *L'humanisme médiéval dans les littératures romanes du XIIe au XIVe siècle.* Edited by A. Fourrier. Paris, 1964, pp. 217-47. Rpt. from *Journal des Savants* (1963):161-90.

*_____. "Les Traducteurs et leur public en France au moyen âge." *Journal des Savants* (Jan.-Mar. 1964):5-20.

Morgan, B. Q. "What is Translation For?" *Symposium* 10 (1956): 322-28.

Mounin, G. *Les Belles Infidéles*. Paris, 1955.

_____. *Les problèmes théoriques de la traduction*. Paris, 1963.

_____. "L'intraduisibilité comme notion statistique." *Babel* 10 (1964):122-24.

_____. *Linguistique et traduction*. Brussels, 1976.

_____. *La machine à traduire: histoire des problèmes linguistiques*. The Hague, 1964.

Mund, A. "La Traduction lyrique: Art, Science et Technique." *Babel* 14 (1968):144-51.

Nabokov, V. "The Art of Translation." *New Republic* 105 (1941):160.

_____. "Problems in Translation: *Onegin* in English." *Partisan Review* 22 (1955):496 512.

_____. "The Servile Path." In *On Translation*. Edited by R. A. Brower. New York, 1966, pp. 97-109.

Newmark, P. "Standards of Translation." *Journal of Education* 89 (1957):248-50.

_____. "An Approach to Translation." *Babel* 19 (1973):3-18.

Nida, E. A. *Comment traduire la bible*. Translated by J.-C. Margot. Paris, 1967.

_____. "Linguistics and Ethnology in Translation Problems." *Word* 2 (1945):194-208.

_____. *Toward a Science of Translating with Special Reference to Principles and Procedures Involved in Bible Translation*. Leiden, 1964.

Nida, E., and Taber, C. *The Theory and Practice of Translation.* Leiden, 1969.

Nietzsche, F. "Zum Problem des Übersetzens." In *Das Problem des Übersetzens.* Edited by H. J. Störig. Stuttgart, 1963, pp. 136-38.

Nöel, J. "Linguistics and Translation." *Revue des langues vivantes* 32 (1966):525-31.

Oettinger, A. G. *Automatic Language Translation.* Cambridge, MA, 1960.

Paepke, F. "Sprach-, Text-, und Sachgemäßes Übersetzen: Ein Thesentwarf." In *Interlinguistica: Sprachvergleich und Übersetzung. Festschrift zum 60 Geburtstag von Mario Wandruszka.* Tübingen, 1971, pp. 610-16.

Paris, J. "Translation and Creation." In *The Craft and Context of Translation.* Edited by W. Arrowsmith and R. Shattuck. New York, 1964, pp. 77-91.

Pascher, G. "Traduzioni e tradizione." In *Le traduzioni dei libri liturgici, Atti del congresso tenuto a Roma il 9-13 novembre 1965.* Vatican City, 1966, pp. 89-108.

Passgier, E. *Choix de lettres sur la littérature, la langue et la traduction.* Edited by D. Thicket. Geneva, 1956.

Pattison, E. W. "Translation." *University Quarterly* 2 (1860): 124-35.

Peirce, Charles Sanders. *Collected Papers.* Edited by Charles Hartshorne and Paul Weiss. 8 vols. Cambridge, MA, 1931-58.

Phillimore, J. S. *Some Remarks on Translation and Translators.* English Association Pamphlet 42. London, 1919.

Pocar, E. "Lektor und Übersetzer." *Babel* 10 (1964):20-23.

Poggioli, R. "The Added Artificer." In *On Translation*. Edited by R. A. Brower. New York, 1966, pp. 137-47.

Politzer, L. "A Brief Classification of the Limits of Translatability." *Modern Language Journal* 40 (1956):319-22.

Postgate, J. P. *Translation and Translators*. London, 1922.

Pratt, A. W., and Pacak, M. G. "Automated Processing of Medical English." In *Preprints of the International Conference of Computational Linguistics*. Stockholm, 1969.

Procházka, V. "Notes on Translating Technique." In *Prague School Reader on Aesthetics, Literary Structure and Style*. Washington, D.C., 1964, pp. 93-112.

Purvey, John (attrib). "On Translating the Bible." In *Fifteenth-Century Prose and Verse*. Edited by A. W. Pollard. New York and London, 1903, pp. 193-99.

Quine, W. V. *Word and Object*. Cambridge, MA, 1960.

_____. "Meaning and Translation." In *On Translation*. Edited by R. A. Brower. New York, 1966, pp. 138-72.

Rabin, C. "The Linguistics of Translation." In *Aspects of Translation*. Edited by A. H. Smith. London, 1958, pp. 123-45.

Rado, G. "Approaching the History of Translation." *Babel* 13 (1967):169-73.

Raffel, B. *The Forked Tongue; a study of the translation process*. The Hague, 1971.

Ray, Punya Sloka. "A Philosophy of Translation." *Babel* 8 (1962): 182-88.

Rescher, N. "Translation as a Tool for Philosophical Analysis." *Journal of Philosophy* 53 (1956):219-24.

Reyburn, W. D. "Cultural Equivalence and Non-Equivalences in Translation." *The Bible Translator* 20 (1969):158-67; 21 (1970): 26-35.

Rhodes, I. "Syntactic Integration Carried out Mechanically." *Automatic Translation of Languages, papers presented at the NATO Summer School, Venice, July 1962.* London, 1966, pp. 205-09.

Richards, I. A. "Towards a Theory of Translating." In *Studies in Chinese Thought.* Edited by A. F. Wright. Chicago, 1932, pp. 247-62.

Richens, R. H., and Booth, A. D. "Some Methods of Mechanised Translation." In *Machine Translation of Languages.* Edited by W. N. Locke and A. D. Booth. New York and London, 1955, pp. 24-46.

Ronai, P. "The Trials of a Technical Translator." *Babel* 4 (1958): 210-12.

Rose, Marilyn Gaddis, ed. *Translation Spectrum: Essays in Theory and Practice.* Albany, 1981.

*Rosenthal, J. T. "Aristocratic Cultural Patronage and Book Bequests, 1350-1500." *Bulletin of the John Rylands University Library of Manchester* 64 (1981):522-48.

Ross, Stephen David. "Translation and Similarity." In *Translation Spectrum: Essays in Theory and Practice.* Edited by Marilyn Gaddis Rose. Albany, 1981, pp. 8-22.

*Rothwell, W. "Lexical Borrowing in a Medieval Context." *Bulletin of the John Rylands University Library of Manchester* 63 (1980):118-43.

Rouse, W. H. D. "Translation." *Classical Review* 22 (1908):105-10.

Rudhart, J. "Réflexions philosophiques à l'occasion d'un exercice de traduction." *Cahiers Ferdinand de Saussure* 21 (1964):55-85.

Rüdinger, H. "Problematik des Übersetzens." *Neue Jahrbücher für antike und deutsche Bildung* 1 (1938):179-90.

Rychner, J. "Observations sur la traduction de Tite-Live par Pierre Bersuire (1354-6)." In *Journal des Savants* (1963):242-267.

St. Jerome (Sophronius Eusebius Hieronymus). *Ad Pammachium* (Ep. 57). In *Sancti Eusebii Hieronymi Epistulae, Corpus Scriptorum Ecclesiasticorum Latinorum.* Vols. 54-56. Vienna and Leipzig, 1910-18. Vol. 54, pp. 503-26.

_____. *Ad Sunniam et Fretellam* (Ep. 106). In *Sancti Eusebii Hieronymi Epistulae, Corpus Scriptorum Ecclesiasticorum Latinorum.* Vols. 54-56. Vienna and Leipzig, 1910-18. Vol. 55, pp. 247-89.

_____. "Preface to Eusebius." *Patrologia Latina.* Vol. 27, pp. 33-40.

_____. "Preface to Pentateuch." *Patrologia Latina.* Vol. 28, pp. 147-52.

_____. "Preface to Isaiah." *Patrologia Latina.* Vol. 28, pp. 771-74.

_____. *Commentarium in epistolam ad Ephesios. Patrologia Latina.* Vol. 28, pp. 439-554.

Saussure, Ferdinand de. *Course in General Linguistics.* London, 1960.

Savory, Theodore. *The Art of Translation.* Philadelphia, 1960.

Schadewalt, W. "Das Problem des Übersetzens." In *Das Problem des Übersetzens*. Edited by H. J. Störig. Stuttgart, 1963, pp. 249-67.

_____. "Antike Tragödie auf der modernen Bühne." In *Hellas und Hesperien*. 2nd ed. Vol. 2. Zürich and Stuttgart, 1970, pp. 622-71.

_____. "Aus der Werkstatt meines Übersetzens." In *Hellas und Hesperien*. 2nd ed. Vol. 2. Zürich and Stuttgart, 1970, pp. 671-80.

_____. "Die Übersetzung im Zeitalter der Kommunikation." In *Hellas und Hesperien*. 2nd ed. Zürich and Stuttgart, 1970. Vol. 2, pp. 680-88.

Schleiermacher, F. "Über die verschiedenen Methoden des Übersetzens." In *Das Problem des Übersetzens*. Edited by H. J. Störig. Stuttgart, 1963, pp. 38-70.

Scholz, K. W. H. *The Art of Translation*. Philadelphia, 1918.

Schorp, A. "Quelques critères de qualité dans les traductions techniques." In *Quality in Translation: Proceedings of the Third Congress of the International Federation of Translators*. New York, 1963, pp. 333-47.

*Schwarz, W. "The Meaning of *fidus interpres* in Medieval Translation." *Journal of Theological Studies* 45 (1944):73-78.

*_____. *Principles and Problems of Biblical Translation*. Cambridge, 1955.

_____. "Translation into German in the Fifteenth Century." *Modern Language Review* 39 (1944):368-73.

_____. "The History of the Principles of Bible Translation in the Western World." *Babel* 9 (1963):5-22.

Searle, John. *Speech Acts: An Essay in the Philosophy of Language.* Cambridge, 1969.

Selver, Paul. *The Art of Translating Poetry.* Boston, 1966.

*Segre, C. "Jean de Meun e Boro Giamboni, tradutorri di Vegezio, Saggio sui volgarizzamenti in Francia e in Italia." In *Atti della Accademia delle scienze di Torino 2, Classe di scienze morali, stor. e filol.* 87 (1952-3):119-153.

Seuren, P. *Operators and Nucleus.* Cambridge, 1969.

Shattuck, R. "Artificial Horizon: Translator as Navigator." In *The Craft and Context of Translation.* Edited by W. Arrowsmith and R. Shattuck. New York, 1964, pp. 215-33.

Shillan, D. "An Application of Contrastive Linguistics." *META* 15 (1970):161-63.

*Shoaf, R. A. "Notes Toward Chaucer's Poetics of Translation." *Studies in the Age of Chaucer* 1 (1979):55-66.

Simpson, E. "Methodology in Translation Criticism." *META* 20 (1975):251-62.

Sliosberg, A. "Quelques considerations sur la traduction médicale et pharmaceutique." *Babel* 17 (1971):14-21.

Smeaton, B. H. "Translation, Structure and Learning." *Journal des traducteurs / Translators' Journal* 3 (1958):122-30; 4 (1959): 9-14.

Smith, A. H., ed. *Aspects of Translation.* London, 1958.

Smith, J. M. Powis. "Some Difficulties of a Translator." *Journal of Religion* 5 (1926):163-71.

Snyder, W. H. "Linguistics and Translation." In *Translation Spectrum: Essays in Theory and Practice*. Edited by Marilyn Gaddis Rose. Albany, 1981, pp. 127-34.

Souter, A. *Hints on Translation*. New York, 1920.

Spivak, Gayatri Chacravorty. Translator's Introduction to *Of Grammatology* by J. Derrida. Baltimore, 1976, pp. ix-lxxxvii.

Spolsky, B. "Comparative Stylistics and the Principle of Economy." *Journal des traducteurs / Translators' Journal* 7 (1962):79-83.

Steiner, G. "To Traduce or Transfigure." *Encounter* 27 (1966): 48-54

_____. *After Babel*. London, 1975.

Steiner, T. R. *English Translation Theory 1650-1800*. Assen and Amsterdam, 1975.

*Stone, H. "Cushioned Loan Words." *Word* 9 (1953):12-15.

*_____. "The French Language in Renaissance Medicine." *Bibliothèque d'Humanisme et Renaissance: Travaux et Documents* 15 (1953):315-22.

*_____. "Puzzling Translations in the Thirteenth Century Multiple Equivalents in Early French Medieval Terminology." *Romance Notes* 10 (1968):174-79.

Störig, H. J., ed. *Das Problem des Übersetzens*. Stuttgart, 1963.

Storr, F. "The Art of Translation." *Education Review* 38 (1909): 359-79.

Süskind, W. E., and von der Vring, G. "Die Kunst der Übersetzung." In *Die Kunst der Übersetzung*. Munich, 1963, pp. 9-40.

Swadesh, M. "On the Unit of Translation." *Anthropological Linguistics* 2 (1960):39-42.

Sykes, J. B. *Technical Translator's Manual.* London, 1971.

Taber, C. R. "Explicit and Implicit Information in Translation." *The Bible Translator* 21 (1970):1-9.

Tallgren, O. J. "Savoir, comprendre, traduire." *Neuphilologische Mitteilungen* 25 (1924):162-86.

Tarnóczi, L. "Congruence entre l'original et la traduction." *Babel* 13 (1967):137-43.

Taton, R. *Ancient and Medieval Science.* Translated by A. J. Pomerans. London, 1963.

Tennyson, Alfred. "Attempts at Classical Metres in Quantity." *Cornhill Magazine* 8 (1863):707-09.

Terracini, B. "El problema de la traducción." In *Conflictas de lenguas y de cultura.* Buenos Aires, 1951, pp. 43-97.

Testard, M. "La traduction du latin." In *Problèmes littéraires de la traduction.* Louvain and Leiden, 1975, pp. 29-55.

Thalmann, M. "Gestaltungsfragen lyrischer Übersetzung." *Die neueren Sprachen* 33 (1925):321-32.

Thieme, K. "Die geschichtlichen Haupt-typen des Dolmetschens." *Babel* 1 (1955):55-60.

Thieme, K., Hermann, A., and Glässer, E. *Beiträge zur Geschichte des Dolmetschens.* Munich, 1956.

Thierfelder, F. "Darf der Übersetzer den Text des originals verändern?" *Babel* 1 (1955):51-54.

Thillet, P. et al. "Translation Literature, Greek and Arabic." In *New Catholic Encyclopedia*. Vol. 14. New York, 1967, pp. 248-56.

Thomas Aquinas. "Contra errores Graecorum." *Divi Thomae Aquinatis doctoris angelici opuscula omnia*. Vol. 1. Antwerp, 1612.

Thompson, L. S. "German Translators of the Classics between 1450 and 1550." *Journal of English and Germanic Philology* 42 (1943):343-63.

Thomson, S. "The *Dulcis Jesu memoria* in Anglo-Norman and Middle French." *Medium Aevum* 11 (1942):68-76.

Todorov, Tzvetan. *Mikhail Bakhtin: The Dialogical Principle*. Translated by Wlad Godzich. Minneapolis, 1984.

Tolman, H. C. The *Art of Translating*. Boston, 1901.

Trevisa, John. "Dialogue between a Lord and a Clerk upon Translation." In *Fifteenth-century Prose and Verse*. Edited by A. W. Pollard. New York, 1903, pp. 203-10.

Tyrell, R. V. "Translation as a Fine Art." *Hermathena* 6 (1887-88):147-58.

Tytler, A. F. *Essay on the Principles of Translation*. New York and London, n.d.

Ulmer, Gregory L. *Applied Grammatology: Post(e)-Pedagogy from Jacques Derrida to Joseph Beuys*. Baltimore, 1985.

Ure, J. "Types of Translation and Translatability." In *Quality in Translation: Proceedings of the Third Congress of the International Federation of Translators*. Edited by E. Cary and R. W. Jumpelt. New York, 1963, pp. 136-46.

Ure, J.; Rodger, A.; and Ellis, J. "Soma=Sleep: an Exercise in the Use of Descriptive Linguistic Techniques in Literary Translation." *Babel* 15 (1969):4-14.

Valeri, D. "Qualche nota sul tradurre poesie *Lirici tedeschi*, 1959." *Babel* 11 (1965):7.

Valgimigli, M. "Poesia e traduzione di poesia." In *Del tradurre e alteri scritti.* Milan, 1957, pp. 22-59.

_____. "Del tradurre da poesia antica." In *Del tradurre e alteri scritti.* Milan, 1957, pp. 3-21.

van Doren, M. "The Uses of Translation." *Nation* 170 (1950):474.

van Hoof, H. *La Théorie et pratique de l'interprétation.* Munich, 1962.

_____. "Recherche d'un modèle d analyse en traduction." *META* 16 (1971):83-94.

van Kesteren, Aloysius. "Equivalence Relationships Between Source Text and Target Text." In *Literature and Translation.* Edited by J. Holmes, J. Lambert, and R. van den Broeck. Leuven, 1978, pp. 44-68.

Vernay, H. *Essai sur l'organisation de l'espace par divers systèmes linguistiques: Contribution à une linguistique de la traduction.* Munich, 1974.

Vinay, J. P. *A la recherche d'une traduction.* Montreal, 1952.

_____. "Stylistique et transformation." *META* 11 (1966):3-14.

_____. "The Theory of Translation: Myth or Reality." In *Translation and Interpretation, a Symposium.* Edited by M. B. Batts. Vancouver, 1975, pp. 35-46.

Vinay, J. P. "Traductions." In *Mélanges offerts en mémoire de Georges Panneton*. Montreal, 1952.

Virtue, L. M., and Baklanoff, N. W. "The Technique of Translation." *Modern Language Journal* 36 (1952):396-401.

Walmsley, J. B. "Transformation Theory and Translation." *International Review of Applied Linguistics* 8 (1970):185-99.

Wandruszka, M. "Implicitation et explicitation." *Revue des langues romanes* 31 (1967):316-30.

————. "L'aspect verbal, problème de traduction." *Travaux de linguistique et de littérature* 6 (1968):113-29.

————. "Nos langues; structures instrumentales--structures mentales." *META* 16 (1971):7-16.

Warren, T. H. "The Art of Translation." *Quarterly Review* 182 (1895):324-353.

Weightman, J. G. "Translation as a Linguistic Exercise." *English Language Teaching* 5 (1950):69-75.

Weil, H. *De l'ordre des mots dans les langues anciennes comparées aux langues modernes: Question de grammaire générale.* 2nd ed. Paris, 1844.

Weisgerber, L. "Das Dolmetschen und die sprachliche Verwandlung der Welt." *Babel* 1 (1955):7-9.

Wellard, J. H. "The Art of Translating." *Quarterly Review* 250 (1928):128-47.

Whibley, C. "Translators." In *Cambridge History of English Literature*. Vol. 4. Cambridge, 1932, pp. 1-25.

Whorf, Benjamin Lee. *Language, Thought and Reality*. Edited by J. B. Carroll. Cambridge, MA, 1956.

Widmer, W. *Fug und Unfug des Übersetzens*. Cologne and Berlin, 1959.

Wilhelm, J. "Zum Problem der literarischen Übersetzung." In *Interlinguistica: Sprachvergleich und Übersetzung. Festschrift zum 60 Geburtstag von Mario Wandruszka*. Tübingen, 1971, pp. 617-27.

Wilss, W. *Übersetzungswissenschaft: Probleme und Methoden*. Stuttgart, 1977.

Wils, J. "Aspects of Sacral Language." *Babel* 9 (1963):36-47.

Winston, R. "The Craft of Translation." *American Scholar* 19 (1950):179-86.

Winter, W. "Impossibilities of Translation." In *The Craft and Context of Translation*. Edited by W. Arrowsmith and R. Shattuck. New York, 1964, pp. 93-113.

Winthrop, H. "A Proposed Model for Studying Message Distortion in Translation." *Linguistics* 22 (1966):98-112.

Wirl, J. *Grundsätzliches zur Problematik des Dolmetschens und des Übersetzens*. Vienna, 1958.

*Wittlin, C. J. "Les Traducteurs au moyen âge: Observations sur leur techniques et difficultés." In *Actes du 18ᵉ Congrés International de Linguistique et philologie romanes*. Vol. 2. Quebec, 1976, pp. 601-609.

Witty, F. J. "Translation Literature, Early." In *New Catholic Encyclopedia*. Vol. 14. New York, 1967, pp. 248-56.

Woledge, B. "La légende de Troie et les débuts de la prose française." In *Mélanges de linguistique et de littérature offerts à Mario Roques*. Vol. 2. Paris, 1953, pp. 313-24.

Woledge, B., and H. Clive. *Répertoire des plus anciens textes en prose française depuis 842 jusqu'aux premières années du XIIIe siècle*. Geneva, 1964.

*Workman, S. *Fifteenth-Century Translation as an Influence on English Prose*. Princeton, 1940. Reprint New York, 1972.

Wüstenfeld, F. *Die Übersetzungen arabischer Werke in das lateinische seit dem XI Jahrhundert*. Göttingen, 1877.

Wuthenow, R. R. *Das fremde Kunstwerk*. Göttingen, 1969.

Young, D. "Summing up of a Round Table Discussion on Translation and Translators Held by the International PEN Club." *Babel* 10 (1964):154-58.

Zeydal, E. H. "Can We Rely on Translation?" *Modern Language Journal* 25 (1941):401-04.

Zilahy, S. P. "Quality in Translation." In *Quality in Translation: Proceedings of the Third Congress of the International Federation of Translators*. Ed. E. Cary and R. W. Jumpelt. New York, 1963, pp. 285-89.

*Zink, M. *La prédication en langue romane avant 1300*. Paris, 1976.

Zuber, R. *Les "belles infidèles" et la formation du goût classique. Perrot d'Ablancourt et Guez de Balzac*. Paris, 1968.

Index